AF473682

The Life of Bryan *A Celebration of Bryan Robertson*

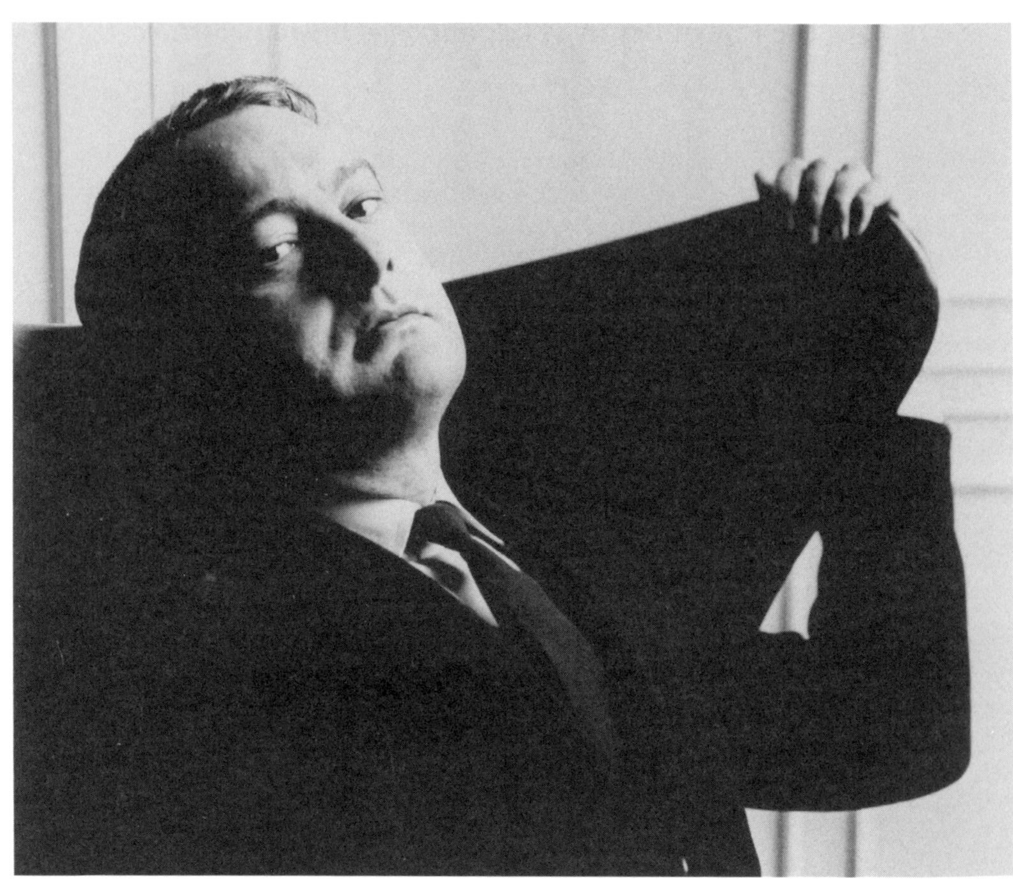

Andrew Lambirth

THE LIFE OF BRYAN

A Celebration of Bryan Robertson

Unicorn Press

First published in Great Britain
in 2019 by Unicorn Press
60 Bracondale · Norwich · NR1 2BE

tradfordhugh@gmail.com
www.unicornpublishing.org

A CIP record of this book can be obtained from the British Library

ISBN 978 1 916495 73 9

Designed by Robert Dalrymple
Typeset in MVB Verdigris
Printed & bound in the UK by TJ International Ltd,
Padstow, Cornwall

Frontispiece: Lord Snowdon, *Bryan Robertson*, 1964
24.2 × 29.1 cm, gelatin silver print
© Armstrong Jones / National Portrait Gallery, London

Contents

Preface

'Art is not a luxury, it is the most acute and basic expression of the spiritual state of any society in any epoch.'

Bryan Robertson (1925–2002) was an outstanding figure in the twentieth-century art world, a curator and writer of international significance, a public-gallery director who changed the face of British art. Like many such figures (and indeed artists), they are apt to be forgotten after their death, as they are swiftly replaced by influential and charismatic successors, who in turn give way to the next generation. Robertson will live in the history books, but he was a remarkable man and inspired such love, respect and affection that a more detailed account of his achievements is called for.

This is not a biography – Bryan would have been aghast at such an idea, I am convinced – but more of a celebration of an art-world mover and shaker seen through the prism of his own writings and recalled through the memories of his friends. I have used his own words wherever possible, from letters, reviews, books and articles, and interspliced these with accounts of his friendships and the kind of unparalleled support he gave to artists. The book is not a straightforward narrative, though it is roughly chronological; rather it is a compendium of Robertsoniana, put together on the collage principle of unexpected and flavourful juxtapositions.

My words are set in bold type, as here; those of Bryan himself and the other contributors in regular type; **and throughout the book, some of Bryan's pithy 'soundbites' are added in the margin, as above.**

Robertson is known as the greatest director the Tate Gallery never had. In 1952, at the age of twenty-seven, and against formidable competition (which included David Sylvester and Lawrence Gowing), he became Director of the Whitechapel Art Gallery, a post he held until 1969. While there he effected a revolution in the British museum world, bringing the more innovative and radical American and European contemporary artists to these shores, as well as programming a series of exhibitions devoted to British artists in mid-career, and young artists just starting out. He was the first to show Jackson Pollock, Mark Rothko, Robert Rauschenberg and Jasper Johns in depth in England, matching this with historical re-evaluations of J.M.W. Turner, George Stubbs, Bernardo Bellotto and Thomas Rowlandson. The Europeans he showed included Piet Mondrian, Nicolas de Staël, Kazimir Malevich and Serge Poliakoff, and such British artists as Barbara Hepworth, Alan Davie, Ceri Richards and Keith Vaughan. Among younger painters and sculptors he identified Anthony Caro and the New Generation of John Hoyland, Bridget Riley, Allen Jones and Patrick Caulfield, and stage-managed an extraordinary flow of exhibitions which transformed the Whitechapel and made it *the* gallery to visit.

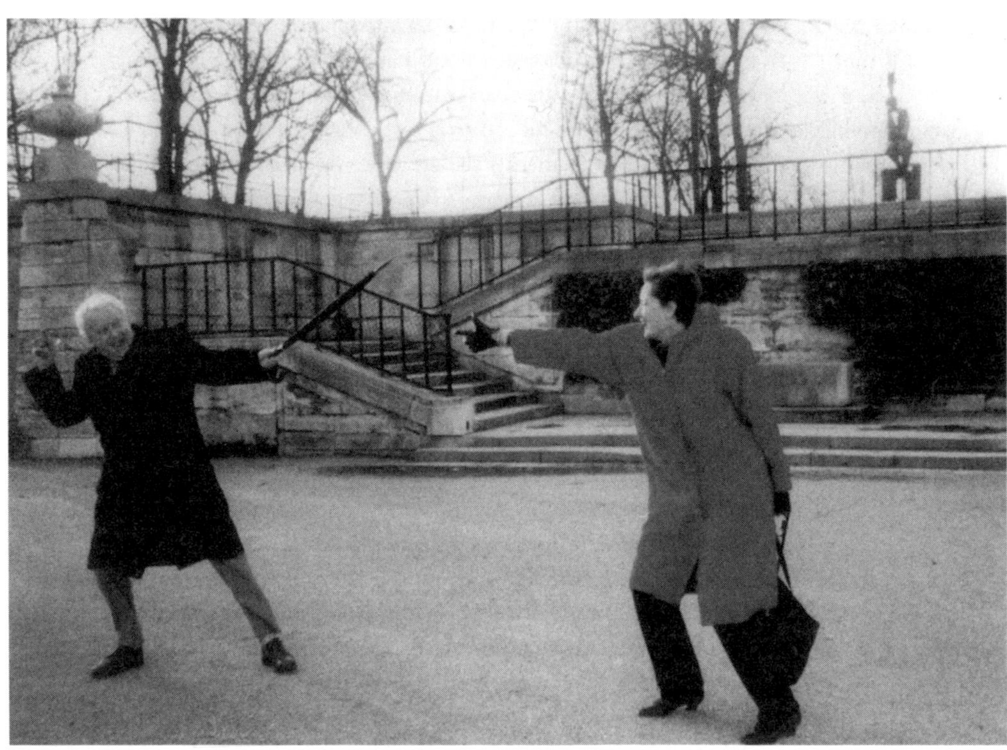

1 BR duelling with Elaine Finch in the Jardin des Tuileries, Paris, late 1980s

Bryan Robertson was a man of vision and flair, and this book will celebrate his lasting influence over the way we look at and think about art. It is not an academic study of trends in 1950s or 1960s British art, nor is it a detailed examination of the successes and failures of Robertson's Whitechapel administration. It is intended as an evocation of his spirit – tumultuous in enthusiasm and humour, deeply cultured with a touch of mischief, unexpected and even anarchic, but above all generous. That's why this book has been written: to record and honour Bryan Robertson's generosity of spirit. Long may it be remembered.

Prologue

I interviewed Bryan in September 1999 for an article I had been commissioned to write for *RA* magazine, the Royal Academy's quarterly journal, to which I was then a regular contributor. The idea was to preview a pair of exhibitions he was curating in Cambridge, one at Kettle's Yard, the other at the Fitzwilliam Museum. Michael Harrison, the genial and distinguished Director of Kettle's Yard, had approached Bryan to select a loan exhibition which would more or less cover his professional career, beginning at Cambridge and going on to Whitechapel and his later work as a freelance. In other words, fifty years of organising exhibitions and writing about them. Similarly, the Director of the Fitzwilliam, Duncan Robinson, had asked Bryan to choose his favourite works of art from the museum's permanent collection to make a display. For the show at Kettle's Yard, called *'45–'99: A Personal View of British Painting and Sculpture*, he opted to focus tightly on English painting and sculpture – cutting out all American art (his favourites Rothko, Pollock, Robert Motherwell featured nowhere), all Australian art (despite his enthusiasm for Sidney Nolan, Arthur Boyd, Brett Whiteley) and all French art (like de Staël and Poliakoff). And to strike a balance, for his exhibition at the Fitzwilliam, *A Critic's Choice*, he focused entirely on French art, but included manuscripts, enamels from Limoges, wood-carvings and ivories along with the paintings.

The impact of both exhibitions was to be intensely personal and thought-provoking, but that was for the future. Meanwhile, I had to conduct my research and find out enough to make a good article. I knew of Bryan as the legendary Director of the Whitechapel Art Gallery in the 1950s and 1960s, and as a distinguished writer and critic who found it impossible to deliver copy on time. (At *RA* magazine, the editor gave him ridiculously early deadlines, and still the articles were late, though always full of interest.) By this point in my own career, I had been writing professionally for some fifteen years and had interviewed quite a number of artists, some of them monsters of egotism, but I was still totally unprepared for Bryan. At least artists actually allowed you to ask occasional questions, and some even answered them. Talking to Bryan was something else – perhaps a little like being in the passenger seat of a runaway articulated lorry.

Question and answer was not his idea of an interview: he overrode most of my questions and it was scarcely possible to get a word in edgeways. When he did deign to listen to an interruption of his monologue, my point would only ever be obliquely answered, or in passing at best. But none of that mattered, because the energy and optimism and humour

were all-engulfing. Like a cataract, Bryan poured on, regardless of bemused onlookers. I have tried to reproduce the cascade and sparkle of his speech in the edited version of our conversation which follows.

Initially working as a very junior sub-editor on *The Studio* magazine in London between 1944 and 1946, Bryan spent most of 1947 living in Paris, returning to England at the end of the year. Then, at the invitation of one of the directors of the Lefevre Gallery in London, he went to work there in 1948 for a year.

I realized that working in a dealer's gallery was for me impossible because my character is by no means marvellous – absolutely not – but I found that I simply couldn't pretend to like things I didn't like. It sounds very pious and holy but it's the truth. First of all, if you work in a [commercial] gallery, the only way you can have any fun is by owning it, or buying yourself a partnership, and that means putting in a lot of money which I hadn't got. I would only have ever been a salaried employee, and therefore you have to enthuse over shows that you don't always feel any commitment to at all. But I didn't regret working at the Lefevre because it taught me a great deal about French painting, because you were living at close quarters with very good examples of all sorts of people – Monet and Renoir and Pissarro and Cézanne and everybody. And at that time – which was one of the reasons I went there – the Lefevre was one of the great strongholds for an extremely strong bunch of English painters. They showed Ben Nicholson, Barbara Hepworth, occasionally Francis Bacon, John Tunnard, Edward Burra always, John Minton, Robert Colquhoun, John Craxton, Keith Vaughan and others I can't remember. Lowry always.

In 1949 he answered an advertisement in the papers for someone to run the Heffer Gallery, part of the bookshop, in Cambridge. He stayed there for the next three years and, though not initially impressed by the place, he soon realised that it offered a rare opportunity to put on ambitious exhibitions without too much interference:

I thought it would be marvellous to run a gallery, but when I went there my face fell as it was part of a ghastly department store selling artists' equipment and greetings-cards and stationery, on the top two floors. But it was actually a good gallery when you got there, with top lighting, and I put on a lot of shows. My first show was I believe a three-person show of Merlyn Evans, Francis Rose and Cecil Collins. Cecil Collins lived locally and I met him and saw his work at the Lefevre Gallery.

But what I'm most proud of at Cambridge – this really was something positive – was a show that I put on of modern French painting in my second year. Believe it or not, it was the first show of modern French painting ever to be seen in Cambridge. The Fitzwilliam Museum then was run very tightly and rather grandly and distantly as a department of the university, which only allowed the public in under vague sufferance. They made no effort to ingratiate themselves with the public or put on special shows, or indeed do much towards instructing the young, who came in and out in a rather lost sort of way. In fact, it was a rather dim place in lots of ways, though full of beautiful things and run by an admirable director, Carl Winter, who did his level best to get things going, but it was a slow and uphill business – had no money either in those days. But to get to the point, the modern French show sounds grandiose and my God it was!

It wasn't just scraps and bits and pieces from dealers' galleries; it was largely the core of the collection of Mrs Kessler, who lived up in Rutland and whom I was very friendly with. She was the wife of August Kessler, who was one of the chairmen or founders of the Anglo-Iranian oil company, and she was wealthy and cultivated and Dutch and an enthusiast. She had commissioned Dufy to come over and paint herself and her daughters and sons-in-law on horseback in the park in about 1932. She was a dashing woman, very gutsy, very courageous, very outspoken and totally adorable. And she had a magnificent Gauguin, of a Brittany girl with her hands clasped in prayer. She owned a great Renoir reclining nude – a great one – a magnificent Braque still life, a magnificent Matisse still life, a great Cézanne, *Les Grandes Arbres* – it is a fantastic painting – and of course a great painting by Dufy, *Le Grand Champ de Blé* – a pink and blue horse out in a field of corn and weeds, with wonderful calligraphic scribbles for butterflies and birds and bees, on an enormous scale. It's in the Tate but they hardly ever show it, of course. It's one of his great paintings.

This was the nucleus of the show to which I added a marvellous Chirico from Roland Penrose, the *Melancholy of Departure*; a very good Derain – one of the few things I borrowed from a dealer's gallery; a Provençal landscape from Gimpel; and a very good reclining nude by Picasso from the early thirties, a sort of sexy, voluptuous girl looking in a mirror, when breasts get mixed up with apples. The show was a knock-out. Nikolaus Pevsner wrote a text for the catalogue and it was really very good. That was in 1950 and I was twenty-four.

I loved it – it was my introduction to art. As a schoolboy I grew up reading Wilenski's *Modern French Painters*. I would go to exhibitions in the war years when we were all thinking that Paris was occupied and France was down, to concerts of French music and exhibitions of French painting that had been scrabbled together by the French Embassy. Even as a schoolboy reading French books – in English translation, of course. A great deal of Mauriac, I adored Mauriac and the great novels, now forgotten, of Roger Martin du Gard, the Thibault family saga, a sort of Galsworthian aspect of Proust, if you like. *Roman fleuve*. French writing, French music – I just gravitated to, I loved it, and French art, of course. The first art I ever responded to as a child was French art, seen through the windows of an artists' colourman in a south London high street where I grew up, and they were reproductions of *Le Lac d'Annecy* of Cézanne – well-made prints – the *Street at Sannois* by Utrillo and a big blazing, rather angry painting of Rouault, *The Old King*. I was transfixed! Absolutely! [Aged eight or nine, it was a formative experience.] Eventually I bought one – I bought the Rouault when I was about twelve. And I remember as a schoolboy using lunch money to go and buy gramophone records. Of *La Mer* or *Daphnis and Chloe* – the old Boston Symphony Orchestra. In other words, I was bewitched by French culture very early on.

At this point I had the temerity to ask if Bryan thought he was good at meeting people. A fairly fatuous question, admittedly, but to justify my existence (if nothing else) I was desperate to interrupt the flow. I didn't succeed. He just gave me a look and proceeded.

My family background was fairly ordinary. We weren't poverty-stricken, we were very hard up. My father was often unemployed, there was often very little money. We were what's called fashionably now 'upwardly mobile'. All the children – I was one of three children – all got scholarships to go to good schools. I went to a very good ancient – and looking back quite magnificent in education – grammar school. Now of course, ludicrously, abolished, gone. My brother went to a very good school, so did my sister. We all read like mad, my mother read a great deal, the house was always full of books, dense with books you might say, and we went to the theatre a good deal, and the cinema chiefly. Not the music hall – Victoria Palace 'Crazy Gang' would have been the nearest we got to it in those days. But there was no visual thing to draw me. I think it came through art classes at school and magazines, and seeing those reproductions in the shop window. An excellent teacher, Arnold Keith, who I remember with great gratitude and affection. His brother Bernard Keith was a very good either viola or cello player, I always get muddled with those instruments, rather disgracefully. He was a well-known soloist with orchestras. Arnold Keith was the pointer towards the Tate.

The first job that I did when I left school was in publishing, because I knew that I wanted to write. I'd been writing a great deal. I have to say I was asthmatic. I hate saying this as it sounds like violins and strings and sob stuff, but I really wouldn't have missed it for anything. Although it was painful and very frightening when you're a child, and in those days there weren't drugs to help much, it meant that I spent a great deal of my life in bed. And what do you do when you're in bed? You read. So I read like a madman. I read voraciously, devouring books, so I was pretty well read and cultivated by the time I was sixteen or seventeen. Precociously so, sometimes rather meaninglessly so – you get a bit ahead of yourself really, emotionally as it were, without quite comprehending.

Anyway I joined a firm of publishers, the Oxford University Press, for only about a year and a half, and then sent an article to *The Studio* magazine, an essay on some soppy idea, ludicrous, linking up music with painting. Can you imagine the sort of half-baked embarrassing thing? It was to do with a painting by Edward Wadsworth, called *Brown Ballet*, and Arthur Bliss's *Colour Symphony*. How about that? Of course they sent it back as if with scalded fingers and said they didn't think they could publish it, but there was a job going for a junior sub-editor if I'd like to come and talk to them, so I did. That's how I worked there and that opened everything up because I started going to exhibitions far more.

I wanted to write about painting, funnily enough, about visual things. It takes you a long time when you are young to realise how you work and how you act, and it took me a long time to realise that I was totally visually motivated, and lived through my eyes. Not much behind them [chortles] – not a great deal of brain; not too much intellect or powers of analysis, but a good deal of reaction to things seen. So I worked on *The Studio*, and that of course was a kind of nightmare because it was a very philistine set-up, very old-fashioned, but it got me out and about among the galleries, borrowing photographs, asking questions, getting to know artists, going to interview or talk to them – all that stuff. I wrote very early on a piece on David Bomberg. That's something I'm quite proud of because it was written when the war was still on, and it was just about his big charcoal drawings of the city under air attack. Those drawings of the churches and St Paul's at night. They were marvellous, I'd never heard of him but I thought they were wonderful. So I got a piece about him printed and then the article on the young English painters at the time. And that brought me in contact with the Lefevre Gallery and that's why they wrote to me after I'd been in Paris for a year, to say 'We've heard you're in Paris. If you're thinking of coming back to England, what about coming and working here? There's a job for you.' The only time I've ever been invited to do anything, I think. It was rather nice when you're twenty-three.

I think also what had been helpful – I'd better come clean about this – was Kenneth Clark. In writing about the work of the young English painters I came across the work of a very good artist, now forgotten, called Mary Kessell. Mary Kessell lived in Hampstead and she did very beautiful drawings and rather fine, rarefied paintings, a little in the manner of Odilon Redon. I thought they were really very remarkable and I sought her out. We became great friends, extremely close friends. She was an intelligent and lively young woman of about thirty. We used to meet at least once a week and go and see plays and have supper together, and she talked continuously about somebody called K. I didn't know who she was talking about, I really didn't. I thought it was a woman for a long time, a woman called Kay. And one evening I went to supper with Mary and there was this charming fellow in braces and an open-neck shirt doing something at the stove and he was introduced as K Clark. And of course it was easy to see they were lovers and I didn't realise it. She was one of many girlfriends he had, and he became extremely friendly and very helpful indeed. He was Director of the National Gallery, the war was coming to an end, he wasn't yet bringing work back from Wales, he was living a lot in Portmeirion and so on.

So I went to Upper Terrace House where he was living and saw his paintings and nearly fell over, because he had absolutely the most amazing collection. People don't really seem to remember or understand – he had one of *the* great collections. In those days he had the great Matisse of the woman lying on the bed in a tall walled studio with a view of Notre Dame, now in the Duncan Phillips collection. And he had a great Renoir, *La Baigneuse Blonde*, of a young girl with beautiful little breasts and a pearlescent skin sitting naked on a rock, long, long fair Titian sort of gold hair. A lyrical painting, really pearlescent – the best sort of Renoir. A good Courbet. He had a thoroughly awkward Seurat called *Le Bec du Hoc*, which is a big rock, and the top of the rock absolutely flattened to be in false alignment with the horizon. That was a kind of awkward and edgy painting. That was one of the least ingratiating of Seurats.

He sold the Matisse painting because he found it a difficult painting to live with domestically – slack-breasted, heavily contoured with great black slashing lines around the thighs and belly, sprawled erotically on a bed. The whole thing is charged with some kind of erotic feeling. Perhaps he felt ... though God knows his private life was ... very planned and carefully conducted, but he certainly wasn't a puritan. He was amazingly erudite and had more knowledge than anybody I've ever known. He'd read more and seen more.

Here I managed to interject another question, asking if he thought Clark was a genuine scholar.

Totally, oh, totally. I think he suffered all his life from jealousy. It's very difficult if you are a salaried person working in a regional museum and you want to write a book on Leonardo. You know that in Warsaw there is a great painting called *Lady with an Ermine*, and on that salary in Leeds or Huddersfield, you had to wait a bit before you got the airfare to go. Or even the train fare. And photography is expensive, and the hotel. The whole thing is very tricky. Kenneth Clark could wake up on a Monday – he was after all a great Leonardo scholar – and decide that he had to go to Warsaw and look at this painting. And on Tuesday morning he'd be there – on a first-class flight, with a Rolls-Royce or Daimler meeting him at the airport, dinner with the director, and on Wednesday he'd be back in his house in London with a whole set of expensive photographs, slides, X-ray photographs and God knows what, to get on with his work. You see what I'm getting at?

There was a great deal of jealousy, and rival critics and rival historians put down what was a tremendous ease of manner and a great facility in expressing complicated things very simply, put it down to lightweight thinking, but it wasn't lightweight. It just came from extreme clarity of expression and a very good mind. His writing is wonderfully clear. He can express complicated things, and as you read them you think 'Oh yes, quite right, I've always thought that'. Well you hadn't. He'd done it in such a well-mannered way that it was not somebody being pompous or over-intellectual in a kind of *de haut en bas* way. It was expressing something very directly to you and treating you as equals.

The Nude [published 1952] is a masterpiece and says things about the way the nude has been depicted in history in ways that had never been said before, or observed before. It's an extraordinary book. So read *The Nude*, read *Landscape into Art* – absolutely wonderful books. I have a real affection for him because he did so much behind the scenes that nobody knows about. He paid for, he bought, the houses and studios where Henry Moore, John Piper, Victor Pasmore and Graham Sutherland lived and worked their whole lives. He never asked for the money back. He gave enough money for David Jones to live without worry all his adult life. He heard that Edith Sitwell was in financial distress and he was extremely upset because he loved her. She was worried about money and was putting up for sale at Sotheby's an enormous portfolio of drawings and watercolours by Tchelitchew, who had been her platonic but much-adored friend and imaginary lover. K was very distressed by this so he bought the whole lot anonymously and sent them back to her. She was simply furious because she had genuinely wanted to get rid of them – they'd been a frightful nuisance for years!

There were very many other people he helped – an enormous list – quite extraordinary. He was not mean and when I went to Paris [1947] a cheque arrived in the post which of course frightened me out of my wits, for something like £100, which in those days was a lot of money, more like £1,000 now. I was terrified and I sent it back with something frightful like an eight-page letter explaining why. The sort of thing you do when you're twenty-one. It was something to the effect that he had probably an exalted idea of my attainments or potentiality. I was just flustered by the whole thing and nervous. And to his eternal credit he sent it back. Anyone else would have thought 'silly arse' and got on with his work. He didn't – he sent it back with a short postcard saying 'Dear Bryan, I do understand how you feel. I believe Paris food is frightfully good right now but it is extremely expensive. Why don't you spend it all on two or three good meals and get rid of it quickly?' I didn't realise at the time, but that showed real style, because I was being in fact boring and the letter was unreadable. So I had that [money] to begin with anyway, but that didn't go so very far come to think of it.

A slight pause for breath, and his mind clicked on to a new track:

A lot of artists that I put into exhibitions really owed nothing to me whatever. They were very well known and established long before I put them on. For example, in the mid-60s [it was actually in 1960], I put on at the Whitechapel a really very fine Henry Moore show, because he was doing wonderful work then. This was the first time the London public had the chance to see the big two-part inventions, the split-up figures. They were known only through photography and articles, and they couldn't be seen in London because nobody could show them. In those days the Tate didn't do special shows like that. So we put them on at Whitechapel – I happened to be the manager of some useful premises at that moment for Henry Moore. But he owed nothing to me, he was an international figure then. So he's not in the show at Cambridge.

Barbara Hepworth is. Not because I think she's a greater figure than Henry Moore but because when I approached her with the idea of a show in 1952–3, she was at a very low ebb. Ben had walked out on her, her gallery had thrown her out, the Lefevre Gallery; the partner who had been so friendly and good to me had died, and that broke their connection with contemporary art. They just wanted to revert to showing expensive French pictures. They told Barbara Hepworth that her work mucked up their carpets and they didn't sell it. I would say that the English public respected her but didn't really like the work, which only had a very tiny following. And her son had died in Korea, and she was at a very low level. The show really did put her across in a way that she never had been before. As a result of that she got to know good collectors and a link-up with Gimpels and then Marlborough, and all kinds of *réclames*, very good reviews, and it got across that she actually did things that were rather beautiful, and not terribly intimidating after all. So she was in the right context, in the right top-lit big spacious gallery in London, for the first time. So the [Kettle's Yard] show begins in terms of sculpture with her.

There again, Caro had got not much reputation in England really. He'd been working on those early expressionist pieces and the work had changed, he was working on those big metal things, and therefore the show at Whitechapel. I have to say that wasn't particularly cleverness on my part, it was just intuition and faith. Because you couldn't *see* any of the things. When you went to see him he'd just got bits of old tramlines lying around, they couldn't be assembled very easily. Also I'd written a great deal on Hepworth and on Caro – it [the Kettle's Yard show] is about people I've written a lot about too. And then comes Tim Scott because he had a very spectacular show, then Bryan Kneale for the same reason, then Nigel Hall – someone again I'm tightly involved with and have written on a great deal.

And Michael Sandle, whose work is his biggest and most barmy and most eccentric and wild. In fact one of his works I bought twice – once for the Arts

Council and once for the museum I ran in America – the *Monumentum pro Gesualdo*. I bought it to the great dismay of the Arts Council, who nearly fainted with shock and horror when they saw this thing. They gave me a modest budget to spend for a year, ten or eleven thousand pounds, and they said 'Make it go as far as you can, and, if you can, buy things that are readily transportable that will go in travelling shows'. So for some ridiculously knock-down sum, £1,000 or £1,500, I bought the *Monumentum*, which really needs the Albert Hall to show it properly off! It's a huge, complicated thing in about seventeen packing crates. And there it stood for about two years because no museum or public gallery in England would take it, even on indefinite loan with no strings attached. They just screamed and jammed the phone down. So the Arts Council was stuck with this, so I rang them up and bought it for the museum in America.

Clearly Bryan wasn't including that particular sculpture at Kettle's Yard, given the constraints of space, and Sandle was in fact represented by a substantial mixed-media work on paper. Phillip King, whose work Robertson championed for many years, actually had a show in 1957 at the Heffer Gallery after Bryan left, but his inclusion at Kettle's Yard is justified by the major exhibition he had at the Whitechapel in 1968, and Robertson's continued support, for instance in writing the catalogue for King's 1997 Forte di Belvedere retrospective in Florence.

Hodgkin is in [the Kettle's Yard show] though I never exhibited a single painting of his at the Whitechapel Gallery. I thought he was a different generation to the others and working in a different way. He was slightly outside that group and actually I didn't like the early ones with Mr & Mrs X in their patterned wallpaper interior. I thought they were a bit soppy. I liked them more when he got on a bit. I've written about him a lot. Also I bought the first painting by Howard to go in an American museum. I'm totally committed to him but I wasn't so keen on the early ones. There you are: a peculiar, bigoted list in which all the great names are conspicuously missing, of course. No Francis Bacon, no Lucian Freud, no Frank Auerbach, Kossoff, Hockney.

Playing back the tape, nearly twenty years later, Bryan's voice drowning out my questions grew higher and higher with excitement or emphasis, rising almost to a wail, pursuing his own thoughts and his own past, with almost desperate speed and emphasis. I got the impression that these were very close recollections – as if he could see in front of him the paintings he described and the people he mentioned. Frequently he would make a statement which would have stood well on its own, but then he kept adding to it, qualifying it, the words and sub-clauses piling up like a tottering tower of bricks that seemed forever on the verge of collapse.

They're all slightly one-off people. They're all slightly isolated individuals – they don't quite link up with other people. They're all friends, which is rather nice, and slightly over-cosy. On the other hand, I can truthfully say that there's not a single painter or sculptor whose work I enthused about, whose work I didn't know long before I got to know them. I became friends with them through their work. You can't know somebody who you like personally but can't stand their work, you can't do it.

In a rare pause, I asked him what were the principal things to have changed in his fifty-year career.

Oh money, money's the big change. There wasn't an awful lot of money in the forties and fifties. The big change in art came when huge sums of money began to change hands. It didn't change hands over poetry. If you were a poet in the 1960s and wrote a poem, you still got paid 5 guineas or whatever it was. With painters and sculptors, big money started to move around in the sixties. The sixties, for what it's worth, being not the 1960s as they're generally thought of, but roughly speaking 1956 to 1966, or '57–'67.

Did more money improve the situation, I asked, taking advantage of this unexpected lull.

It's swings and roundabouts, but mostly good, as a matter of fact. I don't think money ever does harm, it's the people who use it who are silly, but that's a truism, too stupid to think about. I think there are inflated values, that's ludicrous, but who pays attention to them except millionaires? There are instances at auction where Robert Ryman is in the millions, Mark Tobey in the thousands – ludicrous, but so what? Truth will out, finally, things find their level eventually. I think money's useful, why not?

The presentation of art has got better, venues for art have increased, writing about art – despite the meanness and the ignorance of literary editors – has increased on the whole, and there's some good stuff being done. There was some awfully dull stuff, you know, in the fifties. And don't forget that all through the fifties and the first half of the sixties, I had to endure the nightmare of John Berger, who I think should be in gaol. First of all he's a very nice fellow, second he's rather a good writer, thirdly he means every inch of what he's up to, absolutely passionately, but he is more wrong-headed and more vituperative about what doesn't fit in with his cast of mind than you could have believed possible. He said of the Pollock show that it was a kind of masturbatory ludicrous activity, irrelevant to everything. He abused every single artist that didn't look like social realism, and what he put forward were dreadful people, like somebody called Peter Peri. A dear old boy, doing these ghastly toy-like things in coloured concrete, which he called pericrete, an invented material. Berger would write columns about this, and yet write a column destroying Henry Moore headed 'Piltdown

Sculpture', meaning fake – fake emotion, fake art, fake work, fake sculpture. Oh come on, he was a nightmare! He was dreadful!

It's this whole thing of being a committed critic – I hate it! Much better to be wonderfully uncommitted, to be open, absolutely open. I was particularly enraged by inheriting an exhibition that he'd dreamed up with my predecessor at Whitechapel. It was called *Looking Forward* and was an exhibition of the realist painting of that time, and was put on about 1954 or 5 [it was actually in 1952]. It had some rather good worthy things but I have to say that when you walked into the gallery, you couldn't see anything. Everything was a kind of monochromatic haze of subfusc greys and browns and ochres and no colour. It was very drab, and the show was ill attended. People would walk in and spend about fifteen seconds and walk out again. I realised that what people wanted in East London was colour and vivacity and something to lift them up. When you're queuing up for a bus in the pouring rain after working in a factory or at a garment-maker's bench all day, you don't want to go home and find on your television screen or on the wall an image of a miner clutching a blow-lamp in the semi-gloom of a Warsaw railway station at 4am. Do you see what I'm getting at? It's a kind of intellectual conceit of providing the masses, so-called, with everyday reality. They don't want it – they want to escape from that.

I thought perhaps that experience might have given him a clue as to the way he wanted to go, but Bryan was having none of that.

No, it only fed my innate prejudices. One of the things I hated, coming to Whitechapel, was finding sullenly entrenched the poor old Euston Road School of painters, entrenched in the Slade. And the Slade was rather a good school and produced some good people, and some good work went on in it, but it was absolutely solid for tonal painting and school of Bomberg, it really was. Some of that work was rather good but I abominated it, because it was all brown and black and no light and no colour. And, I thought, a slightly souped-up and phoney expressionism which had become a stylistic strait-jacket. It was real for Bomberg, it was magnificently real for Soutine, who was *the* great painter of the century in terms of that kind of expressionist distortion of form. But they were doing it gratuitously, and it seemed to me a folly. And paradoxically there was an area of inverse snobbism in the whole Euston Road approach to art which I loathe. It seems to me to be full of ex-public schoolboys painting their cleaning ladies.

I'm oversimplifying things wildly, but do you see what I'm getting at? Mass Observation, out of which it flowed, was not inverse snobbism at all, that was a genuine sociological thing. That was when bright young men from Oxford or Cambridge went and lived among the colliers to see what life was like. That was serious work, no more snobbish or far-fetched than young men coming down from university and going to work for a year or two at Toynbee Hall, in the Clement Attlee place, to help the poor with their legal problems. The Euston Road thing seemed to be slightly affected and contrived, and also terribly rearguard and reactionary. Painting in the 1950s in the manner of Degas, you know? It seemed to me foolish. And I think what I've been drawn to all my life is clarity and composure and balance and equilibrium and something that transcended life. And I think that comes from a rather poverty-stricken background with a good deal of tension through unemployment and the miseries of the thirties, which was a terrible time to be a child in unless you were born into a well-off family. It's as remote as prehistory now, but it wasn't at one time. And also being asthmatic. I think I wanted something to take me out of my life. That's why I've always adored Matisse, Bonnard, all that stuff, and a lot of the Americans, and for heaven's sake a lot of the English when they got going and cleaned their palettes.

And of course French art has everything that I love. It has composure, equilibrium, a wonderfully sophisticated sense of the world, of life, and of the land – even when they're dealing with landscape, even in *Les Très Riches Heures du Duc de Berry*, to do with horticulture or husbandry of the land, there's a kind of sophisticated intelligence behind it. How you cultivate a vine. How you put plant pots around in a garden. How you compose the elements on a breakfast table. It seems to me they've got it and it just touches my heart – I love it. And I fear it's the sophistication – I like sophisticated things.

He described his plans for the Fitzwilliam installation:

There are six walls and six paintings. There will be a very beautiful and erotic Delacroix nude, a very straight and untypical, rather mysterious Courbet, and then a very good Renoir, again untypical, of a woman standing with cows, a wonderful Bonnard, a lamp – one of Howard Hodgkin's favourite paintings, I discovered by chance – a wonderful Monet of a terrace with apple blossom or almond blossom. It's maximum intensity, isn't it? I think this one is the most energetic and concentrated and focused. It bristles with life and energy. And then below the paintings, below each wall, will be a table, and each table will take a different showcase covered with a cloth. There's going to be a book of hours, an illuminated manuscript, Limoges enamels and some ivories. All French, and they'll make people look for once at small things. I've got a passion for illuminated manuscripts and books of hours, though I haven't got much scholarly knowledge of them. I can tell a French from a German from an Italian from a Spanish, I can do that. It's the intensity that I love.

There was to be nothing from the twentieth century at the Fitzwilliam, which may have been a surprise to some people. 'It's what I've made my

living from and what I've enthused about. But if I were suddenly rich, one of the first things I'd buy would be a Sung bronze which I love with an absolute passion. And certainly a Persian illuminated manuscript, and a whole lot of other things to do with ancient art, not the twentieth century.' Robertson never really wrote about these enthusiasms for earlier, less modern, art:

I did once write a long piece on Mantegna's *Triumphs of Caesar* which David Piper anthologised in a book of essays, in which I comment loudly for their proper siting and lighting, which eventually got done.

I like things that are condensed and compacted. I'm being pretentious here. Although I speak French well, I read it slowly and cumbersomely and with difficulty. I like the French classical style because it's got that loaded compacted concentration. It's very lean and sinewy and I like that. It implies a great deal – a lot is in those simple sentences. It's in Radiguet. It's not in Proust, he wrote in a different way. It's in the wonderful *Manon Lescaut* novel. That's a perfect example of French writing. I like that in painting. French painting's got it too – this very rich and luxuriant economy. It's a kind of extraordinary worldly awareness – it comes in the way they use colour. When Patrick Heron puts a bright blue on a painting, it is Cobalt no.3, used very strongly. When Matisse uses blue it seems to have 300 years of French sophistication and feeling about sky, sea, space and the blueness of blue, and to be of course very different. In other words it's been digested and sieved through an extraordinary complexity of civilisation and culture.

With this last paean to the cerebral and emotional, the outrageously funny, break-neck, helter-skelter kaleidoscope of thoughts and impressions, prejudices and perceptions was at an end, and I was dismissed from the presence. I had far too much material for the short article I had to write, but the experience of listening to Bryan in full spate was not to be missed. I felt inspired, refreshed, full of energy. I wanted to get out there and see some art, or a film, perhaps a play, read a good book, talk to artists – in short, to celebrate the cultural world that lay entrancingly all around. Bryan had that effect, and I hope this book will too.

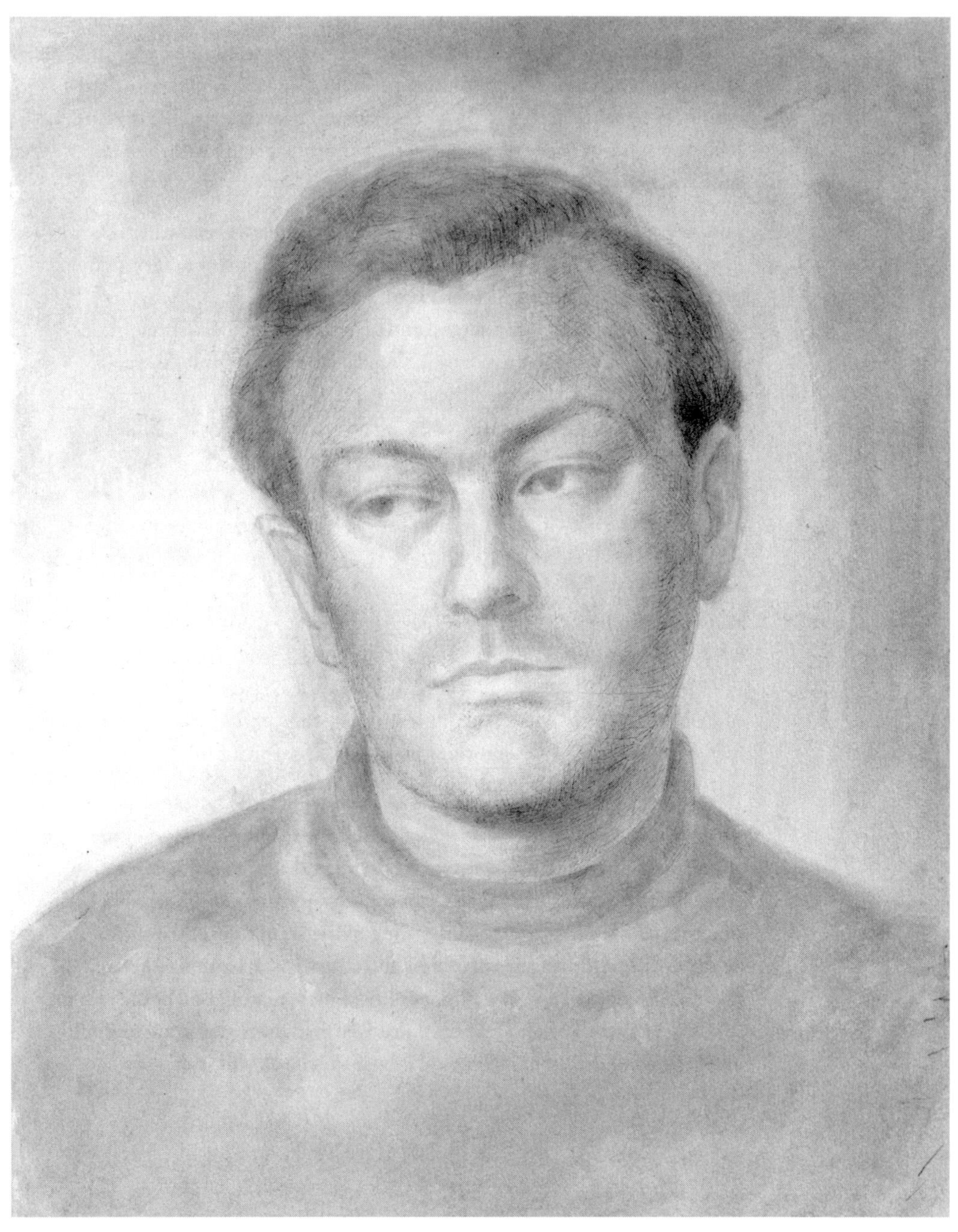

2 Elisabeth Vellacott, *Bryan Robertson*, 1952, 54.5 × 43.2 cm, pencil and wash

Bryan's background and early years

I only interviewed Bryan's sister, Peggy (Margaret) Little, once, and that was during a telephone conversation in 2011. She made it clear that Bryan would not have relished the thought of a detailed biography of his life, and our conversation helped to direct the final form this book has taken. In accordance with his wishes, this is not a biography – more of a celebration of Bryan's remarkable achievements with a few curriculum vitae reference points and facts (accurate wherever possible) to provide a framework and chronology. Thus, although Mrs Little said that her brother was very much against biographies that dwelt on childhood, it is recognised that Bryan was terribly ill all his young life and this had an extremely important effect on him. Apparently he had measles at eighteen months and that led to his lifelong asthmatic condition which (in those days) meant long periods of bed-rest. This turned him to reading and self-education, to literature and art, to visual and intellectual excitement. Colour was always important to him as an art critic, and this enthusiasm dates from his early years of semi-invalidism.

The following remarks are informed and illuminated by my conversation with his sister, whose deep affection for her brother was much in evidence. Bryan's interest in art was fostered by his mother, who quickly realised that his visual and tactile responses were highly developed. He loved feathers, fur and velvet, and was acutely conscious of the way people looked. His mother borrowed all the picture books in Streatham Library she could find and took them home for Bryan. (Ironically, Streatham Library was one of several public libraries in South London founded and built by the philanthropist Henry Tate, who was also to be responsible for the Tate Gallery, the museum that Robertson in mid-career so longed to direct.) Peggy Little, who was seven years older than Bryan, was clearly very fond of him and spent much of her spare time with him. His fight for breath was a constant torment. She recalled: 'When I was coming home from school I could hear his breathing before I got into the house.' Occasionally he was well enough to go to school. She remembers he went to a very good local elementary school before he got ill and had to stay at home. Teachers came to the house with lessons which they took away and marked.

As soon as he was able to get up and go out, aged five or six, his mother would take him to the cinema. He loved watching films and became fascinated by the medium. He would read a novel then talk it into a play with Peggy and put into it all the actresses he'd seen in the movies. He developed an encyclopaedic knowledge of actors, actresses and dancers, absorbed both from the films he revelled in and from reproductions in books and magazines. Peggy described him as 'a prodigious reader'. Although the household he grew up in was by no means well off (his father, Albert Robertson, was a caterer's manager and often unemployed), Bryan had an older brother, Gerald (who was to die in the Second World War), and several bachelor uncles, and it was a lively and boisterous home. Bryan's grandfather had been the headmaster of a large school for poor children in Holborn around the turn of the century, and had also helped to start the first soup kitchens in Holborn and Clerkenwell. That sense of public service was to be strong in Bryan himself, who demonstrated a similar evangelical commitment to educating the English in art and contemporary culture.

By the time he was sixteen, Bryan was up and about more, largely due to the stronger and more efficacious drugs that were now available. He was able to attend Battersea Grammar School (between 1936 and 1942) on a scholarship, but was soon ambitious to widen his horizons. He went to work as an office boy for Oxford University Press at Neasden, a suburb in north-west London, from 1942 to 1944, but hated it. After that he began to work as a very junior assistant on *The Studio* magazine, which he disliked also, though finally he was meeting people in the art world. Peggy said that Bryan met an artist she remembered as Peter Kapp (perhaps the Edmond Kapp to whom Bryan was later to give a retrospective exhibition at the Whitechapel in 1961). There was talk of Kapp employing Bryan but nothing came of it. Then in 1945 Kapp went to France and offered to put Bryan up for a night or two in Paris. Peggy remembered packing the kapok pillow that Bryan couldn't travel without, and the fact that he was so ill on the boat.

Although Bryan did not enjoy his time at *The Studio*, it gave him the opportunity to start publishing reviews and articles, and to meet artists. In a draft letter from 54 Conifer Gardens, Streatham, SW16, to Rodrigo Moynihan (probably in early 1947), Bryan wrote introducing himself:

> There are a few things that you should know about me. I'm in my early twenties (that sounds better than 'nearly twenty-two') and although I was on the volunteer reserve of the RAF for over a year, was not, in fact, in the services during the war. At my final medical they discovered that I was asthmatic. Since then I've been cured of asthma by penicillin, of all things.
>
> Until a year ago, I worked for *The Studio* magazine. I cannot write as fully about this as I should like to, but without any exaggeration it was the most miserable experience imaginable. It all ended with a big row and I left last January. However, they published a couple of my articles; one on David Bomberg and another one on the younger British painters which was cut

and altered, without my permission or knowledge, almost out of recognition. I did a certain amount of book reviewing for them, while I was there; and, I suppose, gained some useful experience.

The Bomberg article was still being quoted by others nearly thirty years later. This example is from the Fischer Fine Art 1973 Bomberg exhibition catalogue, in a section entitled 'Selected Criticism':

In 1946 Bryan Robertson was to report Bomberg as saying that it was 'one of the despairs of his life that the Palestine and Petra paintings are the only paintings that could gain him status in the art world, and the only paintings that could be sold. His vital experimental work, which he rightly regards as his real work, could only appeal consistently to a small circle of friends'. This was in an article in *The Studio* devoted to Bomberg in which Robertson talked of his having 'already achieved greatness by his sincerity, craftsmanship and intensity of expression'.

The catalogue writer, who, in fact, was David Sylvester, continued, citing a 1964 Bomberg exhibition at Marlborough Fine Art:

This 1964 show served to win several new supporters, though one of the most interesting notices was that in which Bryan Robertson expressed certain misgivings about the landscapes: 'There is some discrepancy, some blockage, almost continually present in his work which repeatedly confuses form, and even volume itself, with weight, and space with density. Now the density of Bomberg's work, achieved through a limited tonality, precludes any real sensation of space ... Bomberg was more conscious of the pull of gravity than of an object's projection into space and its consequent displacement of space.'

What is interesting, whether you agree with the judgements or not, is that Robertson recognised Bomberg's importance as early as 1946, when most critics ignored or overlooked him. (One of Sylvester's later regrets was that he did not realise Bomberg's importance when he was a younger man.) The Bomberg episode was typical of Robertson's prescience, even though he was not really an admirer of the kind of work Bomberg made.

Bryan often alluded later to his Parisian period:

As a young man living and studying in Paris just after the war, in 1947, Henri-Pierre Roché – later the author of the novel *Jules et Jim* from which Truffaut made his famous film – took me to Brancusi's studio in the Impasse Ronsin. This was a decisively clarifying and uplifting experience, with Brancusi revered as the supreme innovator in twentieth-century sculpture. I had the good fortune to visit Brancusi once or twice each year from then on until shortly before his death, but that first visit in February 1947 profoundly affected my view of art and creative responsibility.

Peggy Little described Bryan at this time as 'rather handsome on the George Sanders line' and 'a very sophisticated young man'. After his Paris sojourn, he worked at the Lefevre Gallery, dealing with a fine selection of French artists and modern British painters. It was there he met Cecil Collins, who became a good friend. Robertson wrote to him in the summer of 1949: 'Back in the autumn I had a breakdown in health and had to leave the Gallery to undergo some very intensive cures. I went over to Paris for three months, later, and recovered completely and since then have been reviewing exhibitions for this new *Art News and Review*. The real point of this letter is to tell you that I have been appointed Director of the Heffer Gallery, in Sidney Street [Cambridge].'

Undoubtedly, Bryan's sister was very supportive, not just in his early years. They remained extremely close and for a time shared a flat together at 49 Trinity Church Square, London SE1. (They bought the contents for £500 and the rent was £3 12*s*. a week.) Later his friend Deanna Petherbridge recalled that Bryan used to talk about teaching himself to read, of being ill in bed and learning for himself. 'I think that patterned his whole life,' she observes. 'He felt himself to be different and outside as an invalid. So he cultivated invalidism of a sort all his life, in a way.' As an adult he was often ill, but perhaps illness was also sometimes a convenient excuse when he had let someone down on a deadline or failed to turn up for dinner. Certainly, recurrent bouts of illness provided a kind of structure to life: dedicated engagement with the world alternating with invalidish retreat, when he would quite likely be gasping for breath in a darkened room, waiting for the attack to pass.

As is so often the case with daughters, it fell to Peggy to look after the Robertson parents when they grew old. Bryan was aware of this, and in a draft letter of around 1965 he wrote to Barbara Hepworth about his sister 'who I'm very fond of (an entirely amiable, undemanding and v. intelligent women with a splendid gaze on life), has had a very tough time for 10 years, trapped with ageing and increasingly dependent parents'. Subsequently, Bryan often went to stay with Peggy when she settled with her son, Marcus, in Hythe, on the Kent coast. There were, of course, both pros and cons to this. In later years he wrote in a draft letter to a female friend:

One of the weird penalties of being a bachelor is that you never get to have a proper Xmas of your own, in your own house, on your own terms, in your own style. It's always been with parents, and then with Peggy. She wouldn't like to leave Hythe in tricky winter gale time or I'd love to lay it all on here.

Also, I think that she feels it's her job and one of the things that she can do – and she does it marvellously of course. But it leaves me feeling peculiar, as if I've never grown up or something. Perhaps it's why I like to give dinner parties, to make up for it and do my host thing!

Cambridge, 1949–1952

At the Heffer Gallery Bryan discovered his true métier as a curator and organiser of exhibitions, and began his professional career that was later to change the face of British art.

In a draft letter from Bryan to John Piper (dated 19 July 1949), he wrote:

I have, very recently, taken over a large art gallery, here in Cambridge, which is owned by Heffer's, the book people. There is a large potential public for painting here, as well as crowds of enthusiastic undergraduates, but people in general do not know much about contemporary painting and, in fact, Cambridge has been almost completely cut off from modern art, in the past.

The gallery is large and quite exceptionally good – I plan to commence activities in October with a large and comprehensive retrospective survey of Modern British Painting 1900–49, beginning with Steer, Sickert, Ethel Walker and the Camden Town painters and ending with Moore, Nash, Sutherland, Hodgkins, and all the more interesting younger painters.

May I please have a fairly large picture from you? They will all be for sale, and if you can leave the picture somewhere in Central London I can arrange for transport. The show would be incomplete without it – I hope that K. Clark will write a short foreword and Henry Moore may lecture here, at the gallery, while the show is on. I leave the choice of the picture to you – but preferably a fair-sized recent one, and as rich in colour as possible – the cumulative effect of a big show of British painting is a curious one of extraordinary restraint and greyishness and I want to dispel it whenever possible.

Writing in 1965 for a catalogue introduction to the work of the sculptor Betty Rea, Bryan struck a reliably rich vein of reminiscence:

Betty Rea and I first met each other in Cambridge in 1949. I had just arrived there with the intention of bringing modern art into a city which seemed very cut off from it, and with an equal desire to help the local artists by presenting their work properly in various shows. And to lecture, learn and advise. (Mostly, I learned, inevitably.) Above all, to try to remove the barriers of provincialism – artists living outside London, unless established and famous, can feel rather lonely and isolated.

This description of my motives may sound pious, but it is accurate. I was twenty-three, and Betty Rea at first viewed me with some suspicion as a city slicker, which of course I was, since I had not lived for any length of time in a small city since childhood. Life in London, Paris and parts of Germany had intervened in the mean time. She also displayed some scepticism over the practicality of my plans, and here time proved her wrong, to our mutual pleasure.

At that first meeting, I thought Betty Rea was a rather prejudiced lady, which she was on occasion: but nothing could be more hilarious or captivating than the wild way in which she would fling any preconceived idea out of the window, for ever, once its lack of validity was understood – as Russians shatter their glass against a wall to implement a toast. I also thought that she might be too committed to certain social and political viewpoints to make good sculpture, and here time proved that I was wrong.

Bryan soon built up a loyal support group of friends in Cambridge, of which Cecil Collins and Elisabeth Vellacott were two of the chief members. Writing to Collins (9 June 1949) before he took up his new post he had this to say:

I want to put contemporary painting on the map, in Cambridge; the Fitzwilliam is a lovely place with all sorts of good things in it, but the British section – modern – is very poor, and I don't think that there has been much opportunity for people in Cambridge to see the best modern painting. (I'm thinking of starting with a large and comprehensive show called, tentatively, '40,000 years of Pornographic Art' – anything to wake them all up and get the Gallery really well known!)

I shall of course be living permanently in Cambridge and I hope that we shall see something of each other. I shall come up to London quite often to continue my art criticism and keep in touch with artists and various officials that I know.

Six months later he was writing:

Saw Howard Bliss and Sir Edward Marsh yesterday in London at the Arts Council show private view (which I have to review by Monday morning) and they are both coming to the private view on January 11th. Also, Henry Moore is coming over and to the party. I am having your small oils framed very specially in inset box frames – they will look very beautiful indeed. How are the other gouaches coming? MUST have them immediately after Christmas for framing (by 31st December).

Another letter, this time undated, from the Cambridge period suggested certain disagreements:

Now Cecil, my poppet, I must – at the risk of protracting the controversy still further – say one more thing. Whatever my drawbacks and limitations,

I am one hundred per cent for all artists and whatever I do is always determined by what seems best for the present and potentially, for their interests, and if you saw me wangling framing bills, cutting down percentages and squeezing in all kinds of mild irregularities, you would realize that I put the interests of the artist first and the interests of the gallery, if not last, very far down the list. Now let's forget it and go out and pick daffodils.

And finally, a diplomatic tribute to artist and wife: 'I know that you and Elisabeth have done a great deal to help me; in fact, if you had not been living here before I arrived, my position would have been impossible and I owe you both a lot ... You must never think that I am not always very conscious of those facts.'

One young artist Bryan was to get to know first when he came to Cambridge and who went on to great things was Elisabeth Frink. She was introduced to the Heffer Gallery by a couple of supportive collectors, Walter Brandt and his wife. (Walter was a brother of the photographer Bill Brandt.) In Bryan's own words:

They owned notable works by Sutherland and Moore and one day asked if they could bring to see me the gifted daughter of some friends who was just about to commence her studies at Chelsea School of Art. I agreed, and in this way met for the first time a tall, silent and shy girl of very evident gifts, Elisabeth Frink. She was about eighteen and embarrassed by the kindly enthusiasm of her mother's friends. Although I was only twenty-three myself, about the same age as the undergraduates who frequented the gallery, I doubtless seemed like a formidable stranger to the young Frink in the un-private noise and bustle of a department store gallery.

Robertson was so impressed by the powerful drawings of naked horsemen and menacing birds that he included some in a mixed show he was putting on. This was for Frink her first taste of public recognition, albeit for drawings rather than sculpture.

The biggest triumph of Bryan's Cambridge period was the show at Heffer's of modern French painting. Referring to his highly developed Francophile tastes he later wrote:

By the time that I arrived in Cambridge to work, I was a tremendous French snob of the deepest dye, the embodiment in sentiment of that charming eighteenth-century jingle:

The French have taste in all they do
which we are quite without,
for nature, which to them gave *goût*,
to us gave only gout.

In Paris my affections had spread to Fouquet, Clouet, the painters of *Les Très Riches Heures du Duc de Berry* and other pastoral celebrations. Earlier, in the war years, I was immersed for ages in Delacroix's *Journal*, borrowed pre-war copies of *Verve* and *Cahiers d'Art* and pined for a vision of Paris, as yet unknown to me and still occupied. But I had written on 'the young English painters' for *The Studio* magazine in 1945 – Minton, Vaughan, Craxton, Ayrton, Colquhoun and MacBryde among others of that period, so that a concern for English painting was developing.

This stood me in good stead at Heffer's, but within a year I somehow managed to present also the first exhibition of modern French painting in Cambridge. The Fitzwilliam was not so active in those days and not at all the beautifully presented and welcoming institution of today. Charles Gimpel had introduced me to a great collector, the Dutch-born Anne [Anna] Kessler, living at Gunthorpe in Rutland, who hung on her walls masterpieces by Cézanne, Renoir, Gauguin, Matisse and others. [These were the paintings which made Bryan's show so remarkable.] A sporting Mrs Kessler, to save transport costs, helped to load paintings into an old Rolls-Royce in which a friend had driven us up to Rutland: we stored them overnight in Elisabeth Vellacott's cottage in Round Church Street. I cannot imagine antics like these today.

Another Heffer's show to have a lasting effect was an exhibition of lithographs and etchings produced by 'La Guilde de la Gravure', a post-war guild founded in 1949 to make accessible all forms of fine-art printing, all for sale at three guineas a piece. Robert Erskine saw this collection as an undergraduate and realised that original art could be sold inexpensively through the medium of prints; in effect, this exhibition was the inspiration for his St George's Gallery in Cork Street, which effected something of a revolution in the public perception of original prints.

Bryan later listed some of his achievements at the Heffer Gallery:

I showed pots by Lucie Rie – then hardly known – Bernard and David Leach, Katherine Pleydell-Bouverie, Constance Dunn and others; lithographs by Colquhoun and MacBryde and work by Sutherland and Moore, with shows of paintings by Merlyn Evans, Francis Rose, Cecil Collins, who lived locally, and Charles Howard, an American artist of rare distinction living nearby. I chose as a new assistant a lively, elegant and cultivated young girl just down from Newnham called Jane McIntire. Within a few years, Jane had embarked on a love affair with a great man of letters and eventually became Jane Grigson, married at last to her beloved Geoffrey. While we worked together, in arduous conditions but often hilariously, I passed on to her my affection for the paintings of André Bauchant, the French so-called primitive painter: one of Jane's first cookery books had a beautiful Bauchant painting on its cover.

Despite Bryan's achievements in putting on memorable exhibitions and spreading the good news of the Heffer Gallery, after four years the proprietors decided to discontinue the art connection and turn the gallery back into a display of office furniture. This added to Bryan's despondency at the poor visual taste he'd found in Cambridge, among dons and undergraduates alike. He determined to pursue his fortune in a more civilised spot. In a letter to Kenneth Clark from Cambridge (dated 29 February 1952) he wrote:

I have just heard from Hilary Wayment, the British Council representative in Cambridge, that the present Director of the Whitechapel Art Gallery, in London, is leaving his post to take over the curatorship of the Walker Art Gallery. Assuming that the post of head of the Whitechapel Gallery becomes vacant and is not already filled by a second-in-command, do you think that I would stand any chance at all of getting the job?

I hope that you will forgive me for troubling you again. Your advice was most reassuring and useful to me and I have written a great many letters to provincial museums – but so far, without success: the position being that most museums badly need more staff but cannot at the moment afford to increase their staff. I absolutely long to have this job at Whitechapel and know that I could do great things there. You may remember that I applied for the position some years ago, when I was twenty and had more enthusiasm than experience, but was of course too young for the responsibility. Lord Bearsted was very nice about it at the time but I think was rather amused that I should apply for it at that age. He was extraordinarily kind about it, I remember.

I am a little out of touch with the London art world through living here for three years, so if you know anything about the position and think that I would fit the job, I should be extremely glad to hear from you, and very grateful.

The one thing that has sustained me through the past few years of rather wearing and distasteful commercial dealing, has been the educational side of organizing large-scale exhibitions and arousing interest among the public. It's something that I really can do, with great gusto, and love doing, so that Whitechapel is a very alluring thought.

Mentors

In the draft for his unpublished memoirs, compiled late in life, Bryan mentioned three men as his mentors: Colin MacInnes, Kenneth Clark and Merlyn Evans. He planned to explore their influence over his thought, tastes and standards, and their continuing relevance to him. They were an ill-assorted trio, but perhaps that was the point: individually they appealed to different sides of Bryan's character, and together

they provided a benchmark of behaviour and opinion which was a useful measure for navigating the depths and shallows of the art world.

Colin MacInnes

The English author and journalist Colin MacInnes (1914–76) was born in London but spent much of his childhood in Australia, returning to the UK in 1931. An early ambition was to be an artist, and he studied for a time at the Euston Road School under William Coldstream, Victor Pasmore and Claude Rogers. The war changed him fundamentally; his biographer Tony Gould referred to him as shy and sensitive before it and sardonic and ferocious after it. Post-war, MacInnes worked for BBC Radio before earning his living as a writer. In November 1947 he became art critic for the *Observer*, in which post he lasted just six months before resigning. Later he was an occasional writer on art for the *Times*. In January 1951 he joined the BBC Radio programme *The Critics*, broadcast on the Home Service (which later became Radio 4). Gould, writing in his 1983 biography, described it as follows:

> Though it was a less highbrow affair than its successor *Critics' Forum* (on Radio 3) is today, the format of the programme was much the same: a film, a book, a play, an art exhibition and sometimes a radio programme were discussed by a team of critics, each of whom was responsible for starting up the discussion of his particular topic.

MacInnes was generally the art critic, and a considerable success at performing in a middlebrow context.

Solitary and often bloody-minded, MacInnes alienated so many of his friends and well-wishers that eventually he retreated from the world, not only on a social level. (He commented: 'If chastity were not a virtue, it would be quite attractive.') He was a man of the 1950s, that era before the Beatles and sexual intercourse (according to Philip Larkin), a period which at best reflected the innocence and optimism associated with the premiership of Harold Macmillan. Gould wrote that for three or four years at the end of the 1950s and the beginning of the 1960s, MacInnes

> achieved near-celebrity status. But then he rather lost touch in a world he found increasingly unsympathetic, first in its smug and strident materialism and then in its depressingly familiar return to harder times. MacInnes maintained, for the most part, a high standard of journalism, but the chemistry which had transformed journalistic experience into contemporary fables was missing; and in his later fictions he retreated into a kind of historical make-believe, the ingenuity of which cannot conceal the barrenness, not of invention, but of purpose.

In the prefatory notes to his essay on Ella Fitzgerald in *England, Half English* (1961), MacInnes wrote:

I was staying, at this time [1958], with Bryan Robertson, whom the reader will meet more fully some pages later. I asked my kind host to help me, and he there and then jotted down two pages of notes on Ella Fitzgerald's particular magic. I joined these ideas of his together, added some notions of my own, and posted the robbery to Bernard Wall [then editor of *The Twentieth Century*, the magazine for which the article was written].

The second appearance of Robertson occurs in the prefatory note to the Sidney Nolan essay that MacInnes reprinted from the Whitechapel catalogue of 1957:

The invitation that came from Bryan Robertson, in the spring of 1957, to write again about Australia in a catalogue introduction to Sidney Nolan's retrospective exhibition at the Whitechapel Art Gallery was … a most welcome one. It revived my wounded interest in the Australian theme, and enabled me to say some of my admiration for Nolan as a man and artist. Bryan, with the sure impresario touch that is one of his many talents, asked me to write as freely and fully as I could about Australia, as well as about the paintings of its splendid son.

'The shifting focus in recent art from an interest in form to an investigation of space is accompanied by an expansion of the act of painting into a new realm of exuberant panache, a departure best exemplified in England by the work and outlook of Alan Davie.'

MacInnes wrote the bulk of his remarkable novel of adolescence, *Absolute Beginners* (1959), in Robertson's flat in Cundy Street, just off Ebury Street in Belgravia, between April and October 1958. Actually the two didn't see very much of each other: Bryan was out working all day, leaving before Colin got up, and returning just as Colin was going out for the night. Somewhat inevitably, MacInnes left after a row. Although he was difficult to the point of impossibility, it seems that Bryan adored him. The artist Stephen Chambers recalls hearing that MacInnes was the love of Bryan's life. But in Gould's book, Bryan commented on his friend's sex life:

He could not, it seemed, have a sex relationship with an equal. Psychologically, this no doubt related to his mother's rejection of him – it's a classic pattern … His attitude to his sexual partners was rather like the attitude of some artists towards their dealers: 'Wouldn't have them to dinner.' He was by nature a warm, tetchy queen; but he would have hated such a description, regarded the type with scorn, not been at ease with it.

The curator and exhibition organiser Richard Riley told the following story:

Alan Davie had a national touring show and it came to the Whitechapel about 1958. Bryan shared a flat with Colin MacInnes, and Bryan was entertaining Alan and Billie his wife at the Whitechapel, and they were discussing the exhibition. There came a point when they'd done everything they needed to and they had a gap before the opening, and Bryan didn't know

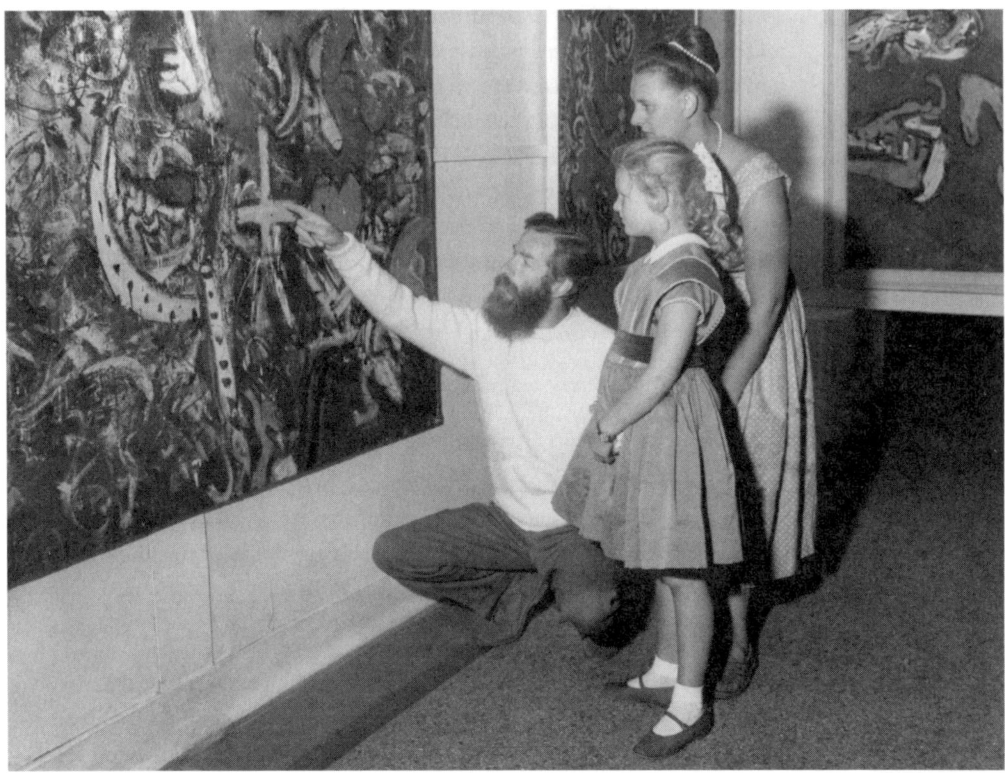

3 Alan Davie at his Whitechapel Gallery show in 1958.
Whitechapel Gallery Archive

what to do with Alan. Alan wasn't really a great conversationalist and they'd run out of things to say. So Bryan thought 'Oh, I'll take him back to the flat for a cup of tea'. Unbeknown to Bryan, Colin MacInnes had decided to have a wild gay party, so when they opened the door there were young men running around in next to nothing. But he took the Davies in – they were into Tantric sex and stuff – and they just sat in the midst of all this, perfectly fine, drinking tea.

The essentially solitary MacInnes was good at playing the mentor. Ray Gosling, who became a widely acclaimed broadcaster and journalist, was happy to acknowledge his relationship with MacInnes: 'I was but one of many protégés – he loved taking people up'. But MacInnes dropped people with equal rapidity, unable to put up with anyone for long. He was both mentor and promoter. Gould comments that MacInnes 'was a bit of an artistic impresario himself, discovering, or re-discovering, and promoting talent'. This was something he had in common with Robertson. Likewise, MacInnes, who actually gave away most of his possessions, announced: 'It is impossible to be generous unless you have nothing.' Robertson, who owned lots of books and works of art, nevertheless managed to be generous though he never had much money.

Again, MacInnes, like Robertson, was more comfortable being the host rather than a guest. Gould tells a story of MacInnes going through a pile of letters and throwing things away unopened if they looked like bills. This could have been Robertson, who had a similar dislike for opening his mail, though he might have stored the unopened envelopes in a black plastic sack rather than immediately throwing them away. MacInnes liked women, flirted with the idea of bisexuality and once proposed a *mariage blanc* to a young woman, who allegedly replied 'Oh Colin, why *blanc*?' This is remarkably like Robertson's own flirtations with the idea of marriage to favourite artists.

Towards the end of his life, MacInnes even relinquished his beloved London and went to stay with Robertson's sister Peggy and her family at Hythe in Kent. Gould recounted the move:

> Bryan Robertson remembers Colin phoning him to say that he was in trouble, even that someone was trying to kill him, though that may have been an exaggeration; it could have been simply that he owed money he was unable to pay back. Whatever the cause, he sounded scared. He said he needed to get out of London for a fortnight or so, and did Bryan think he might go to Hythe and stay with Bryan's sister there? Peggy Little agreed to his coming, and what began as a temporary respite turned into a more or less permanent arrangement; though he was loath to admit that he had found a home, the house on the sea-front at Hythe ('where no one is over twenty or under sixty', as he described the town) became precisely that for him in his last years.

In the autumn of 1975, when MacInnes was ill, Robertson tried to persuade him to see a doctor, a famous heart surgeon. MacInnes refused, but eventually accepted that he should go into hospital for some tests, staying with Robertson beforehand. Gould wrote:

> By now he could not tolerate the slightest cold or draught, so the central heating had to be full on. In addition, he was a 'total insomniac' and probably had not had a proper night's sleep in 20 years. He took catnaps during the day and kept Bryan up till 1 or 2am every night and then, if Bryan was obliged to get up in the night, called out to him and started up again where he had left off. 'It nearly killed me,' Robertson recalls.

In hospital MacInnes learned he had cancer of the oesophagus, and went back to Robertson's house to discuss it with him, including the possibility of suicide. Robertson persuaded him to have the suggested operation because at least it offered him a chance of recovery. Sadly, he was not cured by the operation, and he went back to stay with Robertson for a further three weeks. His behaviour was 'pretty manic', wrote Gould quoting Robertson. 'Suffering', Bryan concluded, 'is not ennobling'.

Robertson gave him the confidence to travel, and MacInnes visited Paris and Amsterdam before returning to Hythe. He died on 22 April 1976.

John Ryle, reviewing Gould's biography, *Inside Outsider*, in the *Sunday Times* (11 September 1983), commented: 'For the reading public MacInnes more or less invented youth culture, and his fleeting authority as a highbrow journalist in the 1950s and 60s was founded on his ready familiarity with the newly visible urban presence, not only of youth gangs, but also of black immigrants and homosexuals from whom they borrowed much of their style.' The artist Paul Huxley, who knew MacInnes and was a close friend of Bryan's, recalled their similarities when I interviewed him on 6 April 2016: 'Colin was wonderful on those programmes [*The Critics*]. I only met him once or twice but he reminded me of Bryan – physically and in the way he spoke. I think Bryan not only looked up to him, but I think he was so influenced by him that he became a bit like him.'

Kenneth Clark

It appears that Bryan Robertson first met Kenneth Clark (1903–83), known as K to his friends, in the summer of 1948 (Bryan's chronology actually says 1946 so the exact year is uncertain), an encounter engineered by Mary Kessell, Clark's mistress, whom Bryan had come to admire as an artist and like as a friend. They took to each other and were to remain lifelong friends, with Clark helping Robertson whenever able. One of the first instances of this must have been when he recommended Bryan as a writer to the publisher Eric Gregory, who was setting up an arts magazine. Later he was to write a reference in support of Bryan's application to be director of the Whitechapel, and the support was to continue, in terms of speaking up for him and offering counsel and advice, for the next thirty-five years. But first, Bryan felt it incumbent on him to apologise for a letter he had written to *The Listener* the previous year, attacking Victor Pasmore, one of several contemporary artists to whom Clark gave financial assistance.

That first letter (dated 25 December 1947) addressed the Letters page of *The Listener* thus:

Sir,

I would very much like to know the basis for Mr John Russell's contention that Victor Pasmore's new pictures represent a 'heroic encounter' between Turner, Whistler, Degas, and Mr Pasmore. Such a gifted and intelligent critic as Mr Russell should know better. It is difficult to find any signs of a real understanding of Seurat's mastery of form and construction in the small spotted areas of paint in Mr Pasmore's canvases, and the reference to Degas is mystifying. One can occasionally enjoy Mr Pasmore's pretty pastiches, but this talk of heroic encounters is surely going too far.

And it is disappointing to find that the rest of Mr Russell's article constitutes yet another example of the present extraordinary complacency and blindness in our art criticism. We have several excellent painters working in this country and possibly one great sculptor, but it has for some time been obvious that there is in England, as in other countries, a decline in painting, and at a time when so much depends upon intentions and possibilities and there is so little in the way of actual performance and accomplishment it is surely foolish and short-sighted to attempt to create a false impression of the melancholy clutter of mediocrity only too often exhibited nowadays as contemporary British painting.

Yours, etc Bryan Robertson

In Bryan's letter of apology to Clark (dated 24 October 1948), he wrote:

Dear Sir Kenneth,

I am leaving for Paris on the 1st of December – since July I have been going through all the stages of a nervous breakdown and often thought that I should never live to go on with my studies or look at a wonderful picture or listen to Heavenly music again. Please forgive this precipitative beginning – this is my fourth attempt to write this letter to you and I feel that I must simply say what is in my heart and mind and hope for your understanding.

First of all, and most important – I believe that you have done more for British painting and the understanding of Italian art in this country than any other man alive. I think you are a very great man – whenever I think of Ruskin, which is very often, I think of you. (I've suddenly realized that you probably don't even remember my name, and if you do happen to remember it, may think that this letter is absurd, in assuming that anyone should care to know my opinion – but I must go on.)

I want to apologize very humbly, for a loathsome letter written by myself about Pasmore, and which was published in *The Listener*. It was written at a very miserable and – now, and was then – humiliating time in my life and was actually levelled at a certain kind of art criticism which always irritates me; but as I was to my great shame under the influence of other people, I can only hope that you have either never seen or heard of the letter; or if you have, will accept this apology for attacking in a muddled and vaguely fortuitous way, one of the most enchanting painters in the country.

Ever since I can remember, I have wanted to be as complete a person as possible; a writer; and to help in any way possible the cause of art in this country. I've been particularly miserable at a dealer's gallery, for eight weary months, in order to find out everything possible about the painters … Preposterous as this sounds, it linked up in my mind with certain aspects of Ruskin's work – but it wasn't at all like that, in practice.

I do not want to bore you – so will be brief. In Paris I shall find some sort of job to achieve a degree of security, spend as much time as possible in museums, cathedrals and galleries in and around Paris, study as much as I can and perfect my still wildly ungrammatical, if fluent, French.

The worries and troubles of my family have obsessed me for years – have decided to ignore it, from this day forth – as I can do nothing to change their lives, and the doctors tell me that I'm ruining my life.

This letter is not very coherent and does not say half as much as I should like to say. But I feel and sense something of the glorious transition from mental and physical illness and misery to a realization of my gifts and everything I must do to perfect them …

Please don't answer this letter. If I had a letter like this, I'm quite sure that I shouldn't know what to say; and as we all know that you are always excessively occupied, I should be happy if you would accept it as a token of intense admiration, mixed with feelings of great gratitude for certain things in the past.

Yours sincerely,
Bryan Robertson

After they had been brought together, what was it that kept them friends? Bryan's admiration for Clark was clear from the start, but it was very soon reciprocated, as Robertson began his remarkable series of Whitechapel exhibitions. And although Bryan might not immediately have seemed to be an obvious friend for K, in fact they got along well together. As Caryl Hubbard noted, and she had worked for Clark in her early years, K liked people like Bryan and particularly valued their directness. Coupled with which, both men liked and admired artists – a rarer quality in the museum world than might be supposed.

Like Bryan, Clark believed that art and beauty are everyone's birthright, an idea ultimately deriving from John Ruskin, about whose writings Clark was something of an expert and devotee. Robertson greatly admired K's own writings and, as Simon Pierse has succinctly put it (*Australian Art and Artists in London, 1950–1965, An Antipodean Summer*, 2012), 'shared his instinctive approach to art criticism'. As Bryan was to write to K in 1960: 'You're always about thirty paces ahead of everyone else in observation.' Interestingly, Clark saw himself, to a degree, as self-created, rather as Robertson was largely self-educated. 'I am the type of local boy makes good,' said Clark. There are other parallels of taste and interest. Clark was involved with the Royal Opera House, as Robertson was to be, and he had a circle of New York ladies who gave him dinner and looked after him when he visited the city. Bryan had a similar fan club whose financial generosity helped him survive the lean years later in life. Perhaps surprisingly, Clark liked the work of Pollock and Rothko, despite his reservations

about abstraction, and he became (like Bryan) a friend of Motherwell. K was, however, on occasion a trifle imperious, if not downright regal. Clark's biographer, James Stourton, quoted Michael Gill, the soon-to-be-producer of the BBC 2 documentary series *Civilisation* (aired in 1969 and written and presented by Clark) on the great panjandrum arriving at the Whitechapel to see the Rauschenberg exhibition in 1964: 'When Clark swept through with the actress Irene Worth, he delivered brilliant, perceptive and, I thought, ultimately condescending opinions on each complex image in turn.'

In the following years, as Bryan's own career trajectory became more fragmented and unsatisfactory, Clark continued to be a hugely supportive friend and mentor. In 1965, K recommended Bryan as a broadcaster to the BBC, and in 1975 had a word with J.W. Lambert, literary and arts editor of the *Sunday Times* (1960–76), to see if there was any work for Bryan. This led to some book reviewing but nothing regular. Clark wrote to Bryan about the possibility of him making a short series of films on abstract art, regarding it as an important project as so many people were at a loss when faced with abstract art. Clark envisaged a series of three to five films, dealing with cubism, Mondrian, abstract expressionism and subsequent developments, and trying to assess what was of value and what not in contemporary abstraction. Bryan was perfectly placed in terms of personal experience to present the films. Clark wrote: 'You are obviously the only person who could do this with knowledge and authority. Would you like to pay me a call here toward the end of the week? I would like you to see my new chambers, which are really very pretty.'

Although the respect was mutual, in later years Bryan seemed to grow more desperate in his need for reassurance and for work. In a letter dated 28 July 1977, Bryan tried to persuade Clark to come to Australia with him to make some TV programmes about the landscape. He also invited K to come to lunch with Moore and Sutherland, and also with Hoyland and Caulfield. It was almost as if he was trying to bolster his own self-confidence at a time when it had taken a beating. The tone of these later letters to K is slightly facetious and even hysterical, imploring. 'I do need fresh air, early nights and a bit of peace,' he wrote, 'as my house has been a common lodging house for months, The Palace Flop House and Grill, with Motherwell, now Clement Meadmore, & sundry young artists who subside in my spare room after they've gollopped [*sic*] all my wine.'

Merlyn Evans

The artist Merlyn Evans (1910–73) was born in Cardiff, but grew up in Glasgow where he went to art school. He developed a vigorously linear style that drew upon abstraction as well as surrealism to communicate an overtly social and political subject matter. Emigrating to South Africa in 1938, his work with its characteristic interweaving of organic and mechanical imagery made increasingly explicit reference to atrocity and war. He joined the South African army in late 1942 as an engineer and served in North Africa and the Middle East. These experiences influenced his artistic style by introducing an ethnic element.

The friendship between Robertson and Evans does not seem to be much documented, despite the thoroughgoing monograph on the artist by Mel Gooding (2010), who dedicated the book to the memory of Robertson, 'lover of art and friend of artists'. Robertson seems to have first met Evans in 1945 through their mutual friend Mary Kessell. Gooding writes that Bryan had seen Evans' work 'as early as 1946, and had followed his career closely ever since, visiting his studio, providing encouragement, and using his considerable influence to secure attention and interest in his work'. Robertson wrote Evans a characteristically enthusiastic letter about his 1953 exhibition at the Leicester Galleries:

The opening of your magnificent exhibition this afternoon marked your final and complete emergence as a great artist. That is to say, to be reckoned with only in the company of those great and wonderful men of our country: Picasso, Braque, Brancusi, Matisse, Moore and Léger. I do not know how this show will sell – I think, very well, actually – but the time is assuredly not far distant when you will be able to sell anything that you care to produce. It is an immense triumph.

Three years later, Evans' retrospective at the Whitechapel opened. In the catalogue preface Bryan wrote that Evans 'may in some ways be considered as one of its [abstraction's] earliest and most convinced practitioners in England'. He went on to state:

Evans is the outstanding engraver in this country, and a major draughtsman. His paintings, essentially Celtic and romantic in spirit despite occasional classical ventures, reveal in a most powerful manner the musings and speculations of a mind entirely absorbed by the twentieth-century world and capable of relating it on occasion to other periods in history and other societies. His pictures are humanist in conception, forceful in execution and urgent in their implications. The Prisoner concerns us all, so do the Refugees and the Victims of the Demolition, and so does the Trial. Evans has made images which depict the roots and the structure of violence, however oblique the references may be to its actual manifestation.

Writing in the catalogue for another exhibition, *The Graphic Work of Merlyn Evans* (at the Victoria and Albert Museum in 1972), Robertson commented:

It is hard to write directly of the imagery in Evans' work because what he creates is the image behind or beyond words. But in old-fashioned terminology, it might have been possible to consider his work literary if the advent of Johns and Rauschenberg had not made this phrase obsolete. Like that of Ernst or Picasso, Evans' work has always had a subject. Abstract in presentation and formal device, this subject is hardly representational but it is often figurative, in different ways, and frequently symbolic. The nature of the imagery is plain to see and Evans has never indulged himself in cryptic or misleading titles. But, if we consider different facets of this nature for a moment, we may best be rewarded by following the advice of Polonius in *Hamlet*: 'By indirections find directions out.' And this is perhaps the most relevant and courteous approach to the very dignified, Celtic, and elegiac sensibility of the artist.

Although little is recorded about the friendship of these two men, it is clear that Robertson found much to admire in Evans, in terms of standards of human conduct and approach to the fundamentals of art and life. In his Kettle's Yard '45–'99 exhibition catalogue in 1999 Bryan recalled the man and the art:

With an exceptional mind and intelligence, Merlyn was formidably erudite about modern art and an active member of the Royal Institute of Philosophy. He was a great draughtsman and an extraordinary painter whose work, although winning international prizes in print-makers' shows, always seemed to be outside prevailing fashion. He is one of the very few artists to have made substantial images in paintings and drawings inspired by war, some of them made when resting up from the battlefields. In later years, he dealt in more abstract terms with themes of social and political oppression: a visual conscience of our time. His friendship over thirty years, and his shared knowledge, expanded my awareness of art and life.

Bryan Robertson: a personal memory by Edwin Mullins

Here the arts writer and journalist Edwin Mullins recalls his relationship with Bryan:

Moving to London in the late 1950s straight from university I found myself, like so many others, drawn to places that seemed to give off the pulse of a youthful city, one that had at last shed its old cultural insularity and its post-war greyness. For street-life and trendy clothes there was of course the King's Road, Chelsea; there was Ronnie Scott's newly opened jazz club, and for theatregoers the Royal Court in Sloane Square where you could Look Back in Anger with John Osborne; while for art lovers the place above all others was the Whitechapel Art Gallery, down in the East End, where – some of us were aware – Picasso's *Guernica* had once been exhibited.

One lunch-hour I left my sub-editor's desk and took the underground to Aldgate East. Right next to the station a policeman was standing by the entrance to the Whitechapel Art Gallery, gazing watchfully at a steady stream of visitors who were making their way inside. There had been protests and trouble recently, I knew. This was 1958, and the exhibition was the work of a contentious American artist whose 'drip' paintings had never been seen in London before, and were raising some outraged eyebrows in the British art establishment. The artist was Jackson Pollock.

The man responsible for the exhibition was the Whitechapel's young director, Bryan Robertson. There were many who wondered why a fringe gallery in the East End had shown the initiative of putting on such a show rather than the Tate Gallery, particularly since the Whitechapel then received no public funding from the London County Council or the Arts Council. Its director clearly had a way of attracting support from individuals and corporate bodies who recognised that he possessed a vision and an understanding of the direction contemporary art was heading that the museums and art institutions in this country conspicuously lacked, from the Tate Gallery downwards.

I never met Robertson on that visit to the Pollock show, though I would like to have done so. I was well aware of his reputation and his innovative achievements. My very first visit to the Whitechapel two years earlier had been to the pioneering exhibition he had mounted, boldly entitled *This is Tomorrow*, which had given me my first bewildered glimpse of artists like Eduardo Paolozzi and Richard Hamilton. After the Pollock exhibition I regularly took that same District Line train to Aldgate East in my lunch-hour to see whatever Robertson was showing now. And that was how I got to know him. The gallery was usually fairly empty, and he would sometimes join me for a beer and a plastic sandwich in the nearby pub. Gastro-pubs were things of the future. And we'd chat about the artists he liked, and gossip about the art moguls and critics he didn't like. He was always delightful company, and I'd return to Fleet Street rather late but in the best of humour.

The highlight of those lunch-hour visits to the Whitechapel was the Mark Rothko exhibition which Bryan put on in 1961. I had yet to visit the United States, and like most British art-lovers was only familiar with American abstract painters through art magazines, which gave no idea of the huge scale of their work. The Rothko exhibition bowled me over. It was like seeing Giotto's Arena Chapel for the first time. Bryan saw the look on my face, and laughed. 'You need a drink', he said.

Three years later another of Bryan's exhibitions sent shock-waves across the London art world. Following on from his earlier ground-breaking show

This is Tomorrow he now put together a selection of work by young British painters who had recently graduated from art school and were still virtually unknown. I remember Bryan ringing me at my flat to announce: 'You've got to come. This is a bit special.' By this time I'd became the *Sunday Telegraph*'s art critic, and Bryan was organising a special preview for critics he considered likely to be sympathetic to the show; I noticed some significant omissions. The exhibition was called *The New Generation*. It was still being hung as I arrived, and Bryan was bustling about giving sharp orders while breaking off to welcome about six of us who had been invited along. It had the air of a final rehearsal before the first night, and Bryan was doing his best to emulate Diaghilev, his hero. Finally the paintings were all hung, bottles of wine were produced, and introductions made by a now calm and entirely charming Bryan Robertson. It was my first meeting with several artists I came to know better, and my first acquaintance with the work of John Hoyland, David Hockney, Bridget Riley, Paul Huxley, Patrick Caulfield and Allen Jones.

This was 1964. And for those of us who were at the Whitechapel that evening, and for the official opening a couple of days later, it felt as though *The New Generation* carried a banner for the Swinging Sixties, and that a great deal of dust and cobwebs was being blown away from the art scene. It was a time when people began to feel that London was no longer a cultural outpost of Paris or New York, but at the very centre of things. And for this Bryan Robertson was to a considerable extent responsible.

I was also aware that 1964 was a stressful year for him. He had now been at the Whitechapel for twelve years. He was still only about forty, and he harboured ambitions: or rather, he had one ambition above all. Bryan was too discreet a man to talk openly about personal hopes on the occasions when we'd meet for a drink or a pub lunch. Nonetheless they leaked out. The Director of the Tate Gallery in London, Sir John Rothenstein, was retiring. He had been a powerful presence: a likeable and generous man, but in the eyes of many disastrously insular in outlook, having overlooked countless opportunities to enrich the Tate's collection of works by major European and American artists of the twentieth century. The gallery's holdings of foreign masterpieces were considered by Rothenstein's critics to be shamefully meagre. The art historian and friend of Picasso, Douglas Cooper, described the Tate's foreign collection to me as being displayed 'down a ship's ladder in the basement'.

Because the mood had changed in favour of a more international outlook it was widely held that Bryan Robertson was the candidate best suited to succeed Rothenstein. But there were other names in the hat, particularly that of the painter and art scholar Lawrence Gowing, who was a loud and persuasive figure with many supporters. Robertson was by comparison a loner. The Tate trustees backed away from the political arena and played safe by appointing Rothenstein's deputy, Norman Reid. As it turned out, Reid proved to be one of the Tate's most respected directors; nonetheless Bryan was left a deeply disappointed man with seemingly nowhere to go.

Studio International echoed the sentiments of many in describing Robertson as the greatest director the Tate Gallery never had. He remained at the Whitechapel for a further five years. The pioneer work continued. There was the first Robert Rauschenberg exhibition in this country, over which Bryan and I metaphorically came to blows since I could never see the point of Rauschenberg, and Bryan seemed to me to talk a lot of nonsense about him.

In 1968 he resigned from the Whitechapel. He had been its Director for sixteen years. The same year I gave up being the *Sunday Telegraph's* art critic. We had dinner together and Bryan asked me what I was going to do. I said I wanted to make television documentaries on painting and sculpture, and perhaps write books. Then I asked him the same question. He said he didn't know altogether, but he would like to curate exhibitions here and in the United States. This of course he did, including a spell of five years as director of the State University of New York museum, and later demonstrating the catholic nature of his taste by putting on the delightful Raoul Dufy exhibition in London for the Arts Council – for which I teased him, 'you're going soft, Bryan'. But it wasn't a national museum like the Tate Gallery, which I always felt he should have had.

Inevitably I saw him less. Our paths rarely crossed. But then in the mid-1970s the BBC asked me to become one of the regular presenters of a new daily arts programme on radio, *Kaleidoscope*. We took it in turns. Each presenter tended to have his own speciality, and art exhibitions were generally left to me. In the role of interviewer rather than critic I could talk to whoever I wished, and over the next seven or eight years I chose Bryan whenever he was in this country and available. One lively dialogue I enjoyed with him related to an exhibition in his old haunt, the Whitechapel Art Gallery. The subject was the work of one of my favourite artists of the twentieth century, the German expressionist Emile Nolde. Under the Nazis, Nolde's work, like that of most other gifted young Germans, was classified as 'Degenerate Art', and he was forbidden to paint. He secretly defied the order, producing tiny watercolours which could easily be concealed from prying Gestapo eyes. These became known after the war as Nolde's 'Unpainted Pictures', and Bryan's successor at the Whitechapel had shown the wit to obtain a loan of them.

As Bryan and I sat opposite one another in the studio at Broadcasting House it transpired that both of us had been to Nolde's remote house at Seebüll in northern Germany close to the Danish border, and that we shared the moving experience of having stood in the tiny attic room with its slit of a window overlooking the drive along which the Gestapo would be visible as they approached the house. *Kaleidoscope* was broadcast live, and I have sharp memories of a green light flashing urgently in front of me and frantic waving of the producer's arms from beyond the glass screen as Bryan and I shared our enthusiasm for Nolde's spirit and his Unpainted Pictures.

It may not have been quite the last time I saw Bryan, but it is the occasion I like to remember as encapsulating my feelings of appreciation and affection for him. There have been few people I have known and worked with whose understanding of art has been so broad and generous, and whose enthusiasms were so easy to share.

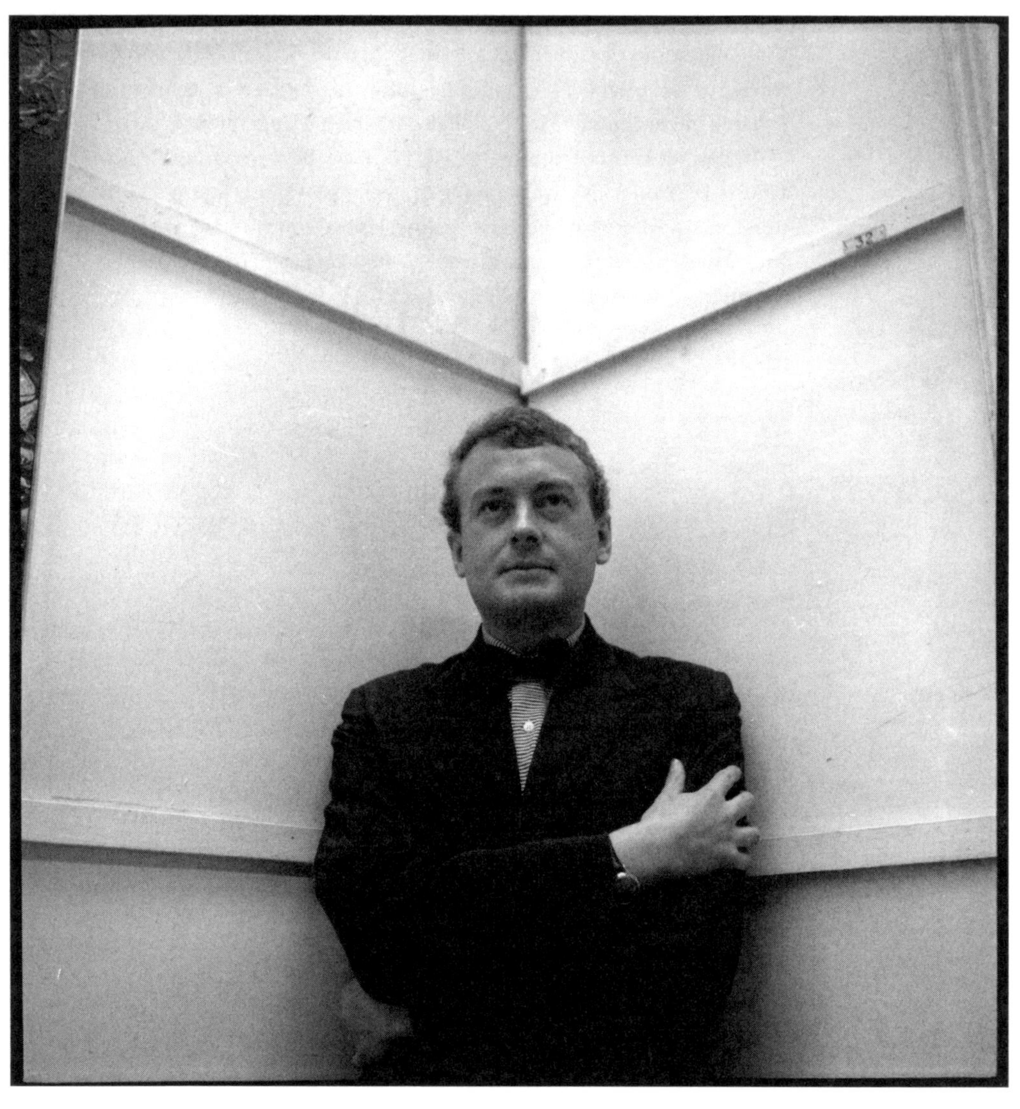

4 Ida Kar, *Bryan Robertson*, 1958, 5.71 cm square film negative

The Whitechapel years, 1952–1969

When Bryan Robertson took over as Director of the Whitechapel Art Gallery in April 1952 it looked, he later wrote, 'like a grim, scruffy East End mission hall. The walls were covered with grubby coffee coloured hessian, riddled with gaping holes, alternating with beetroot red hessian; the supporting pillars were chocolate brown, the terrazzo floor was grimy and the whole place reeked of poverty and good works among the poor.' The first thing that Robertson did was to redecorate, transforming his gallery into an airy white space with a pale blue ceiling and doubling the daylight, a forerunner of the notion of the gallery as a 'white cube' which was to take such powerful hold in the 1970s and then the 1990s. In this, as in so many other things, Robertson was a pioneer.

Robertson's decision to put on group shows without a thesis (something difficult to imagine nowadays) simply in order to show good art was similarly innovative. Mary Yule, who has extensively researched Robertson's Whitechapel years, described his policy thus:

> Through a careful orchestration of juxtapositions, Robertson presented a view of richness and variety in British art, placing it, where he felt it was merited, on equal terms with distinguished foreign art. He sought to show a range of simultaneous discourses and wherever possible tried to make links between the visual and other arts. The stress he placed on illustrating the notion of simultaneity was influenced by his reading of R.H. Wilenski's *Modern French Painters*, in which Wilenski sited the French modern masters within a context which refers to music, dance, opera and poetry.

Against an array of talented competitors – including Lawrence Alloway, Quentin Bell, Peter de Francia, Lawrence Gowing and David Sylvester – Bryan won the job as Whitechapel supremo at the perfect time. Man and era came together with precocious fortune.

Robertson was a maverick who refused to conform to accepted tastes, and this was his great strength. He was determined to show artists he believed in, whether they were outside the critical mainstream or not. Robertson cleverly interspersed his more radical exhibitions with shows of more straightforward artists, such as Derek Hill, Thelma Hulbert, John Craxton and Mary Potter. The result was a richly varied programme that strategically enhanced the differences of what was being shown. This passionate plurality was very much at odds with the restrictive modernist orthodoxy practised (and loudly preached) by the influential critic Clement Greenberg. Robertson refused to be so limited, and through his wide-ranging vision he managed to reposition British art, bringing historical work within the purview of the modern, and commanding

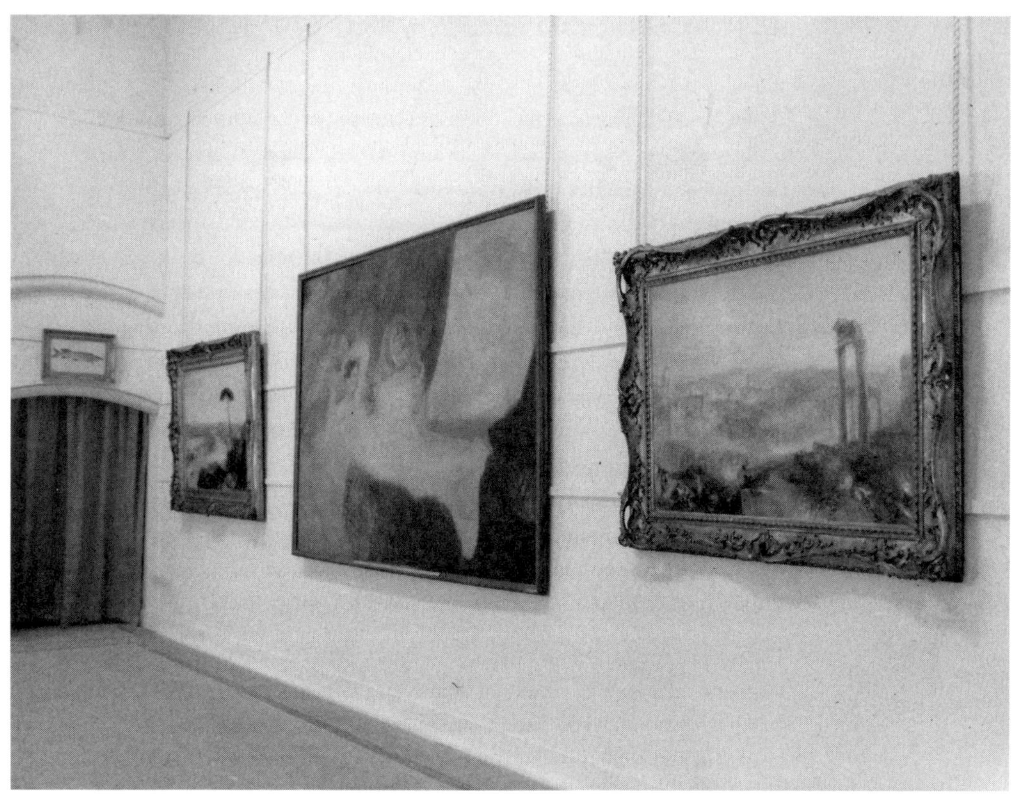

5 Installation view of the J.M.W. Turner exhibition at the Whitechapel Gallery, 1953
Whitechapel Gallery Archive

proper respect and attention for the latest work by young artists, as well as by painters and sculptors in mid-career. In the mid- to late sixties, he was closely involved with three exhibitions of British art in America: *The English Eye*, curated by Bryan with Robert Melville at the Marlborough-Gerson Gallery in New York in 1965; *London: The New Scene* at the Walker Art Center, Minneapolis, in 1965; and *New British Painting and Sculpture* at UCLA Art Galleries, Los Angeles, in 1968–9, curated by Herbert Read with Bryan. All these helped to spread the Robertson gospel of excellence further afield, and to identify his judgement even more firmly with the art of this period.

The J.M.W. Turner show which Robertson mounted in February and March 1953 was very grand, containing 224 exhibits (oils, watercolours and pencil drawings) largely unfamiliar to a London audience. Amazingly, this was the first major Turner exhibition in a public gallery since the artist's death in 1851. Patrick Heron, in the *New Statesman and Nation*, wrote: 'Mr Robertson has transformed a dingy cavern of a gallery into a luminous cave, whose off-white, pale blue and grey-mauve ceiling and walls re-echo with perfect "acoustics" the blue and gold "chords" emitted by these Turners.' Kenneth Clark contributed to the exhibition very practically by lending an oil and a copy of Turner's *Liber Studiorum*, his collection of prints. In the catalogue, Bryan wrote: 'I gratefully acknowledge, in particular, the advice and information given by Sir Kenneth Clark, whose scholarship and enthusiasm for Turner greatly enriched the content of the exhibition at a decisive stage in the selection.' The exhibition was a huge success, attracting almost half-a-million visitors. Robertson's Whitechapel was well and truly launched.

The Whitechapel remained remarkably independent, if operating on a minuscule budget. Before the Hayward Gallery opened in 1968, the Whitechapel was one of the best spaces in which to exhibit art, particularly sculpture and large-scale paintings. Robertson had a real flair for exhibition installation, and would think around a show trying to make each one a special event. For instance, he very much wanted Samuel Beckett to write a text for the 1958 Colquhoun retrospective, and when this was sadly not forthcoming, commissioned George Barker to write a poem instead. 'Sonnet, as Panegyric for Robert Colquhoun' was duly printed in the catalogue, adding a further and unexpected resonance to the reproductions and explicatory texts. And for Ceri Richards' 1960 exhibition, Bryan organised a piano recital in the gallery of Claude Debussy's *Cathédrale engloutie*, a prelude that had struck a deep chord in Richards' imagination and given rise to many remarkable paintings, prints and constructions.

Bryan reacted against the drabness and austerity of post-war Britain, what the Kitchen-Sink realist John Bratby called 'the colour and mood of ration books – the general feeling of sackcloth and ashes after the war'. If he was drawn more to colourful abstraction, its 1950s unpopularity giving way to 1960s popularity, this was because he felt that abstract art was extending the visual language more than figuration. He took to heart Ezra Pound's injunction to 'Make it New', and reacted explosively to the Whitechapel's immediate past. He referred to the puritanical 'left-wing scoutmaster' Hugh Scrutton, his predecessor, but at least Scrutton had left the gallery in financial solvency, a concept entirely foreign to Robertson with his extravagant and disorganised approach. If Bryan's radical vision for the Whitechapel was a refreshing and cleansing hurricane, he nevertheless took too little care for the future, storing up administrative and fiscal problems for himself and his heirs. But the Whitechapel successfully surfed a key historical moment under Bryan's leadership, and there is always a price to pay for such swashbuckling. Accountants don't like panache.

The 1955 Michael Ayrton exhibition catalogue contained the following statement of intent (from the preface by Robertson):

In many ways, the most useful kind of exhibition that can be offered to the public at the present time is the comprehensive and reasonably definitive show covering the work of one artist. Accordingly, plans have been made to present two kinds of one-man exhibition: the first, devoted to the assembled work of some of the great archetype figures in modern art and the second kind to form a gradual survey of the work, to date, of some of the younger British artists interspersed with retrospective exhibitions covering a longer period in the lives of some older British artists. The recent Barbara Hepworth and Piet Mondrian exhibitions have been part of this programme; and plans have been made for some time to organize, at a later date, an exhibition of sculpture by the Spanish artist, Julio González [this plan was not realised].

'British painting and sculpture has never been more vigorous or more varied than it is today [1954] and our artists need and deserve every possible encouragement. It should never be forgotten that every work of art created today represents a very considerable act of faith.'

Our own younger artists need and deserve all the help and encouragement that can be given to them; and the trustees feel that a series of large exhibitions, covering approximately ten years in their careers, could be useful both to the artists themselves and the general public. Artists particularly need this kind of occasion when they are in their thirties and forties. There has been a swing of the pendulum since 1945 in favour of the art school student: a great deal has been done, in many ways, to make their lot a happier one and to give them increased opportunities. Nobody would wish to see this changed; but in their middle years artists need, with even greater urgency, every chance to exhibit their work in this country and abroad, and the trustees hope that the additional opportunity of seeing a large body of their work gathered together in one place may be helpful. For it is at this time in their lives that artists may find themselves temporarily becalmed in the doldrums of uncertainty or engaged in the laborious process of re-orientation which so many have to face – or they find themselves, for the moment, outside the approval of fashion and the mode; all this when they are beset by the enervating problems of existence and looking after the upkeep of their homes and studios.

The beliefs Bryan expressed here – particularly in the second paragraph – are central to his philosophy of directing a public gallery, and ring as true – if not truer – today as they did in 1955. There is still a desperate need for a gallery and a director with the vision to show artists in mid-career or late middle age, when they might be out of fashion and largely invisible, caught in that slough of despond between early success and the veneration delightedly accorded the survivor: Grand Old Man or Grand Old Woman. All the public galleries in London today show the same kind of internationally fashionable art, or else blockbuster Old or Modern Masters exhibitions, so desperate are they for box-office revenue. Bryan's great gift was that he put the artists first, didn't care about money (the

Whitechapel had a free admission policy anyway), and concentrated on making very beautiful exhibitions of art he valued.

In August 1956 *This is Tomorrow*, an exhibition at the Whitechapel that Bryan had very little to do with, was famously opened by a robot. The show was proposed and organised by a team of artists and intellectuals and was devoted to the possibilities of interdisciplinary collaboration over the design of the future. It was led largely by the Independent Group, an ICA faction, but the ICA was far too small and cultish for the remarkable extravaganza the organisers (who included Theo Crosby, Richard Hamilton, Reyner Banham, Eduardo Paolozzi and Lawrence Alloway) had in mind, and the Whitechapel made the perfect venue. The show has entered the history books as the forerunner of pop art, a multi-disciplinary collaboration which was in some ways a watershed in British art. Robertson can take little credit for it, nor did he attempt to, but it certainly helped to put the gallery on the map.

The *Times* referred to the Whitechapel as 'An East End Gallery with a European reputation', and on 24 August 1957, wrote:

The gallery is financed partly by grants from the councils of adjacent boroughs, and from the London County Council – but not, as yet, from the City of London; partly by other public bodies, including the City Parochial Foundation, and also the Arts Council, which makes occasional grants for particular exhibitions; partly by the annual subscriptions of the 250 'Friends of the Gallery'; and partly, even now, by private benefactions, of which those of the Bearsted family have been conspicuously generous.

From all these sources the gallery's average annual income, since 1951, has been only £4,500: which, when one considers the expenses of the salaries of a staff of seven, of maintaining the large building, and of mounting exhibitions of quality in a worthy manner, is manifestly insufficient.

The article concluded with a long response from Robertson to a question from the anonymous *Times* correspondent about the tastes of contemporary visitors. He answered with typical enthusiasm and wonderful idealism:

They come … not for instruction but for pleasure. They like the exotic, the spectacular; for the taste of the East Ender is, if not higher, certainly 'slicker' and more sophisticated than it was. It is sometimes said that 'everybody really yearns for art'. It would help us greatly if they did, but in fact just as some persons are tone deaf, others are quite indifferent to painting. All one can do is hang the best work of its kind upon the walls, open the doors wide, and leave it to the people to come in. What one may hope for is that the architecture and the situation of the gallery are such that classical and contemporary art are made as accessible as they can be to anyone who may wish to look; and also that at Whitechapel we may be able to extend the living artist's public to a wider, unfamiliar world.

The influential art critic Denys Sutton, writing the same year in the *Financial Times*, compared the Whitechapel most favourably with both the Museum of Modern Art (MOMA) and the Whitney Museum in New York. As Mary Yule was to conclude nearly half a century later:

In his first five years at the Whitechapel, Robertson achieved what he had hoped for, an elevation of visual standards and the creation of a context of great distinction for British and European art. By 1957 the Gallery had 'a European reputation' and was set to embark upon the next stage in placing British art on an equal footing with the best of foreign art.

An art-world contemporary, such as Alan Bowness, made sure he saw everything at the Whitechapel, bought the catalogues, and made notes in them for future reference. Bowness was a kind of establishment counterpoint to Robertson, seen as a more official, respectable figure because he had studied at Cambridge and the Courtauld. Robertson had no such qualifications but, interestingly enough, two of the other most celebrated post-war curator-critics, Lawrence Alloway and David Sylvester, didn't have university educations either.

Perhaps the disinclination to delegate that marked Robertson's rule at the Whitechapel came from his character as autodidact. He worked on his own, was very much his own man, making his own decisions. Although he did have some help from time to time – and he certainly had assistants: in 1952, Miss Joan Holland, by 1957 Ann Forsdyke, later Tejas Englesmith (perhaps the best known) – the impression many had was that the Whitechapel was run by Bryan alone and was his personal fiefdom.

Bryan was astute at positioning the Whitechapel in the 1950s and, at a time when there was a shortage of good exhibition space, he excelled at introducing artists, both British and foreign, contemporary and historical, to the public. He saw this great opportunity in that decade, and lost no time in seizing it. The Arts Council couldn't take all the exhibitions that were being offered to them, so Bryan established some very valuable alliances, including one with the Stedelijk Museum in Amsterdam, which was then under a brilliant director called Willem Sandberg. Sandberg liked Bryan and they got on well together, and a number of Bryan's most important exhibitions, his Mondrian and Malevich, for example, were largely done with the help of Sandberg.

Bryan's other strong point was establishing an American connection. He realised quite early on that American painting was going to be of more interest to people than French, and in a sense his de Staël exhibition in 1956 represented the end of an era. Bryan was prescient in this, as many

people in the 1950s still expected something great to come out of Paris. This is evident from the writing of such very different commentators as Patrick Heron and John Berger. History was swift to justify Robertson's prediction, and American painting did develop, much assisted by American money and the CIA. At the American Embassy, Stefan Munsing was the cultural attaché charged with promoting American art. Bryan made a friend of him. Meanwhile MOMA in New York was busy putting together a whole programme of touring exhibitions of new American painting that could easily be diverted to the Whitechapel. Very often they were packages – organised in New York by Peter Selz or one of a group of similarly competent curators – and Bryan took them over and made a catalogue. He did not always originate his shows personally, but he had the wit to recognise the wonderful opportunity he was being offered, and from such international alliances he was able to put in place a remarkable sequence of exhibitions.

Bryan liked to hang an exhibition without any interference from the artist. Very often this meant that he actually put on the walls considerably fewer pictures than might be listed in the catalogue. (Sometimes, out of a list of eighty works, Bryan would hang as few as fifty or sixty.) Occasionally this could lead to complaints from disgruntled lenders, but it did mean that Bryan allowed himself a free hand to make the most beautiful hang possible. This rather autocratic approach paid dividends because of Robertson's eye: he was responsible for incomparable and surprising installations of paintings and sculpture.

Shortly after assuming the mantle of Director, Bryan wrote the following letter to Kenneth Clark, using K, as he often did, as a sounding-board:

At a time when our finances are low and prospects for increasing them somewhat remote, I suppose that my plans for shows may well seem rather high flown. But there are one or two points in connection with the public here that I think might rather interest you.

First of all, the public that comes here is not exclusively East End. It used to be. So far as I can tell from records at the beginning of the century and up to the twenties, large and quite spectacular exhibitions were put on regularly of oriental art, paintings by old masters – all kinds of things. This was possible because of an immense army of voluntary help which could always be relied upon: lecturers, financial backers, transport, benevolently disposed printers – all kinds of help. Also, of course, running costs connected with the building were much lower: general bills, salaries, rates, etc.

In those days when there was no radio, no television, hardly any cinema and precious little else in the way of indoor amusements we could rely upon a large purely East End audience. Nowadays, everything is different. There is certainly radio, television and cinema (one sees television aerials emerging from obviously very poor houses in the back streets) but there are also the Settlements, such as Oxford House, Toynbee Hall, The Jewish Settlements and many others, with their vast constructions of clubs, welfare groups, societies and all the rest of it for every kind of person and age group. [Bryan gathered personal experience of Toynbee Hall: he stayed there for his first year as Director at the Whitechapel, getting to know the area.]

With the increased activity and strength from all these bodies during the past twenty years, one must also take into account a definite, though not especially spectacular improvement in living conditions: LCC flats, better schools and houses and so on. Add to these improvements, the fact that nowadays there is a large army at work in the East End, of schoolteachers, students (resident at the settlements), welfare workers and other civilised people who add notably to the public.

All this means that today, the Whitechapel Gallery has to face competition from radio, television and cinema (a more potent seduction for the kind of people around here than for people in other areas, who take art exhibitions, concerts, and cheap seats at the ballet and theatre in their stride), and is simultaneously deprived of voluntary help both from voluntary workers and individuals who might help with money – for these latter quite rightly point to the Borough Councils, the LCC and the Ministry of Education, and say: Try and get some more money from them – we are taxed to the hilt.

Add to this, the fact that East Enders have changed quite a lot. They always were extraordinarily mixed; nowadays they are much more so, for the public here now include all those who are a bit better educated, plus that vast army mentioned above who are educating them.

To be brief, our audience is more alert and wants a higher standard to lure them in here than ever before. And it is nowadays only one-third East End. One third is composed of art school students who love this Gallery because there is always something worth looking at and the atmosphere is less formal than in most West End Galleries; and one third is drawn from the ordinary London art public – those who trail around the London Galleries regularly. The other third being a much sharper East End audience. Plus quite a large number of business people from the city, which is very near. But I am sure that you already know all this.

So you see, that although one would obviously avoid mobiles or unnecessary embellishments, the only shows that bring people in are the really good ones; of all kinds, provided it is the best of its kind. Anything else is no use, and we have found that during the past three years, the finest shows have always brought larger audiences, increased interest in the affairs of the Gallery, and a definite and marked increase in subscriptions. Really, after years of effort and pleading, we are almost adequately endowed for ever.

I shall do my best to get a little more from the appropriate authorities to ensure full solvency, although I cannot avoid a campaign for subscribers as well, much as I dislike the idea of doing it. And here, may I say in confidence that exhibitions in the past have cost far too much money: expenses can be cut by half in this direction. [Rather a case of wishful thinking ...]

All I really am aiming at is to increase the impact of this Gallery on the lives of the people here, and not to aim at any one section. For the public here is mixed enough always to appreciate the best of its kind, whatever that may be. I do not think that they would be dismayed at *Twentieth Century Form* provided I can give them explanations in the form of an introduction to the catalogue and lectures during the course of the exhibition. I shall try hard to get them really excited about it all and curious about its implications. After all there is no other art Gallery in this part of the world: the West End Galleries are rather remote for them and sometimes a little intimidating, and our work should be educational.

This letter is much too long, I know, and I apologise for it. But the problems and factors here are somewhat unique, and I am fascinated by the background and potentialities. In mentioning the Mexican show to you, I had a wild hope that the Mexican Government might pay for its transport (which I realised would be excessively expensive) because of the propaganda involved for their country, but those plans have fallen through anyway because the exhibits are going to Sweden and eventually back to Mexico. Please do not bother to reply.

The Whitechapel exhibitions in 1952 were ones inherited from Robertson's predecessor, Hugh Scrutton – *Looking Forward: British Realist Pictures*, curated by John Berger (who was to become one of Bryan's most sacred *bêtes noires*), and *East End Academy* (the local talent-spotting exhibition, which was to metamorphose over time into the Whitechapel Open). The year 1953 had much more of Bryan in the mix, with the great Turner exhibition which opened the year – and for which he was much praised – followed by *Twentieth Century Form*. This was pure Bryan, and it was during its planning that he made the acquaintance of the architect Trevor Dannatt (born 1920). In 2017 I asked Dannatt what it was like to work with Robertson:

It was in 1952 I think that Leslie Martin, whom I'd got quite close to, suggested me to Bryan Robertson for this exhibition on *Twentieth Century Form*. Bryan wanted somebody to do the architecture and we got on very well. He was a very engaging character and threw things up in the air, you know – quite mad, most of it, but there was always something very interesting coming up from it. I liked him very much. He had the gift of persuading people to lend, I think. He got very major works for *Twentieth*

Century Form. The exhibition showed works for the first time in England by Mies van der Rohe, Eero Saarinen, Naum Gabo and others.

'The fifties were a time of exceptional strength in European as well as American painting. It seems in retrospect to have been the most cathartic period in European art since 1910.'

For the exhibition (its full title was *Twentieth Century Form: Painting Sculpture and Architecture*, and it ran from April to May 1953), Dannatt selected the architecture exhibits and wrote an essay for the catalogue. In the director's acknowledgements, Dannatt was effusively thanked – 'without whose expert knowledge and patience this exhibition would not have been possible'. Robertson pointed out, in his preface, that the show was in no sense a complete survey of its subject but offered 'a plain man's guide to some aspects of modern art'. It also intended to show how 'certain clear-cut and stabilised forms of pictorial or sculptural expression have influenced architecture, and vice versa'. The third and final object of the exhibition was 'to demonstrate to people who are not usually interested in or sympathetic towards the art of their own time, that a great deal of the aesthetic endeavour of this century is less remote from modern life than is often realised'.

Dannatt was friendly with a group of avant-garde abstract artists who used to meet in Adrian Heath's house in Charlotte Street, Fitzrovia. Among the artists were Victor Pasmore, Robert Adams and Eduardo Paolozzi, and Dannatt was asked to design the series of exhibitions they mounted in Charlotte Street between 1952 and 1955, which gave him an opportunity to experiment with unconventional methods of installation. He was thus somewhat prepared – by this experience as well as by working on *Twentieth Century Form* – when asked by Robertson to design the first major Jackson Pollock exhibition in Britain for the Whitechapel. In this he excelled himself by proposing a solution that was both discrete and dramatic, as Roger Stonehouse describes it: 'an abstract geometrical landscape of blockwork monoliths upon a matting floor and under a billowing white fabric sky.'

Dannatt had designed the layout for *Twentieth Century Form*, and recalled the planning of the show:

It was not very ambitious, being done more on a shoestring, but I think I had quite an input on it. But when we came to Jackson Pollock [1958], we spent a lot of money on the installation, which was quite lavish. I went with Bryan to Berlin to see the exhibition and how it was installed on its tour before the Whitechapel. We spent two days in Berlin and were very well entertained by the Americans. It wasn't quite my scene – more Bryan's, going to nightclubs – but I enjoyed it. He was fun to travel with. He came in his tennis shoes. I don't know whether he was scared of flying but I remember very vividly – I was sitting next to him on the plane – he came out in a terrible sweat as we landed in Berlin.

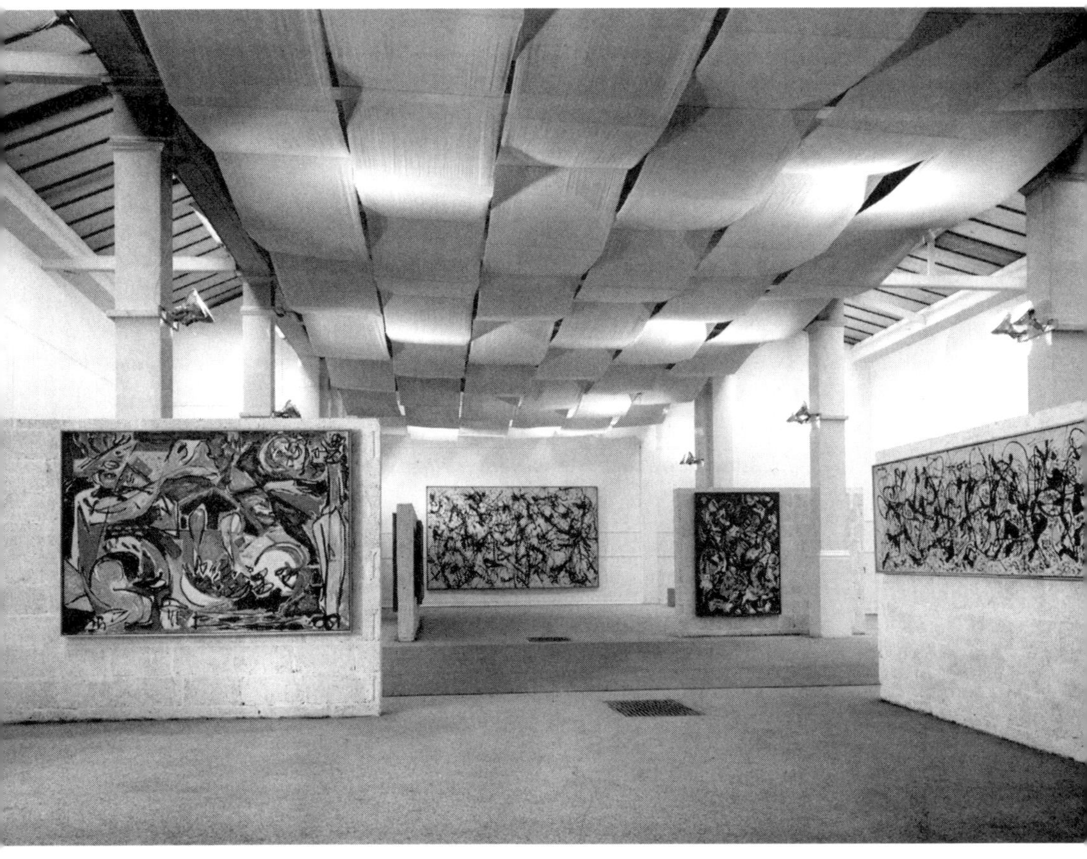

6 Installation view of the Jackson Pollock exhibition at the Whitechapel Gallery, 1958

It was terribly exciting to work on that exhibition. I hadn't heard of Pollock before. Bryan made all the arrangements for the move and I measured every picture and noted their qualities. Then we came back and I suppose I produced some sort of sketch scheme. We built four walls in a sort of dynamic, rather Mies van der Rohe composition. The ceiling was a little folly I indulged in. I remember him saying 'Are you going to throw rhinestones up on to the ceiling? You could have it covered with rhinestones.' He was like that – a sort of fount of ideas who somehow had his finger on the pulse of the art scene in an extraordinary way. The nice thing with Bryan was that it was all great fun. We worked together and he chattered a lot of the time. I was a sober young architect and tried to keep him on the rails, I suppose. But we got on very nicely together.

The Pollock show was selected by the poet and friend of the artist Frank O'Hara, and travelled from the São Paulo Biennial to seven European cities, sponsored by MOMA's International Circulating Exhibitions Program. Dannatt described the setting:

We put a bench seat in front of one of the paintings and concealed lights in the seat – low-level lighting. I played with different fabrics hung on the walls behind the paintings. [Black and grey fabric was stretched behind certain paintings, and pleated 'like the underbelly of a mushroom', as Bryan put it.] Part of the compositional theme was the ceiling, and the carpet ran contrary to it. The ceiling material was white, the carpet brown, I think. The false walls were crude block-work, roughly painted white. The use of fabric was intended to dissolve surfaces and reduce the ceiling height. The aim was to produce an ambience reflecting the essential ambiguity of Pollock's work – dynamic yet calm. The setting was, in effect, an abstracted landscape: the floor matting was the grass, the block-work was rocky outcrops, with muslin clouds above.

Dannatt went on to discuss his later work at the gallery:

Then there was the Rothko exhibition subsequently [1961], but I had less involvement in that. I did do the installation, but I can't remember it in the way I remember the Pollock. I think there wasn't such a diversity as there was in the Pollock exhibition – early Pollock is very different from his mature paintings. We found places for individual works. I suppose this is what working together is – we discussed the big pictures and where we should put them and how to light them. Though we spent a lot of money, it was nothing compared with what is spent today on installation. Through my previous work on exhibition design, we had very good contractors who were all terribly co-operative. It was a terrific thing for me because we were playing with space and organising vistas and deciding what went where. I did the lighting, such as it was. That was really on a shoe-string compared with what's done now. And there was good natural light at the Whitechapel.

Both the Pollock and Rothko exhibitions were enormous successes (the Pollock show was seen by over thirty thousand visitors and was extended by two weeks), but in the eight years between *Twentieth Century Form* and *Mark Rothko*, Robertson had run the gamut of responses for a widely varied exhibition programme. In 1953, he had followed up his first historical success (Turner) with three more shows of British Old Masters: James Gillray, Thomas Rowlandson and John Martin. In 1954 he gave Barbara Hepworth her first retrospective museum show in London, then followed up with an intriguing survey of *British Painting and Sculpture*. The year 1955 saw a selection of works from the Bearsted Collection. Lord Bearsted was the Chairman of the Whitechapel trustees, and was really responsible for keeping the show on the road. He was immensely supportive of Robertson. Bearsted's family home was Upton House in Warwickshire, made over to the National Trust in 1948, and full of top quality Old Master paintings. An exhibition of *American Primitive Art*

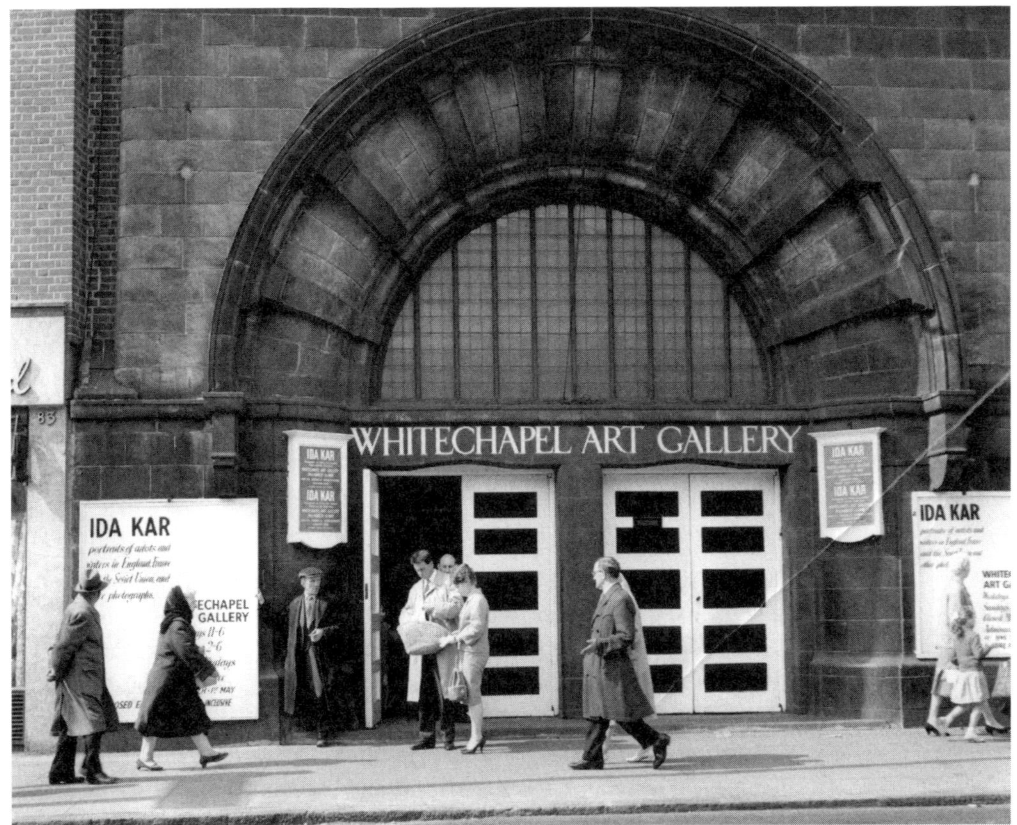

7 Ida Kar's photograph of the exterior of the Whitechapel Gallery during her exhibition, 1960, 19.2 × 24.1 cm, vintage bromide print

(1670–1954) followed, then an important Piet Mondrian retrospective. A Michael Ayrton show came next.

Amongst the subsequent exhibitions at the Whitechapel as the 1950s moved towards the 1960s, and Bryan Robertson brought the gallery to its peak of innovation and explication, were Josef Herman, Nicolas de Staël and Charles Howard in 1956; Stubbs, Bellotto, Sidney Nolan and S.W. Hayter in 1957; Robert Colquhoun and Alan Davie in 1958; Jack Smith, Kenneth Armitage, Kazimir Malevich and Cecil Collins in 1959; Ceri Richards, Ida Kar, Prunella Clough and Henry Moore in 1960. The range (and I haven't mentioned the group shows such as *Pictures for Schools* and the *Women's International Art Club*) was formidable and exciting.

The Pollock show at the Whitechapel (1958) preceded the *New American Painting* exhibition at the Tate in 1959, and for many English people was their first real taste of abstract expressionism. Bryan's own fascination with Pollock, which found its most substantial expression in his 1960 monograph, was passed on to others through criticism and

'It has taken Medley almost thirty years to realize, with proper confidence, that he is not a visual painter in the usual sense of the phrase but an abstract-philosophical painter concerned with the shifting convolutions of space, time and memory.'

lectures as well as the Whitechapel show. A student then was Nicholas Elam, former British Ambassador to Luxembourg:

I do recall – almost as if it were yesterday – Bryan's coming to talk to the Oxford University Art Club (some time between October 1958 and June 1960) carrying a Jackson Pollock original under his arm – an amazing revelation for us youngsters at the time. It was quite a small one – I think no more than two feet by three – and it was framed. I don't believe I have ever seen one that size since, so it probably ended up in a private collection. Rather than giving a lecture, he chose to talk to us in a very informal group – a formula we adopted for regular use thereafter, notably with artists exhibiting at the Bear Lane Gallery.

How many tutorials on Pollock have been illustrated by original works?

Robert Medley, whose work was the subject of a retrospective at the Whitechapel in November and December 1963, recalled the experience in his memoir, *Drawn from the Life* (1983):

The great thing about the Whitechapel during those years, when Bryan Robertson was its Director, was that there was nothing institutional about it. It did not represent an official or establishment view of things: it was a place for living art. And because it was a public gallery, with remarkably high and consistent standards, it was an important and prestigious place to show. An exhibition there was an opportunity to take stock and also to indicate new directions. It was an opportunity for which many artists of my generation and the next have felt a special debt of gratitude to Bryan, whose remarkable eye, and breadth of critical sympathy, have made him an outstanding figure in the world of modern art.

Barbara Hepworth

Writing about Prunella Clough in the magazine *Modern Painters* (summer 1996), Robertson reprised the history of women artists in recent Western art, and made the following observation about Hepworth. He noted that she earned for herself 'a reputation as a glacial and humourless grande dame – a view of Hepworth at total variance with my own experience'. Bryan enjoyed a warm relationship with the sculptor, based upon his very real appreciation of her work, and the solid support he gave it. Hepworth was the subject of the first solo show he gave a living artist during his tenure at the Whitechapel, and this came in 1954, when her reputation was at a very low ebb. Also in 1954 Bryan was responsible for the installation, on loan, of a large Hepworth limestone carving entitled *Monolith (Empyrean)* on the South Bank, outside the Royal Festival Hall. It was carved as a memorial to Hepworth's son Paul Skeaping and his navigator, who were killed on active service with the RAF in 1953. The sculpture was purchased by the London County Council in 1959, and remained on the

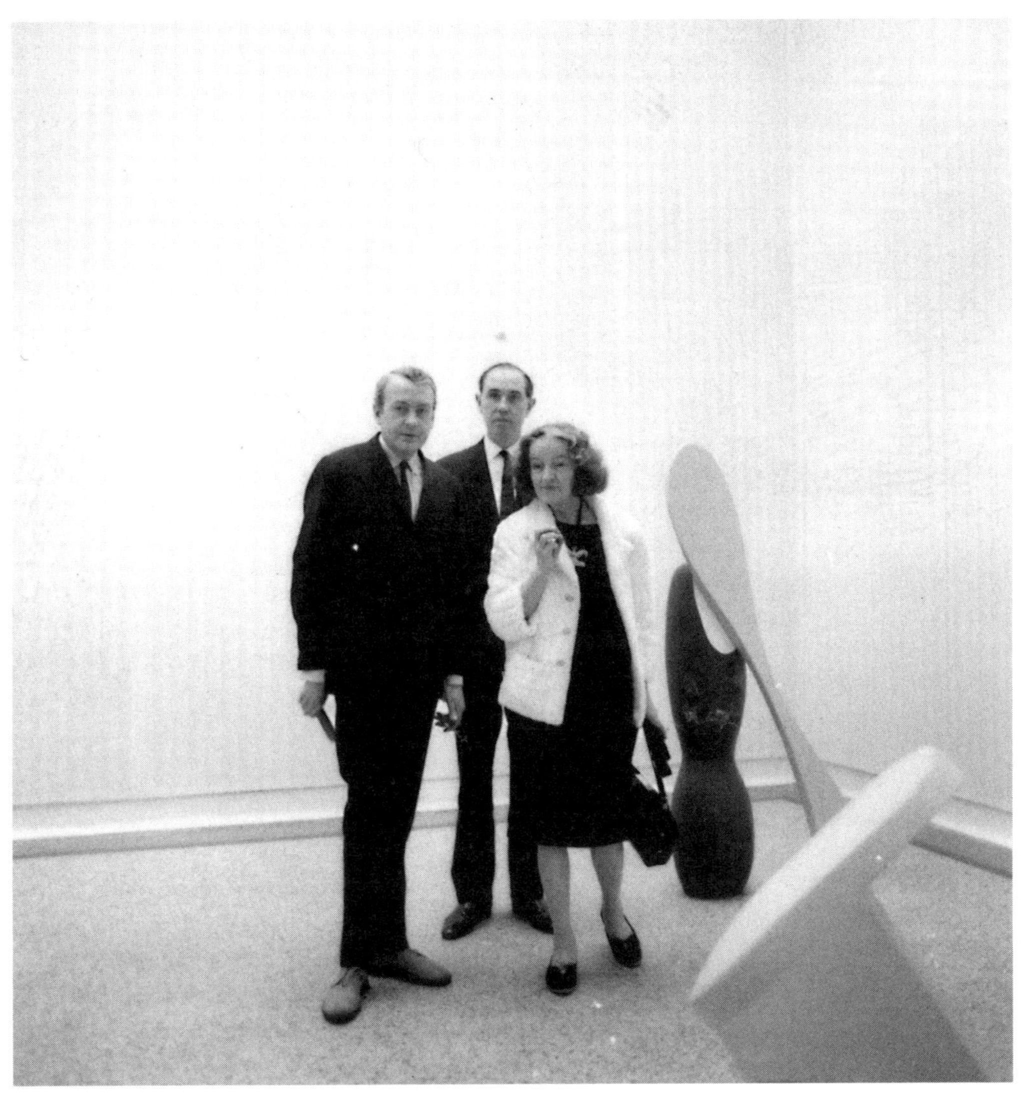

8 BR with Barbara Hepworth at *The New Generation 1965* exhibition, Whitechapel Gallery
Photograph by Martin Koretz, Whitechapel Gallery Archive

South Bank until 1961 when it was relocated to Kenwood. Later, writing in the *Spectator* (17 September 1965) on one of his favourite themes (or hobby-horses, as he himself called them) of 'why aren't our artists being made better use of?', Bryan asked why Hepworth hadn't been commissioned to design 'a great sculptural bridge'. This kind of public support was invaluable to a sculptor who had previously felt rather left out in the cold. And that first Whitechapel show (Bryan was to follow it with a second solo Hepworth show in 1962) helped considerably to put her back on the map again. It was a landmark exhibition, and the catalogue was equally crucial as a prototype of what was to follow.

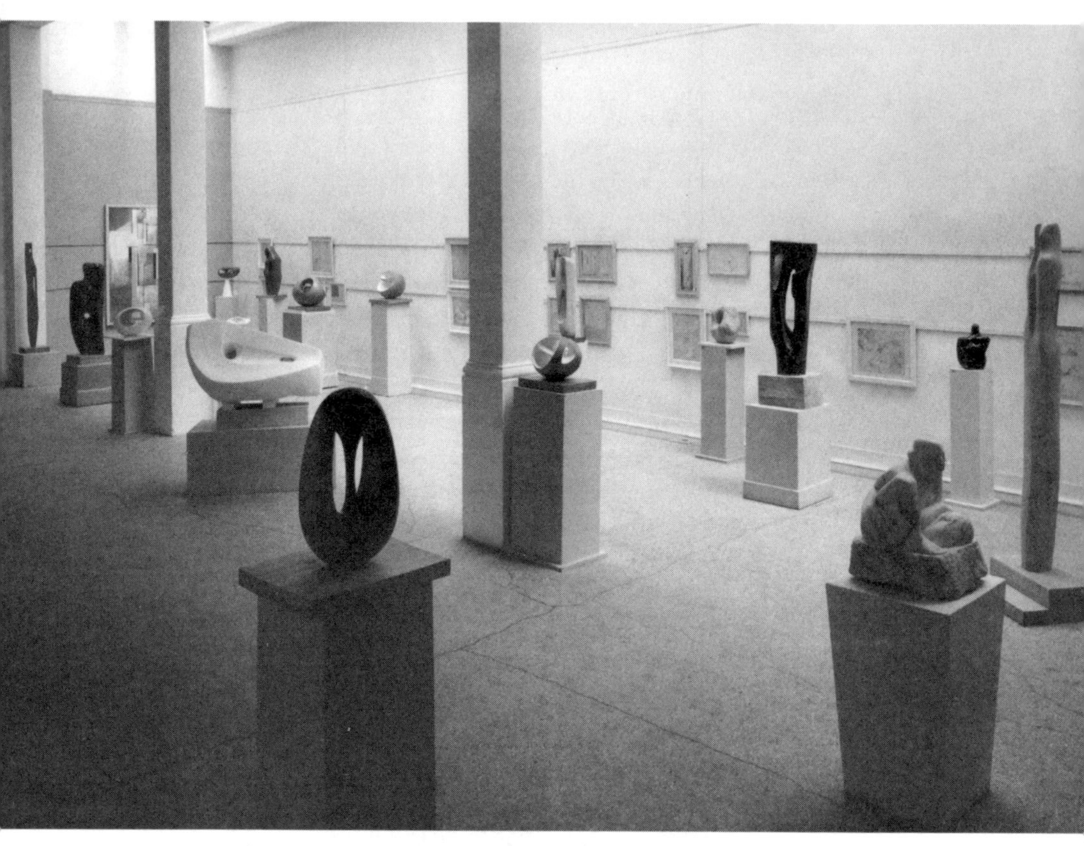

9 Installation view of the Barbara Hepworth exhibition at the Whitechapel Gallery, 1954
Whitechapel Gallery Archive.

Robertson developed a recognisable style for his catalogues, which combined seriousness with accessibility, documentation with readability. Substantial illustrated publications, they set a pattern that was much admired and emulated. In the 1954 Hepworth catalogue Bryan wrote of the exhibition: 'It represents most of the work created during the past twenty-seven years by a distinguished British artist. It is also the first presentation in East London of a large number of works by any artists working in an advanced idiom. The trustees hope that it may help to narrow the gulf which exists today between these artists and the public.' He continued:

Future generations will know more easily the extent and degree of Barbara Hepworth's accomplishment; but at this moment we can pay tribute to her imaginative powers, and the years of devoted and single-minded pursuit of highly personal ideals. The intellectual discipline which she has imposed over her visual discoveries has clarified and strengthened the meaning of the carvings and drawings assembled in this exhibition, which in their entirety constitute a tangible mythology of great subtlety and beauty.

The Hepworth exhibition represented a new departure for the Whitechapel: works were, for the first time, for sale. In a letter to Hepworth (18 June 1954), Robertson wrote:

At this moment, needing a big sale and cash badly and feeling frustrated, you'll probably not believe this – but this show has accomplished a tremendous amount. 17,040 people have seen it. Daily average over 51 days was 333 daily. 1,124 catalogues were sold – apart from a vast number of complimentary ones given away. A definitive catalogue is now in existence. A great many people have been converted wholeheartedly to your work, who were dubious or ignorant before. A *vast* new public has made contact with it. The Festival Hall project is of vital importance and will produce all kinds of things, I'm certain – and you stand to get a decent sum of money. You have been damned unlucky over sales but the fact remains that in spite of tough buyers and their unerring flair for picking works which you can't make money from – nine drawings (at high prices, for these drawings *are* expensive for most people) and three carvings have sold – possibly five.

The letter continues full of advice about possible Hepworth shows in America and France.

In the catalogue for Hepworth's 1962 show Robertson wrote:

This is one of the most important exhibitions of sculpture ever held in this country, an attribute shared with the recent assembly of work by Henry Moore [for his 1960 Whitechapel show]. We may well feel a special sense of occasion. Factually, the exhibition has been designed to show us those large carvings and bronzes completed since this artist's retrospective show at Whitechapel early in 1954, practically a decade ago. These are too large to be seen within the more restricted confines of a smaller gallery. But the present occasion has far greater implications than that; for it comes at a time when the artist's maturity is complete and indeed at a moment when the full flood tide of inspiration and attainment is at its richest and most potent. This has been clearly recognized at the highest level in many parts of the world, and reached a climax in 1958 when the artist received the international grand prix at the São Paulo Biennale. But the last exhibition at Whitechapel brought the artist complete recognition in her own country and a radical increase in personal stature. This came at a time when she had received in the past only tacit recognition for her extraordinary gifts, rather than the total acceptance and rather surprised reaction which that retrospective show aroused in the minds of all visitors.

The following draft letter was addressed to Hepworth, and dated 25 March 1970, in which he describes his plans for a Rothko memorial trust:

I have been thinking of the death of Mark Rothko, and wondering if something creative for the future could be devised by his English friends through which his art and his presence among us might be kept alive, for as long as possible. If some gesture were made it should, I feel, embody an ideal that Mark might have relished. As he had great affection for England (for Mark, all Englishmen were the fellow countrymen of Shakespeare) I believe that it would be particularly apt if a gesture of commemoration came from England. Mark was always so generous to his many English visitors, and he has given, very recently, a superb bequest to the Tate.

Might it not be a fitting way to honour Mark Rothko's memory by sending one young English painter or sculptor to America each year, with a return ticket and just enough money to live simply for about six weeks? Perhaps, a young American could be brought to London, as a regular alternative.

Our young artists will always want to go to America, for a visit at least. There, among much else, they can see Rothko's paintings. The number of scholarships or bursaries which take young artists to the States has diminished sharply in recent years: the Harkness Fellowships are severely cut; the Stuyvesant 'Young Generation' bursaries that I planned have come to an end. A new scheme is badly needed.

If a sufficient number of Mark's friends collaborated by financing the project annually, no intimidatingly large sum of money would be required from anyone. The contributions could be relatively modest. I am willing to make a beginning with £25 from myself, and undertake to continue this payment annually. The total sum that I envisage is not alarming, as a whole. The award of bursaries might be registered as a charitable trust.

This was the beginning of the Mark Rothko Memorial Trust, inaugurated by Bryan, which planned to send an artist to America every year, funds permitting. A portfolio of prints was published in 1973 to help generate income, and the contributing artists included Henry Moore, Patrick Caulfield, John Hoyland, Allen Jones, Victor Pasmore, Bridget Riley and William Scott. No Barbara Hepworth. By this point relations had soured between Hepworth and Robertson, largely because of Bryan's attempts to secure a major Hepworth for the American Museum he was then directing (p.169). This was a shame as their friendship had been warm, and characterised by generosity on both sides. Barbara had given Bryan a rather beautiful wood-carving (which he later sold) and was even inclined to be flirtatious in her dealings with him. Handwritten at the end of a short typed note to him from St Ives: 'It was marvellous to see you after so long – and to see you looking so well & young & *handsome*. B.'

Bryan's health

However much Bryan may have blamed forgotten social engagements or missed professional meetings on his health, it is evident that he continued to suffer from asthma and related respiratory problems during his time at the Whitechapel. Passages in draft letters to Cecil Collins and Rodrigo Moynihan in the 1940s and 1950s explained that he was suffering from flu or bronchitis and was thus unable to honour their appointments. This was typical. A note (dated 10 December 1954) from Bryan to Cecil Collins declined an invitation because of pressure of work:

I am now all right, but have been away with bronchitis and over and above everything else, the past month has been a nightmare in every way. A complicated move from Mount Street back to my parents' house and now, tomorrow, a move into a new flat with my sister – which has meant three weeks of writing, telephoning, tearing about and generally feeling rootless, flustered and wretched.

In a letter to Barbara Hepworth (dated May 1961) he lamented 'a dreadful blank, fatigued and derelict winter' of too much travel (to Australia, South-East Asia and America). Undoubtedly he was demanding much of himself and his qualified physical resources. Not surprisingly, from time to time, his health broke down under the strain.

John Kasmin (born 1943), but always known simply as Kasmin or Kas, is an art dealer and collector who led the field in the 1960s, opening a large white space in New Bond Street, a kind of commercial counterpart to what Robertson was doing at the Whitechapel, and showing a number of the same artists. He comments:

As I got to know Bryan, I realised he did suffer from very bad asthma, and it was a strong constituent element in his make-up. Although he didn't talk about it a lot, his feebleness of health must have been a very big factor in the slight aura of muddle that surrounded him. It must have been very odd working for him. I think he didn't share things very much with other people. You had to talk to him. Even though it was so long ago – we're talking about 1962 – I remember that the scale of what he was promising, the sort of encouragement and enthusiasm, was so strong it always overcame every worry that you had at the time. The next day there would be another worry. But things arrived and everything happened. All very last minute, very fraught.

Nan Youngman (1906–95), artist and educationist, was a long-standing friend of Robertson's. They originally met in Cambridge. A card to Nan Youngman (dated 2 June 1986) from Robertson in Paris said that last year

was 'a lousy year for me with incessant illness, none of it grave but all of it debilitating & repeated infections on the chest and antibiotics. Much better now.'

Prunella Clough

By 1958, Robertson and Clough were, as her biographer Frances Spalding notes, 'reasonably well acquainted'. After a dinner with Prunella and his sister that July, Bryan proposed out of the blue a retrospective at the Whitechapel. Clough wrote to him the next day: 'With some incredulity I have been thinking of what you said on the doorstep.' But she admitted that she had plenty of paintings and would endeavour to do some more which 'would stand up to the scale of the gallery'. In fact, she was quietly pleased at the prospect: 'if you really feel inclined for a gamble I'll not be the one to refuse.' In his letter of reply, Bryan rose to his usual heights of enthusiasm, writing: 'I've felt very strongly for a long time that you are one of the best painters in this country – and more to the point, in the International context – and the thought of your exhibition gives me immense pleasure. I am full of anticipation.' In a postscript he exhorted: 'You must let rip, with a vengeance!'

When the exhibition, which opened in September 1960, came to be installed, Bryan insisted on hanging Clough's industrial paintings on a black-painted wall, which, to her surprise, worked extremely well. In the preface for her Whitechapel catalogue Bryan wrote:

Prunella Clough's ancestry is divided between Yorkshire and Irish and Scottish origins. It is tempting to read something into this lineage, to find material confirmation of that side of her nature which is practical, down to earth and equipped with a keen social conscience as well as an almost militant integrity; and the reverse side which is quirkish, imaginative and poetic, and animated by a highly strung, exceedingly refined temperament. All these qualities seem to establish themselves in her work, but none of us is entirely conditioned by inheritance and the first and most immediate characteristic of her painting, in all its phases, is the strong flavour of emancipation and individuality. The erratic moves of fashion and those subtle pressures which spring into being every season from the cultural promoters, or even the mere proximity of provincial interpreters of the international vanguard: all this has been steadily ignored. There is, of course, no special merit in taking up a remote position for its own sake; but Prunella Clough's comparative isolation as a painter is involuntary and not the result of any consciously adopted attitude. In this, she shares equal ground with most of the other genuinely gifted artists in this country, who are in a similar situation.

All the work in this exhibition is at once intimate, and impersonal or at least detached, in feeling; so that one is continually faced by paintings which

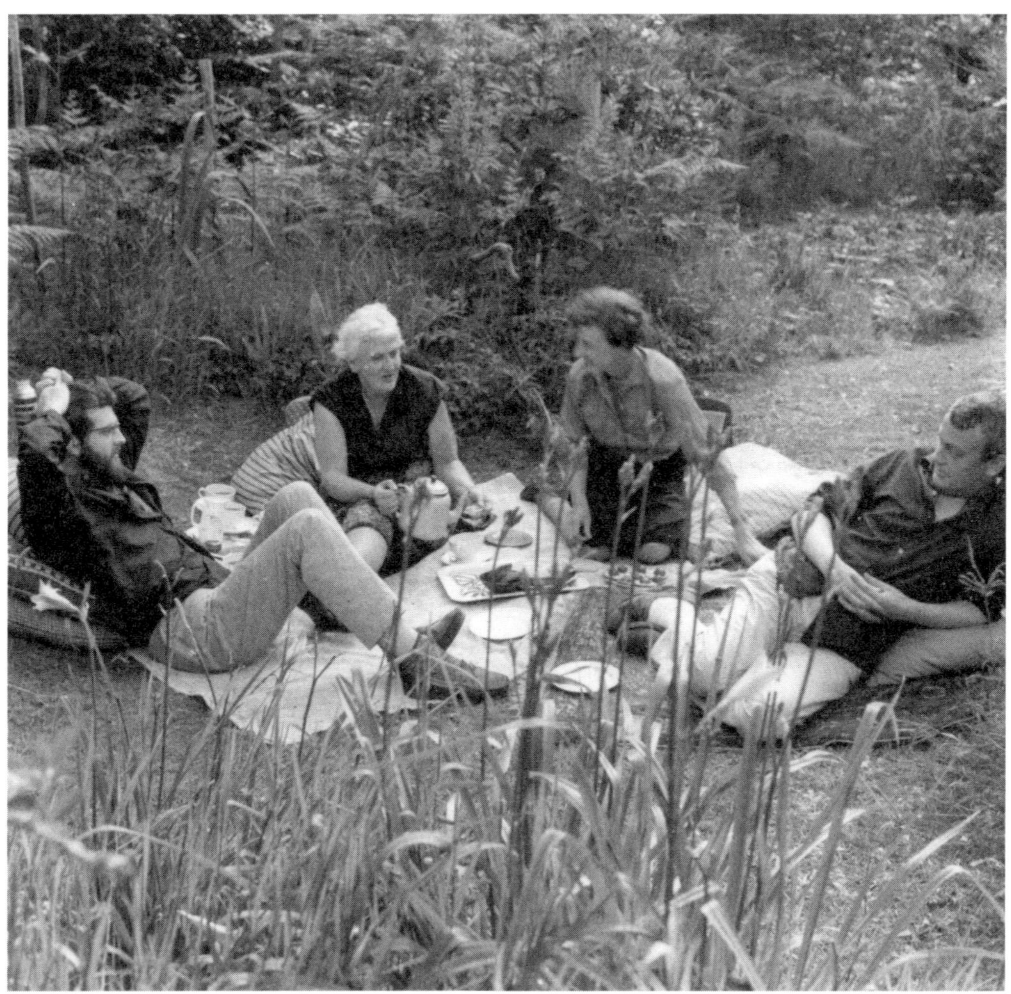

10 BR (right) at a picnic with (from left) John Hitchens, Molly Hitchens, Prunella Clough, *c.*1961.

haunt the memory because of their highly original perception of the world around us and yet in that same recollection dissolve into an almost anonymous sobriety of mood and atmosphere. These are slow paintings, curiously weighted and with their own density and gravity, and they take time to register. Once this is accomplished, they do not diminish or contract. They expand, for Prunella Clough has succeeded consistently in loading the particular and the localised with an extraordinary element of generality. She has also had the courage to concern herself with urban subject matter of a singularly unpromising nature, in any usual sense, and she has been very true to it, evading any easy exits or compromise solutions.

The following is the entirety of a characteristically brief letter from Prunella Clough, dated '65: Saturday morning':

Dear Bryan,

Very sad not to see you (and your telephone still out of order); sorry about the asthma. Went to see Pat Heron instead, also in bed with bronchy trouble.

When you are fit for it I shall tell you how *awful* you are the way you don't answer letters – and that won't be news. (This is apropos of whatever you said on the telephone; I mean attack first; not that I knew what you were on about.)

Paris tomorrow; back Wednesday. I'll ring over Easter,

Yours,

Pru

And this is Bryan to K Clark (dated 6 September 1966):

Very belatedly thank you for your hospitality to Prunella Clough and myself some weeks ago ... Prunella loved Saltwood, and the occasion. One day I must tell you how incredibly good, wise and generous that lady is, apart from her qualities as a painter. Her life is one long throwaway gesture, ostensibly, so her virtues and real intelligence are usually camouflaged.

Clough was close to Bryan, but just how close it is now difficult to establish, as this notoriously private artist destroyed many of her most intimate papers. Certainly she had some influence over him, as the painter Trevor Sutton recalls. (He describes Bryan as 'loved by some and somewhat feared by others'.) He remembers one occasion when Bryan was having a dig at him and Prunella came to Sutton's defence. Bryan's tendency to get 'out of order' perhaps needed to be checked from time to time, and Clough was clearly equal to the task.

Here's another letter, of 13 August 1989:

Dear Bryan,

Had we seen each other last week (and incidently [*sic*] forgive me for being so brusque not to say deeply unappreciative about Tippett, of course he's o.k. and a good Prom, simply not being in the mood.) I was going to explain that having shifted a bit of another Eileen Gray royalty in a certain direction, it then came back to me because the occasion for which it was going to be used had been cancelled. So here it is floating homeless and purposeless. Are you with me? Well never mind. I am just redirecting it as the Post Offfice says, in your region. I mean for redecorating. Wasn't that what you said you were going to do? Aram's sales simply appal me, though it's ever so nice, because of the Responsibility. So you will do me a favour of putting this towards the enormous cost of indifferent house paint etc., seeing as how for an anchorite I am enormously rolling.

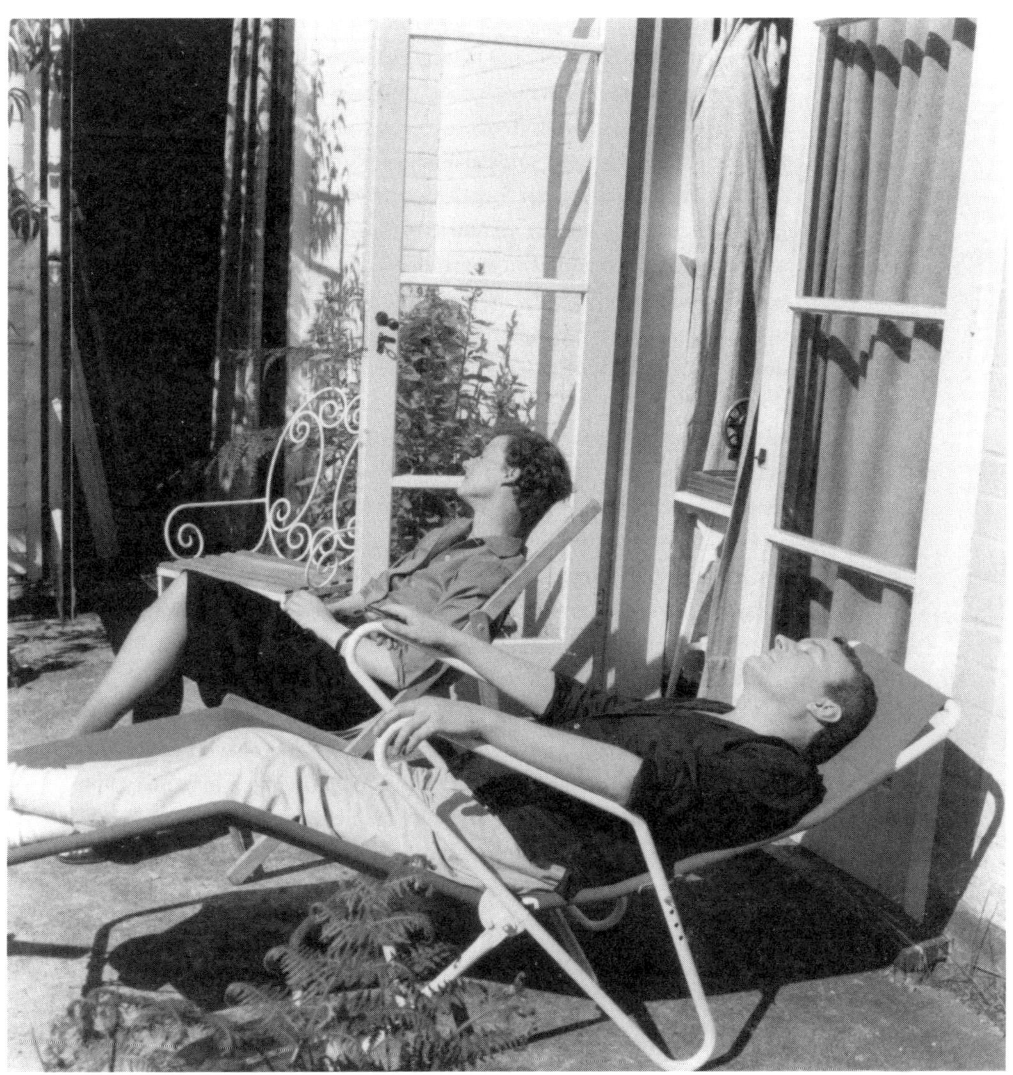

11 BR with Prunella Clough sunbathing at Ivon Hitchens's home in Sussex, *c.*1961.

Have a great time looking at the grass & sea & we will take up where we left off, dear Bryan, best wishes for acrylic writing.

Love Pru

Do find out what your postcode is.

In his obituary of Clough for the *Independent* (29 December 1999) Robertson wrote:

The death of Prunella Clough a few weeks after her eightieth birthday removes from British painting one of the best and most original artists to emerge in the second half of this century. Clough is honoured and held in affectionate esteem throughout her profession for the consistently original and independent nature of her paintings and graphic work. An exceptionally wide range of friends and admirers – collectors on a formidable scale, fellow artists and students, architects and designers – cherished also the unassuming elegance and gallantry of her character as it was revealed through the integrity of her friendship and professional conduct.

The essence of Clough's art and its strong driving force was the invention and constant extension of an utterly personal abstract language with which to distil and to celebrate the most commonplace and transient ephemera of our urban and semi-industrialised scene. Industrial tips or artisans' dumping grounds with rusting, abandoned machine parts or broken implements often provided Clough with inspiration, but her sources were always seen, and abstractly revealed, in close-up. A discarded handful of old nails and fragments of wire mesh were enough, rather than the big bulk of a machine: the parts seemed more eloquent to her than the whole.

Clough brought to this unpromising material a subtly calculating eye and a pictorial intelligence intent upon metamorphosis, rejecting nostalgia in favour of a crisply articulated synthesis between visible fact and subjective memory, essences and remnants. This visual synthesis is bathed in an imaginative light which owes nothing to time of day or night and only reflects the mood and constructed density of the final image.

The best of Clough's paintings have an extraordinary and unexpected magic because of the sheer sophistication and refinement of her handling of pigment, surfaces and textures which create the reduced, quintessential character of her icon-like images. It is as if, under a cold white English sky, a painter with Bonnard's wry sensuousness had focused on slag heaps, deploying a palette restricted to earth colours, greys, blacks and ivory white.

And he concludes his assessment of her achievement thus:

Clough's essential claim to her strong position in modern British painting comes most centrally from the rare beauty and individuality of her work. But there is also the historic fact that she is the first woman painter in Britain to have achieved recognition entirely on her own terms. In this sense, she opened things up quietly but very considerably for her admired friend Bridget Riley, among others. Last, her work has also an original social dimension because it gives us a sequence of visual epiphanies, a magisterially eloquent record of our detritus as icons and hieroglyphs for the future.

As constant in death as she had been in life, Clough left Robertson £20,000 in her will.

Keith Vaughan

After the spate of historic shows in the early days, which culminated in the George Stubbs and Bernardo Bellotto exhibitions in 1957, Robertson's Whitechapel years are famous for three kinds of exhibition: showing young artists (the New Generation), British artists in mid-career (a lot of whom would not have been given major museum shows elsewhere), and the best of modern art from abroad. This last category began with the masters of modernism (Mondrian, Malevich, and so on), moved into contemporary Parisian developments (such as de Staël) and then segued into the great series of American artists from Pollock and Rothko to Rauschenberg and Johns. Of the mid-career artists, Keith Vaughan (1912–77) was perhaps the best known.

Vaughan was one of the great journal writers, and even in his lifetime substantial portions of a grand total of some 750,000 words were published. His stance was primarily confessional and, although he wrote with the definite intention of being published and read, he did not attempt to enhance his image, preferring an unusual degree of honesty and frankness. Much of it is self-communing and analysis of work, but his friends are mentioned too in the lengthy narrative of the years between 1939 and 1977, published in 1989. One of the most revealing to feature Robertson was the entry for 1 January 1967. The following extract is taken from it:

an extraordinary New Year's Eve with Bryan. He had asked me to dinner and 'then maybe we might go on to a party if we feel like it'. Rings at 6.00 to confirm I am coming – mentions, jokingly the Quiche Lorraine & Daube de Boeuf – asks me for 8.00. No idea what to expect. Will others be there? Rings about 7.30 to ask me to make it 8.30, 'You'll see why when you arrive.' Arrive 8.40. Bryan, tired, dressed in rags, smell of paint, all windows open and piercingly cold. Keep my coat on. Explains he has had a terrific day with painters, decorators etc. working in the kitchen, which is in total disorder. But the table in the dining room is immaculately laid for two. He is dying for a drink and starts the process of making a Martini. We sit at opposite ends of the laid table drinking. I have put on a suit, thinking it might be a dinner party, and feel rather tricked. Admiration invited for the painted ceilings, pictures (idiotic Lee Krasner fills the whole of one wall – dull Ceri Richards on the other – remember with irritation the small oil he 'bought' from me and never paid for and which is now for sale at the Redfern, with the gouache he did buy – so much for his admiration for my work.) Suggest, as he's had such a tiring day he might like to come out, but don't press this, since the table is obviously laid for a proper dinner. About 10.00 he starts to prepare the first course – yoghourt with cucumber, pimento, herbs etc. Sit down finally to eat this ravenously at 10.45. He then announces that he has some delicious veal, vegetables etc., with which he intended making a marvellous stew but it would take about four hours.

Agree that it would hardly be worth starting now. Insist am not really hungry – which I was. Consume cheese and biscuits and wine, all of which is delicious. Suddenly notice it is midnight. We can go to Craxton's party or Neurath's. Choose Craxton's. Rings and says will be along in half an hour or so. Then wonders if it's worth it. Instead we go upstairs with a glass of brandy and he plays on the gramophone the whole second Symp. of Sibelius by Karajan – loud and impressive which brings tears to his eyes. I sit rather soporifically and just let the thing go. About 1.30 I refuse drinks and leave.

The sort of social evening which I could never dare inflict on anyone, but which B. can do and almost make it seem agreeable, until one looks back afterwards. Arrive home ravenous and make myself two turkey sandwiches.

The friendship between Vaughan and Robertson went back to the mid-1950s. Robertson, in his impassioned support of artists, sometimes tended towards hyperbole, particularly in private letters. No doubt his words were intended primarily as reassurance, or the bolstering of fragile egos often under attack from self-doubt or the persuasive arguments of opponents. Typical of this almost fulsome encouragement is Robertson's letter to Vaughan of 5 July 1957, quoted by Ian Massey in his excellent introduction to *Keith Vaughan: The Mature Oils 1946–1977* by Anthony Hepworth and Massey (2012). Robertson writes:

You are the biggest hope we have in English painting bar none. You have more in your little finger than Hitchens or Davie or any of the other real *painters* in this country. Also, you're properly obsessed. You must make some great pictures: you are getting nearer and nearer to it. But you must develop some grandiosity of feeling – about yourself. YOU ARE THE MOST IMPORTANT PAINTER IN ENGLAND. You are too humble, and your humility gives grace to your painting; but an excessive diffidence could cripple and stultify your development; which so far has come magnificently. You must think big and inculcate this into your painting. I don't just mean big pictures in scale. And your handwriting, your wrist must become more flexible as well as your sense of colour & light & depth & texture & space. And FORM SHAPE. This is immensely important.

Recognising the sensual basis of Vaughan's work, Robertson continues:

Perhaps you should play some Berlioz every morning or hit the bottle or something. But whatever you do, it must *come*. It's like some long protracted sexual exchange which gets nearer & nearer to an orgasm – but not quite there. The thing is, start the orgasm, and keep it going for the next twenty or thirty years. It's perfectly possible. Technically you have a great deal

& everything is subordinate to poetry – of a strictly visual kind in your pictures. So do start to give it hell.

Massey observes that soon after this Vaughan effected a dramatic change in his approach, working directly on to the canvas from his sensations, rather than from preparatory studies, though drawing remained an important part of his practice.

It's difficult not to conclude that Robertson's pep talk had helped Vaughan to develop his work further. Clearly, he heeded the warning in Robertson's last paragraph: 'Your alternative is to retain your diffidence and dwindle into an intelligently academic painter of the kind Gowing would approve of. You really shouldn't settle for so little when you have so much waiting to be unleashed. You must believe this – of your potentiality. It's terribly true.'

Vaughan and Robertson spent time together socially. In November 1959, they visited Michael Ayrton and his wife Elisabeth at Bradfields, their Essex home. ('Excellent weekend with Ayrton and Bryan Robertson in Essex,' wrote Vaughan in his journal on Wednesday, 18 November. 'Beautiful temper of Ayrton's mind – his articulateness – mental poise – Better than anyone I know.') It was this trip that ignited Vaughan's love of the north-east Essex countryside and led directly to him buying Harrow Hill Cottage, near the Ayrtons, in 1964. In his journal after this visit Vaughan compared Ayrton's articulateness and mental poise with Robertson's. Ayrton, he writes, 'never muffs a thought – or blusters or covers up. Bryan does this all the time – but has shafts of penetrating wit which always take me completely by surprise.'

Bryan's wholehearted support for Vaughan was manifest in the size of the catalogue he produced for the 1962 Whitechapel show: at over sixty pages it was twice the length of the average exhibition publication. It contained not only an essay on Vaughan's achievement by David Thompson and an eight-page biographical note, but also nineteen pages of extracts from Vaughan's journal. This is taken from Bryan's preface:

Slowly and gradually, over a period of twenty-five years, the painting of Keith Vaughan has come to a full and surprisingly luxuriant maturity. Surprising, because so much in the artist's earlier work pointed to a darkly romantic but essentially phlegmatic and terse restraint, echoing perhaps the quiet evenness of manner and understatement which characterize the man. The stillness and sobriety of these early landscapes, with figures momentarily becalmed in what appears to be a psychological mood as much as a landscape, has shifted and expanded over the years to yield a most passionate and eloquent statement about the human figure and what happens to it when it is seen, remembered, or imagined, in space.

Figures can exist in landscape on equal terms; or they can emanate from the landscape; or the landscape can be felt as a subsidiary projection from the figures. Vaughan's work has explored many aspects of these themes and we find him at this moment in a state of equilibrium, with the figure and the landscape – or space – fused together, and resolved. But at such a pitch and with such intensity that a new abstract image emerges, fortified by the earlier presences so that when we find only a painted space the movement contained in it is charged by their imprint.

The very slowness of Vaughan's evolution has provided a special strength to everything he touches. A stoic puritan by nature, with all the withheld temperamental force that this attribute implies, the work echoes a similar compressed energy. Sensuality is there, but ever since it has moved out from the image itself into the actual handling this sensuality has in turn taken on a concentrated, take-it-or-leave-it precision and formality. Here is the work of a poet, not an orator or a rhetorician.

Perhaps there was a degree of envy in the relationship between these two very different people. Vaughan wrote in his journal for 23 February 1964: 'With my age, fame, wealth I should be living packed and adventurous days (like Bryan Robertson) dashing from place to place, meeting new and interesting people.'

The Vaughan scholar Gerard Hastings kindly supplied the following information about a TV broadcast:

In 1966, shortly after Vaughan had published *Journal and Drawings*, the BBC filmed an interview between him and Bryan Robertson, the Director of the Whitechapel Gallery. At the same time an exhibition was held at the Redfern Gallery on Cork Street, showing many of the featured drawings. The previous year Vaughan had been awarded a CBE and the continuing attention temporarily lifted him out of his customary melancholy. The film of the interview has since been lost. Vaughan discussed being filmed in his journal in early November 1966:

WEDNESDAY, 2 NOVEMBER 1966

BBC TV people here this morning with Bryan to arrange the short programme about my book which they intend to put out. Busy and productive activity with others. Very pleasant. Enough to banish all my depression. If there were more of this in my life, instead of the long days alone trying to find some creative spring of energy within me, I should be a lot better off. But I can't very well apply for a job at the BBC & to take on the extra day at the Slade wouldn't be as good because that again is a solitary activity for the most part. At least it is not sufficiently programmed.

SUNDAY, 6 NOVEMBER 1966
Waiting to do my TV recording with Bryan – discussion part. Tedious. And one knows that after rehearsing it 3 times & defending oneself against Bryan's quite unintentional aggression & domination, one will be at one's worst when the actual take is made.

Hastings, in his edition of Vaughan's final journals, *Drawing to a Close* (2012), wrote:

In spite of Robertson's social panache, humour and amiable character, Vaughan harboured deep reservations about him. Robertson could be inconsiderate and thoughtless with his friends. For example, Vaughan lent him £2,000 for an agreed period of ten days but nothing had been mentioned about it even five weeks later. He was somewhat disgruntled to then be 'treated' to an absurdly expensive meal at the Café Royal a little while later. Though Robertson paid the bill, Vaughan considered that he was using his money to do so. Eventually he resorted to writing an official sounding letter reminding Robertson of the loan. He makes no mention as to whether or not the money was returned. The friendship nonetheless prevailed.

There was bound to be ambivalence built into the relationship between artist and curator. To Vaughan, Robertson was not only a loyal supporter – who continued to promote his work long after the artist's death – he was also the enabler and champion of Vaughan's usurpers: the young and thrusting painters who wanted to dethrone him. On 7 April 1964 Vaughan wrote in his journal:

The New Generation exhibition at Whitechapel. After all one's thought and search and effort to make some sort of image which would embody the life of our time, it turns out that all that was really significant were toffee wrappers, liquorice allsorts and ton-up motor bikes. So one could have saved oneself the trouble. I understand how the stranded dinosaurs felt.

There must have been some doubt in Vaughan's mind which side Bryan was really on – his or the new boys? The fact that it could be both was not something that an artist of Vaughan's particular character could easily accept.

Bryan wrote an encouraging letter (dated 15 November 1975) during Vaughan's final illness:

I can imagine all the shock and tension, and doubtless pain, of the last month or so and I am sorry that you have it all to endure – but thank God the outcome is life ... The great thing is that you still have the chance to go on adding something to British painting at a time when, mostly, artists seem to be standing still or actually diminishing it, and I am thankful for this. Affectionately, Bryan.

But this earlier excerpt perhaps catches the unusual tone of their friendship rather better. From a draft letter (dated 5 July 1957):

My dear Keith,

Thank you for the other evening. I enjoyed it tremendously, and it effaced all thoughts of the preceding fiasco.

Would you be very kind and (if possible and not needed vitally for a show or an early sale) reserve for me that smallish blue painting – horizontal – with a figure – do you know the one? I love it [small diagram].

I'm haunted by it and have lost too many of your paintings in years gone by. Not having one is a physical deprivation, dear Keith, so do this if you can. It will be until late this year, after I've repaid – very gratefully – your generous loan of £75.

Mark Rothko

The following extract is taken from Bryan Robertson's catalogue preface to the 1961 Mark Rothko exhibition at the Whitechapel Gallery:

A painting by Mark Rothko brings us to the final extremities of an utterly simple statement. This conclusion is so massive in its registration, so purged of extraneous details, so relentlessly single-minded in its pursuit of plastic self-sufficiency, that we are carried beyond the end into a new and transcendent beginning. The substance of life itself and its structure, with all the attendant references which normally fill a painting, are dissolved in light and colour. Above all, there is space – remote from known perspective or analysable volume, but implicit in the light and colour of the picture plane and between or around the static or scarcely moving shapes: a calm space of untroubled density, glowing, vibrant and serene …

There is no sign of the artist searching for himself in the execution, no evidence of strain or struggle. This is highly objective painting. We are offered a statement of extreme refinement, formed and articulated with absolute certainty and control.

Late in life, Robertson struck a strong vein of reminiscent commentary, in which he saw artists in terms of each other perhaps more clearly than ever, and became an expert at locating them in the context of their art and times. For instance, he wrote in a lengthy review in *Modern Painters* (autumn 1998) of the 1998 Rothko retrospective at the National Gallery of Art in Washington DC, and the Whitney in New York:

In its fresh disclosures, the Washington show was an event of great beauty and of the first importance in the annals of twentieth-century art if we

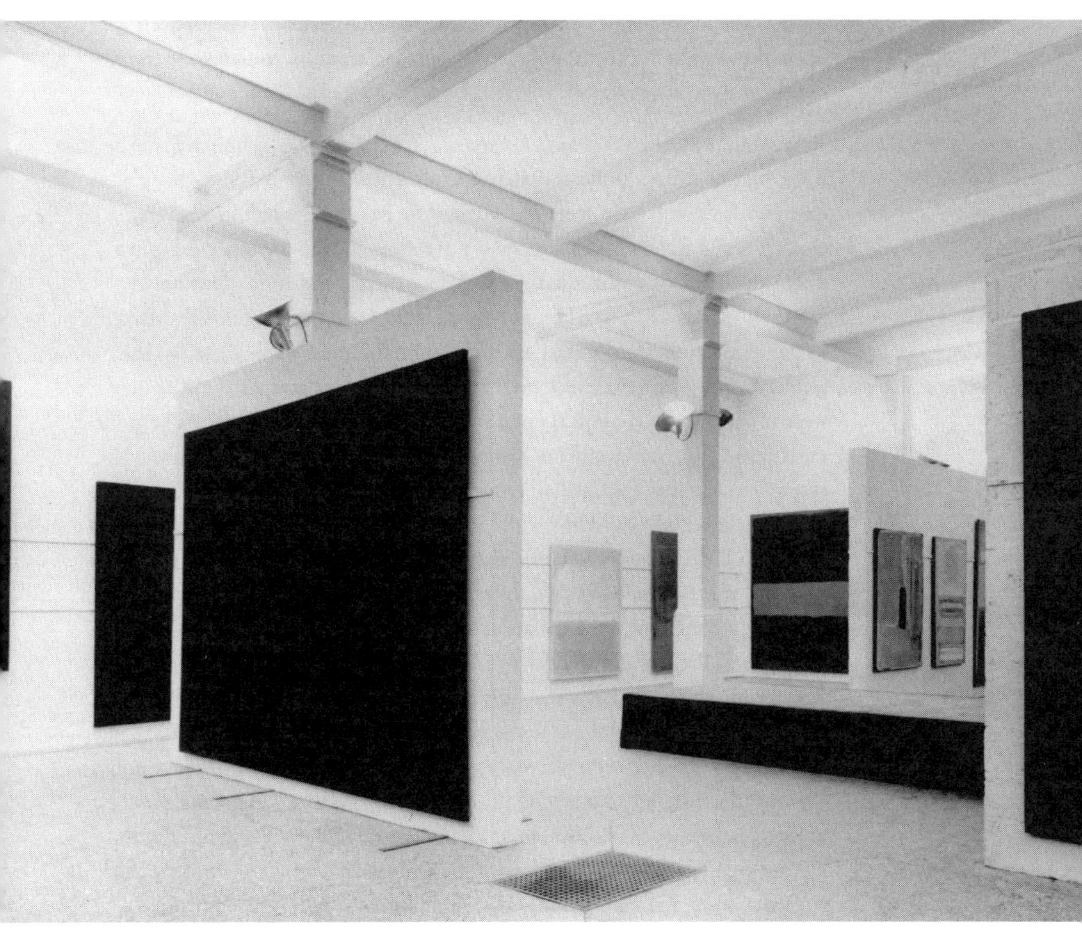

12 Installation view of the Mark Rothko exhibition at the Whitechapel Gallery, 1961
© 1998 Kate Rothko Prizel & Christopher Rothko ARS, NY and DACS, London/ Whitechapel Gallery Archive

esteem Rothko as highly as I do. For if Pollock was the most innovatory painter, formally speaking, since Picasso – with Mondrian on his own, in a tributary – then Rothko hit a new nerve in the original abstract projection of a profound emotional charge, and this charge underlay an equally fresh distillation of sensual experience, visually and atmospherically structured and balanced, in terms of light, colour, and colour-and-light as space.

He observed that Rothko had rather faded from English awareness, commenting sharply: 'The disastrously hung and poorly lit Tate exhibition of 1987, with its faulty installation and subfusc lighting left a depressingly weak impression of a Frigidaire serving as a morgue. The show was further undermined by talk of the poor physical condition of certain canvases.' And then, with a certain inevitability, he cast his mind back to the Whitechapel show of 1961, by saying that however good the Washington exhibition, it did not have 'the palpable feeling of

metaphysical resonance and transcendence' that visitors commented upon during the Whitechapel run. Robertson went on to compare the exhibitions in more detail:

In Washington, the show seemed spacious, expansive; at Whitechapel, the hanging was deliberately compacted. Only a minority of readers, those now in their fifties, will have seen this exhibition, but those who did have that experience will remember it with some feeling, for the show caused quite a sensation in London at the time. Artists of all generations spent hours at the show, day after day. Henry Moore made two very long private visits in rapt contemplation of the paintings when the gallery was closed to the public; so did Kenneth Clark on three separate occasions. Both these men were greatly moved; Clark surprisingly so, perhaps, since for all his genuine and lifelong love of Mondrian – notably the *Pier and Ocean* plus/minus sequence of paintings – he had come to believe, mistakenly in my view, that totally abstract art could not really advance or develop and tended to end up as a form of decoration, a theme that he explored in his lecture on 'Iconophobia'. Another visitor was Georges Salles, a man of letters and a poet, close friend of Ionesco and many artists, who was then the exceptionally intelligent Director of the Louvre and head of all the museums in France. Salles flew over from Paris specially to see the show. These men and many other visitors who had seen clearly how Abstract Expressionism could touch a nerve, were more deeply stirred by the impact of Rothko's work through the way in which it also engaged the emotions. This was something new in abstract painting. Moore spoke often of Rothko's great gifts in later years.

During the crowded opening of the exhibition, Rothko was entranced to find a young man, a Muslim, who came into the gallery and unrolled a long mat on the floor, on which he crouched, forehead touching the mat, at the appointed hour and facing in the right direction for his faith. Sandra Lousada, a photographer, took a sequence of brilliant colour slides, now sadly lost, which showed people moving across the paintings or standing still, gazing, and quite palpably ennobled in some strange way, their movements and stance somehow eloquent, given an isolated dignity when seen silhouetted against and within the glowing squares and rectangles of intense colour and light. This may seem absurd but it was indeed moving to witness people in relation to these paintings within that rapt atmosphere. I thought at the time that the physical effect of the paintings on people was not unlike the way in which men and women move more easily and naturally, decisively even, in great squares than in narrow alleys and mean streets.

After considering the differing content of the two exhibitions, Robertson went on to describe the way in which the Whitechapel show was hung:

In 1961, after meetings in New York the previous year, Rothko and I had been in correspondence about the way in which he liked his paintings to be hung and lit. He made it clear that he disliked seeing his work strung out 'on the line', with painting after painting visible on the same wall. Abstract paintings suffer particularly in this way, for viewers tend to stand at a distance and survey the wall as a bland whole. Figurative paintings force the viewer to go close up to each painting, to look first at a landscape, for instance, and then at a church interior, and then at a still life. Rothko preferred people to encounter his paintings, one by one, in as much 'separateness' as could be contrived. Ideally, he stipulated, each painting should be seen rather close to, with room to move back for more extended viewing of not more than perhaps twelve to fifteen feet. This was in order to establish a close and exclusive environment of colour and light in which the spectator could be totally engulfed, saturated and more fully prone to contemplation. Ideally, also, the works should wherever possible be placed at reasonably distanced right angles to each other, so that the paintings might form a sequence of intimate, open-ended, rooms.

Then Robertson discussed lighting and how Rothko preferred it to be muted:

What Rothko could not explain to me ahead of time, back in New York before the MOMA show came to the Whitechapel, was the physical, optical way in which his paintings made their own light, *from within* the colour, when there was no artificial lighting around at all. This was most magically and dramatically demonstrated when, during the run of the show, he and I were leaving the gallery in the quiet of the late afternoon after the place had closed to the public. The attendants had gone home, and the space was only dimly lit from Whitechapel's top natural lighting. Coming down from the offices, the place seemed not only empty but rather dead. I made a move to turn on some lights while we exited, but Rothko stopped me. 'Wait a minute,' he said. 'Come and sit down.' We sat down in the centre of the deserted gallery with a good view of two big paintings. As my eyes gradually adjusted to the – apparent – gloom, the deep and intense colour slowly began to appear, as if a living organism with its own life force like a steady heartbeat or pulse. All of this must read as a somewhat trite experience, an ordinary physical fact, of rich colour slowly asserting itself in the half-light, but I remember it with some emotion after more than thirty years as a kind of magical revelation – sitting there in the gloaming, and looking at these glowing testaments to the human spirit, floating in space in their own inner light in a silent and gradually semi-dark gallery.

Robertson described how Rothko approved of the lighting in the gallery but requested that one of his paintings be lowered fractionally. Although Robertson pointed out that this would put it dangerously within reach of the machine which washed the floors each morning, Rothko said he'd risk it. Robertson wrote:

I thought privately that he was being too finicky but I was more than willing to humour him in any way on the eve of his private view. The men were summoned and the painting was slowly, very slowly, lowered, at about one sixteenth of an inch at a time, it seemed. As I stood watching with Rothko, he asked me to observe the lower edge of colour – a soft yellow. As the painting descended, the thin band of yellow changed quite dramatically, from a dull yellow to a lighter, sharper, tougher yellow altogether. The shift in light from the colour, and its intensity, was startling: we could all see the difference, which of course affected all the interior relationships in the painting although it had dropped only about three-quarters of an inch in height. It was plain that Rothko had hypersensitive knowledge of colour and light and the way they can be affected by direction and angle. At the time, it seemed revelatory.

Robertson's article is full of brilliant analysis and illuminating discussion. He concluded thus:

As a mature artist, Rothko disliked art being confined by nationality, but his concern for tragedy, for the human state, and much else in his make-up must have sustained a profound awareness of the most appalling human tragedy of the twentieth century. I do not for a moment think that his paintings are *about* the Holocaust, or should be seen as memorials of any kind, but the emotional qualities to be found in his paintings are not those of Matisse or Bonnard, however radiantly and luxuriously the colour comes across to us. Do the paintings veil or do they disclose something – the something being a state of mind, a mood, a feeling, a 'drama' of light, colour and proportions? But if I, as a schoolboy, a non-Jew, living in England could be as stricken as I was at the post-war disclosures of Belsen and Dachau, then is it not possible for an American-Jewish artist, working in New York, of Russian origin, filled with a compulsive sense of the world's tragedy, to be also very often in mind of the Holocaust and the tragic awareness that it left us all with forever? If Rothko's paintings do reflect this awareness in any way, then he achieved a noble transcendence of suffering, for, in addition to their evident sensuousness, his paintings to most people seem also to be radiant with stoicism and implicitly convey a sense of something larger, beyond common experience.

The New Generation exhibitions

Perhaps the best known, and certainly one of the most influential, series of exhibitions that Robertson mounted at the Whitechapel were the *New Generation* shows, from 1964 to 1968. In 1963, a partnership was formed between Robertson and the Peter Stuyvesant Foundation, in order to promote worthwhile new art from young artists, and the *New Generation* phenomenon was unleashed. There were in fact just four exhibitions (and catalogues): *The New Generation 1964*, *The New Generation 1965*, *The New Generation 1966* and, finally, *The New Generation: 1968 Interim*. The following extracts from Robertson's prefatory texts in the catalogues illustrate the context in which the work of these young artists (from Caulfield and Riley to John Carter and Victor Newsome) was seen. Robertson's own excitement is evident. In 1964 he wrote: 'My only motive in selecting it has been to make the best and liveliest exhibition, and to provide a reasonably broad cross section of work from our younger artists.' But he concluded: 'Of all the shows that I have organized at the Whitechapel Gallery over twelve years this one has given me most pleasure to construct.'

13 Exhibition view of *The New Generation 1964* at the Whitechapel Gallery
Whitechapel Gallery Archive

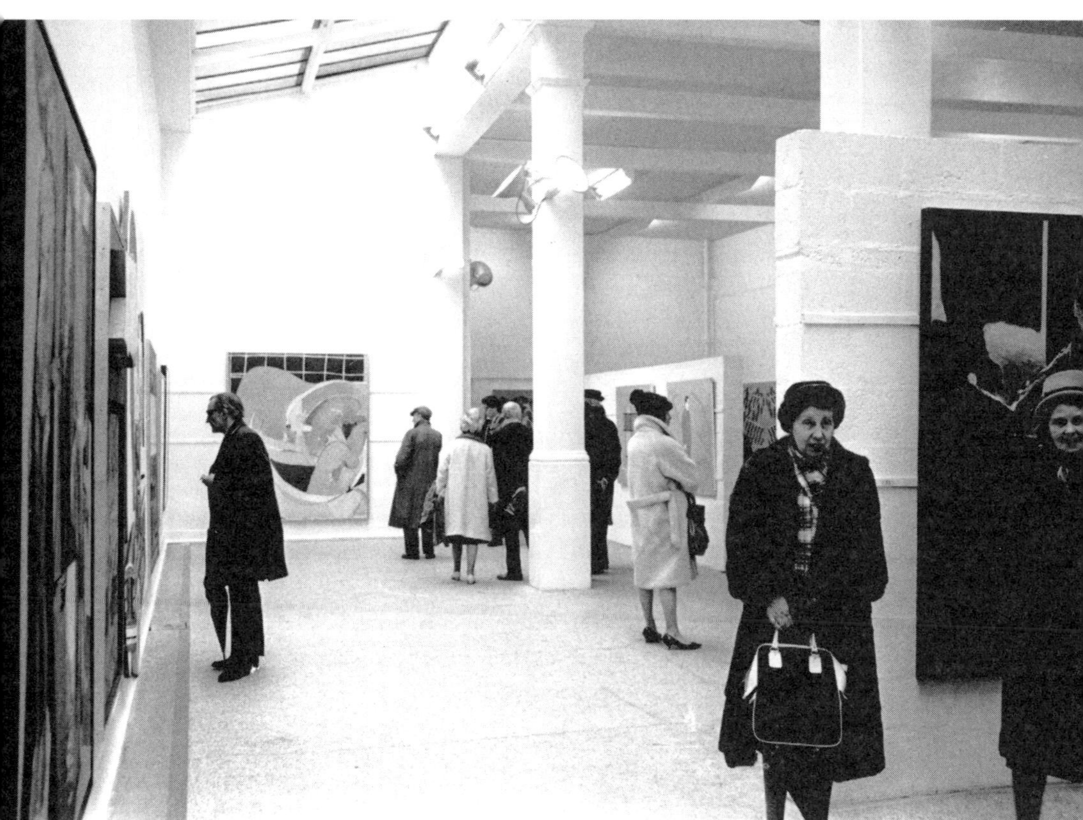

The following is taken from the catalogue of *The New Generation 1964*:

Most artists in England have alarmingly modest incomes from their work: that is, from painting or sculpting. Even the handful of very successful artists only have the incomes of averagely comfortably off businessmen. They do not complain much of this, in fact most artists scarcely realize the gloomy fact: they are too busy working in their studios. But English artists are also over preoccupied with teaching, as well, which they mainly do strictly for money and security, and this time-consuming activity, so deeply entrenched in England, is really no substitute for direct patronage. To be fair, English artists – even at a young and presumably energetic age – do not seem disposed to tackle the risks and uncertainties which their American or Continental contemporaries endure for a while: our young artists possibly demand a higher standard of living, or at any rate a greater degree of security. They have every right to want to live well, and with proper facilities, but it is a pity that teaching alone, in most cases, can provide them with the means.

'The true heroes of the decade, apart from the artists, were the dealers, Alex Gregory-Hood, Leslie Waddington and John Kasmin who, with unflagging belief, put on memorable sculpture exhibitions during the sixties, with very hard-won financial remuneration, if any.'

As private patronage for modern art in England is still inadequate, though it is improving, there is clearly a tremendous need for commercial patronage. The banks, the insurance companies, the large business corporations of all kinds, should face up to the challenge and the great accomplishments of present day culture in England. There is a rich field to sponsor and encourage in the visual arts; and America has set a superb example in the way that modern art can be used in business houses and in new buildings. To tour the collection of modern art in the Chase Manhattan Bank in New York, for example, is an exhilarating experience. There have been a few stray signs of benevolence in certain quarters in London during the past few years, but there could be so much more. We are still at the beginning of public patronage in England.

The Stuyvesant Foundation has taken an unprecedented step, of unique generosity, in subsidising the present exhibition as well as offering travel grants to six artists, and forming the nucleus of a permanent collection by purchasing a work from each of the artists selected for awards.

Robertson's animus against artists teaching is reflected in an anecdote told by the sculptor Bill Pye. He remembers Bryan saying that artists shouldn't have to teach, but they should be borne through art schools on a litter, and the most promising students be allowed to touch their raiment.

This extract comes from *The New Generation 1965*, the sculpture show that was such an unexpected selection of unknowns:

The quality of English light and weather does not encourage that sculptural sensibility which alone can foster a national consciousness and tradition. We see things tonally, in receding planes, and this has produced great

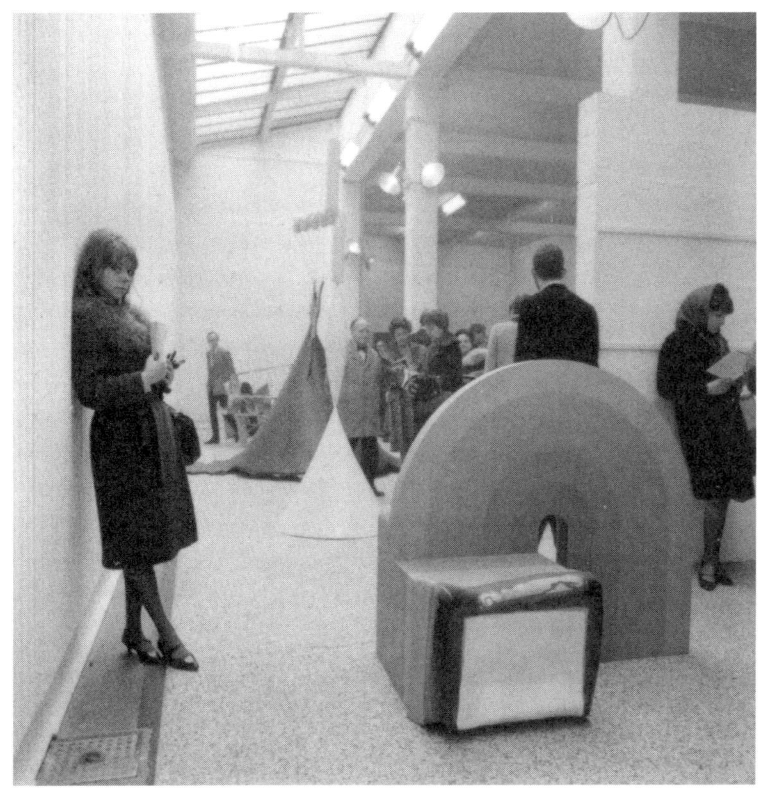

14 Exhibition view of *The New Generation 1965*, with Phillip King's sculpture in the background
Photograph by Martin Koretz, Whitechapel Gallery Archive

landscape painting. We do not see things so well three-dimensionally. The brilliant light of the Mediterranean helped to produce Greek sculpture, and Donatello. The clouded light of England produced architecture instead; something useful and functional, which supported the English notion of art as a utilitarian activity – but not sculpture with its increasing freedom of expression, its dependence on the drama of pure light, and its need for space to be given up to the luxury of sculpture as an art form existing imaginatively in its own right ...

The supremely important question is, of course, vision. Breaks from tradition, the disruption of a prevailing art form, new materials, new concepts – all this can only follow the promptings, the summons, of a strong vision. Vision comes from our experience of life, and it is only possible to react creatively to life and to experience with feeling. And here lies the quintessential problem which looms behind the formation of vision: the present deep confusion among many artists between feeling and sensation (I do not mean sensationalism: that can be left to the purveyors of old-fashioned shock tactics in the form of sick 'assemblages', debased and meaningless as they are). By sensation, I mean what happens when you look at an 'optical' painting, for instance, or the intellectualized titillation offered by that kind

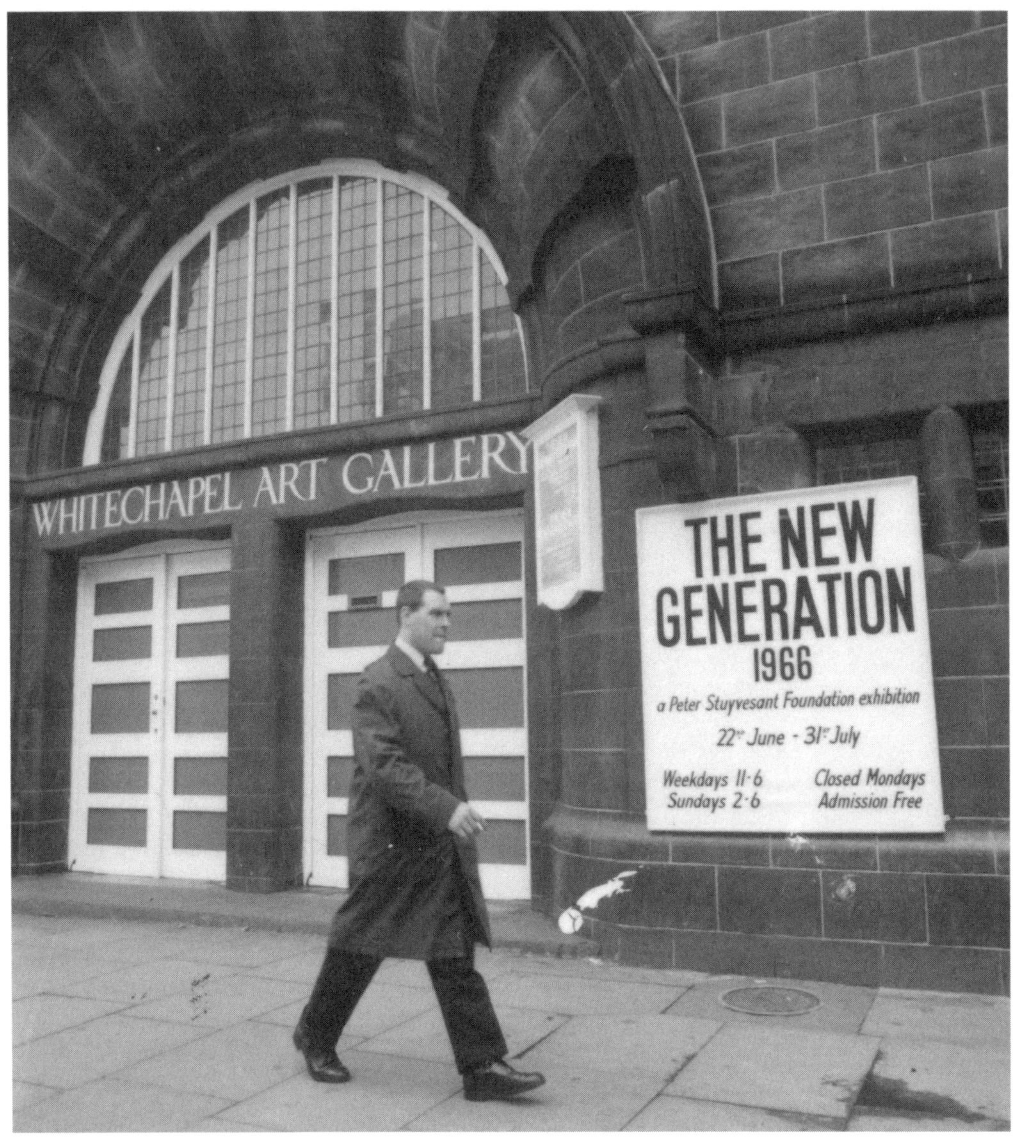

15 Exterior of the Whitechapel Gallery with poster for *The New Generation 1966* exhibition

Photograph by Martin Koretz, Whitechapel Gallery Archive

of pop art which is no better, and certainly no more pointed, than the best and most intelligent forms of advertising or pictorial journalism.

Great painting and great sculpture can only come from feeling. This alone produces a true vision. We cannot expect young artists to have had either the degree or the extent of any experience of life which can transform feeling into a mature vision. A sense of urgency, easily understandable, and a craving for immediate success, are opposed to the idea of a gradual, carefully nurtured, artistic evolution. But it is possible to wonder whether this younger generation of painters and sculptors are trusting their reactions to life sufficiently to allow for that depth of feeling which leads to creation. The alternative is to rely upon sensation. And the 'cool' approach, the 'anonymity' of touch, the 'non-association' of colour, the elementary formal pursuits, experiment as opposed to genuine exploration – all this may be a necessary progress towards an extension of abstract sculptural language. But it seems also to touch upon that 'distancing' ploy used by young people now when they are talking to somebody else in the room – the loud pop music blaring away, the television flickering in the corner. And the fear of silence. A distrust of commitment, engagement, the future, or even perhaps of feeling.

And this is taken from *The New Generation 1966*:

It is clear that in 1966 there is no slackening among young English artists of the vitality, the invention, and the sheer professionalism that have distinguished the two preceding shows. It would be absurd to look each year for radical innovations or a complete aesthetic revolution. Art lovers sometimes tend to be over-satiated with experience and consequently rather too avid for new excitements, sustained at a steady pace. The fact remains that this year a fresh co-ordinating factor hovers over the exhibition as a whole:

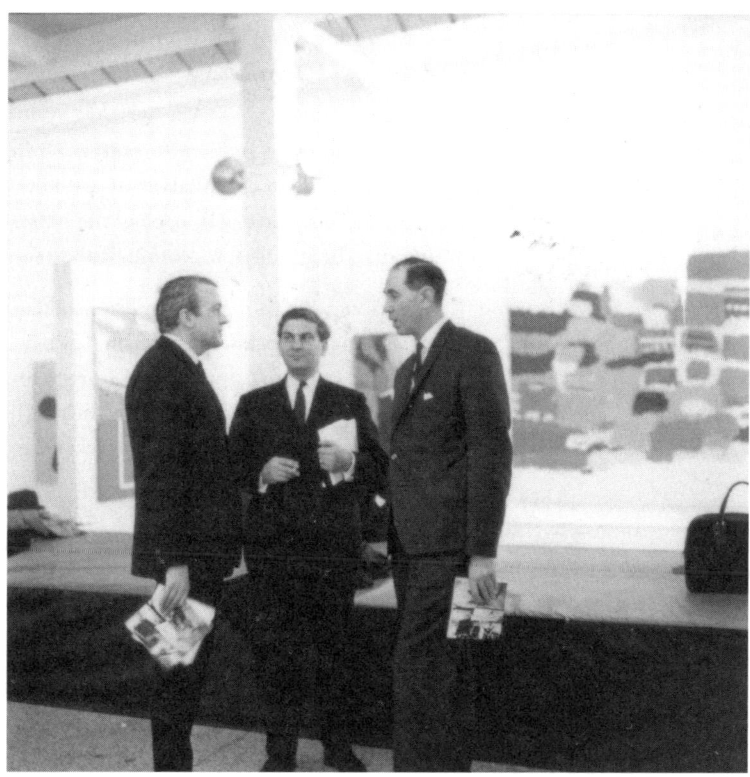

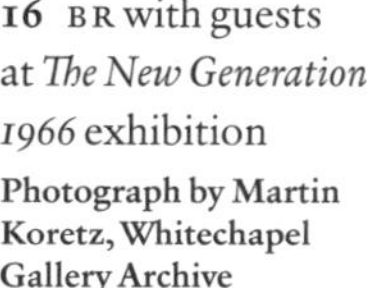

16 BR with guests at *The New Generation 1966* exhibition
Photograph by Martin Koretz, Whitechapel Gallery Archive

the fusion, in fact, between painting and sculpture in the form of shaped canvases, and a kind of painting which is sculptural, as well as sculpture which is painterly. We know these tendencies quite well by now, but in the present context they appear for the first time on reasonably equal terms. To make a rigid division has become, for the time being, a pedantic interference with a fluid situation.

As professional stakes get higher and the transmission of an artist's ethics becomes increasingly more direct and swift, with the inevitable build-up of competitiveness, I want to pay tribute to the extraordinary generosity that artists display towards each other, unostentatiously; and explain that the work of several of the artists included in this exhibition was first brought to my attention by the kindness and enthusiasm of either near-contemporaries or older artists. In this connection it is a pleasure to record my indebtedness for advice from Derek Boshier, Thelma Hulbert, and Bryan Kneale. From the very beginning of the series, this professional camaraderie has been an immense help to me, and I am grateful for it. I should not have known Patrick Caulfield's work so quickly without David Hockney's enthusiasm, or Michael Vaughan's – or Paul Huxley's – without the interest shown by Patrick Procktor. Bernard Meadows and Anthony Caro were equally useful when last year's sculpture show was planned. Neither artist was interested in extending their own point of view: their concern was objective and this is characteristic of the information given by the other artists on the earlier occasion.

With *The New Generation: 1968 Interim* the pattern shifted, and the exhibition presented was a kind of compilation of previous *New Generation* shows in that it featured new work by each of the artists who had exhibited so far rather than breaking new ground. Robertson wrote:

The present exhibition is a marking-time and consolidatory action designed to offset any possible air of expendability which may have been projected at the scheme as a whole. It is also a practical measure to bring the public up to date by showing one new and major work by each of the artists who have exhibited so far, before the ideas behind the project are extended next year.

They weren't, of course, for Bryan resigned his directorship. To scotch any rumour that he had run out of new artists to select, he mentioned a handful (including John Walker, Nigel Hall and Ken Draper) at the end of his piece.

Earlier in the preface he had written:

The first ideal [of showing young artists just out of art school] has only partially been realized: most of the artists represented in the first and second exhibitions were either well known or just known at the time of their *New Generation* participation; only in the third show, of 1966, was the idea more fully realized when a sizeable group of artists without existing reputations or professional history were included. This show was limply received by the critics, mistakenly in my view, because they mostly reacted in a surfeited journalist's manner to familiar factors: of youth, commercial sponsorship, and the painting-sculpture merger, which had already received their attention in earlier years. The show itself contained some impressive work and was the first New Generation show that truly embodied its title.

Knowing the importance of his coup at raising proper sponsorship for these exhibitions, Bryan was careful to thank his supporters:

At this point, I should like to emphasize that the generosity and trust of the Peter Stuyvesant Foundation in permitting all this sensible but rarely indulged activity still fills me with wonder. There is no precedent for their benign gesture in England; with my own experience of youth in the economically despondent 1940s and fifties, I know how much English art owes to the stalwart officers of the Foundation. It is just conceivable that their optimism in implementing the *New Generation* scheme, as well as their other concerns, has indirectly but decisively affected the course of art in England.

Four young sculptors

Anthony Caro (1924–2013), Bryan Kneale (born 1930), Tim Scott (born 1937) and Phillip King (born 1934) were all artists who benefited from the general and specific support of Bryan Robertson. All were given one-man shows at the Whitechapel and their careers were hugely boosted by this show of confidence in the work of a generation of largely unknown young sculptors.

Anthony Caro

Anthony Caro's 1963 exhibition at the Whitechapel was absolutely crucial to the development of his reputation in England, and in general. In effect, it marked a breakthrough. Caro himself (in a telephone conversation with Mary Yule) admitted that if Bryan hadn't exhibited the work then it would 'probably not have been seen in London for a long time'. As his widow Sheila Caro recalled in an interview at the artist's north London studio in April 2014:

The Whitechapel made Tony really. He wasn't an established artist. Bryan was important in that he was at the Whitechapel, he was in touch with all that was going on, and he wanted to show Tony's work. The *New Generation* sculptors coming so soon after – the sculptors Tony had taught – was a huge affirmation of his position in British art. Bryan would talk about them and write about them. He believed absolutely in what he was doing. *Private View* [that compelling survey of the London art world published in 1965 and jointly written by Robertson and John Russell] documents the milieu with which he was intimate.

We first really got to know Bryan when Tony had his show at the Whitechapel. He made it really the most exciting place in London. It was the place to go to. Tony was terribly excited because he hadn't shown in a big gallery. Bryan asked him to go to lunch and talk about it – the date was fixed and everything. Half way through Bryan went to the bathroom, came back and said 'Now I've changed my mind – I'm putting it off'. But Tony came home almost having a breakdown. I don't remember a reason. Of course it was reorganised. Bryan was adorable and wonderful fun but he wasn't always that steady. He was a little bit unreliable but a wonderful entrepreneur with wonderful ideas.

The art dealer John Kasmin played a crucial role in the Caro-Robertson-Whitechapel triangle. Bryan knew Kasmin's mother-in-law, E.Q. Nicholson, from her Cambridge days when she visited the shows he organised at Heffer's. Her closest friend in the art world was Cecil Collins, so their social worlds nicely overlapped. Kasmin's first job was working as 'gallery boy' at Victor Musgrave's Gallery One, which Bryan often visited. Colin MacInnes lived at Gallery One while he was writing his novel *City of Spades* (published in 1957 and the first of his 'London Trilogy'). Kasmin observed that MacInnes was open about being gay, and seemed much freer than the buttoned-up Robertson. 'Colin was one of the first people to wear blue jeans with a Harris tweed sports jacket and get away with it in polite society.' After a stint at Marlborough Fine Art, Kasmin started his own company with Lord Dufferin in 1962, and almost immediately began forming a stable of artists:

I got to know Bryan much better when I took on Tony Caro and made a world contract with him when I started my own business. He was already in both an exciting and staggeringly frustrating relationship with Bryan, preceding the exhibition at the Whitechapel. So I got to know Bryan in another way through Tony, trying to help and be somewhat of an intermediary.

My first images of Bryan were of this man with a wonderful track record who had brought Pollock and Rothko to England, who was about to do an exhibition of the only sculptor I thought worth being involved with. Tony's work was not only thrilling to me, it was so totally different from anything else. I was incredibly excited and proud to be his dealer, while he was amazed I was willing to put money into being his champion. I immediately encountered these curious qualities of Bryan's – his tremendous enthusiasm and this amazing apparent disorder. Thinking about it, it's possible that he used his perpetual and chronic asthma as some sort of prop or cover for his endless procrastination. He had a way of really very decisively not making decisions or facing the work of the day on the table. The show must have been at least a year in planning. Tony was in a state of nervous collapse at times – how will this exhibition ever happen? What was happening with the catalogue, with this, that and the other.

Eventually the exhibition took place, between September and October 1963, and history was made. The following excerpt is taken from Bryan's preface to the catalogue:

Most public galleries have flights of steps to climb, which gradually transfer you from life to the separate world of art. This pause between street thoughts and the exploration of art is not altogether happy. You get the sensation of ascending, physically and mentally, to a higher plane. Your spirits don't always rise to keep you company, for the art plateau is above life and remote from normal human activity. The feeling is not dissimilar to entering a church or the head office of a bank. In either case you are conscious of a challenge to come.

The floor of the Whitechapel Gallery is on the same level as the street outside: you can get in or out very quickly. At least one psychological barrier between you and art has been removed. Similarly, in this exhibition Caro's sculptures stand on the floor without the intervention of pedestals or bases. Their impact is direct and immediate. Caro dislikes the idea of sculpture presented with artificial aids, separated from the ground – and from life, and so trapped inside an archaic aesthetic vacuum. At the same time, although he is also out of sympathy with the precious-object precious-material convention, these new sculptures are certainly objects for contemplation. They do not reflect any anti-art principles. Their astringent formality, at once strong and delicate, should remove any thoughts of brutalism or *art mécanique*.

Writing for the catalogue of a much later Caro exhibition, at Annely Juda in 1994, Robertson evoked the excitement of the Whitechapel show:

It must be hard for anyone under fifty to fully understand the raw shock of Anthony Caro's new coloured sculptures in metal when they were first seen by the general public in London at the Whitechapel Gallery in 1963. Quite an agreeable pitch of exhilaration accompanied the shock because this bright new sculpture seemed straight away to clear one's eyesight. But for many lovers of sculpture or followers of modern form the first impact of some of the larger, heavier, darker coloured and quite un-caressable I-beams straddling the floor was a daunting experience.

Caro's colour was fully polychromatic, brilliant, intense, quite unpredictable and supported the sensation of buoyancy and levitation for some sculptures as opposed to earth-bound, ground-related gravity in others. Colour made some sculptures appear to be weightless. This new use of colour further reinforced other sensations of movement, even speed, by implication, as light-filled yellow, for example, moves faster through space or along the ground than sluggish, more opaque and more equivocal purple, and so on.

Here was pure colour used for the first time in sculpture in quite new, basically functional and constructive ways as well as fulfilling an emblematic, emotional or decorative – but never descriptive – purpose.

It is interesting to observe in passing that Moore, a huge figure in his lifetime, has had no influence on sculpture anywhere whilst Caro's example has plainly had far-ranging consequences for sculpture. I have seen this for myself in Australia, in Canada, in parts of the US where David Smith is otherwise by far the strongest influence – on the early Walter De Maria and Mark di Suvero, for instance – and even in Southeast Asia. I don't think this has anything to do with the relative status of Moore and Caro so much as the way in which some artists leave a situation open for followers, and other artists close everything up, or their work appears to come at the end of a tradition and to seal itself off from any possible extension – like the paintings of Rothko, for example.

Caro's inventiveness in the art of assemblage is providing one of the great ongoing spectacles of my lifetime. Nobody since Picasso has created so much richly innovative work or covered quite such a range of feeling. This word, feeling, in itself is of crucial significance. Robert Motherwell once expressed to me his reservations over much contemporary art by saying that what he disliked was the preoccupation with sensation as opposed to feeling, which for him was the vital element.

Ultimately what Caro discloses is the image behind and beyond the possibility of words, in formal situations of such original and unexpected disposition that they become events of almost ceremonial balance and precision – like the moment when behaviour assumes the formality of conduct. Caro is achieving something here that words cannot express, yet with odd inflexions which appear sometimes to act as a memento, almost, of something that has really happened: a human gesture, a place, or site, a situation which struggles to locate itself in our memory.

Sheila Caro remembered Bryan with deep affection:

We all just loved him and loved going to dinner with him. He gave wonderful dinners – he always mixed people up terribly well. We met Tim Marlow for the first time there. It was always a party you wanted to go to.

He took us to the theatre. He was lovely actually – I was terribly fond of him. I think his judgement was very good. I remember a lecture with David Sylvester – they were sitting on the stage opposite each other, both talking. David waited every time till Bryan gave his opinion. It was funny. Bryan came out so much the top dog, the most perceptive of those two.

Bryan Kneale

Bryan Kneale first met Bryan Robertson through the Redfern Gallery around 1960. The following quotations are adapted from a series of interviews with the artist in his Crouch End studio conducted between 1997 and 2017.

It was about the time I started to make sculpture and they asked Bryan to write the foreword to the catalogue of my first sculpture show. He said 'No, under no circumstances'. They said: 'But you haven't seen the sculpture.' So he saw the sculpture and not only did he like it but he offered me a show at the Whitechapel on the strength of it. And he did write the foreword to my catalogue. He must have seen some of my paintings and taken against them in some way, I don't know. He never spoke to me about it ever. And when we had the show at the Whitechapel [1966] he insisted on having some of the paintings in it. My paintings had changed rapidly from being

17 Bryan Kneale and BR at the New Art Centre at Roche Court, Wiltshire, 1991.

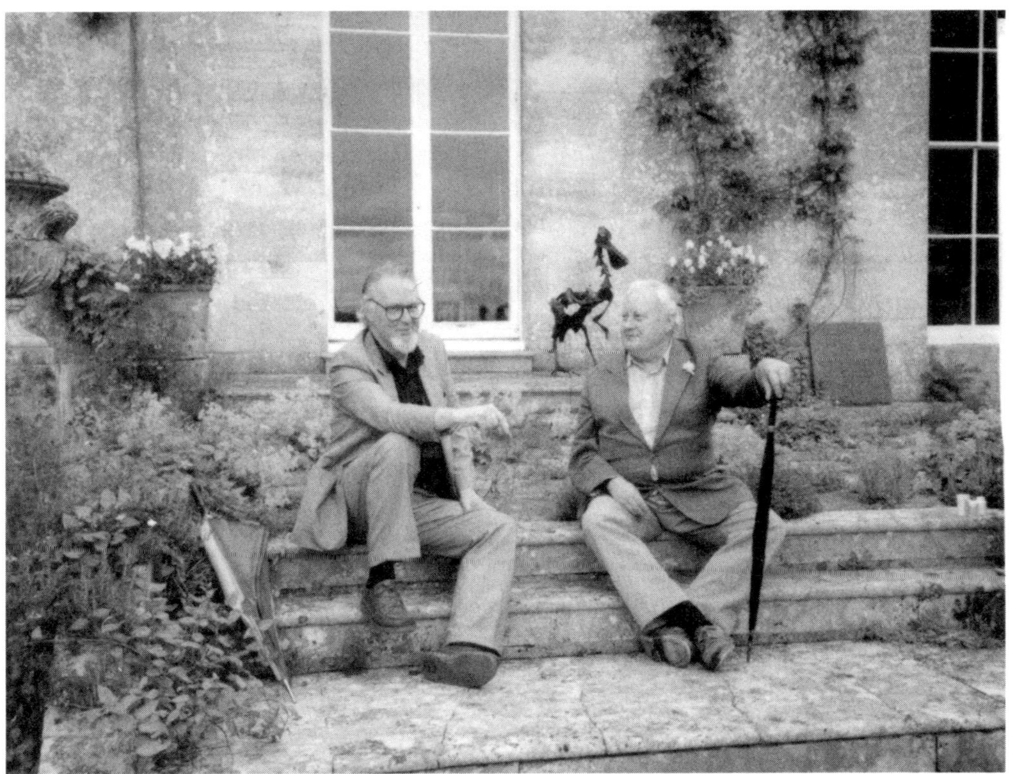

entirely figurative to being non-figurative and then leading straight into the sculpture.

The following excerpts are taken from Bryan's 1964 Redfern Gallery catalogue introduction.

'In the same way as I deplore so-called "commitment" in art appreciation, or art criticism, because it is invariably synonymous with promotion and the rigid avoidance or suppression of any kind of viewpoint which contradicts or departs from the promoted set position – and art is an immensely complex vehicle – so do I enjoy Kneale's refusal to stay inside the confines of a limited formal or technical arena.'

In general, the work combines soft organic and hard inorganic shapes in a series of awkward, unsuave, and always rather startling relationships. Kneale makes us think again of certain basic human activities in a new way: like putting on or taking off a shoe for instance – an astonishing juxtaposition of material and shape, if you think of it for a second, and nothing to do with any mere mechanical process. He is concerned with the effect one shape has on another and with what links them; and his sculptures have to do with mood, with presence, with physical identity in general terms, rather than with any references to a mechanomorphic or quasi-human personage. We are in the world, in fact, of David Smith and Anthony Caro, and confronted by another link in the chain started forty years ago by González and Picasso.

The work is full of paradox, for usually the moment of perfect balance in any one of these sculptures is at once the moment of maximum life and maximum repose. There is little interest in texture and none at all in decorative effect. Colour is used to accentuate the character of a particular form. The references do not come from art so much as from things: objects – like doors, locks, aeroplanes, a car, engines. Kneale is interested in the flow of events which produce a lock and a key and the abstract relationship between a lock, a door and a handle. He is also interested in disruption: for instance, the way a room is changed when you put a sculpture in it.

Back to Kneale (a raconteur of the first order):

I was delighted with his reaction and the Whitechapel offer. He was extremely amusing apart from anything else. Before I had the show he said: 'You've got to have a suit. I always insist on the artist looking good. You know Prunella Clough always dresses in a terrible old cap and great big boots and a men's overcoat. I said to Prunella she must smarten herself up for her show and she went off in a huff. Then on the night of the Private View, she'd been to Paris and had a wonderful gown made, and she was dressed in white satin and looked wonderful beyond words. Next day she was back to the boots and the cap.' Anyway he insisted on taking me to a rather weird tailor in Shaftesbury Avenue who dressed actors and who assured me that if I wanted to be famous I must always come to him to have suits made. So he put me in a suit which Bryan immediately drew all over with tailors' chalk – he knew what he was doing: he knew all about cutting cloth. It was a bit of a surprise. The suit was duly made and it was definitely designed by Bryan Robertson and I wore it.

Bryan had very little money to run the Whitechapel and his salary was minuscule, less than £2,000 a year, I think. This didn't deter him from spending money. It was always a complete mystery to me how on earth he got away with it. There was a wall across the gallery and he decided it had to come down. Then he said that the walls should be covered with treble thickness white muslin. When I got there just before the show he said 'The musliners can't do it'. So in came an army of sculpture students from some art school or other who'd got the date wrong of my show and we gave them staplers and they did it, because the muslin had arrived but the musliners couldn't install it. I just assumed that was the sort of thing that happened, but when I look back on it – it was the thing about Bryan, things happened magically. And sometimes they were disastrous.

The most alarming thing about my show was when my sculptures arrived – there were tons of heavy sculpture, some of them very big – the lorries arrived with all my stuff, and then suddenly another set of lorries appeared with someone else's show. Bryan had got the dates wrong. I think it was Dick Smith. Bryan came down and said: 'Oh take it all away, Dick, we'll have your show another time.' He'd done my catalogue and everything – he'd just forgotten to tell Dick.

Bryan transformed my career. I'd been showing at the Redfern – obviously quite a limited space – and suddenly I had the whole of the Whitechapel to play with, which was very exciting. In fact the whole thing was rather weird. The show took place in February and March 1966 and in 1965 he asked me to have the show. When he offered me the show, I assumed it would be in two years' time as I was preparing for it. It must have been about September or October when I rang him up and said, 'Well of course we've got plenty of time yet'. He said: 'Oh no you haven't – you've got three or four months.' Then it was panic stations, right up to the very end to produce this huge piece of sculpture which was painted. The weather was horrible and the paint wouldn't dry, so we had to raise the temperature in the studio. It was a blacksmith's shop and we had a big furnace going and gas jets all over the place, and oxyacetylene burners going full blast. It was so unbelievably hot we had to lie on the floor gasping. Then suddenly the paint went off. We actually had turned the place into an oven.

The following excerpt comes from Bryan's preface to Kneale's Whitechapel catalogue for the 1966 show:

This exhibition is a great tour de force in the sense that from a total of fifty-two sculptures on show, covering the period 1959–1966, no less than twenty-four works have been completed since November 1964. Eighteen of these new sculptures stem from the last four months: that is, from October 1965. The very nature of this kind of metal sculpture with its obvious physical demands precludes any easy display of facility: there are no short cuts. At a time when art in England is, in my opinion, magnificent in its power, range and sheer momentum, Kneale's accomplishment has a genuinely heroic ring to it ... Kneale is adding, in my view, a fresh emotional and constructive dimension to recent extensions in English sculpture ... Kneale's situation and potentiality as an artist are completely open like Johns, Caro or Rauschenberg, and his own distinctive force, or weight as a sculptor, still rest in the future.

Kneale ripostes:

Bryan Kneale's work 'creates involvement by means of the interval, as in the "cool" art of the Orient, and not by the connection used in the visually organized West.'

I remember being down at his place one day. He was very cunning. The phone rang and he asked me to answer it. It was *Vogue New York*. 'He's not here,' I said. 'I can hear him wheezing from here,' the man said. 'Put him on.' 'Oh yes,' said Bryan. 'I've just finished the article.' He was quite naughty like that ... But he was very supportive: he bought a sculpture for the Tate and brought people to the studio to buy work. He had a tremendous eye for all sorts of things. I particularly liked talking to him about George Stubbs. Stubbs is one of my special artists and I know him quite well. Stubbs has always been there in my thinking. Bryan had a great passion for him.

And finally, here is Robertson on Kneale again (Serpentine Gallery exhibition, 1978):

The best description I can offer of the great body of his work produced in the last eighteen years, which I believe to be one of the most impressive achievements of this period in England, is to say that Kneale's sculpture is an inventive morphology of shape and form which looks often as if Stubbs had made a new *Anatomy* from the eloquent detritus of our mechanical and technological civilization.

Tim Scott

The following is from an email sent by the artist Tim Scott in March 2016:

'A likely story, as Bryan Robertson would say.' This little phrase has tripped into the family chatter at any time that the outrageous or the unbelievable crop up; bringing back with them, as it does, memories of his acerbic wit and the sheer perceptiveness of his opinions.

Sitting at his very large dining table in Barnsbury Street, down which marched an eclectic but very beautiful collection of little objets d'art; listening to his endless exposés of the foibles of the art world, the theatre world, and indeed of any aspect of culture in general, one was aware of a mind that was singular in its breadth of interest and wide-ranging in its depth of understanding. When Bryan engaged any specific subject in his observations, the result was often hilarious, always entertaining and very often profound.

I first met Bryan as a youngster setting out on the path of attempting to be a sculptor, when he was selecting candidates for his Whitechapel *New Generation* shows. As part of the St Martin's 'gang', he came to see my work, such as it was, in the basement of my house in Peckham. I remember very little of what he said at the time. I think, as with most visitors in those days, he had great difficulty in reaching what was perceived as 'somewhere near Dover'; transport facilities then were on the primitive or non-existent side. Anyway, the upshot was that I was selected, and I remain eternally grateful to him for giving me this 'first break' as an artist. In fact, it was the forerunner of what was to become an alarming state of affairs, as, for the next forty years, Bryan became the *only* English critic to visit my studio, which he did on several further occasions.

My next major encounter with him after the group showing of the Whitechapel *New Generation* sculpture in 1965, was at my first one-man show at Leslie Waddington's new gallery in 1966. I was in the gallery setting up the five pieces that constituted the show (the pieces were large and the gallery fairly small), when Bryan walked in. I don't think I have ever experienced someone viewing my work as positively as he did on this occasion. I was, of course, thrilled that someone could show such enthusiasm, and mean it, and we became 'friends'. I was to learn from many further discussions with him that one of his outstanding characteristics and assets was his ability to become so completely enthralled by whatever he was contemplating, that the spirit of it quite literally became contagious.

The most extraordinary personal outcome of this encounter was the offer by Bryan of a one-man show at the Whitechapel, which took place in 1967. This prospect was, naturally, a daunting creative task for me, and one of which I had never dreamed. As it turned out, in comparison to the previous one-man show at Waddington's, the critical reception of the Whitechapel show was very muted and lacklustre. What matters here is that again it was Bryan who came to the rescue. He wrote a wonderful review in the *Spectator* and, as I have said before, remained the sole English critic to consistently continue his support. From this period on, I did not have that much to do with British backing as my main protagonists were now in America and then Germany. However, I continued to see Bryan on and off socially whilst teaching full time in Britain and subsequently throughout the nineties in Germany.

There is no doubt in my mind that Bryan was the outstanding critic and art impresario of his time in this country. There are literally dozens of British artists who owe their reputations and their careers to his support and promotion. Many of us were extremely upset that he failed to nail the job at the Tate; the subsequent history of modern painting and sculpture in Britain would very likely have turned out to be far more serious and thought-provoking than it has without him. What was so splendid about Bryan's presence was the fact that one could absolutely rely on anything that he undertook to come from the heart as well as the head, and that, above all, he believed in it.

Phillip King

Phillip King was included in *The New Generation* sculpture show of 1965 and then in the *1968 Interim* show. That same year, he was given a one-person exhibition at the Whitechapel. It was a version of his show that year at the Venice Biennale – an incidence of recognition which speaks volumes. The catalogue for his solo show contained Bryan's preface, King's own 'Notes on Sculpture', extracts from a questionnaire by John Coplans, and a further piece on King's work by Bryan. There were twenty illustrations, of which eleven were colour plates. This was a substantial publication, and Bryan concluded his preface by saying: 'The trustees of the Whitechapel Gallery hope that as a document this catalogue will be useful for many years as a source of information for everyone concerned with Phillip King's work.'

The following is an extract from Bryan's essay on King's work:

The enigmatic character of King's work springs from a built-in, subliminal element of paradox. Each sculpture is so very much more remarkable than its bare, factual existence as a physical object in space. An essential logos, or personal system of clear rules, is so charged by imagination that wholly unexpected conclusions are revealed: each sculpture will shift suddenly into a different identity whilst its structure is examined. The disclosure has the impact of a dramatic event. It is as if two plus two were made to yield five, incontrovertibly and with splendid finality, for the nature of King's imagination has something of that double-edged rationale which informs music and mathematics, and brings them so close together. At the same time, King avoids the pedantic vacuum of the demonstration piece, or 'composition as explanation'. There are no traces here of a didactic exercise, though a certain degree of compulsion decides all formal choices: notably, a tendency to suggest vertical or horizontal movement in an otherwise becalmed form by a curious manipulation of apparently static elements.

King's sculpture is tremendously alive, in an almost human sense, though he respects certain self-imposed rules which, above all, relieve his work of rhetoric. Surfaces are smooth, though anything but anonymous: there is considerable play with reflective and non-reflective surfaces, and qualities of colour which move from synthetic freshness or sharpness to a density that is more obviously inhabited by mood or association. Higher-pitched colour 'moves' more quickly than deeper registers. Mattness or shininess is connected with resonance – also with light. Expansion and contraction are set in motion by a combination of all these actions, in the way that Rothko's canvases appear to 'breathe' through the gentle pulsation of light, contained and then released, by the colour.

King recalled his friendship with Bryan in an email of March 2018:

I had my first show at Heffer's in 1957, five years after he had left and while I was still an undergraduate. I must have met him around '63, '64, but never asked him how he got the Whitechapel from this modest beginning.

My Whitechapel show, probably one of the most important events in my career, came quite late in 1968. The reason was not his uncertainty about my work, as from the 1965 show at the gallery he let me know I was one of his favourite sculptors, and his support was constant from then on. I was so grateful after that show that I gave him one of two versions of *Twilight* (1963), which he kept in the sitting room, where it proved quite difficult to get around [it] to get to the seating area around the fireplace.

He was a home-loving man and took great care with all the numbers of works of art he had acquired, and up to that time no other home I had been to had so much art in it. He was a very generous and loyal friend; I suspect I had dinner at his place more often than he at mine. He would occasionally write long spidery handwritten letters always to express some support or other.

Many of his friends were artists whose work he liked and I am sure he was equally loyal and supportive with them. His great love of art was given extra depth by the love of other art forms like music, ballet, literature, and he was probably the most cultured man I have yet come across. This was evident in the radio programme *The Critics* where he always shone on almost any topic.

He felt a duty to educate his mostly ignorant artist friends in the most inoffensive manner as a kind of joke. In one case amongst others he persuaded me to read Shattuck's *The Banquet Years*, one of the best books I have read on a group of artists, which I have recommended many times to other people.

He was an emotional man, though he kept this quite hidden; there were never any sexual innuendoes except in jest. I was most intrigued by a bit of gossip that he had proposed to Bridget Riley. I can't imagine it happening, only Bridget knows.

Once he got to like you and your work he never wavered much. There were a few years after I had separated from my first wife when he found it difficult to cope with divided loyalties and we saw less of each other. But in the end he was reconciled with my new partner.

For me the final impression is of someone with great enthusiasm and humour who wanted to communicate what he thought of as the most important and the best; so much so that he must have pushed a lot of people out of their comfort zone including me, in the end all for their betterment. Last of all he was a great cook and gardener though the practical side of life was not always his forte.

Bryan's support for King's work continued unabated over the subsequent decades, and one of his most considered statements on King did not appear until 1997, for the catalogue of the major retrospective at Forte di Belvedere in Florence. Here are three quotations from that essay:

For the past thirty years, I have enjoyed the privilege of living day by day with Phillip King's *Twilight*. This extraordinary invention, strange in its time and place of London in the early sixties and disconcerting still after all this time, continues to add immeasurably to my imaginative apprehension of the world around me, seen and unseen. For all of its mysteriously poetic presence, the sculpture transmits a tonic and bracing strength: an energy which commands attention at all times but does not invite speculative contemplation. You have to accept *Twilight* instantly as a fantastic object in its own right without casting around for a story or a metaphor. *Twilight* is sharply self-assertive and self-sufficient: it has no need of an alibi …

King has of course travelled a very long way since that astonishingly mature and original debut in London through the sixties: at the Rowan Gallery in 1964, at the Whitechapel Gallery (which I directed in the fifties and sixties) in the historic *New Generation* show of 1965 and in his Whitechapel retrospective in 1968, when King also represented England at the Venice Biennale. King has made during the past thirty years some of the strongest, most beautiful and original sculpture of my lifetime. My own standards in sculpture are very high and not easily satisfied. [And here Robertson mentions his first-hand knowledge of Brancusi and his works – a lifelong benchmark of excellence.] Phillip King is the only sculptor in my experience to have fully lived up to and extended in new ways the aesthetic concentration and refinement of Brancusi. There is no superficial resemblance. I am only touching on the originality and strength of a basic gift and an artist's aesthetic purity …

I do not believe that art is about progress; science is about progress, art is concerned with change. When Scott Fitzgerald sent his friend Gertrude Stein the manuscript of *The Great Gatsby*, he enclosed a card in which he expressed the hope that, in asking her to read the new book, it might at least be better than his last book, which Miss Stein had admired. *Gatsby* was returned to Fitzgerald within a couple of weeks with a few constructive and helpful comments about syntax pencilled in the margins and a note which said, 'Thank you for letting me read your new book. It is a beautiful and very good book, but of course it is not better than your last book for we do not get better as we get older but different and older and this book is different and older.' I agree with Gertrude Stein: the notion of an artistic progression ever upwards towards some fixed, immutable, optimum point of excellence is absurd. Our journey through life is not a linear evolution from A to B. If you are any good at all as an artist, you are good in different ways at certain stages right through your working life. Late Titian is not better than, say, the *Venus of Urbino*, it is just different and older.

Final years at the Whitechapel

Things had begun to go wrong and the mood of retrospection was hard to shift. Before he left the Whitechapel, when he was feeling particularly beleaguered in his job, Bryan wrote an article in the *Spectator* (dated 20 May 1966) spelling out some of his achievements:

When I first started at the Whitechapel Gallery fifteen years ago, I lived for a year nearby to explore East London and try to understand its mental climate. I worked at various clubs, old people's homes, even found myself lecturing to prison inmates ... I came pretty quickly to the obvious conclusion that East London was just like everywhere else, except livelier ... As the standards of its inhabitants are both sharp and high, I decided to ignore the gallery's environment and make a series of spectacles, celebrations if you like, which would not disgrace any national institution...

The miracle is that the gallery has survived. Until [1966] there was about £600 per annum with which to mount between six and eight vast shows every year, each one of which cost between £1,500 and £3,000 to stage ... The constitution of Whitechapel is unique: there are no useful parallels ... There must always be free admission. Canon Barnett founded it, believing that it was important for a gallery to exist in that part of London 'to show the best modern art of the day' and that 'paintings hidden from the multitude are unknown tongues, speaking truth'. I hope on balance the redoubtable Canon would agree that a lot of language has been unleashed in recent years ... nearly 60,000 people thronged the Rauschenberg in a month. 23,000 came to see the [1966] *New Generation* display. The annual attendance is startling.

If anyone doubts that the public for art is classless, they have only to visit the Whitechapel on Saturday or Sunday and observe elegantly clad art-lovers from Belgravia or Kensington rubbing shoulders with mildly demented parents with kids ... from Bethnal Green, all mixed up with art students from everywhere, people up from the country who might usually be found in Wildenstein's or Agnew's, and quite a lot of inquisitive local swinging youth, Teds fifteen years ago, now Mods replete with cool gear, incredulously – sometimes enviously – assessed by the office workers in their tweeds. The point is that this gloriously mixed public enjoy each other as well as the art and actually speak to each other – I loathe the hushed 'reading-room' atmosphere of museums, discourage it strenuously, and it helps that you can smoke and stub a cigarette out on the floor.

Art is not a luxury, it is the most acute and basic expression of the spiritual state of any society in any epoch, and its revelation should be an integral part of life, of common experience, because it finally makes the shape of everything around us. But I dislike wagging forefingers and telling people what to think ... and this is why a certain ambience generates itself at the Whitechapel – there are no slogans, no explanatory captions by works of art and no lectures. Good art speaks for itself. Exposure and patience is all.

The policy formed itself. I wanted to do something about English artists who are too often judged, and mercilessly, on the evidence of a small one-man show every few years; but whose work surveyed over a decade, for example, makes good sense and explains itself more readily. And sanctimonious as this sounds, I've always wanted to give a bit of dignity to English artists by providing them with the grand occasions in their middle years, or younger, if they're worth it, that used to be reserved for Picasso or Braque – or might follow their own demise. And make catalogues which would be useful to everyone and be worthy of the seriousness of the occasion. As I've always believed that England's basic trouble has been an inability to come to terms with the twentieth century, and it's surely crucial to understand now, not 1900 or 1935, I also wanted to bring Londoners up to date with modern art on a broad front. Commitment to a narrow section of modern art so often means ruthless promotion and my own taste is wide – to the consternation of artists, who cannot believe that after hanging their own show and trying to help them through the angst-ridden months of a large retrospective, you can hang with equal enthusiasm work that's diametrically opposed to their viewpoint.

But at least English artists have been presented on equal terms with their foreign contemporaries. It's hard to realise the inferiority complex that once plagued English artists in their part-supposed, but often very real, isolation. We have not been told enough about the greatness of the English tradition and its interaction, from the days of illuminated manuscripts, with continental evolution. I'm glad the work of the gallery is so well known abroad. I hope that Whitechapel has had an effect on English artists: we're in the middle of an extraordinary period in English art, and I'd like to believe that Whitechapel has provided some of the background stimulus, as well as the celebrations.

After Bryan had announced his resignation in November 1968, there were various responses in the press. Bridget Riley, writing in the *Spectator* (dated 3 January 1969) made the first public statement by an artist of the *New Generation* circle about how much they – individually and collectively – owed to Bryan:

Bryan Robertson, who left the Whitechapel Gallery this week, became its director in 1952. One cannot help feeling that this is the end of an era, and one must not let the occasion go by without at least an attempt to say what that era achieved. The British contemporary art scene immediately after the last war was marked by an infectious apathy and a vicious insularity. There was little information available and less wished for. There were few, if any, travelling exhibitions, scarcely any art books or periodicals, and the most meagre opportunities for showing recent work. This state of affairs was underwritten by the curiously ambivalent British attitude to foreign artists – that, on the one hand, no native artist could hope to compete with them on equal terms, while, on the other, what these foreigners were doing was so suspect as to be better ignored.

Students who entered art schools in the late forties and early fifties found them staffed by a generation whose horizons were inevitably bounded by pre-war concepts. I clearly remember the shock with which I discovered, in the late fifties, that art had not stopped with the surrealists. And, if the intervening twenty-odd years were a blank, the enormous upheaval in American painting which was happening at this time was hardly rumoured over here.

What Bryan Robertson did at the Whitechapel was simply this: he made people aware of developments outside these islands, he provided a focus for British artists and he encouraged them to work in an international context …

And here, as one who took part in the 1964 show, I must try to explain how Bryan Robertson's personal friendship with an artist, while losing nothing of natural warmth, is all, in a sense, part of the principles on which he has run the gallery. By taking every opportunity to introduce us to visitors to this country – writers, painters, musicians, poets, he encouraged the exchange of ideas and, what is more, on an equal footing. This sense of confidence, at any rate at the beginning, was very necessary. But above all, his unique blend of enthusiasm with critical attention creates a perfect climate for such meetings …

There was also a letter from Professor Sir William Coldstream and others to the *Times* in December 1968:

Sir, – Last month Bryan Robertson retired from the Whitechapel Art Gallery and we should like to take this opportunity to declare our appreciation of his unique and vital directorship. The exhibitions that he presented were informed by a selfless dedication to contemporary painting and sculpture and also by a passionate interest and concern for the artists themselves.

These exhibitions, which in retrospect give an astonishingly wide survey of the various aspects of contemporary art, were rarely generalized. His interest was prompted by the specific and personal, not by 'groups' or 'movements'. It was precisely this quality that made the work he achieved at Whitechapel so important. He performed for us all, the public as well as the specialist, a singular service which cannot ordinarily be provided by public bodies or committees. It is no overstatement to say that his directorship of Whitechapel is of historical importance in the development of British art and artists.

Yours faithfully,

William Coldstream, Barbara Hepworth, John Hoyland, Jasper Johns, Phillip King, Bryan Kneale, Robert Medley, Henry Moore, Robert Motherwell, Serge Poliakoff, Robert Rauschenberg, Ceri Richards, Bridget Riley, Tim Scott, Mark Tobey, Keith Vaughan, Mark Rothko

In the Tate Archive, there is a handwritten note by David Sylvester about Bryan's application to the Whitechapel:

The beauty of the way Robertson ran the gallery was that he ignored its location. I took the opposite line when I applied for the job. (We both, by the way, cited Henry Moore as a referee, with the difference that I had the great man's permission to do so and Robertson didn't.) The policy outlined in my application was entirely orientated to the gallery's being in the East End and read as if it had been drawn up by the Workers' Educational Association. I don't know what Robertson said in his application, but once he had got the job he set out simply to make the place the best gallery of contemporary art in Britain, and he wholly succeeded.

John Hoyland

John Hoyland (1934–2011) became a close friend of Bryan's, doing a marvellous imitation of his voice and telling scurrilous, inventive and affectionate stories about his habits and proclivities. Here are some of the anecdotes more fit to print, taken from an interview with the artist in his London studio in May 2011.

I was in the Situation Group and Bryan, for his own irrational reasons, had taken against them. I guess looking back on it, he had a wider perspective on art in Britain, and he also had a wider perspective on what was going on internationally. You know he lived in Paris for a bit. Paul Huxley and I were friends at the time, we were students together and buddies, shared our ideas. He was my closest friend and in those days people had a generosity they don't have any more. Bryan was choosing the *New Generation*, and he was very reluctant to see me because he had this already pretty thought-out idea about Situation artists. He wouldn't even look at me until Paul persuaded him to look at my work.

Anyway, Paul, with some difficulty, got Bryan to go and see my work. I was still in Primrose Hill and had an overwhelming amount of pictures.

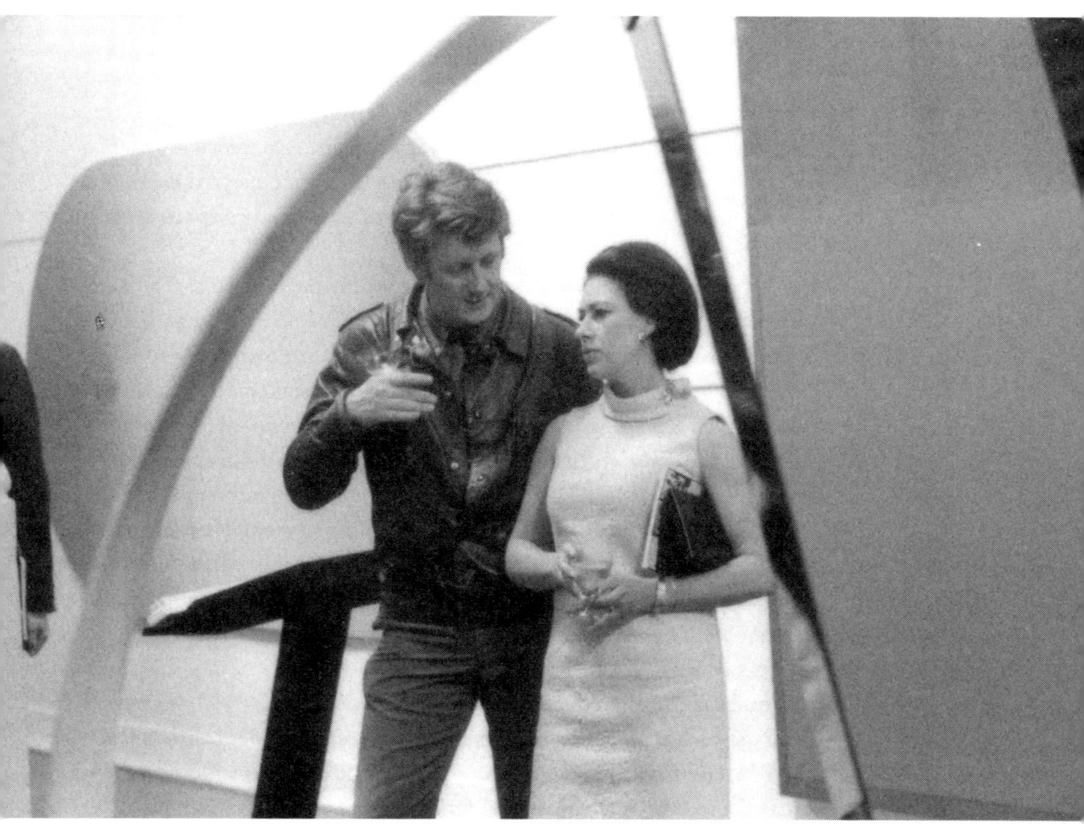

18 John Hoyland and Princess Margaret at *The New Generation: 1968 Interim* opening at the Whitechapel Gallery
Whitechapel Gallery Archive

For some reason he said he liked them and he put me in that show (*New Generation 1964*). I can't really remember how the social side grew, which it did of course. Bryan was a great party-giver. He used to live in this flat behind Sloane Square. I used to call it the Château Beef, it was like a French building. He had no money, he was really skint all the time, and yet I met Rauschenberg there, Jasper Johns, Michelangelo Antonioni. Lindsay Kemp came to dinner one night, dressed something like a clown – an extraordinary man. Bryan mixed people up, had no idea of classing or tiering them, but wanted them to get on and be useful to each other.

One of the fringe benefits of the *New Generation* shows was the Stuyvesant travel scholarships. Paul got the big one [in 1964] and went with Bryan [to America]. They travelled together. Bryan of course had a lot of connections which he persistently destroyed. I heard something about Errol Flynn that David Niven said and it applies to Bryan – the one thing you could rely on Bryan for was that he'd always let you down. Like when he got the date wrong for my exhibition opening and people turned up on the wrong day. Anyway, so Paul went off with Bryan, and he met all the museum people and dealers and I was envious. But I had my trip – I got one of the other scholarships. It was all chosen from the *New Generation* shows. The other hugely enviable prize that everyone could kill for was the Harkness, which was two years in New York or wherever you wanted to go. Free apartment and free studio and materials. Paul got it. He went to New York. I was stuck here living with the wife and kids in Kingston with a garage for my studio. Teaching and painting. I think the Harkness was what inspired Bryan to set up his own fellowships. I think that gave him a solution of what to do with what he left.

I suppose I became a little bit of a Paul substitute, in so far as if he wanted a younger companion to go to the theatre or opera or something – because he was always trying to educate me (impossible job!), giving me books to read and telling me I didn't know anything (which was true). There was a book called *The Girls* by a French author. So I commenced my meteoric rise through the cultural echelons of Britain. As I say, Bryan was always skint, but he would always pay. We'd go to a restaurant and be presented with a bill – and also the one from the previous visit. He'd be sweating because he was a bad asthmatic and in those days there was only these Ephedrine tablets and apparently they had to give you three times what you needed so you would sweat. He'd get the bill and I'd say, 'Let me do it, let me chip in'. 'No, no, no – a mere trifle.' And he would never let you pay.

And then he offered me a show at the Whitechapel [1967]. I was the youngest who had one. I had about a year to prepare it, but I already had it, so I did two more shows. You know I was the only person who had a show that changed halfway through? All the big green paintings. That was all very well received. Meanwhile I'd been kicked out by Marlborough, and I didn't have a gallery.

My other cliché about Bryan was that the reason why he couldn't work in the establishment was because he was a nine till five man – nine at night till five in the morning! He couldn't fit in with the civil servants of the London art scene and people probably thought he was too dangerous and reckless. William Scott once said to me, 'You know Bryan Robertson? He shows friends, top artists and a few unknowns'. Because *he* obviously didn't get a show there.

When I first met Bryan, he was very taken with Australian art. Brett Whiteley was Boy Genius – and he was, in some ways, he had his moments – and Colin MacInnes was living at Bryan's house. He was very gay though I don't know if they were lovers or ex-lovers. They were very much of the moment before the *New Generation* shows. I think MacInnes introduced him more to literature because he was at home with that.

Tony Caro was in full flight with his entourage of artists and they were making all this exciting new stuff and Clem Greenberg came over. He looked around and he said, 'The worst painter in America is better than the best painter in Britain'. That went down well. In some ways, looking back on it, I know what he meant ... Of course Helen [Frankenthaler] was given the news about the new discovery of English sculpture and she was kind of leggy, nice, not beautiful but attractive. So sometime Bryan said, 'Oh, Helen Frankenthaler's coming over, she wants to see the new English sculpture.' He got in a panic because he didn't know any of them – they were another side he'd shut out ... So he said, 'You know all these guys, don't you?' I did. Bill Tucker was living in a squat in Primrose Hill, I was living five minutes away. Everybody was so broke, with no anticipation of ever selling anything or owning a car. Phillip King lived in Swiss Cottage, as did Mike Bolus and David Annesley. I had a little Beetle and you could park in those days. Helen came over to me, where she had to climb in the window to get in the studio. (There were too many paintings.) She said, 'God, you're painting real paintings!' As though it wasn't possible in England. Anyway I took her around to the sculptors' studios, and when she left she wanted to return the hospitality. Told me to look her up in New York ...

He put me in another key show at Marlborough Gallery [in New York] where Rothko is reputed to have said, 'If you've got to have School of Rothko, he's the best'. Now, I don't necessarily think that was meant as a compliment. Going back to Bryan – he could be extremely trying, but he was so generous, not just to me, but to everybody. He was hilarious – we used to laugh all the time. Tears used to run down my cheeks. Especially on the phone. When he laughed, it was like the organ of some great cathedral.

Did I ever tell you about my trip to Italy with Bryan? Well, Bryan rang me. He'd been asked to revise his first book, on Pollock. I've never read it from end to end, but people say it is full of omissions and mistakes, but he rattled it off for the money. He said he wanted to write a book on me and he had to do some revision on the Pollock book. He said Thames & Hudson had offered him a villa near Florence, so he said I could come down and we could start on my book. I thought it sounded a good idea. And he said, 'Bring a black tie, we're going to all sorts of amazing parties in Florence'. In those days, the plane dropped you at Pisa and the bus took you to Florence. Getting on the plane I'd seen this rather nice black girl. It turned out she was a stripper and a dancer and a singer on river boats on the Arno in Florence, a sort of nightclub thing.

So I got off the bus, and Bryan wasn't there. It was the middle of nowhere, so I rang the villa and the guy said he'd gone out. So I got back on the bus and went on to Florence with her. I booked into a hotel. Eventually I got hold of Bryan the next day, [and said,] 'Where have you been? I've been ringing hospitals and the police, I thought you might have been in an accident.' Anyway, he'd got these T&H people round his little finger. He'd got them cooking special meals. He'd hired through them the biggest, most expensive golden Mercedes. He said, 'It's the only one I could have – it's the only one with air conditioning for my asthma'.

Anyway, it came to leaving and he didn't want to leave because he hadn't done anything on the book and he had to do a *Spectator* thing. I said, 'We're going to miss the plane – it's getting late. Better get going.' We went back to the villa to pack up what he'd bought: loads of records and rolls of deckchair material. He'd spent all his money, and he was spending my money by this time. So we get in the car and it's getting dark. We got to the airport ten minutes before take-off. She said: 'The flight's closed.' I was so fucking angry. He said, 'Well, we can go and stay at the villa as long as we want'. I said, 'Fuck off'. And I walked away. I got a taxi into Florence but because I didn't have any money I could only go to the most expensive hotel, the Excelsior, and there wasn't a flight out until the Monday night. So I had to spend three days paid for on my card – which in those days cost me an extra £500 or something – just because he was so wantonly not going to do what he was supposed to do. Kind of childish, peevish. I didn't speak to him for three years. He came along to get on the same plane as me, with records falling out from under his arm, books, all his stuff, and I'm not with him, not helping him with anything. I never spoke to him on the plane.

Then Thames & Hudson threw him out because he hadn't produced any writing, so that was that out the window.

Bryan gave up pretending he would write the proposed Hoyland monograph, and Mel Gooding was assigned the job instead. But Hoyland couldn't keep up the effort of being angry with Bryan forever, and although he couldn't remember how exactly the ice was broken, they started talking again:

I remember thinking it was ridiculous, looking back on it. Maybe I'd accepted that he was not to be relied on.

Did I tell you about when I met Graham Sutherland? He was there at Bryan's and Bryan was making a Martini in a big glass jug. All his sweat's dropping in it, then more lemon, more lime, more gin. The pretext for this lunch was that Graham wanted to meet the younger generation – me, Howard [Hodgkin], Patrick [Caulfield]. We sat down and I was opposite him. He was talking about Menton. I said, 'I suppose you went there Graham for the light?' 'No, my dear boy, for the life.' Then he said: 'You must all come down to the house, we'd love you all to come down.' Howard, notebook: 'Would June 3rd be all right?' We were just pleased to be asked, but he was on the case, old Howard.

I remember Bryan used to wear Grecian 2000 and when he was sweating it all used to run down his face, a sort of battleship grey colour. And of course he was very fat by the end, but he was very slim when I first met him, like a model. But even up to three or four days before he died, when he was conscious he was joking and laughing. He had great spirit. I think he was the most fearless person I've ever met. Not just intellectually, but physically he wouldn't be afraid. He was fearsome. He didn't give a shit about the Establishment or what people thought. He undoubtedly had a great effect on my career. Of course these things affect you more than you realise at the time. He was a remarkable guy. I always thought Bryan's great strength was a kind of female intuition. He'd come over and say 'Can I see that purple one?' but I hadn't done a purple one. He'd remember things that didn't exist, and yet he wrote, years and years ahead, about Bali, about water, the celebrations.

The following quotation is taken from the John Hoyland 1967 Whitechapel catalogue introduction (for once Bryan wrote the main essay, a token of his feeling for Hoyland's work):

Apart from the obvious size and radical colour of John Hoyland's paintings, their main characteristic is energy and the concentrated force that its intelligent and sharply directed use declares. Force rather than passion, because the work seems to be the consequence of intellectual thrust or speculation rather than emotional surrender to a specific event or situation. This speculation attends the slow and thorough deployment of minimal visual factors. Hoyland's paintings are, therefore, structural declarations rather than romantic declamations because rhetoric is avoided together with the possible vagaries of perception or any suggestion of equivocal atmospherics. As all painting is about something, physical, philosophical, or metaphysical, they should also be recognized in essence as active, interrogatory, declarations of an 'intellectual-imaginative' nature expressed in terms of physical order. The paintings are not acquiescent statements which merely confirm an existing or accepted arrangement of formal elements.

To this extent they have also a bristling, loaded warmth, verging on aggressiveness, as opposed to the discrete inflections, studied and final, that might inform a more wholly cerebral statement. Another dimension, more sensual and less temperate, continually dislocates the balance or equilibrium suggested by the paintings, or actively postulated by them – and then denied: ruthlessly, and in no uncertain terms …

Rarely, in recent English painting, have such apparently elementary constituents been invested with so much drama or achieved a transformation into such resplendent spectacles. It is, on occasion, as if three matchboxes and two matchsticks in a large empty space were miraculously transformed into a water carnival in Thailand …

He brings to the act of ordered disruption all the hot impulse and cold device of an expert polemicist. His paintings are radiant, and artful …

Barnett Newman has accurately said: 'Art criticism for artists is like ornithology for the birds.' But contact with the public leads me to believe that visitors to galleries rarely give sufficient time to studying paintings: everyone is visually conscious because we live in an age of visual aids, props, signs and symbols, but with this increased consciousness has come little real awareness. It takes half an hour to listen to a symphony or a piano concerto, three minutes to read one page of a book, but the public expects quicker returns visually and is conditioned to slogan-like visual messages, instantly received, recorded and understood. Verbal interpretations may at least suggest that there is more to Hoyland's work than its immediate effect.

Bryan behind the wheel

Bryan Robertson was an enthusiastic if inaccurate car driver. A late learner, he found himself compelled to take to the wheel when he lived in America, or he would never have managed the logistics of his life there (if he can be said ever to have attempted such a thing). His friends suffered the consequent alarms and buffets and often made amusing anecdotage out of it. Here is John Hoyland recalling the chastening experience of being driven by Bryan. Similar episodes are subsequently recounted by Paul Huxley, Bryan Kneale and Gary Wragg.

HOYLAND:
When he was in America he had to drive – and he'd never driven before. He drove like a Womble of Wimbledon because he didn't have the right glasses, he was too vain. He went out and bought this car, second-hand, that was as big as a Cadillac. Huge. He used to park it illegally in Manhattan every night. He was the worst driver I've ever known. A nightmare. I remember him hunched over the wheel. The car gradually started to get narrower, because he was always going into gaps that weren't big enough. So the car looked like a joke car. He was absolutely fearless or childlike when he was driving. We'd be coming up to the intersection to join a main road, and there'd be a vast truck and he'd be trying to push it out the way. We're about this far from the truck and I'd say 'Bryan! We're going to hit this truck!' 'Oh, don't fuss!' he'd say.

On a holiday in Italy, when he was supposed to be writing a book on Hoyland, Bryan hired an enormous golden Mercedes through Thames & Hudson, his publishers. Hoyland recalled begging Bryan to let him drive, but Bryan wouldn't.

The car business was terrible because we got to the point with the narrow dry-stone walls that every time he went round a corner he hit the wall. In this big expensive Mercedes. Then he nearly hit another car, and again, like the car in New York, it began to shrink. Clearly he couldn't see, or he couldn't judge, or he was inexperienced. But he wouldn't let me drive.

I heard one big clunk and he said, 'Oh, they'll soon tap that out'. 'Tap it out?' I said. 'These have got a hundred layers of paint on them, regardless of getting the bump out.'

Eventually he came back to England and he wanted me to help him choose a car. He couldn't drive with a gear shift, so he bought the nearest thing to an American Mustang, which was a Capri, an automatic Capri. That he also proceeded to remodel. Then I found that he didn't have a licence. He was something else.

HUXLEY:

Bryan wrote to me, when he was living in the country, that he was being urged from all sides to learn to drive, take lessons, take a test, which he dreaded but was fatalistic about. And of all people in the world, Bryan Robertson should not ever have been trusted in a car. But living in America in the predicament he was in ... he had to have a car. He did eventually pass his test and own a car and it was terrifying. He got a bit like Toad of Toad Hall and quite chuffed about it all and quite confident. I don't say I felt in danger for my life – it was other people who were in danger. He was blithely unaware of the trail of disaster he left behind him, as he drove along, cars screeching to a halt and almost colliding because they were avoiding hitting him. He did sadly get arrested once for bumping the corner of someone's car. He was arrested and put in jail. He didn't deny it though he had absolutely no memory of it whatever. He probably never noticed.

KNEALE:

I think Bryan was always full of dreams and illusions as to how things were going to work out [in America]. I remember him saying the first thing he was going to buy was a big American car. But he was a terrible driver, and he shouldn't have been on the roads in anything ... When I met up with him in New York, the car was like a crumpled paper bag. He was given to parking in underground car parks and bouncing off the walls, all the way down and all the way back. I was making a big piece of sculpture in New York State and he drove all the way up to see me. Bryan drove unperturbed hundreds of miles with the silencer trailing in the road behind him. Plus cat. He brought a cat with him.

WRAGG:

On one occasion we were going down to see Peggy, his sister, in Hythe. Bryan had got this red car. We got into it – nice summer day – Bryan started it up, it jolted a bit and went backwards. It stalled a second time. The third time it went forwards before stopping. I said, 'Bryan, have you passed your test?' He said, 'No, but it's all right'. Off we drove and somehow we got down to Hythe. He would be talking to you and not looking at the road.

Paul Huxley

In his book *Private View* (1965), Bryan introduced Paul Huxley thus:

A quiet, intent, rather reserved presence on the scene, Huxley has also, beneath a benignly self-deprecating manner, one of the most incisive and certain intelligences at work in the current situation. His paintings follow an even, steady pace of development and are among the most original inventions coming from his generation. They are also quite possibly the most beautiful in the sense of surface calm and perfection, restrained and unobvious sensuality, and a feeling for colour which continually moves on, fresh, challenging, always beyond that range of decorative, non-associative blankness that characterizes so much of the abstract colour range of his contemporaries. Huxley's colour is 'lived in', 'inhabited', as it were, even though it is abstract. Something happens in the interaction of a form on a differently coloured ground in a Huxley painting which brings an extra dimension to the colour as a whole. The surface calm should not be confused with inertness: these lovingly painted surfaces have a vibrancy and life of their own quite apart from the luminosity in the colour (if it is high-pitched) or the resonance in earlier, darker toned paintings in greens and blacks.

I interviewed Huxley in his West London studio in April 2016:

Bryan first made contact with me in early 1963 and came to my studio to see my work. From then on, he wrote to me and said he loved the paintings and wanted to buy one, and wanted to put me in a show – which he did, *The New Generation* [1964]. He would phone me up and invite me out to dinner. I actually met Bryan through Patrick Procktor. I was teaching at Maidstone School of Art with Patrick and David Hockney. When I had my first show Patrick encouraged Bryan to see it but he didn't, he missed it, so he followed it up by a visit to my studio after the show. After that he was very supportive. It gave me a great boost to have this sort of response from Bryan.

I didn't realise until later that when I met Bryan, he was dragging himself out of the break in his relationship with Patrick. I think it had ended then, and Bryan was the one left licking his wounds. I remember Helen Frankenthaler quizzing me about that when I was with her in New York, and I genuinely couldn't give her any information. I didn't think then that Bryan and Patrick were lovers – I was that naive.

Bryan was an enthusiast and it was evident in what he wrote about in art. He said several times to me that his policy was only to write positively. He had the strongest disregard for critics who devoted their time to being negative, disapproving. He thought – what's the point? If you don't like the art, it's not your job to complain about it. He thought a critic's job was to help to interpret, to show and reveal what's wonderful about things that are wonderful. So he was in that sense a great supporter of artists. I remember him on the radio a lot – *The Critics*, especially, a BBC Radio 3 programme in which teams of four or five people would review a play, a concert, an exhibition, a book every week. He was so good because like his colleagues on those programmes he was so knowledgeable about the whole field of the arts. Bryan was exceptional in that respect. He could talk about music and ballet and film with as much erudition and knowledge of the history behind them as he could about painting and sculpture. He was wonderful like that.

Most of the people of consequence I've known in my life were either through Bryan or someone who Bryan introduced me to. It was quite a network of connections. I taught in the same art school as Merlyn Evans – at the Central School as it was then. There was Merlyn and Morris Kestelman running the department. Bryan was kind enough to take me in like a stray cat when I came back from New York in September 1967 and my marriage had split up. Through necessity I had to return to London – I had two little children I wanted to keep in touch with – and I checked into a hotel. Bryan said, 'Oh for goodness sake come and stay for a while'. He had moved to Barnsbury in my absence. When I left he was living in Draycott Place and then he bought this house from Justin Knowles. So he said come and stay for a few weeks and I stayed for two years. It was terrible of me – I look back on that with cringing guilt, that I exploited his hospitality for so long.

But I think he enjoyed having company. I shared in the cost of living but I didn't pay rent. We ate out a lot and I'd pay the bill sometimes – it was very relaxed. I didn't have a lot of money because I was keeping my ex-wife and children. Bryan was a very tortured person really. He put on a front that was either very entertaining or very domineering or very patient, but it belied really a state of crisis through health and chronic inability to manage ordinary practical affairs such as finances. When I first met him back in 1963, he told me that his doctors had given him three years to live because he had very bad asthma and he practically chain-smoked. He would have been thirty-eight, though I always saw him as an older person. He stopped smoking after I'd moved out, but I spent quite a bit of time with him going out for walks on Highbury Fields to keep his mind off smoking. That was difficult for him to do and took courage. I don't think he had a lot of personal will-power or self-discipline. He loved the good things in life – drink and food – though he was never a drunk.

The medication he had to take for his asthma had strong side-effects and made him very tired. He used to spend sometimes several days in bed, not ill but just resting and sleeping. Then he'd perk up and be himself again – or the face that he gave the public. I got a teaching stint in the early seventies at Cooper Union through Dore Ashton – someone I met through the Motherwells, who I met through Bryan – and went and stayed with Bryan for a bit. He was not in a good state in his health or his mind. He was living in the countryside outside New York for a while and got his apartment in New York on Central Park West a bit later, I think. He'd been in some isolation which was unusual for him. He had two little kittens that were dying and he had to inject them.

When I first went to America it was with him and there was a whole trail of artists who were fighting to get to meet him again and have dinner with him. That was 1964, when he was still very much at the Whitechapel. We went together, he ostensibly to do research for his next monograph – it was going to be on Motherwell. I'd met Motherwell in London when he was married to Helen Frankenthaler and they were very much a forceful partnership in the New York art scene. Bryan had a couple of Charles Eames chairs and I think it was the Motherwells' home that influenced him to get them because they had a couple in their New York sitting room. We went out to Springs to meet Lee Krasner and I became good friends with her. Within three weeks or so I met so many of the leading artists in New York. It was just incredible and something I never expected to happen in my life – all through Bryan's contacts.

They thought I was his boyfriend. I was much younger looking than I was, and even if I say it myself, quite pretty. I didn't care. I think he was gay but largely asexual. I don't think he had a lot of physical sex. Certainly not on a regular basis. He had a brief fling with Helen Frankenthaler. We stayed in the Motherwells' house in New York when they were absent at Provincetown, Cape Cod, for the summer. When we got to Cape Cod, Bryan had to get down to business and spend long sessions with Bob Motherwell and take notes. I split off and met some other artists. Then after a few weeks I left and Bryan stayed on.

I don't think Bryan much liked homosexuals actually. He wasn't attracted to them sexually, he was attracted more to straight men.

Looking back on it, Huxley thinks it must have been torture for Bryan with him living in his house, oblivious to the older man's desires.

But we had a lot of laughs – he was such fun. There were three people who could get me in stitches, all now dead: Bryan, Adrian Berg and John Hoyland. I think part of what kept Bryan alive was his sense of humour. Bryan was not an intellectual – not as much as Adrian Berg, for instance.

Bryan must have spent a lot of time with Lee Krasner and gained great insights into Pollock. His book brought him great prestige. It was the first monograph of those American artists of the New York School. Then the Motherwell challenge came up. He was courted by all those artists to write the next book. They wanted it – they wanted a show at the Whitechapel and a book by Bryan Robertson. That's why he was being chased – Gottlieb kept phoning every day, and Bryan would go, 'Say I'm out, say I'm out!'

Motherwell Bryan obviously decided to respond to, understandably. I'm sure – though Bryan never admitted this to me – it began to feel as if the book would never happen because the intellectual challenge was too heavyweight for him. (Motherwell was an intellectual.) Whether Motherwell abandoned him, or he Motherwell, I don't know. There were reams of notes he took, but Bryan wasn't precious about his archive.

When Bryan went to America for the Purchase job, he left his house as it was. He didn't have the energy or the sense of purpose to deal with it – he just had to leave it. [It was later rented out – Tony Patterson was key in that. Huxley was given the task of going through Bryan's papers and boxing things up to store in the cupboard.] Tony P, as he was called, knew Bryan from the days when they must have been very young and lived in Toynbee Hall. That's when they met. Tony was a lawyer. They remained friends all their lives. Bryan kept Tony as a side-kick who he didn't involve in certain things because he didn't think Tony was up to it. He was rather superior towards Tony P which I understand. Bryan was a great person for bringing people together, but Tony was a case of someone Bryan depended on but didn't hold in very high esteem. Which was a bit cruel as Tony was never a stupid man. But he was a lawyer. He helped a lot of artists and Bryan involved him in the art world. He did my divorce for me and I paid him with a painting, and he did a lot of artists' conveyancing when they were buying property.

Greenberg I met through Bryan. He took the two of us to lunch at the White Tower, which was an upmarket Greek restaurant in Percy Street at the end of Charlotte Street. We were talking about editing. Greenberg was a frustrated artist. I went to his home and saw paintings by him which were very wishy-washy large-scale landscapes. He was a lover of Helen Frankenthaler's before Motherwell. He controlled quite a lot of artists and edited their work for them. A couple of times he was either in my studio or at an exhibition of mine – he wore a hat all the time and, of all the inappropriate objects, he used it to mask things. He created around him a school of artists who enjoyed his advice. People like [Jules] Olitski and [Larry] Poons, they tended to flood canvases with a lot of spilt and stained colour and then they'd have joint sessions when they'd invite Greenberg in and discuss how they would be cropped. I always associated it with photography. Bryan would never interfere like that. I don't think it would occur to him to change something.

Bryan obviously in terms of professional rivalry didn't spend a lot of time with people who were in the same profession as him. He might spend his time with artists principally, or dancers, conductors, composers, poets. I think the meeting up with Greenberg was a fairly rare acquaintanceship. I wouldn't call it friendship.

Then, quite apart from teaching, I started getting into committees. I was invited to join the committee for the Serpentine Gallery and through that I came on to the Arts Council committee. Then I was invited to be a trustee of the Tate Gallery. Bryan was disapproving of it all and one day I said to him, 'You don't think much of this, do you?' He agreed that he didn't and I asked him why. He said, 'Well, if you're a cow, you shouldn't work in the milk parlour'. He was right – it wasn't good for me. I was flattered to be invited to do those things. Perhaps the reason was that I appeared to be relatively unprejudiced with a fairly catholic taste. On the whole I think Bryan might have been right – that you should keep some independence as an artist.

Later 1960s

The fashionable 1960s gallerist Kasmin recalled working with Robertson at the Whitechapel, in an interview conducted at his London apartment in April 2016:

All my involvements with Bryan were to do with shows in the sixties like *The New Generation* or the *Peter Stuyvesant Foundation* [a 1965 exhibition]. I provided work and chatted about what was going on. He seemed to know what he wanted, though some of his motives would have been sentimental and general generosity. He was a kind person and he'd put in things because of his relationship with the artist rather than whether it was necessarily great art. More of a flaw was his slight disorganisation, I would say. I remember Lady d'Avigdor-Goldsmid being jolly upset at what happened to a Rothko of hers that was damaged during the Rothko show. She thought she was roughly treated as a lender, and never lent anything to any show ever again. Most people would say that Bryan was staggeringly gifted but a bit slipshod round the edges. Everyone has faults, and you see faults in anyone making shows if you have strong ideas of your own.

Bryan did so many good things that we remember him with pleasure. He never did anything wrong to me. A lot of our cross-over was to do with Frankenthaler and Motherwell – they were both very fond of him. I think it was Bryan who was instrumental in making one of the ballet companies hire Helen as a set designer. Bryan was an admirer of the naughty and flamboyant, he had a whimsical camp side later on, but it wasn't so evident in the sixties. He was close to Bridget [Riley] and he was quite close to Margaret and Snowdon. They were there at Tony's [Caro] opening. Everybody was close to him. He kept buttoned up about lots of his life. He was evasive. There are lots of people I know who just don't like being pinned down. You ask them what they're doing and they'll never actually tell you.

Inevitably, not everyone was happy with the 'advanced art' that Bryan had made such a success of showing at the Whitechapel. Lord Bearsted, Chairman of the trustees, was worried that some of the exhibitions were too daring, but in general he was hugely supportive of Bryan's programme. But local funding bodies, especially from the neighbouring

boroughs, began to feel that Bryan was too concerned with experimental art and not thinking enough of the local public. Local funding was reduced as it was felt that the gallery had become a 'national institution' rather than a local one. Money had always been a worry, but by the second half of the 1960s became more so. Bryan was very good at overspending, less efficient with administration. He began to distance himself from the gallery after his unsuccessful attempt at the Tate job, and it was almost as if he had lost heart – or interest. The Arts Council, the Greater London Council and the Drapers' Company all gave money to the Whitechapel, but it was never enough. Finally the situation became critical. Unable to afford to stay open, the Whitechapel closed its doors between October 1966 and January 1967.

This was only ever intended as a temporary measure, and the gallery re-opened with what was widely considered to be a safe and popular choice – paintings and drawings by John Craxton. The exhibition was opened by Jennie Lee, Arts Minister and a confirmed Whitechapel supporter, and there was a sense of a revival of the gallery's fortunes. Even though the exhibition did not find favour with the critics, it did with the man in the street. And one influential man was most enthusiastic. This was Hugh Farmar, secretary to the Drapers' Company, who admittedly had a personal interest as he was passionate about saving the wild Cretan goat from extinction. He in particular felt the relevance of Craxton's work, in which the goat was something of a leitmotif.

Robertson left the gallery at the beginning of 1969, with three exhibitions already lined up and (to different degrees) organised: Hélio Oiticica, Helen Frankenthaler and Robert Downing. The Frankenthaler show, with which Bryan was closely and emotionally involved, was the most important to him. Mark Glazebrook, the new Director (of whom Robertson approved), asked him to hang the show, and wrote: 'I am getting proper brick walls constructed again, to be painted white, so that the Gallery will look its usual self again.' Bryan wrote the text for a two-page pamphlet which was intended for an English audience (the show came on to Whitechapel from America). This is an excerpt:

The memory or essence or generalized after-image of Helen Frankenthaler's work in the mind's eye is an unforced state of physical well being in a predominantly benign and easy climate, not unlike the first days of early summer with bright sun and clear blue sky. In this mythical season there are traces or echoes of appropriate physical activity or repose: moving in placid water or through surf, drying in the sun, lying very close to sand and the kind of succulent grass or parched scrub which grows on beaches, feeling and observing the impact of spray, floating across a pond or lagoon either in the water or low in a boat, walking with no fixed purpose but receptively through green fields or woods, observing light flashing through foliage or on water and the darkening or clarifying vagaries of weather or time of day; the cheerfulness and expectancy of morning, the stillness of noon, the imminence of evening and its deepened mood.

The exhibition following Frankenthaler was of sculpture by Robert Downing. Glazebrook wrote in the catalogue: 'Thanks are due to Bryan Robertson who chose Robert Downing as the first of a number of Canadian artists who might show their work at the Whitechapel. The Whitechapel is also grateful to Dennis Young, who, at the request of Bryan Robertson, has written the introduction to this catalogue.' Robertson's hand was still visible in this show, as a letter of greetings from Downing some time later (dated 24 August 1987), indicates: 'Anyway, I simply want to send you all best wishes for the entire day upon which you receive this, and remind you that I am among those grateful artists whose entire life was changed in some magical way, simply by knowing you.'

Forty years on

In 2008, the New Art Centre, now relocated from Sloane Street to East Winterslow, near Salisbury, put on *New Generation Revisited: British Sculpture from the Sixties and Seventies – A Tribute to Bryan Robertson at the Whitechapel*. Ian Dunlop, who had written the catalogue essay for *The New Generation 1965* show, wrote the introduction to this new catalogue, commenting on his own good luck at that early association:

To my surprise, as a young inexperienced art critic trying to scratch a living in London writing for the *Times* and the *Evening Standard*, he asked me to write a catalogue introduction and prepare notes on each of the exhibitors. He was taking a big risk. But that was the essence of Bryan. He was a risk taker; and he believed in the young, and he trusted his incredible eye. Sadly, like so many in the art world in Britain, he was a prophet: 'not without honour, save in his country, and in his own house.' His talent was never fully recognised.

Dunlop also gave his recollections of the context for those long-ago *New Generation* shows:

The art world … in those days was incredibly small and looking back at it from today's perspective it was touched with innocence, even naivety and an admirable lack of commercialism. There were only two or three galleries for younger artists to show their work – Kasmin who showed Hockney, Robert Fraser who showed Richard Hamilton and the Pop school and the Rowan Gallery who showed Bridget Riley and a number of abstract artists.

Marlborough Fine Art represented an older generation and their chief artist was Francis Bacon. Helen Lessore's Beaux Arts gallery still existed and there you could see the work of Freud and Auerbach. With the exception of the New Art Centre on Sloane Street, gallery life occupied a fairly small area in London centred around Cork Street and the West End. There were no galleries in Hoxton or in the East End. There were few collectors, certainly no equivalent of Charles Saatchi. The public galleries and institutions were for the most part completely out of touch with what was going on. There was no Tate Modern, only the old Tate without its additions, run by the reactionary Sir John Rothenstein. The Royal Academy was a joke and the summer exhibition an annual disaster. There was no Serpentine Gallery, few alternative spaces. The main venue for young artists to meet and show their work was at the ICA, then on Dover Street, but the premises were too small to show the large-scale work young painters and sculptors were beginning to produce.

And then there was the Whitechapel Gallery.

Bridget Riley

Bridget Riley (born 1931) was for many years one of Bryan's closest friends and companions, whose career was immeasurably helped and enhanced by his endorsement. As with many people close to him, there were tensions, arguments and the occasional falling-out, but Robertson was in fact an enormously loyal friend and supporter, and a great believer in the value and originality of Riley's art.

Writing about the problems of lighting Rothko's paintings, Robertson noted in an aside in his article about Rothko for *Modern Painters* (autumn 1998):

In 1971, directing a new museum in the US and studying the new methods of lighting for some months at the New York Fashion School of Technology, I returned to London to install Bridget Riley's show at the Hayward Gallery and persuaded Arts Council colleagues to invest a lot of money in the then new tungsten-halogen lights, which were first used, to spectacular effect, in the Riley show.

Bryan Kneale remembered that Bryan hung the Riley exhibition from a wheelchair, and he was clearly not in the best of health when he returned to London. But there was no doubt that he would return: Riley was one of his closest friends, and getting the installation of her Hayward show right was of considerable importance to him.

He had thought much about lighting in his years at the Whitechapel, in particular when hanging the Rothko exhibition in 1961. Robertson was by now keenly aware of the subtleties of lighting and the different effects it was possible to achieve. At Morris Louis's Whitechapel show

in 1965, he had tried the experiment of using only the brilliant natural top-lighting of the gallery (the exhibition took place in mid-summer), but the scheme had to be abandoned after just a week. Although the paintings looked good, visitors didn't understand and thought the place was dead. Robertson commented: 'As a dreadful general principle, art lovers like a bit of showbiz glitter.'

The following extract, a classic example of Bryan not writing about the subject in hand, except indirectly, comes from the Hayward Gallery catalogue of Riley's show:

Art is many things but it is not primarily a means of communication as we normally understand that utility. There are easier and certainly less laborious ways for one person to express an idea directly to another than by painting a picture or making a sculpture. In itself, the action would be unreliable. Conversely, no written or printed document, film or TV programme, the proper media for communication in the usual sense, could ever convey with any compensatory degree of accuracy the true imaginative quality of Piero's *Baptism of Christ* or *The Moroccans* of Matisse. For media is an intermediary device: concerned with visual art, it uses inaccurate or irrelevant language; finally it involves falsification. Art brings into being a convergence of circumstances which enforce an unprecedented act of recognition, a disclosure of unpredictable dimensions which radically extends life and possibly transforms it. In achieving this transformation art begins and ends with perception; conceptual issues arise at some middle stage. Visual art is essentially an act of revelation, almost in the sense of a biblical or legendary miracle. Water gushes forth from a barren rock: it is fundamentally inexplicable but the eye is its first witness.

Life can be lived in the hopeful belief of order, discipline and logic – together with its magical disruptions – but one must know also that the creation of a work of visual art is an intensely primitive activity which touches profound levels, either unknown until that instant or forgotten over the millennium. When this visual act of revelation takes place, the eye of the beholder transmits multiple facets of awareness to the mind. And it is at this precarious, delicate, momentous instant that words, spoken or written, can arrest or rigidly circumscribe an imaginative response to that act of revelation. Artists work through inspiration from perceptual sources: we must receive what they offer us with imagination, and imaginative dimensions are endless. This preamble is written only because, in an age of disbelief when it is hard for many people to concede the possibility or even the relevance, the suitability for our times, of a masterpiece, there is a tendency to relegate art to the inferior role of a stylistic 'information-communication' catalyst or demonstration piece. There is also a general insistence on trivialization, with its attendant demolition of vital barriers, categories or divisions and, above all, historical standards, so that a large body of contemporary art is occupied by problems of process, format, and 'presentation' in a vacuum: marvellous subjects for words, and they need them. This essay is intended only to provide the reader with some facts regarding Bridget Riley's working methods and some insights which may be helpful: ultimately, in the exactitude of their authority, the paintings speak for themselves and do not require interpretation.

Patrick Procktor

The young and wildly talented Patrick Procktor first met Bryan Robertson through Keith Vaughan early in 1961, when he was twenty-four and still a student at the Slade. In February, Procktor's close friend Mario Dubsky, then President of the Slade Society, invited Robertson to the Slade as a guest of the Sketch Club. Procktor's biographer, Ian Massey, records that both young men befriended Robertson, 'meeting him socially for meals and visits to the opera, though at some point the relationship between him and Procktor became more intimate'. And from this point may be dated Procktor's rise to early fame, for Robertson was a loyal supporter. He encouraged Procktor to develop his painting and then in February 1963 wrote to Harry Tatlock Miller, one of the directors of the Redfern Gallery, describing Procktor as an exceptional young artist and offering to help with promotion and publicity. His suggestion was taken up, and Robertson publicly affirmed his support by writing the catalogue essay for the Redfern show later that year.

Near the beginning of his introductory essay in the catalogue, Robertson stated:

The exhilaration, the delight, of Patrick Procktor's moment of self discovery is splendidly conveyed in this first one-man show. All the work before us has an extra edge of freshness in the handling of paint, resonance in the inter-play of high and low keyed colour, and absolute confidence in the projection – at once energetic and self indulgent – of images which spring from life. And the imaginative experience which extends life.

In all this, an unselfconscious element of risk flickers in and out of the paintings but seems only to accentuate the warmth and ardour of these first disclosures from an artist with an immediately recognisable belief in life. And made articulate in his work with a maximum degree of passion and conviction. This belief in life is active and supercharged, never merely acquiescent, and has darker sides as well as its own particular luminosity.

And Robertson concluded:

In and out of life, actively involved, passively contemplative, the spectator and the participant, the fantasy dream and the prosaic occurrence – there is a sense of paradox at work here, of duality and antithesis which continually animates the scene. As if a Roman feeling for the ease and warmth of life were sharpened and deepened by a Greek awareness of fatality and high drama.

This last remark sounds altogether too horribly prescient, given the later dramatic decline of Procktor's career and his tragic death in 2003, less than a year after Robertson's own demise. But for the moment all was champagne and success.

There's a line drawing by Procktor in his 1991 autobiography (entitled *Self-Portrait*), captioned 'Bryan Robertson in Greece, Paris, Venice or Cornwall', indicating the extent of their travels together. Robertson is posing against the wrought-ironwork of a bedroom balcony and is wearing either a bathing costume or underpants. It's not a flattering portrayal – the nose is a little too sharp, the mouth rather prissily pursed, and the torso is already gathering the bulk that would be a distinguishing feature in later years – but there's something recognisable, perhaps the insouciant pose with which he greets the day. Procktor described his relationship with Bryan in his book: 'I was seeing a lot of Bryan Robertson, at the gallery [the Whitechapel], at his flat, and on trips and holidays together.' Procktor had been invited to participate in the first *New Generation* show. He continued:

The plans for the exhibition were partially made in his flat in Draycott Place behind Sloane Square, which was furnished with rather wonderful paintings: a small Michael Andrews of figures in a garden which I thought was quite beautiful, an abstract by Prunella Clough in shades of gold and grey, an Oriental picture over his desk.

We became good friends: Bryan always made me laugh, and taught me a great deal about music. Once he started talking about art he couldn't be stopped and still can't today. If you try to say that Jackson Pollock is an awful painter he won't attend to your explanations … whatever the ostensible meaning or subject-matter of a picture is, Bryan always looks for the abstract, the form.

We went together to visit Keith Vaughan's new studio on Porthmeor Beach in Cornwall, which he had recently bought … We stayed at John Milne's house, 'Trewyn'; he was a sculptor, a neighbour and friend of Barbara Hepworth's, and kept a rather nice boarding house with bright, colourful bedrooms … Bryan and I stayed there, as Keith had before he'd found the studio. Bryan and I went to Paris together for the debut of Rudolf Nureyev with the Marquis de Cuevas Ballet. He appeared as Bluebird in *La Belle au Bois Dormant*, and remains the loveliest dancer I have ever seen.

Bryan and I then travelled to Greece in the summer of 1964 [actually

1963]. We went straight to Venice, and took a boat from there to Piraeus. We stayed in Athens and went to Delphi … Bryan and I argued the entire time – good, serious arguments – about talent, about what I wanted to do, the extent to which he as a writer and critic agreed and differed.

Then Bryan went to Crete while I came back to England. We arranged to meet up again in Amsterdam, which was a first visit for me. I went with my mother, and we successfully found Bryan. We saw a great deal of art, and thanks to Bryan's connections we had lunch with the director of the Kröller-Müller Museum, which is the best collection of van Gogh anywhere. And we went on to Rotterdam, as well as seeing the other great collections at Amsterdam and the Hague.

Procktor then discusses *The New Generation* show and his part in it. A different interpretation of events comes from John Craxton, with whom Bryan stayed in Crete. Massey quotes him as saying that Bryan had written earlier to say that he was coming to stay with a brilliant young painter. 'By the tone of the letter I presumed that he was very much in love with him – *it is the joy of my life* – that sort of thing. Then Bryan arrived alone and in despair. This artist had decided at the last moment not to come, and left him completely in the lurch.'

Earlier, in the build-up to his first solo exhibition at the Redfern, Procktor writes: 'Dear Bryan really did his best for me that year.' He himself bought two of Procktor's paintings (*The Beach: Figures in Black & Red* and *Reclining Figure*), wrote the catalogue introduction and also 'a sort of manifesto essay' for *London Magazine* called 'Against the Rimless Men'. Procktor comments: 'I figure at the end of it as an artist who isn't rimless like the men he describes, in a usage that was never quite clear to me, but somehow as a prefigurer of new potency, no less. Bryan was interested in talking about the larger contexts in which artists work, and this essay was part of that.' Kenneth Clark also purchased *Figures under Water* for the National Gallery of Victoria's Felton Bequest (for which he was official buyer), a move no doubt encouraged by Robertson, who continued to be very friendly with Clark.

Later in his autobiography Procktor described the lunches that Cecil Beaton would give. 'At lunch with Cecil you would meet the Clarks, the Rothschilds, Thom Gunn and Irene Worth. We used to go to the theatre. He liked to mix up his grand friends with the low life, the motorbike leather with the velvet, and anyone who was appearing on stage.'

In 1983 Procktor was commissioned to design *Turandot* at Covent Garden, an invitation that originated with Robertson, who had been acting since 1979 as design consultant to the Royal Ballet and Royal Opera. The recommendation seemed particularly appropriate since Procktor had lately returned from China with a whole body of work

inspired by the country. Sadly, as Massey recounted, Procktor's designs were considered disappointing, and the producer was soon secretly working on an alternative version with an American designer. It all ended badly, and although Procktor was paid the full fee, exhibitions of his designs at the Redfern and in Los Angeles had to be cancelled. The whole episode must have been a considerable blow to his self-confidence and prestige.

An exhibition entitled *Patrick Procktor: Paintings 1959–1989* toured England and Wales between August 1989 and November 1990. The following passages are extracted from Robertson's catalogue introduction:

In retrospect, Procktor's work seems more conventional from the late sixties on – the artist calls it 'more conventionally professional' with often acute portraiture alternating with topography and still life as the traditional subjects. The best of this work has a crispness of touch and lean concentration of imagery which combines to make a peculiarly relaxed and understated strength of its own. Colour is continually fresh and resonant; an interest in patterning, in Oriental and Islamic art, shows itself in some North African paintings and later interiors, but this seems only to reinforce a kind of rejection of more abstract composition and an acceptance of pure form only as decorative pattern. There are exceptions: the *Self-Portrait in Fez* of 1975 retains much of the earlier, wilder, more venturesome spirit with its shadow-like figure and dramatic opposition of interior shadow with exterior light. But in general a far more conservative mood prevails: cheerful, contemplative, and effortlessly sustained with no sign of stress or strong emotion. The closest step to strong feeling is in the extraordinarily happy and affectionate rendering of landscapes or broad sweeping views across harbours or mountains. The quality of line, the ability to draw eloquently with the brush as well as the pencil or burin, the freshness of touch are all retained. But it is hard not to feel that some kind of animating energy has been subdued and the paintings in their comparative urbanity no longer question space, colour or form. They arrive but do not explore …

What the best of all the work has in common is a feeling of latent strength, of energy in reserve. The present occasion may be a retrospective show but it is very much also an account of work in progress. I believe that Procktor very much wants to tackle the traditional work of an artist, as Sutherland did: to paint portraits, to travel and fulfil commissions. His work did not falter at all in the seventies, when painting everywhere was in eclipse, under a cloud of disbelief after the advent of minimalism, and the arrival of conceptual art and performance art. But by then, a decision seems to have been taken, unconsciously or with awareness, to keep the work tightly inside the public domain and to aim for a completeness of statement rather than a more investigative fragmentation. Some of the cool 'openness' of the work of the past two decades seems almost Edwardian in its politeness, in its generally good manners, all day and no night. The restrained spirit of William Nicholson hovers over some of the carefully composed, lucidly presented still-life compositions. None of this can have anything to do with the post-modern stylistic games of the past decade and the neo-conservatism of some recent architecture as well as painting – Procktor had evolved his art to its present clarity and objectivity by 1970. What he has made is impressive and enjoyable. And it has for me, still, the edgy brilliance from time to time of the provisional, of something disclosed with much in reserve – and for any artist this is surely preferable to imagery and style that seems fixed forever in its own system, a trap which has undermined so much of the shallower abstract painting of the past twenty years.

Massey comments: 'Given Procktor's reputation as an artist of topography, that "they arrive but they do not explore", with its implication of sticking to the known landmarks, seems quite deliberately cutting, and given their personal history one might question Robertson's objectivity.' Clearly though he was disappointed in the direction the artist had taken since his euphoric catalogue introduction in 1963. The artist Stephen Chambers recalls being with Robertson whilst he was talking with Procktor over the telephone, describing their conversation as 'quite catty, very much like ex-lovers. I was with Bryan on three or four occasions over the years that I knew him (mid-1980s until his death) when I'd be in the room whilst these calls were taking place. I wouldn't talk to him about the conversations but they had the irascible tone born of exhausted familiarity. I didn't need to be told of a former intimacy; this was evident.'

In late January 1995, Robertson wrote to Procktor from Rhodes:

I've been living here since early October, not returning till end of April. I'm doing the same thing next October, so that I shan't be in London quite so much in future. I'm writing hard, memoirs, so shake in your boots. I'm so very sorry to have missed your show, although I've vivid memories of some outstandingly fine paintings in the studio. I was very impressed by their balance of strength in design & drawing with intimacy of mood & tone & richness of pattern. Like Vuillard on roller skates or should I say, on the skids ... much love, dearest Patrick, from your old admirer Franchot Tone X

Not long before he died, Bryan secured accommodation for the ailing and alcoholic Procktor in the Charterhouse, where such distinguished 'bachelors' as Robert Medley and Simon Raven had comfortably ended their days. Perhaps wisely, given his outrageous behaviour at another venerable

institution, the Royal Academy, where he could be virulently outspoken when under the influence, Procktor refused the offer.

Lord Snowdon and *Private View*

Private View, published in 1965, was a revolutionary book, the first of its kind to offer a survey or conspectus of the art world, and still rather exceptional. Large in format and beautifully and boldly designed, it offered a rich mix of words and images evocatively encapsulating the London art world at a crucial moment of its development. The photographs, which work so brilliantly with the text to illuminate the artists and their worlds and offer a splendid balance of documentary and portrait, were by Lord Snowdon, and the two writers, Bryan Robertson and John Russell, took it in turns to write about the artists. When I asked Lord Snowdon in two conversations at his London home in July 2012, then the only surviving contributor of the talented trio who were responsible (with designer Germano Facetti) for *Private View*, what he thought of Bryan Robertson, he was unequivocal. 'I loved Bryan,' he said. There were qualifications, however, about working on the book. 'It was a nightmare to do,' said Snowdon. 'Every time you arranged to do one sitting with Bryan or John, the other one would be in Paris. It was a disaster, but great fun.'

One or other of the writers ended up accompanying Snowdon on the studio visits and briefed him about the artists. His photographs nearly always tell you something new about the artist – a juxtaposed texture or stretch of landscape, an interior or a physical gesture, visual echoes – all these things Snowdon made telling. Sometimes the psychology of the artist was revealed (as in the photos of Lucian Freud), sometimes the character of both art and artist (in the John Piper entry). One of the more memorable images features the art historian Anthony Blunt, not yet unmasked as a Russian spy, holding up a slide to the light which casts another image – a portrait by Picasso – across his face. I asked Snowdon if that had been chance or intention. 'I think that was luck,' he replied, 'it was the sun'. In the end, looking through the book, and examining the plates in some detail for their rhythms and references, Snowdon summed up: 'It is quite fun, isn't it? I think it's probably more fun now than it was at the time.'

Robert Medley was one of the artists featured in *Private View*, and he described in his memoir *Drawn from the Life* (1983) how a photo shoot could disrupt the smooth running of a day at Camberwell School of Arts and Crafts (where he was then Head of Painting):

> Snowdon's visit to the College was memorable for its professionalism and informality. He already knew Tony Fry and Patrick Procktor (who had

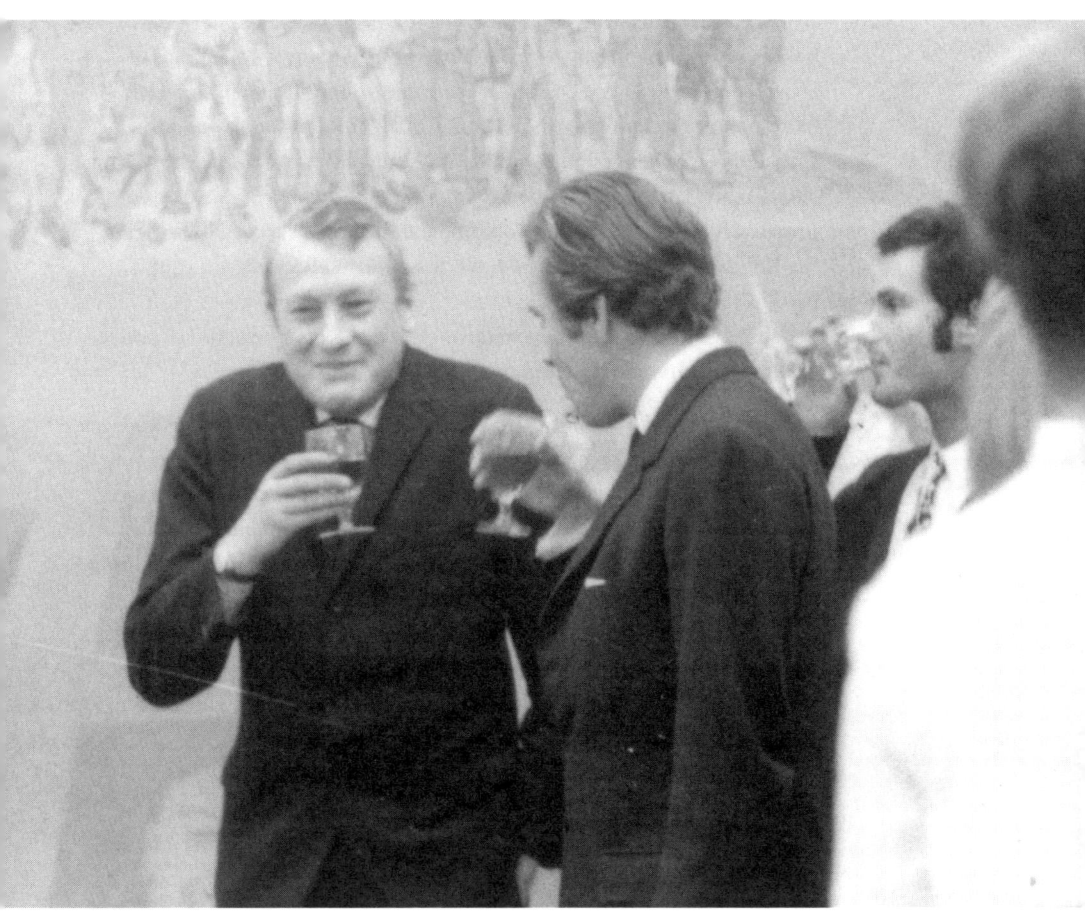

19 BR with Lord Snowdon at *The New Generation 1966* opening at the Whitechapel Gallery
Photograph by Martin Koretz, Whitechapel Gallery Archive

recently joined the staff) and felt at ease and among friends. It had long been our custom to lunch at the pub round the corner from the school, where we could discuss school matters in congenially uninstitutional surroundings. Snowdon wanted to photograph one of these informal staff meetings and so we went to the pub for lunch as usual and, engaging a long table, we gave the landlord no indication that we would be feeding so royally famous a person. It was not until we were leaving that the penny dropped. Such anonymity could not be preserved in the studios but the students continued with their work with predictable *insouciance*, though I could not help noticing that some had taken the unusual step of brushing their hair. Snowdon was given freedom to move about the school at will and he was delighted by the informality. It was fascinating to see him at work. Behind the camera he seemed to disappear completely. When I finally came to fetch him away I had difficulty in finding him, so invisibly had he melted into the activity of the students.

Bryan contributed brief and pithy introductions to the artists with whom he was most in sympathy, and these texts are in many ways models of evocative compression. Of course there are Robertsonian digressions – for instance he can't resist quoting Max Beerbohm that living in England is like being in the middle of a lettuce when he should be writing about Ivon Hitchens – but his writing is nearly always vivid and often provocative. Between them, Robertson and Russell succeed in bringing the English art world of the mid-1960s to life, in all its beguiling and intriguing diversity.

Here are three paragraphs of quintessential Robertson, full of praise but by no means entirely eulogistic:

Extrovert, gregarious, sharp-witted, and intellectually both serious and well versed, Patrick Procktor at twenty-nine has a keen satirical and theatrical sense as well as a concern for the reality – including the tragedies – of life. He is also, with all his out-going sociability and incessant quest for information and diversion, an unusually self-sufficient man, maintaining an almost guarded privacy. All these contradictions, or varying attributes, can be found in his figurative work, which has passionately upheld as a mainspring the Marxist viewpoint of relating art to society – though this sometimes conflicts with the obscurity of his autobiographical subjects. These seek a solution in a combination of realism, fantasy and abstraction.

Procktor relishes what he calls 'the open situation' that now exists, stylistically, in art everywhere; and he is sufficiently eclectic by nature to make skilful and intelligent use of this situation and to exploit its potential freedom of expression. But committed as he is to figurative painting, this free-wheeling can easily lead to superficial and unconvinced references to abstraction, from which to bind together the figurative elements in a composition.

He has learned from other figurative painters in England: Vaughan (his teacher, at one time), Bacon, Hockney, and above all from Kitaj. All these artists are trying to find the answers to similar problems, the main one being an attempt to project a new image of man in a relevant and meaningful context without relapsing into a devitalised and academic formula or accepting total abstraction.

Besides being a visual feast – and the full-page colour portrait of Procktor is just one of many delights – the text is sprinkled with provocative remarks and lively opinions. For instance, here is Robertson on the best way to show art.

But, of course, taste can't be imposed. Or can it? I believe in *exposure*. If people have the chance to live with something for a reasonable period of time, and if it's any good, they'll gradually understand it and like it. Maybe even love it. At the moment there's precious little chance of that happening. Modern art is made to seem unreal and remote from life because the public rarely ever sees it except inside the artificial vacuum of a temporary exhibition. I think the budget for permanent acquisitions should be increased, with a corresponding decrease in funds for temporary shows. I know they're educational; but there's a fine line which divides education from a new form of indoor entertainment, and I think a lot of people go to modern art exhibitions now in the same mildly curious but basically blank way in which they watch television.

A sentiment which is truer now than ever before.

On 22 October 1965 Bryan wrote to Kenneth Clark:

Here is the book I've been working on for three years, believe it or not, signed by Tony (who wanted to) and me later when we meet. Hope you'll be amused to read that you start the book off – v grand – in the first section, and I also hope you'll not be too discomfited by the photo, which I think is superb. (I hope I look as swinging, cool etc. etc. as you, when I'm a bit older!)

There are also several references to you in various sections of the text. We all owe you a lot, so there it is. I must say, there's never been such a comprehensive study of any art world in any capital city before. The Americans have bought 40,000 copies I'm happy to say, so it should do English art a bit of good. It's right up to date. I know you have vague reservations about JR but I must also say he was splendid and most punctilious to work with – I love the text. My sections are irreverent and sharp, I hope. See you soon. Love B

Roger Cook

One of the youngest painters to be included in *Private View* was Roger Cook (born 1940), who did not react well to the limelight of this exposure and promptly gave up painting. He spoke to me with refreshing frankness in a telephone interview of May 2016.

I was teaching at Reading, with a senior person from the St Ives School, Terry Frost, and Terry wasn't in that book, and he was really furious about it. I discovered fairly quickly that he was going around saying I was Bryan Robertson's bum boy. That was really so horrible. If it had been true, it might have been all right, but it wasn't true. Bryan obviously knew I was gay but he never ever made any passes at me or anything like that. He did have a relationship with Patrick Procktor who was my best friend at the Slade. I first met Bryan through Patrick because I was sharing a flat with Patrick and Bryan used to come round. Then Bryan saw my work. At that time I was a sort of op minimalist. My first show at the Rowan Gallery was more op art, and was very much appreciated by Bridget Riley. Then I took out all the optical trickery and became a monochrome minimalist. Bryan was just wonderfully supportive to me. I was in the *New Generation 1966* show, and through Bryan I got a Stuyvesant scholarship to New York. I still feel terribly guilty [at giving up painting]. Various artists that were loyal to Bryan were angry with me and felt that I'd let him down.

One of the reasons that I wanted to pull out of the art world was this gossip that I was having a relationship with Bryan. I never discussed it with him – I was young and upset. I was quite naive about the art world. Bryan introduced me to some extraordinary people. I had dinner with him and Lee Krasner in the Ritz in her suite. Of course he had my painting on the wall of his flat, and he had parties there and I met Robert Motherwell. The painting of mine that was in *Private View* was reproduced as a square. The copy of *Private View* that I've got has a note from Bryan apologising about this. It should be a diamond. Bryan owned something similar, which he bought at a very reasonable price. It was a great honour and he was very proud of it. He showed it off. I think there was a great generosity of spirit in Bryan. I feel very sad that I then lost touch with him.

He was very generous in introducing me to people. He was extremely literate, not just in terms of art but in literature and music. I remember one evening at his flat he suddenly decided we should write a joint letter to Aaron Copland who he knew. I don't remember whether we'd been to a concert and heard a Copland piece but he sent the letter. I don't know whether we ever got a reply. He was very urbane and sophisticated in his tastes, and it was really wonderful for me to have known him. He obviously enjoyed the art world – he was a very sociable man. But I was just too young to handle the art world, actually.

Patrick [Procktor] was like a brother to me. He was very much more sophisticated and quite a bit older, he'd been in the Navy. I was so close to Patrick that I've got lots of anger with him still, when he became such a terrible alcoholic. I think he probably didn't treat Bryan very well. He used Bryan probably for his own ends, and probably Bryan was in love with him rather than the reverse. Patrick was very witty and urbane and no doubt they had some nice evenings together, but sexually I should imagine it was very frustrating for Bryan.

There was a launch of *Private View* the book at the Royal College and I was teaching that day at Reading. Suddenly the Secretary came running through the building and said, 'Princess Margaret's on the phone, Princess Margaret's on the phone!' I said, 'Don't be ridiculous'. She said, 'She really is – she's wanting to invite you to the Palace tonight and they've got a painting of yours hanging in the living room'. I panicked and contacted Robert Medley and asked him to chaperone me because I was terrified of the situation socially. He said, 'Of course, dear boy, of course I will'. I was on the pavement outside with Robert and this sports car came up with Snowdon

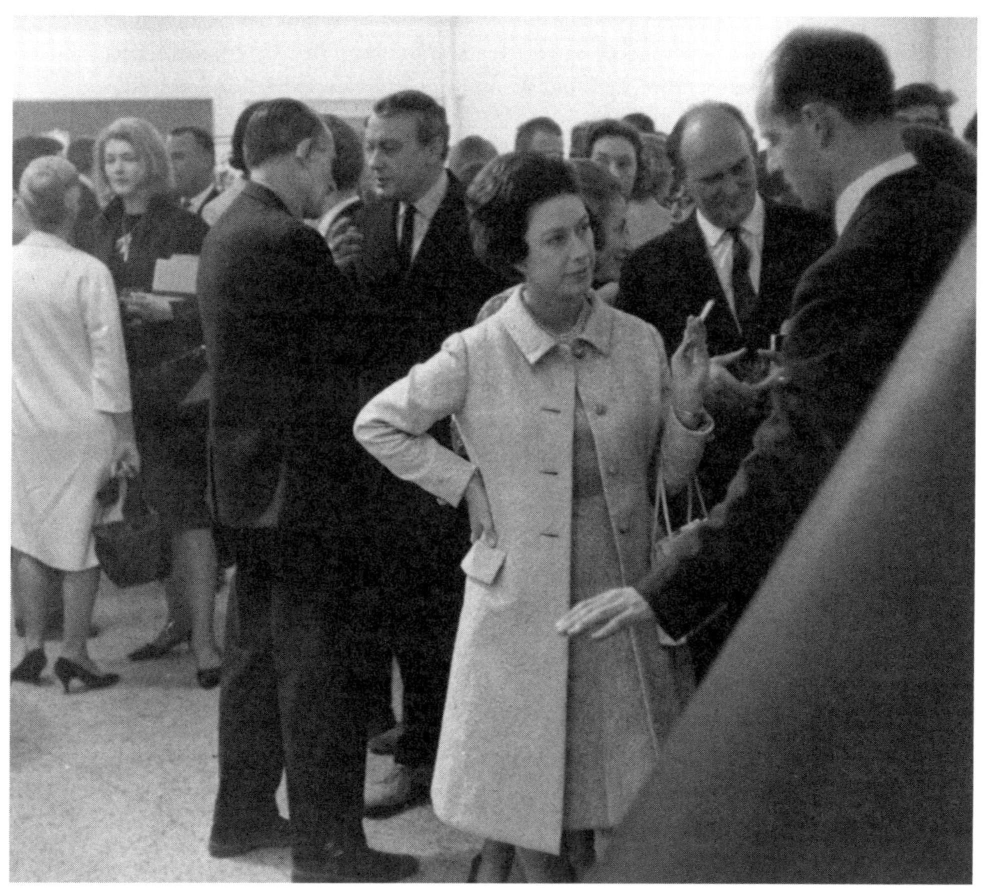

20 Princess Margaret talking to Phillip King at *The New Generation 1965* opening at the Whitechapel Gallery
Photograph by Martin Koretz, Whitechapel Gallery Archive

and Princess Margaret in it, and they said 'Jump in the back, Robert,' and he left me on the pavement. Then John Russell and his terrifying wife took me by the arm and we were driven in the ceremonial Rolls. Vera Russell said to me, 'You know they want to buy your painting?' I said, 'They can't – it's already sold to my dealer, she bought it for herself'. Then when I got to the palace, it was one of those terrible things that happens to abstract painters. I saw my painting in the living room, and the colour was a sort of burnt orange and it exactly matched the furnishings. And I knew they weren't wanting to buy the painting for the right reasons.

Patrick wasn't at that do – he hadn't been invited – so I imagined there was a kind of falling out with Bryan at just about that time. It was a wonderful, very informal dinner in the basement with gingham tablecloths. Princess Margaret greeted me as almost the guest of honour because I was the youngest artist there, and I had to sit next to her. It was all pretty agonising, really, and eventually I was taken on a tour of Snowdon's dark rooms by one of the equerries. They were very extraordinary heady days.

Frank Bowling

Frank Bowling (born 1934), the Guyana-born British abstract artist, spoke very directly about Bryan in an interview in his London studio in April 2015.

I first met Bryan about the time that I got kicked out of the Royal College of Art for marrying Paddy Kitchen. He was one of the people who tried to change Robin Darwin's [then Rector of the RCA] mind about this. So I went to the Slade and Paddy became Lawrence Gowing's personal assistant when he moved to Chelsea. Bryan's circle of friends included Colin MacInnes – I didn't get along with him, he was a very aggressive pooftah and I felt very uncomfortable in his company – and Robert Medley, who was running Camberwell at the time. Robert gladly gave me a part-time job teaching. I got on with him like a house on fire.

Bowling, like one or two other others you might have expected to be included like Howard Hodgkin, was not among the *New Generation* artists:

It was really very hurtful and when I challenged him about it, he said I was getting too much. I got the Shakespeare Centenary job, I was given a lectureship at Reading by Claude Rogers and I was trying for the Harkness. I didn't get the Harkness either, even though Bryan was my referee and he'd tried to fix it. At that time we were very close and he used to call me up if he had to go and see a movie for *The Critics*, or the theatre, and then he introduced me to Richard Buckle who was handing out the various jobs for the Shakespeare Quatercentenary and I got the painting job with Peter Blake, Ceri Richards and Leonard Rosoman. They had offered it to Francis Bacon and he didn't want to do it, and also to Sidney Nolan, who didn't want it. My studio wasn't big enough for those enormous paintings so they gave me a studio at Alexandra Palace.

The view that I had of myself as this young blood who was up in the forefront was dented because of the disappointments. Bryan just took it, as was his way, shrugging. Later I mentioned that disappointment in some conversation with Rasheed Araeen in *The Other Story* [the 1989 Tate exhibition of British, African, Caribbean and Asian modernism] and Bryan by then was very angry about lots of things and he said he was going to sue me for the remarks I made [about having been] left out of *The New Generation* without any explanation. A piece he wrote [on me] for the *Sunday Times* colour magazine was spiked and his theory was that Britain wasn't ready for a young gifted black artist. That was quoted and he went up in smoke. He was very angry.

I tried to patch it up after that and wrote him a letter. His attitude was, 'After all I've done for you to say what you did'. Bryan was very sensitive and easily hurt. I could have said other things that he might have taken as a joke but might have been more damaging to his career. I went [with him] to the Paris Pullman off the Fulham Road and saw *Last Year at Marienbad*, I think it was, and Bryan went to sleep soon after we got to the cinema and didn't wake up until the movie had finished. We walked back but he hated Finch's and wouldn't go in there, he wouldn't go in the Queen's Elm and we walked all the way back to Sloane Square before he would go into a pub and have a drink, and I told him the story of the film. And he was amazing about the film.

I used to go to shows with older guys (Liz Frink's first husband, her biographer Stephen Gardiner, etc.), and Bryan was one of those guys. He took me to concerts at the Wigmore Hall. He was a mentor to me about art but I felt leery of the crowd that was going down to the Cotswolds. There were too many openly aggressive queers in that lot. (Cecil Beaton, Jeremy Fry, Richard Buckle, Howard Hodgkin, David Hockney – all those people.) It was a time when the homosexual crowd ran the country scene. They were outrageous and I got frightened by them, I think. Bryan was gentle and sweet, he was not an aggressive pooftah. You'd go round there for drinks and he'd walk around in his slippers because he had bad feet. I think he got along with John Hoyland best of all, because John was very up with all those different kinds of girls and I think Bryan kind of enjoyed watching all that. A sight queen, as we used to call them – he liked to look.

Bryan, knowing that I wanted to go to America, bought the painting *Big Bird* for the CAS [and the CAS gave it to the Victoria Gallery and Museum, Liverpool, in 1975], that's how I got a small amount of money. He was very helpful in different ways. I think he felt very strongly that I was one of the better younger artists around, and he made a point of being friendly towards me. Like Francis Bacon was. And he was outraged at the way Robin Darwin behaved towards me for getting married to Paddy Kitchen. Bryan went out of his way to follow up what I was doing. He was always having me round. We saw the Beatles in Alexandra Palace with Richard Buckle and Bryan nodded off in that. He fell asleep the moment he got bored.

I think he had this guilt thing about being a homosexual. When Patrick [Procktor] started running rings round him he was like an animal in bright lights, he was mesmerised by Patrick's excesses. Patrick was so bold and insistent. I spent about a month at the Slade and he was always after me. Bryan wouldn't have dared do a thing like that. He was much more passive. He liked being in the company of women, too. He was into culture in a way that I only found when I went to America and met Clement Greenberg. Clem was this amazing guy who would go anywhere to see art if he heard that there was something interesting to see, he would check it out. Bryan had that feeling about him. He was always interested. He had this marvellous openness to culture, but I think he was frightened by the establishment, too, I think they intimidated him.

Maturity: character and characteristics

Bryan was a curator and writer – not an arts administrator, though his public-gallery jobs in England and the USA required a degree of administration that he avoided where possible. Artists were at the centre of his concern, and luckily for him the art world in general, and arts funding in particular, were less hidebound and controlled then than now. However, rather unexpectedly Bryan proved adept at obtaining corporate sponsorship when it came to the *New Generation* exhibitions, and he persuaded the Peter Stuyvesant Foundation to put up £60,000 to purchase a collection of modern art over a period of three years. (Much of the art coincidentally came from the Whitechapel exhibitions, which aided revenue there.) But with Bryan, it was always much more a question of flair – of relying on intuition and luck – than long-term planning.

Bryan had, however, a well-developed sense of mission – a determination to improve visual standards in Britain, and to give people wonderful exhibitions to visit. His chief skills were in interpretation and presentation, not in paper-clip counting, and many observed that the speed at which he could read a painting, and respond to something entirely new and previously unseen, was phenomenal. He was, in some ways, a classic outsider, a nonconformist, a man who knew his own mind. And that was where he got his strength from – his individuality. His maverick status was consolidated by being erratic and evasive, with an established habit of not answering letters. He was also excitable, touchy and fussy, with a tendency to show off – that was the theatrical side of him. But this maverick outsider status carried within it other dangers. For instance, that he could become the victim of his own myth.

He loved digressions and distractions, and would happily stop in the street to talk. Artist Bert Irvin (1922–2015) recalled:

> His exhibitions at the Whitechapel were a great inspiration, and an overwhelming influence. They meant absolutely everything to us. His lecture on Jackson Pollock was very good indeed. And in America he'd been to an Elvis Presley concert and was very impressed. He was always very encouraging when we did meet. I remember being in the street in Highbury for an hour and a half talking. He recommended going to the Festival Hall Poetry Library and reading more.

Bryan had a certain vagueness that could be quite charming to begin with – but how long would one put up with it? He may have appeared to be absent-minded, but then his mind was also as sharp as his tongue could be. Luckily humour was never far away, for Bryan had a good sense of the comedy of life. He loved young people: their youth, vitality, talent and optimism. He made a habit of 'adopting' one or two and spent a lot of time with the favourite of the moment – whether Paul Huxley, Gary

Wragg, Ken Draper or Stephen Chambers. In return, many of his friends loved to imitate him, as if wanting him back in the room, especially John Hoyland, Draper and Tim Marlow. It was odd, then, that Bryan should have been so bad at continuity in relationships. He tried to keep a dog or cat from time to time and couldn't ever manage it. Sustained relationships were beyond him – he was good at concentrated bursts of energy, but not the daily expenditure of keeping a relationship going. Even friendships usually ended (or suffered a hiatus) in an explosion or because Bryan withdrew. Like many of us, he was a bundle of contradictions.

One of the things Bryan was known for was a dislike of expressionism. Writing in the catalogue for his '45–'99 exhibition at Kettle's Yard in 1999, he summed up his reasons, juxtaposed with a description of the kind of art he really valued:

Life seems quite expressionist enough without having to endure a painting of a grimacing or shrieking face on the wall. I love the passion, energy and wild sensuality of Soutine; I greatly appreciate the early, psychologically penetrating portraits of Kokoschka and Jawlensky's early figure groups, but the muddy paintings of the so-called 'School of London' artists seem turgid and dated, with a patronising view, from the painter, of 'little people'.

What I look for in art of any period is imaginative energy, radiance, equilibrium, composure, colour, light, vitality, poise, buoyancy, a transcendent ability to soar above life and not be subjugated by it, the avoidance of rhetoric, a resolved formal tension. I have tended to prefer abstract art to figurative art in the twentieth century because so much modern figurative painting, unsurprisingly, is inherently morbid and this, again, seems self-indulgent to me and redundant. My strictures may sound narrowly self-protective, but they are part of a reservation which also dismisses various sorts of academicism.

Later in the same essay, he praised individualism:

I mistrusted groups, movements and labels. What impressed me most was the work of a handful of individuals, unclasssifiable, out on a personal limb which ignored fashion but wasn't backward looking: Prunella Clough, Keith Vaughan, Edward Burra, Merlyn Evans, John Craxton, Cecil Collins, Jack Smith and a handful of others. All of these artists, with a few others of comparable individuality, had retrospective shows with considerable success. Burra exhibited once in mixed company at Whitechapel in 1954 [at the *British Painting and Sculpture* show], and we became friends, but to my regret I never got around to presenting a full-scale show of his work.

Bryan had a highly pronounced appreciation of luxury as a part of life – enjoying fine food and wine, a well-made, fashionable suit, and taxis instead of public transport – and reacted against the English

determination to see passion in painting as equalled by thick paint and roughened surface. (He preferred bright colour and svelte finishes.) He was a great catalyst, as Hoyland was swift to point out, making things happen and people do their best work. And yet he was elusive in so many ways as a person, and quite reserved. (He said: 'I am more comfortable with formality than informality.') John Carter, discussing how difficult it might be to paint or draw Bryan's portrait, as both Elisabeth Vellacott and Bridget Riley did, observed: 'He had quite a strange face and quite curious eyes. His eyes were never vivid in any way. I always think of them as somehow recessed and pale. Not in any way striking. And also one never saw his teeth – in my memory, he always managed to smile or laugh without showing any teeth.'

And yet he also had so much understanding. The writer and critic John Spurling recounted that Bryan once said to him that all any of us really wants is to be recognised and praised. He suggested therefore that we each of us make a disc to play to ourselves at times of discouragement, on which the pronouncement of our name is followed by cheers and thunderous applause. Perfect!

Bryan's slight phobia about opening letters developed into a sustained cash-flow problem. In the Tate Archive there is a letter (dated 17 February 1967) from Sweeney and Palmer Ltd about the non-cashing of a cheque sent to Bryan on 18 November 1966, for £11, in settlement of the commission due on the purchase of a sculpture from the Grabowski Gallery. When Stephen Chambers cleared up Bryan's house after his death, he found a pile of uncashed cheques an inch deep. Occasionally Bryan made an effort to rouse himself. In April 1969 he wrote to the BBC Talks booking manager:

> I am very sorry to trouble you with this matter but I should be very grateful for your help. In having a great clear out of papers with my secretary I have come across a number of contracts which have not been filled in and returned to you. I think it likely that I have not received payment from some of these; on the other hand it is also probable, having mislaid other contracts at the time, I may in fact have received duplicates from you and thus received payment for certain other programmes. I do apologise for this laxness on my part, but I would be very grateful if you could sort the matter out for me and let me have any fees that may be still due to me, or renew the dates on those contracts which are still valid so that I may apply for payment.

A gentleman from Fulmar Television left a note: 'I came round this afternoon to see you but must have made a mistake about the time or day. Or something came up. I will telephone later this evening.' And good luck to him. The number of plaintive comments about phones being out of order

or not answered suggests a tendency for procrastination and avoidance. (Among those who complained were Lord Snowdon and the *Spectator*.) Also coupled with this was an inability to return photos or slides which had been sent, admittedly often unsolicited, or to respond to publications such as *Who's Who* when they wanted to update information. Even standing outside his house (as some attempted) did not always produce a face-to-face result.

Books were not written (there's a sharp demand from Nikolaus Pevsner in 1966 for missing text, coupled with the threat of cancelling the contract for a Pelican History of Art volume); others were borrowed and not returned. A 1991 letter from the Librarian of the Courtauld Institute asked Bryan to return a Lee Krasner exhibition catalogue, a loan made (as a favour) in July 1986. The Librarian goes on to say that he has already written more than once, but that there has been no reply.

From a draft letter to an unknown recipient (dated 7 June 1979), explaining that a major drama with neighbours has taken up much of his time and energy, Bryan wrote:

I am exhausted having had only a few hours sleep in the last two weeks, roughly, and at the most concentratedly busy time of my entire life, with very big issues at stake and bewildering sums of money. To make it worse, I have no secretary. And an Ansaphone machine I had installed for my sanity doesn't work. It takes 1 message and none of the others that follow it. A long testimonial for Jennifer Durrant was written but untyped and unposted. I had to read it to them over the phone. A long recommendation for Tim Scott for something else, of real consequence to him, has been written but is still untyped or mailed. My handwriting is bad anyway and now tired. No time to find another secretary. There is much, much else. When I am at my most demented with it all (it includes a detailed scenario for a 13 part TV series, involving millions, an exhibition to accompany it at Burlington House for a similar figure; the setting up of vast committees of all kinds, setting of strategy for the Barbican Art Gallery, completing a book, and a play in which the Nat Theatre is interested, and films with Melvyn Bragg and a long 10,000 words text for Peter Murray's Sculpture in the Park booklet and a lot of other things) apart from getting to the hairdresser, no haircut for months!, the dry cleaners, exercising the dog, clearing up chaos of papers and books so that my cleaning lady can at least clean – Then there's Harper's & Queen, ballet reviews for New Statesman etc etc etc. You have a wife? I do it all alone, mostly.

His usual good humour may have been the face he wanted the world to see. Later in the same missive he writes: 'There is no time in any day at present for me to blow my nose. I'd consider myself damn lucky if I have trousers on. To be shaved is a bonus.'

Soul-searching was an occasional indulgence, and Kenneth Clark seemed frequently to be the recipient of it. A letter (dated 5 February 1961) from Bryan to K reads:

I should like to write you a funny letter and make you laugh, but although I'm well enough and have kept away from bed, my spirits are at their winter nadir and all I want to do is stare into space, full of nostalgia for my wasted youth and gloomy forebodings for the future. I feel like a thumbed man, haunted and harassed. All my friends seem bores, and I long to sweep them all away, dispense with all loyalties, and get to know some new and witty and better-looking bunch of people. Thoughts of foreign travel fill me with apathy; the prospect of the next three or four months trapped in Angleterre fills me with desperation …

A Trappist cell for a few weeks might be a solution, but then I know I'd want to ring everyone up and gossip on the phone. Or escape.

I think we should all be pensioned off in the winter, with books, moderate company, a congenial job to do like writing (but no pressures) and not be expected to keep up appearances. I can find nothing to keep up.

The following excerpt is taken from a later letter (dated 6 September 1966) from Bryan to K:

I've had an odd summer, don't know where it's gone: many trepidations, and sense of unreality, about getting the house [Barnsbury]. With my life half over, it seems, all I can think of these days are unfulfilled promises, artists I've neglected who needed help, books I haven't completed – let alone started, and the lack of written evidence of thought and aspirations as opposed to ephemeral living and the endless screeds of time-devouring journalism, broadcast talks and all the other mercenary, vanity motivated wastage of two decades. Apart from all that I'm enjoying being 41 – but I've begun, for the first time, to be stricter with time and jobs, and to keep boring irrelevancies at bay. It's a continual battle.

John Osborne, when asked at the beginning of the 1970s what kind of person would be ideally equipped to run the National Theatre, replied:

The ideal would be someone like Diaghilev. Someone who is absolutely single-minded, entirely egotistical, who takes no notice of what anyone else is doing or thinking. Someone who concentrates completely on his own plans. He is setting the styles and trends and fashions, not following. He doesn't really care what the public thinks or what's happening at the box office (though it can't be ignored, I suppose). It's a certain kind of artistic temperament and hardly anyone ever has it.

Bryan Robertson had it.

From a horoscope cast for Bryan Robertson in 1965

This was found amongst Bryan's papers in the Tate Archive.

Your Aries Sun and Venus give you enthusiasm, pioneering spirit, independence, assertiveness and much willpower. The Sun and Venus are posited in your House of Unions, meaning that you have a great need to communicate with others in order to find your equilibrium. The good trine between your Sun and Neptune gives you idealism, spirituality and intensifies your emotions; it also makes you musical.

Because of the Sun's challenging aspect to your Cancer Moon and Pluto, there is a tendency to give into too many impulses, chaotic relationships and mis-channelled energies. It tends to explosive excesses of all kinds. Because you are extremely responsive to all emotional stimuli and apt to exaggerate your need of rebellion – acting it out on an emotional plane rather than on the intellectual one – you are apt to run into unique attachments that have little chance of bringing you the kind of stability you so desperately need in order to express your strength and talents to your best advantage. You need much affection as a steadying/controlling power. And you are at your best actually when acting under the direction or in accordance with the advice of a partner/wife or friend although you do not make a good servant and need to be at the head of whatever you undertake in order to be at your best.

According to this horoscope, the following are among Bryan's attributes:

courteous, kind, affectionate – true artistic touch
acquisitive, secretive, shrewd and cautious
many-sided and exuberant; over-confident?
high-strung; predisposition towards exaggeration
nerves and lungs the weakest spots
sensitive, moody and irritable

Like so many forecasts and assessments of this sort, there is much which rings true, and much which doesn't.

The war of the Tate succession

Looking ahead at his career, it seems likely that Robertson positioned himself quite deliberately at the Whitechapel with an eye to taking on the challenge of directing the Tate when the post became vacant. As soon as Sir John Rothenstein announced his retirement in April 1964 (to take place in September), the race was on. One of the chief contenders was Lawrence Gowing, a brilliant writer and art-school teacher and protégé of Coldstream. When the job came up, the short list consisted of six people: Gowing, Norman Reid (who had been at the gallery since the end of the

war and was virtually running it), Hugh Scrutton (Bryan's predecessor at the Whitechapel, who had taken over the Walker Art Gallery in Liverpool), Bryan himself, Alan Bowness and Graham Reynolds (head of the department of prints and drawings as well as paintings at the V&A). The one-time plot to make Douglas Cooper, the combative and much-disliked champion and collector of cubist art, director of the Tate, seems to have been a non-starter.

Gowing was so convinced he would be offered the job that when Snowdon came to photograph him for *Private View*, he insisted on being photographed at the Tate because he said he would be director by the time the book was published. Snowdon refused to photograph him in those circumstances. Bryan was so horrified at Gowing's presumption that he went and told the politician R.A. (Rab) Butler. This backfired because Rab told the trustees of the Tate, and the trustees were then instructed that they couldn't vote for either Gowing or Robertson as both were compromised. Adrian Clark, in *Fighting on all Fronts: John Rothenstein in the Art World* (2018), wrote that, at the time of appointing his successor, 'Gowing was unhelpfully behaving as if he were already the Director and it was also rumoured that Robertson was a candidate. It was assumed that, of the two, Robertson was John's preferred choice, and this led to another squabble with Reid, who in front of other staff accused John of writing to the Board to support Robertson.' (This information is taken from Cathy Courtney's interview in 2000 with Norman Reid.)

Nick Serota, interviewed while still Director of the Tate himself, recalled:

There is this story – I don't think it's apocryphal – of John Rothenstein announcing he was leaving to a board of trustees and the trustees looking round the table and saying 'Lawrence, you'd be the right person to be the director!' One of the trustees was a man named Dennis Proctor who had been a senior civil servant in the Home Office (I had this story from Dennis years later), and he said 'I just had to tell them that this was a public body and they had to have a competition. They couldn't decide amongst themselves'. So almost before the thing had begun, Lawrence had been anointed to be the director.

In the end, with two of the chief contenders disqualified, Norman Reid was appointed, thought by many to be a safe pair of hands. Bryan was bitterly disappointed not to be given the chance of running Britain's leading modern art museum, and it may be said that after this the heart went out of his Whitechapel directorship.

I asked John Hoyland whether he thought Bryan would have made a good director of the Tate. 'I think it would have been a mad six months! He dug up Mark Tobey [at the Whitechapel] and nobody had ever heard of

him. He put on all these amazing shows. Norman Reid was a very nice guy but he didn't have Bryan's flair. Bryan had entrepreneurial flair, more the kind of Diaghilev feeling.'

Robertson's public platform as art critic of the *Spectator* 1965–9 by Hilary Spurling

I first met Bryan Robertson in the summer of 1965. I was twenty-four years old, in my first proper job as arts editor of the *Spectator*, and urgently in need of an art critic. Bryan was forty, and had been running the Whitechapel for twelve years. 'We're in the middle of an extraordinary period in English art,' he wrote, assessing the gallery and its strategy a year later. He had already galvanised the first generation of young British artists to operate on equal terms with the best of their contemporaries anywhere in the Western world. Now the time had come to turn his attention to the public, what he called 'the *real* public, not just the art public, which is tiny, alas'.

We met at this point because I had a vacancy to fill, and nobody in the *Spectator* office had the faintest idea where to look, or who to ask. I had been hired as a kind of dogsbody with the newly invented title of arts editor to make the job sound grander. The background of the rest of the editorial staff was heavily political, mine was literary and theatrical. It was my husband, John Spurling (then a BBC Radio announcer working mostly on the Third Programme), who suggested trying the man at the Whitechapel and, looking back now, I realise that first phone call to Bryan Robertson changed my life.

Like most people of my provincial generation in England, I grew up in a post-war visual blackout almost unimaginable today. The 1950s was an age for all practical purposes before TV with no internet, no glossy magazines, no media to speak of, and virtually no exhibitions or readily accessible art books. Everyone had heard of Matisse and Picasso but no one I knew had ever seen anything by either of them. We knew the twentieth century existed – we were living in it after all – but, as for modernism, the closest I ever got was Reg Butler's *Unknown Political Prisoner* in Bristol City Art Gallery. When I finally reached London, Bond Street galleries were no help. Nor was the Tate in those days. So far as the work of my own contemporaries was concerned, I might as well have grown up blindfold.

This was a situation Bryan set out to remedy. 'Art is not a luxury, it is the most acute and basic expression of the spiritual state of any society in any epoch,' he wrote sternly, appalled by the lack of even basic visual education available to ordinary people at that time in this country. I was a prime example, and from now on I became his guinea pig. I can still remember my excitement and relief when I read his opening salvo in June 1965: 'A new generation of young English painters and sculptors is producing for the first time in my memory a body of work ... which does face up to the present, and is not a later provincial variation on original themes first established in Paris or New York.' Later that year, when I saw my first *New Generation* show at the Whitechapel, I felt as if the blindfold had been taken off at last, and suddenly the whole world exploded in light and space and colour.

'Questions not answers are in the air', wrote Bryan, coaxing and encouraging readers like a ringmaster drumming up an audience for new acts of ever greater daring and agility. He reported what he called 'a change of pace', a general quickening and expanding on all sides of the art scene, diagnosing its disruptive symptoms in the work of R.B. Kitaj ('something solid turns halfway into a flat area'), and even more disconcertingly in Patrick Caulfield: 'a Mondrian-like grid of soothing, if rigid, austerity is confounded by seagulls of the cheapest strip-cartoon variety darting in and out of the cross-bars.' Both represented an exploratory, experimental phase in what Bryan described with a flourish as 'the new and grand journey into the interior of art'.

This was August 1965, and from now on things hotted up. One week he rushed his readers off to Kasmin's gallery in Bond Street to see the latest huge abstract sculpture by Anthony Caro ('bright blue, pared down to essential structure and so animated that it practically winks at you'). Another time it was the first one-man show of a young artist at Axiom ('it will prove historically important', wrote Bryan, urging readers to spend a pound or two on an Ian Hamilton Finlay print). He compared the appearance on the scene of another unknown young artist to Cézanne's arrival at Alphaville. A third had 'the capacity to become a latter-day Monet'. This last was Bridget Riley on the verge of moving from black and white to colour. 'She is a mistress of dislocation', wrote Bryan, reviewing the next stage in her miraculous evolution twelve months later. 'Automatically one's hand goes up to straighten a tie or pull up a sock, such is the graceful, perfect severity of Miss Riley's working studies.'

'I don't believe in "public taste"', wrote Bryan. 'It doesn't exist. The public has no taste whatever until it is offered something as an example.' His aim was to give ordinary people a chance to encounter the best and latest art of their own time, but he had no illusions about the disgust and revulsion likely to ensue. He said good art needed no explanation, but people needed information. He told *Spectator* readers not only where to go and what to see, but how to look at what they saw. Week by week we learned a new visual language as it was being invented. In this context it is worth recalling that, when Henry Moore's *Knife Edge Two Piece* was installed opposite the Houses of Parliament in the summer of 1967, it was publicly denounced as a bronze oddity by the past President of the Royal Academy, Charles Wheeler. At the height of the controversy, six days before Moore's piece was due to be unveiled, Bryan responded with a set of practical, step-by-step instructions for looking at abstract art in general: 'You really have to work at sculpture: walk round it slowly, keeping your gaze fixed in order to see successive changes materialise in the form; you have to crouch down to inspect the quarry from different heights; it is also useful to ask to have the electric light switched off.'

I particularly liked this last tip. One of my many problems on first reaching London – as a scruffy newly graduated Eng. Lit. student with a part-time job as a waitress in the Tottenham Court Road – was having to face the supercilious and perfectly groomed girl behind the desk in every West End gallery, who sized you up and wrote you off before you'd even crossed her threshold. I enjoyed imagining her reaction to hordes of pinstriped City gents with rolled-up copies of the *Spectator* demanding to have the lights put out. Daylight came high on Bryan's list of priorities. He claimed to have personally postponed erection of the Hayward Gallery by pointing out at the planning stage that no provision had been made for daylight. 'Light is to sculpture what water is for fish: an essential complementary element. Without it – with a fixed unaltering light – sculpture is not alive. It needs variation in light, and daylight at that, far more than painting.'

The piece he was talking about was Phillip King's *Through* on its first London outing: a painted plastic cone sliced into nine segments, almost as big as Moore's mighty bronze *Knife Edge*, simple, sober, monumental, and now in the Tate collection. Bryan followed his helpful hints on sculpture a year later with a companion piece on how to look at abstract painting. But his greatest teaching tool, in person and on the page, was ineluctable conviction. Here he is advising readers to go at once to see four immense striped canvases by Kenneth Noland, newly shipped in by Kasmin from the US: 'The sheer delight imparted by these paintings drives all the usual standards from one's head.' A long and detailed description followed, together with background information and a rationale of the aims of purist colour theory ('to free colour not only from all descriptive functions but also from the slightest ... subsidiary activity of any kind') as preached in New York by Clement Greenberg. Bryan ended by evoking Noland's synthetic colour ('fiendishly hard to describe') before letting rip in a characteristically wild, free-wheeling riff of his own that evokes the exuberant impact of Noland's austerely reductive canvases probably better than anything else could:

> I found myself thinking of the 1920s and thirties and the world of flappers, chiffon dresses, young fellows in striped blazers, river parties, Dufy, van Dongen, Coco Chanel, lime fizz, sun-tan cream, beach huts, palm trees and blue skies at Nice or Monte Carlo, Molyneux, Lanvin, brown-bread-and-butter ice at Gunters and so on. The artist doubtless intended none of this.

From 1965 until well after I left at the end of 1969, Bryan used the *Spectator* as his public platform, putting forward in its columns the parts of his programme not already accomplished at the Whitechapel. He called for higher standards, better funding, greater accessibility and more public use of painters and sculptors. He urged collectors to come forward to buy contemporary art (any *Spectator* reader who took his advice seriously in the 1960s will now be sitting on a small fortune). In 1968 he suggested demolishing the Tate or, failing that, radically rethinking its primary function: 'If a public museum is a stunning place to visit, and houses masterpieces impeccably hung, placed and lit, then everyone will go there.'

He called for the Arts Council to pull itself together and take the lead. He repeatedly insisted London must overhaul its standards of opera and ballet design. 'Visually Covent Garden seems to have no sense of the twentieth century, let alone 1965,' he wrote crossly, citing the model responsible for so much in his own career: 'Can nobody get the composer, the choreographer and the right artist together, as Diaghilev did?' In 1968 he greeted the ICA's opening show in its new premises on The Mall with thunderous rebuke:

> wholly unsuitable as an inaugural gesture from what is now the most lavishly subsidised centre in England for cultural trail-blazing ... This arbitrary conglomeration does no service to the younger artists on show and is a betrayal of their seniors ... no relevance whatever to the central concerns of modern art ... panders to all that is most reactionary ... a dated element of schoolboy daring or goading hangs over this exhibition ... Rarely has aesthetic cynicism descended to such depths of futility.

Bryan worked his readers hard. What seems in retrospect an astonishing succession of small but seminal shows in private galleries was firmly signalled ('make sure you go, for I am pretty sure we are considering a masterpiece,' he wrote of Caro's *Prairie*). 'Take advantage of a lull in the action and spend several days exploring the great exhibition of Picasso's sculpture,' he said, reviewing the Tate's 1966 retrospective that changed for ever British perceptions of the modern movement. When abstraction became briefly fashionable, he urged readers to be vigilant for fakery as well as genuine innovation. He warned against shallow imitative practitioners whose sophisticated games too easily degenerated into pictorial journalism or, worse, 'trite comments *about* pictorial journalism,' adding a rider – 'Art is beginning to take its revenge' – still relevant nearly fifty years later.

'Take a notebook, make several visits and do some background homework' was his advice when the Royal Academy explored the achievements of the Bauhaus. He loved that show because of the clarity, scope and boldness of the Bauhaus agenda. 'Four or five men of goodwill don't spring out of bed simultaneously one morning with a common idea', he wrote. 'Always one man formulates an idea with which to implement a plan, and ... finds that it strikes corresponding chords in other men's minds. Such a man was Walter Gropius.' Another was Serge Diaghilev. A third was Bryan himself, who shared many qualities common to both Gropius and Diaghilev: phenomenal energy and determination, ruthless disregard for financial viability, a passionate faith in the present and a clear vision of the future.

Bryan's plan extended to most areas of national life. 'Give it a few weeks,' he said in his Bauhaus review, 'and then start giving hell to the GLC or your local authorities for that frowstily designed building or dud flyover round the corner: for this is the kind of documentary exhibition that clears the mind and gives us courage'. His clear-sightedness was hard to resist. He made you feel you too could see things with his rigorous and discriminating eye. '*Nothing but the best here!*' boomed Bryan, imitating George VI, who had once been kept waiting for his lunch by Kenneth Clark stopping on the stairs at Windsor to admire the Leonardos.

Bryan (who was left-handed) never learned to use a keyboard or fully mastered joined-up writing, turning in copy that was always a hieroglyphic artwork in itself, set out on a white page in sloping lines of black ink squiggles as clear and cranky, elegant and expressive as himself. The whole text was spliced and spatchcocked (like his conversation) with afterthoughts, codicils, mad diversions and extra goodies encapsulated in balloons crammed into the margins and between the lines. Often there were scratchy little diagrams with flags and arrows, looking as he said himself like the messages the pirates left for one another in *Swallows and Amazons*. His ear for words could be as sharp as his eye for painting but, when it came to writing, he had no discipline whatever. He never used one adjective where five or ten would do. His articles were brilliant but (as he admitted to me once long afterwards) they needed a good deal of fine-tuning – tightening up, smoothing down, sometimes splicing and rejigging, above all brutal cutting – and I learned how to do it page by page at top speed en route straight for the printer. Bryan taught me how to look at contemporary art, and where to find it, but he also taught me more about the finer points of editing than anyone else before or since.

Each article was a nerve-wracking high-wire performance both for him and me. Getting copy out of him in the first place was never easy. I had other difficult contributors, but none to compare with Bryan, who never grasped that at or after the last minute wasn't the ideal time to start an article. Once he arrived in person the day after his deadline to tell me with a perfectly straight face that his copy had blown out of the taxi window on the way. He was a magisterial figure of immense style and distinction, nearly twice my age and size, carrying weight in every sense, but he made me so hopping mad that day that I shut him in my tiny office and refused to let him out until he had produced the piece for which the printer was holding the Arts' front page. He sat down meekly at my desk, while I telephoned an irate BBC producer to assure him untruthfully that Mr Robertson had just left to keep the crucial appointment for which he was already thirty minutes late.

Enthusiasm was at the root of a preposterously overcrowded schedule that sometimes proved too much even for Bryan. What drove him from the start was his vehement rejection of prevailing British apathy and ignorance. His early years had been conditioned by corrosive nostalgia, 'a constricting, inhibiting dross, a false currency and an irrelevance to the exchange of urgently new ideas'. It is hard now to credit the closed, hierarchical and elitist nature of the post-war art world.

His style as art critic was low key and casual. 'Always the suspicious puritan, yours truly has cast around from time to time for grounds to criticise the extraordinary Hockney performance,' he wrote in a description of David Hockney's ravishing *Illustrations for Fourteen Poems from C.P. Cavafy* (1966). 'These drawings and engravings are technically and aesthetically stunning.' He treated his *Spectator* column as a convivial conversation with readers for whom he poured out his knowledge, insights and discoveries with unfailing generosity. For anyone who grew up, like me, loving painting as much as books but with no means of access to the art of the current day, Bryan provided an incomparable education.

'I shall always miss that zest and eagerness,' he wrote in 2002 about one of his oldest friends, the actress Irene Worth, in his last letter to me from hospital. 'That ardour – for life, people, objects, food and drink, places.' The same infectious relish was what Bryan brought to painting and sculpture and, although there may have been subtler or more learned critics, surely none ever conveyed with more compelling urgency the imperatives of art.

John Spurling

John Spurling was a long-standing Robertson friend and colleague, a consistent admirer of Bryan's many talents, and a writer who has done much to keep his memory alive. I interviewed him in his north London home in March 2014.

I remember how I first met Bryan, because it was due to me that he wrote for the *Spectator*. I was a BBC announcer then, a radio announcer, and I used to sit in Continuity listening to music and talks and so on, on the Third Programme. Hilary had just got the job of arts editor of the *Spectator*. This would have been 1965. She hadn't got an art critic and was looking for one. I heard two people giving very interesting talks on the Third Programme – Roy Strong, who was then a curator at the National Portrait Gallery, and Bryan Robertson, who I'd never heard of before, Director of the Whitechapel Gallery. So I said to Hilary that I'd heard two extremely good talks and I suggested that she hire Bryan Robertson to do her modern art and Roy Strong to do her old art, which she did. They both used to write for her, and that was how we got to know Bryan.

He became a friend quite quickly and invited us to shows at the Whitechapel, such as the *New Generation* exhibitions.

Interestingly enough, neither of the Spurlings had previously visited the Whitechapel. 'It was quite late on in the Whitechapel's Robertson programme, so we had to catch up with what this amazing man had done. We attended one show and then the next one he did we were on the catalogue cover looking at things in the previous show. Princess Margaret was on the front.' This is the catalogue for *The New Generation: 1968 Interim*, its cover a sequence of contact prints of previous exhibition openings by Martin Koretz. Among the notables are Hepworth, Moore and Rothenstein. The pipe-smoking John Spurling is clearly recognisable in the last shot on the back cover.

Bryan's great talent, above all, was not only that he had a marvellous eye and was extremely good at hanging and lighting, but he also understood artists and their need for confidence. So I think his greatest asset as the director of a gallery and the encourager of young artists especially was that he brought them together. The American abstract expressionists were then the great figures, and Bryan was at great pains to introduce all the new fledgling artists he was discovering to these now grandees so that they felt 'I'm an artist too, I belong in this society'. This was Bryan's enormous talent, and he did it through dinner parties, drinks parties at the Whitechapel, and through giving all these young artists proper catalogues, treating them as serious artists.

I think the first dinner we had with Bryan was with Colin MacInnes in a restaurant. Bryan then was in quite a snazzy flat just off Sloane Square. He came to dinner with us bringing Robert Hughes who had only been a fortnight in England. He was an ebullient figure then, but the most amazing thing was that Bob Hughes left his address book behind, so we were to send it on. Being a gentleman I didn't want to open this address book, but Hilary, not being a gentleman, did and went through it. It was amazing. He'd been a fortnight in London and he had every name you could possibly think of in the whole social whirl. This was networking plus. It was astounding and opened my eyes to a whole new area of the art world. I always thought you just wrote or painted pictures and if they were good enough you'd succeed. This opened my eyes to another side of the thing altogether.

My first real view of abstract painting was at the Stuyvesant Collection at the Tate [1967] and that was largely collected by Bryan for the Peter Stuyvesant Foundation. I went into that show thinking about abstract art what all good Englishmen thought – that it was a complete con and a waste of time.

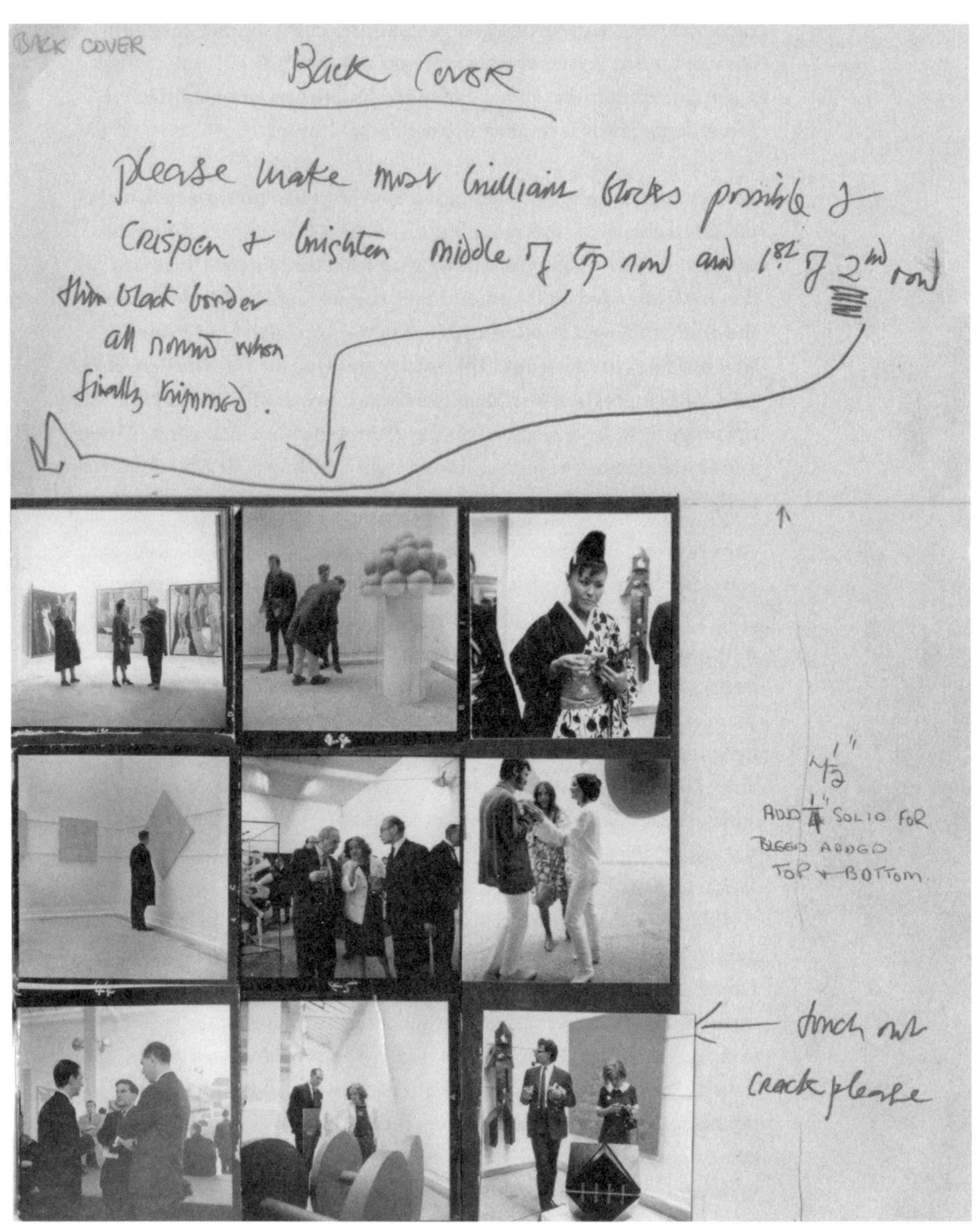

21 BR's instructions to the printer for the back cover artwork of the Whitechapel's *New Generation: 1968 Interim* catalogue, featuring photographs from openings of previous *New Generation* shows. John and Hilary Spurling appear in the photograph on the bottom right.
Photographs by Martin Koretz, Whitechapel Gallery Archive

At the end of the show I'd seen work by Hoyland, Huxley and probably Riley, and suddenly my eyes were opened and I became a complete convert to abstract art. That was Bryan's doing really. I'm sure we wouldn't have gone to it if we hadn't by then known Bryan. I was not then a visual person. I was taught to be one by Hilary, who is a visual person.

Bryan always bought all the latest books. He was a great buyer of books – I'm not sure he was a great reader of books. I often found the cover or marker at about page 20 when going through his books after his death. He also loved passing books on to his friends. Quite late on in his life he sent me a copy of Orhan Pamuk's latest book. I read it and didn't much like it – though I didn't like to say so to Bryan. He'd also sent copies to other friends, including John Hubbard. John, much more outspoken than me, wrote back to Bryan saying thank you for the book but he didn't care for it at all. Bryan said, 'Oh, didn't you? I don't think it was a very good book either.' But he'd bought it because it had very good reviews. I think the reason he didn't get through books was because he spent all his time reading magazines and newspapers.

He got very excited about things. He was a man of huge enthusiasms. That's why he was such a good director of that gallery. He went to concerts and was particularly interested in modern and contemporary music. He kept up with the theatre, but his greatest love was dance. When I wrote my first play after I left the BBC in 1966 my agent sold it to the National Theatre, so my very first production was by the National Theatre Company. Typically Bryan came to the first night and afterwards he said, 'Now we're going off to the Café Royal to celebrate!' For a youngish playwright who was completely dazed by the whole experience this was characteristic Bryan, and I'm sure he did that kind of thing with all his artists too.

Most of the stories one tells about Bryan are slightly comical. If one didn't start by saying that Bryan was a British Diaghilev, was the man who really made English art work in the post-war period, and from whom – I would say – the success of British artists has stemmed, one might portray Bryan as a comic figure. Because he was quite an eccentric and larger than life. Wherever two or three people were gathered together who knew Bryan, he was almost always the main topic of conversation, for his foibles and oddities and whatever the latest story was. But I am in no doubt of the fact that he was 'a very great man'.

He often spoke about his private life. He proclaimed himself to be bisexual, though I think he was mostly homosexual actually. But he did make overtures to at least one lady I know of, Bridget Riley, and he did propose marriage to her. They were very close but had a huge falling-out at some stage. Bryan loved being with women; whether he would have loved being in bed with them is another question. But he loved their company – at least as much as men, if not more. Later on in his life he had huge fallings-out with many of the women to whom he'd been very close. Deanna Petherbridge for instance. With Bridget. He had a coterie of rich ladies from America, and I don't think he fell out with them because he only saw them occasionally.

Bryan was very keen on everything modern and on the modernist programme, as it were – that you went with the new, which was why he was always trying to keep up with concerts of new music, obviously new art and new writing also. If you ever argued against anything modernist, Bryan got quite heated. He didn't like you criticising what was almost a faith. He could be touchy – I expect it depended upon how he was feeling at that minute. One has to bear in mind all the time with Bryan that he was an asthmatic and it affected him all his life. But with Bryan one could never tell whether it was really the asthma which was preventing him keeping his date with you, or whether it was just convenient – as no doubt it was as a child, not to go to school. There's no doubt that he was asthmatic and it was a terrible burden to him and he'd learned to deal with it, but it also I think quite often was an excuse. An excuse probably to himself in a way – if you're always feeling under par it requires an extra energy injection to make you do something. Even when one's in good health, one has to force oneself to one's desk very often to get writing. And Bryan never could force himself to his desk to get writing!

The point about Bryan was that he needed people clearing up behind him. He only had one of them at the Whitechapel (Tejas Englesmith), but at the Tate – if he'd got the job – he would have had several and they would have done all the nitty-gritty which Bryan didn't do. He'd have done all the brilliant stuff at the front, chatting up people who would give art or money to the Tate, and just collecting wonderful stuff. Instead of which he got a nightmare job in America at a new university in New York State. He started buying things for their collection, and then it all crumbled, I think partly because of Bryan's manner of going on and unreliability. His real disaster was that at the same time as he went to America he'd been asked to do for the RA a huge show of British art from the beginning – a really grand showing. Bryan was very keen and full of ideas and lists of artists. And he went off to America with these lists and enthusiasm and then did nothing. Two or three years later the RA said are you going ahead with this show? And he wasn't. He'd done nothing. From that moment on the RA would never use him again. And we didn't get this great show of British art, which if it had been done by Bryan would have been a knock-out. It was a great loss – but the greatest loss was to him. It gave him a very bad reputation from then on.

He did a series of shows when he came back, at the Warwick Arts Trust through his friend Milton Grundy who was a tax lawyer [and Director of the Warwick Arts Trust]. He did that for six years, I think, wonderful shows with wonderful but rather expensive catalogues. Eventually the patience of Milton Grundy ran out – and no doubt the purse. He also did a stint in Hilary's old job as arts editor of the *Spectator*. I can't imagine him being an editor. His own writings – and he did quite a lot of journalism – were always destroyed by not having an editor who'd press him to get going on it before the very last minute. He was always missing deadlines which brought him to the point of panic and made him write dreadful articles, I think, which were just lists of names, comparing the artists he was writing about. That's how he sabotaged himself.

When Bryan did a show it was beautiful (like Dufy at the Hayward), but anyone who had worked with him didn't wish to work with him again. That is very Diaghilev. He liked young people very much. He was one of those people who expands in the presence of young people and they gave him a sense of new energy. Up to a certain point in his life he was always finding new artists to be enthusiastic about. He was always wanting to get in with the new. With Elisabeth Vellacott – he felt she was outside what his life's work had been, she was something from the past. He wasn't good at visiting her in later years yet she adored him. She was very lonely and Bryan was her great sponsor, but latterly I would say he was not one of the greatest backers of Vellacott.

He was a wonderful guest usually – it slightly depended on his mood and who else was there. He came often to dinner with us. He could be a bit grisly. Slightly varying – he was a person of strong moods. When he was on form he was the most charming guest and host. One dinner I went to at his place in the eighties or nineties, when Hilary wasn't there, [the guests] were invited at 9pm for dinner. I arrived at about quarter or twenty past. Bryan let me in. He was looking a little bit harassed and sweaty. A good many of his guests, there were at least twelve of us, I think, were already in the sitting room upstairs drinking very strong Negronis, which was Bryan's favourite before-dinner drink, but absolutely lethal. I noticed as Bryan handed me my drink that the shopping bags containing the dinner were still on the floor of the kitchen, so no preparations had yet been made. We finally dined at about 11.30 or 11.45, I think. There was soup to start with. At that point, the man next to me – I don't know who he was, a small man – fell asleep with his head on the table like the dormouse in Alice in Wonderland. That was the worst I ever knew.

He loved his house. He had a study upstairs but also worked on the dining-room table. When only one or two came to dinner he pushed his papers and books up one end, but if more came then the table would be cleared. He had quite a small patch of garden but would have professional people to clear up the garden and replant it. He couldn't sustain it – it would all have to be redone two years later. The same was true of the pets he had. He had a dog at one stage – that was a disaster – and he also had at least one cat. But he didn't have the staying power to look after them.

Bryan always bought the best and he didn't believe in skimping in any way. He was typical of that kind of person who is always on the edge of disaster financially but was never known to go anywhere by public transport, always a taxi. He had style. He went to the best restaurants, he bought books and he very often 'bought' art. He didn't always pay for it – as with the big Hubbard he had. He bought a good house. He died leaving all those wonderful paintings to galleries – the Fitzwilliam and Kettle's Yard primarily. He was a very warm friend, very loyal and very supportive. His great talent was to give confidence. To the extent that as a critic, he probably wasn't critical enough. If it was an artist he knew and liked he couldn't really say anything bad about them. He didn't have a critic's temperament at all. He was a celebrator and enthusiast, a great maker of things to happen.

Australia and its artists

Some saw Kenneth Clark as the influence behind Bryan's advocacy of Australian painting, and there's no doubt that Clark would have encouraged Robertson's enthusiasm, but he was his own man in this, as in so much else, mounting a series of exhibitions at the Whitechapel to showcase Australian art in general and certain artists in particular. Simon Pierse, in his excellent and informative book *Australian Art and Artists in London, 1950–1965* (2012), identifies that fifteen-year boom period as an extraordinary one in which 'Australian painting was "discovered", augmented, historicized, and finally, re-absorbed back into the UK market'. Robertson was at the centre of this particular whirlpool, presenting a new and dynamic school of painting to the British public. Clark had met and admired Sidney Nolan as early as 1949 when he first visited Australia, but Robertson was not far behind, encountering the Australian's work in Cambridge in 1951 at the Heffer Gallery.

Clark did not discover Nolan, but he did support him, working away behind the scenes to further his reputation in England. As Nolan wrote poetically to Clark: 'One can travel by the stars, but one also needs a compass, and perhaps more than anyone you have provided that for painters.' In 1953, the New Burlington Galleries put on an exhibition proposed by Clark, entitled *Twelve Australian Artists*. Among the artists were Nolan and Arthur Boyd, and several less well-known names along with William Dobell and Russell Drysdale. So the Aussie invasion was already well underway before Bryan's Australian shows in the East End.

In the catalogue for Nolan's 1957 Whitechapel exhibition Robertson wrote:

Nolan works swiftly, with intense concentration, in short, sharp sporadic outbursts of activity. The poetic image, whatever it may be, is clearly established in his mind at the outset and very little in his painting is achieved fortuitously. Paint, colour, structure and tonality are subordinate to this almost obsessively maintained imagery. On occasion, his work in relation to Australia is not dissimilar in flavour and character to the music of Aaron Copland in relation to America, a composer at home among the innovations of twentieth-century musical composition but striving always to create a kind of folk music, relating specifically to America, but deriving a great deal of its vivacity and warmth from indigenous American themes which he expands and transforms by his keen sense of the poetic imagery and atmosphere that spring from certain localities and ways of living …

First of all, it seems clear that Nolan is retaining and developing all his native freshness of approach and clarity of gaze. Everything that he finds in his physical (or imaginary) travels is detonated by an alert and highly personal element of surprise. He is not constricted by art history or affected by the muddled aesthetics and frequently inept findings of contemporary European art. His own work is deeply civilized and at all times the product of a radiant intelligence, but his point of view is his own, owes very little to the work of the immediate past or present in Europe, and will surely develop from its own drive and momentum. Nolan relates everything he sees or reads or hears to life, present-day life at this particular moment. This process might well have been reversed when he came to Europe: so many artists arriving in Europe from other continents try to relate everything they see back to everything they have read and this can end in a kind of self-conscious sterility.

Later, Robertson stated that Nolan achieved 'what can only be termed star status' with this exhibition.

It has been suggested that Bryan mounted the 1960 retrospective show of Roy de Maistre to please his friend John Rothenstein, Director of the Tate, who greatly favoured this artist, and who actually wrote the catalogue essay. However, a show of de Maistre's work fitted snugly into Bryan's survey of contemporary Australian painting, whilst also making a useful link with Francis Bacon, whose mentor the older artist was for a time. In a long essay on Brett Whiteley, composed many years later, Bryan wrote: 'Sitting in de Maistre's studio on an Art Deco couch designed thirty years earlier by Bacon, I became increasingly interested in Australia, Australian art and in the creativity of an exceptional number of Australian writers, designers, dancers and singers who appeared to be reaching a peak of recognised activity.' And in his preface to the Whitechapel catalogue Robertson wrote:

Roy de Maistre is a revolutionary figure in the history of Australian art. The present exhibition has been assembled in order to pay a belated tribute to this simple historical fact and to survey his very personal contribution to European painting.

The strength, the wide range, and the particular flavour of Roy de Maistre's work will be apparent in this exhibition. His presence on the English and European scene for the past forty years has enriched the language of our painting as well as the art of his own native country, which is now producing some of the most original and gifted artists in the world today. The next decade will see the full impact of their work in other continents. Many of them know the part that Roy de Maistre has already played in making their freedom possible, for he has added the formal vocabulary of his time to his own native sensibilities and conditioning and in doing this he has forged a language which is true both to his personal origin and to his original creative impulse as an artist.

In 1961, Robertson mounted a group exhibition at the Whitechapel, *Recent Australian Painting*, which was to anticipate a similar survey at the Tate by two years. The show aroused a certain amount of controversy, both at the time and since, but then nearly all such survey exhibitions have their detractors. Robertson chose to depict Australia as a remote and exotic land (which to many of the gallery visitors it presumably was), and for the exhibition opening filled the gallery with enormous tropical trees and plants. (Robertson the impresario at full-throttle.) He was criticised for skewing the selection towards his own predilection for abstract art (in the wake of his famous Pollock show), but actually the balance between abstract and figurative was fairly maintained. After all, abstraction in Australia had its own established tradition, dating back to the 1930s, and could scarcely be invented, or imposed upon the country, by an English curator. And the artists Bryan particularly admired, such as Nolan and Boyd, could hardly be termed abstract.

However, Robertson did inevitably present his own interpretation of contemporary Australian painting. As Pierse has written:

He shaped the exhibition in such a way that its climax would be three paintings by Brett Whiteley (1939–92), then just twenty-two years old and living in London. Robertson had chosen two of these paintings from Whiteley's Ladbroke Grove studio, paintings which he described as 'of startling maturity, richness and spiritual and imaginative poise, perfectly at ease in their medium and wholly original'.

The catalogue essay was written by the twenty-three-year-old Robert Hughes, still living in Sydney, whom Bryan had visited in March 1960 on his Australian research trip to discuss this introduction. In a typical Robertson way, the matter was raised and then left hanging until the last moment. Hughes wrote early in 1961 to say he was worried because

'I seem to be the only person to have heard anything substantial from you in the past nine months and consequently I am eternally plagued by nervous artists, who seem inclined to blame everything on me.'

Robertson was inevitably criticised for employing so young and inexperienced a writer for this important catalogue, but Bryan was no doubt activated by a conspiratorial fellow-feeling, as well as his admiration for Hughes's gifts. Bryan always admired youthful talent, and he himself had taken over the Whitechapel aged twenty-seven, so there was precedent. In the event, the essay was 'witty, outspoken and controversial', to quote Pierse. Robertson called it 'fresh, lively and crisply written', but requested that certain passages be edited out for the sake of diplomatic relations with funding bodies and Australian officialdom. Hughes later admitted that there were also certain errors of fact in his piece but that, if he wasn't exactly proud of it, 'it was okay for a twenty-three-year-old'.

The exhibition was a great success and the private view a lavish party at which feelings ran inevitably high, before some twenty guests adjourned to Soho for dinner. Barbara Blackman, first wife of the painter Charles Blackman, captured the evening in her autobiography *Glass after Glass* (1997):

I sit next to Bryan Robertson, who curated it all. The Boyds, Rowells, Underhills, Keith Vaughan, Prunella Clough, Francis Bacon, Brett Whiteley, Roy de Maistre all there. Bacon sits opposite but slips through our fingers by getting quickly and rottenly drunk. Vaughan seems to think he is in muddy waters amid this Aussie stream. Prunella has much in reserve. Brett wants everything to have a name and an answer – When was I last chocko? Am I preggers? Is art returning to Braque? Is Prunella lesbian? Is marriage serious? How urgent and irritating the young ones are. Makes me feel like still water, water that reflects, not runs rapids.

In 1962 Robertson was the recipient of a Ford Foundation Grant to visit New York to research recent trends in American painting, and he invited the Australian artist Lawrence Daws (born 1927) to accompany him. It was an exciting trip for Daws, who met through Robertson some of his artist heroes, such as Rothko, Motherwell and Helen Frankenthaler, Hans Hofmann, Johns and Rauschenberg. There was also a week of dinner parties with Lee Krasner and meetings with such of Bryan's friends as the novelist Dawn Powell. (From her 1954 novel *The Wicked Pavilion*: 'Briggs had hoped for assignments in the field of sports but the editor felt that literary training and education were required for that, whereas art was a department where inexperience and ignorance would not be noticed.') Robertson seemed continually on the phone, Daws recalled, 'opening up conduits and networks all over the place' and 'being wooed by Leo Castelli' and others over possible shows in London.

In June and July 1962 Robertson showed the work of Arthur Boyd at the Whitechapel, writing in the catalogue preface:

The best of Australian painting has a startling vivacity and urgency which comes from an energetic belief in life, personal responses to life, and the idea of an expanding future. This painting, whether abstract or figurative, has also an extraordinary quality of unselfconsciousness, like Australian behaviour. If you are born a long way away from the mainstreams of European thought and tradition, you make things up for yourself without worrying too much about your appearance as you go through invented motions of habit, or delve into your own unfolding imagination.

Boyd is also a natural aristocrat with a singularly noble mind and purpose in life. This is matched by his great gifts as an artist which have already been clearly recognized in London. His sets and costumes for Stravinsky's *Renard* at the Edinburgh Festival of 1961 were possibly the most brilliant designs for the English stage in a decade. Meanwhile, his impulse as a painter has acquired a fresh urgency and momentum which this exhibition will, I hope, demonstrate. His presence on the London scene, with a handful of younger Australian painters, is a happy and tonic event which can do nothing but act as a stimulant to British art as a whole.

Nolan was still very much a focus of interest when a Sidney Nolan monograph was published in 1961 by Thames & Hudson, the text divided between three authors. Kenneth Clark contributed an introduction, Colin MacInnes an essay entitled 'The Search for an Australian Myth in Painting', and Bryan the biography and chronology of the pictures. He also edited the book. Here Bryan evaluates and evokes one of Nolan's best-known subjects, the Ned Kelly paintings of 1946–7:

These were the most fully integrated paintings to come from Nolan so far: fresh and vivacious, with a poetic intensity of great depth and feeling. They also combined lyrical elements with some of the pathos of knockabout farce in a new and extraordinary way. The tragedy of the Kelly story was in the paintings, undiminished; but the means taken to underline this tragedy were unorthodox and fantastic. Nolan's ability to register an image in the lightest and most insubstantial manner became clear.

From this time onwards, much of his work was to have something of the quality of a magic lantern image projected on a screen. An anonymity of handling in the use of pigment became a highly personal distinguishing trait in Nolan's technique, but the bland surfaces are always counterbalanced by extreme precision of tonal construction and great freshness and originality of colour. The figures in the paintings are almost without formal structure, like personages constructed by finger painting – which Nolan has often practised in his smaller studies, also using sponges and many other implements to arrive at particular effects of texture.

Later in the same essay Robertson wrote:

His drawings are little known or appreciated, and the occasionally weightless quality of his painting has led some observers to suppose that draughtsmanship in the traditional sense of the word is not among his gifts. But Nolan has frequently shown himself to be a master of pure line, with complete authority over formal structure when the occasion arises. Other drawings reveal, as in the painting, that instinctive capacity to realise all the inflections of tonality. Some drawings provide us with a parallel to an essential aspect of Nolan's personality: the lively and disturbing ability to merge together the soft, dreamy, feathery, graphic sensibility of a Bonnard with the incisive wit and wry wilfulness of line to be found in a drawing by Steinberg.

This aspect of Nolan's art reflects a distinct side of his personality as a man. A gentle and mildly diffident charm conceals the essential toughness of the man's intellect and powers of imagination. Quiet, abstemious, self-possessed, and yet gregarious, Nolan leads a methodical and carefully planned existence, alternating usually between travel or exposure to experience and phases of retrenchment, contemplation and work. As an artist, he never relaxes in the pursuit of visual experience and analysis, but his painting comes in bursts of three or four weeks' duration with many idle weeks or even months between. To meet and converse with, he combines a sharp eye and poetic quick wit with an irreverent humour and flair for the irrational and absurd. His imagination is at once precise and sensible, and extremely fantastic: a tightrope between Cocteau and Groucho Marx, and very Australian.

The coda to Robertson's intense involvement with Australian art came with the publication of the monograph *Brett Whiteley: Art and Life*, published again by Thames & Hudson, this time in 1995. It was essentially Barry Pearce's book, to which Robertson contributed an essay on Whiteley's London years. Bryan recalled their first meeting:

He seemed almost absurdly young and boyish and was in fact only about twenty-one, slight in build, restless, wiry, at once cheeky and delicate in his approach – I was thirty-five, and he didn't at first quite know how to take me, or deal with me – and pink-faced from the Italian sun, wearing T-shirt and cotton pants, with an almost round crop of tight, red-gold curls, subtle and jokey in talk, darting about all over the gallery, filled with wit and bravado and enthusiasm for Europe, for Italian painting – for life. He was naturally intrigued to know that I was planning a big show of

Australian painting for Whitechapel for the following year. Plans were in the penultimate stage. Brett danced and feinted round me like a friendly boxer, full of questions and challenges: a born goader to anyone even remotely in authority.

Robertson is unequivocal about the impact of Whiteley's art:

This was one of the great moments of my life in any studio. The paintings were of startling maturity, richness and spiritual and imaginative poise, perfectly at ease in their medium and wholly original. It was hard to believe that they were by such a young artist. The images weren't merely sophisticated or knowing but totally realised in depth, filled with youthful panache and energy and above all a personal vision.

Bryan also recalled the social scene:

There were a lot of crowded and informal parties at my flat in Chelsea, to which Brett and Wendy came often, as well as to parties at the Whitechapel Gallery after the opening of each show. Brett certainly met Rauschenberg in London at my flat, and Robert Motherwell and Helen Frankenthaler when they were over from New York, as well as Clement Greenberg, Rothko and Newman. For this was still the time when American art was having its maximum impact in Europe and most centrally in London.

Robertson, with characteristic generosity, gave Sunday lunch-parties at his home, introducing the Australians to the British artists. He was known for his stylish hospitality after Whitechapel openings when trays of whisky and gin and tonic were handed around. He also offered practical help, and introduced at least three Australian artists – Lawrence Daws, Charles Blackman and Brett Whiteley – to the directors of the Matthiesen Gallery (John Sing and Stephanie Mason), thus securing for them their first one-man shows in London. But the party was drawing to a close. After the 1960s, Robertson later wrote: 'In art, minimalism, politico-social art, conceptual themes and art-and-language arrived, and painting itself, including Australian painting, was pushed to one side.' And Bryan drafted this in a letter: 'By the mid-sixties (or a little later) I'd switched off from Australian painting – in London that is – because what had been a fairly good situation there for the acceptance of, indeed strong admiration for, Australian painting, had slackened and then dispersed by the arrival of too much weak stuff.'

One of Bryan's less obvious Aussie achievements was to recognise the talents of Robert Hughes and transplant him to London. Although Hughes would undoubtedly have made his way to England sooner or later, Bryan gave him a good reason to leave Australia when he did. He first came over for *Recent Australian Painting* at the Whitechapel in 1961,

and was in London intermittently in the early 1960s, staying in rooms at Albany in 1962 before settling in London in 1965. He wrote for a variety of publications, including the *Spectator*, the *Daily Telegraph*, the *Times* and the *Observer*, and contributed to the London version of *Oz*. Hughes was closely involved with Robertson's *New Generation* exhibitions – both as writer (introduction and notes, 1966), and selecting (with Norman Reid) those artists to whom to award the bursaries. He was living in Bryan's flat at 51 Draycott Place in Chelsea in 1965, and complaining that the telephone had been cut off, as Bryan owed £151 for the last quarter's long-distance phone calls. Later Bob took over the apartment when Bryan went abroad. In the later sixties he lived at Hanover Gate Mansions. In 1970 he was appointed art critic for *Time* magazine and moved to New York, thus leaving England for America at the same time as Bryan. Hughes went on to international success as a writer and broadcaster, with his BBC TV series *The Shock of the New* (1980) and his book *The Fatal Shore: The Epic of Australia's Founding* (1986). Hughes sported a big mop of hair in his early TV appearances, and (according to Paul Huxley) Bryan rechristened his series 'The Shock of the Hair', a welcome variant on the more familiar 'The Shock of the Roo'. In a draft review of Hughes's volume of essays, *Nothing if Not Critical*, published in 1990, Robertson described the author as 'never small-minded or confined by prejudice', and as 'writing the best art criticism for popular consumption in the English language'.

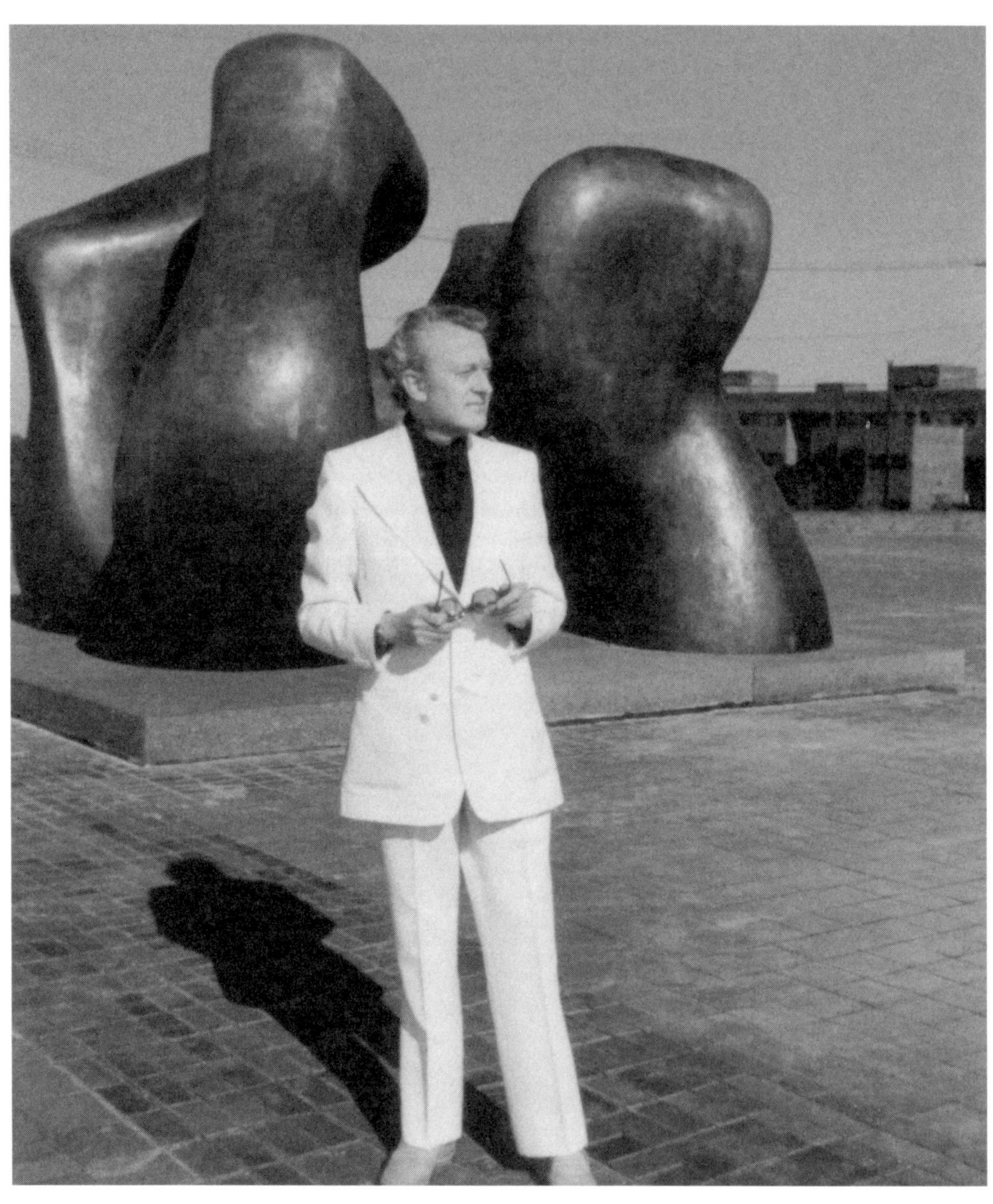

22 BR in front of Henry Moore's *Large Two Forms* (1969) at the Neuberger Museum, Purchase College, State University of New York, *c.*1975.

The decade 1969–1979

1969 – A crucial year

Leaving the Whitechapel, although in some ways a planned and strategic career move, was also immensely traumatic for Bryan. He had lost his power base and his artistic home, and had yet to establish another one. Adventures in America beckoned but there was a time gap before he was due to take up his new job as Director of the Neuberger Museum at Purchase College, State University of New York, in 1970. In the meantime he was involved with a wide-ranging scheme to reorganise the English art world with a new National Archive of Modern Art. It was an ambitious project, and one sadly doomed to failure. Perhaps deep down Bryan realised this. Certainly he was feeling sensitive and vulnerable, but his friends rallied round. The following is an extract from a letter to Irene Worth from Bryan (dated 11 February 1969), thanking her for her support:

Irene, my dearest friend, I do thank you most warmly – and with the liveliest sense of what you've done – for everything you did, when pressed yourself by problems and anxieties no doubt, for me before you went away. I was and am and will always be more touched than you can imagine. And I do cherish you for it all, so much.

The latest as you doubtless know is a huge piece in *Studio International* on me by Maurice de Sausmarez going back to 1942(!); and this very morning the most marvellous tribute in the *Times* signed by everyone I most respect, from Henry Moore to Mark Rothko – 17 signatures in caps. It reads like Magna Carta. I am now St Bryan, and looking increasingly like the classier type of Zurbarán painting. Enough.

I am back in action. Wrote to Lord Goodman, was at once invited to breakfast so that he could give proper time to me and the scheme, thought it brilliant and 'essential for England', has set up a meeting for me, him, John Pope Hennessy, Noel Annan (London Univ) and Asa Briggs (Sussex Univ). Don't know when the meeting will be yet. In meantime I'm talking separately to these people, one by one, explaining the plan. Total enthusiasm and belief so far. Goodman told me I was subject of much concern to him as I had genius (yes!) which had to be used in the right way etc etc, and he was so glad I'd come into the open and 'declared myself'. He was full of plans to implement the scheme. If it comes off, England would have something of crucial importance for the future, way ahead as a concept of any mus. of mod. art. I am transformed. I wrote a long 'head' piece for the *Times* on the horrific plans for the Tate extension, outlining my own plan for the re-distribution and division of the collections. Result – a furore in which every single member of the so called establishment has backed me up to the hilt. What is going on? It's been like a mad house. End result: a motion in Parliament demanding a public enquiry into the affairs of the Tate apropos the extension and the 'confusion of the collections'. How about that? Right now, I can do no wrong. Better watch it. Goodman told me my *Times* piece was much discussed by himself and the Minister, and both agreed totally with it.

A trio of letters

Unedited transcription of these draft letters gives the best and most direct account of Bryan's thinking at this time about his future role in the arts in England and the States. His plans for a National Archive of Modern Art were more theoretical than practical, but his undoubted enthusiasm carried him – and often his interlocutors – along regardless. Bryan did not admire William Coldstream as an artist, but he liked him personally and knew his value as a committee man. Besides being a Whitechapel trustee, Coldstream was Chairman of the National Advisory Council on Art Education (1958–71), which published the Coldstream Report in 1960; Vice Chairman of the Arts Council; and a trustee of the National Gallery. Hugh Willatt, the recipient of the third letter, was a lawyer and arts administrator married to Bryan's old friend the artist Evelyn Gibbs.

[1] To Lord Goodman, Chairman of the Arts Council (probably February 1969)

Dear Lord Goodman,

It was kind of you, as always, to find time to talk to me over breakfast the other day. I have been considering the substance of our conversation, and such issues as are known to me, and have arrived at the following conclusions.

1. I do not want to submit myself to public competition for the Director of Art appointment at the Arts Council because I did so once before for the Directorship of the Tate, and discovered that the machinations at work among the trustees lacked the objectivity and freedom from prior commitment requisite for any public appointment by open competition. This is to put it mildly: Lawrence Gowing, with the advantage of being already a Trustee, had been promised the job and openly arranged his life accordingly long before anyone was interviewed. He was eventually sacrificed, in the light of public as well as official feeling; but the proceedings before and even after that event did not convince me as a scrupulous examination.

2. I feel that my record and authority are now sufficiently known both in this country and abroad: in this light I would, of course, have considered a direct invitation from the Council.

3. You very reasonably asked me how I got on with Coldstream. We have not met for a year or two; he was for a long while a Trustee at Whitechapel so is aware of the strenuous difficulties regarding insufficient income and staff which prevailed there. I believe he recognizes what was achieved in the face of those difficulties, although I imagine the exhibitions policy might not always have reflected his taste. He eventually had to resign from the Whitechapel trustees some years back because he could not find time, among all his other committee work, to attend meetings.

I believe that at this particular stage in art in this country what I think of Coldstream is far more relevant to an increasingly difficult situation in the English art world than any opinion Coldstream may have of me. If this is not recognized, as a symbol of a new attitude at the Council, the new atmosphere there which you agreed might be desirable if introduced by me, will never be generated.

My attitude to individuals concerned with the Council, including Bill Coldstream, is wholly benign. But an old guard has been at work for a very long while in national art life: power is dear to them, their authority and insights are sometimes questionable, at variance with reality or non-existent. It is time this old guard were replaced.

4. I shall not take up the American Directorship, if and when it materializes, for eighteen months. During this time, I shall be occupied with fulfilling commitments for books, and other writing. But I should be delighted if I might be of service to the Council in any advisory capacity that might be useful and should pursue this with diligence, enthusiasm – and, as always, the warmest regard for the Council's purpose as well as for its hard working and devoted officials. At present, I am purchasing sculpture during the current financial year for the Council's collection but as you know, I like to be fully stretched and would like to do more for the Council if there is an opportunity, e.g. Art Panel, I am suggesting certain exhibitions, for consideration.

5. I still hope that my scheme, which you have kindly put forward, for a National Archive of Modern Art, may materialize; and I believe, as you know, that it could provide the ICA with a rationale and concrete usefulness at present lacking in that institution. I will certainly work on the Archive for an indefinite period if it is launched. If I can help the ICA in any advisory way I should also be willing to give time to their problems. There is doubtless no lack of advisory opinion, with money as the prevailing barrier, but policy sometimes stimulates financial backing and my low opinion of the policies so far pursued by the ICA is widely shared.

And now, may I say how keenly I enjoy our meetings whenever they occur; how grateful I am to you for your backing over my own endeavours; and how very greatly I relish the sagacity you have continuously brought to the difficulties faced by the English art world. You have made things better, everywhere, and we all honour you for this, and much else.

[2] To Lord Goodman (dated 18 April 1969)

Dear Arnold Goodman,

It was very good of you to agree, on the telephone the other day, to give me a reference for New York State University, especially as you had not been prepared for the news owing to my initial letter to you going astray – it was sent to your private address about three weeks ago.

To recapitulate briefly: I want very much to pursue the idea of this new art institution for England, through your good offices and the Arts Council and the universities, but the economic position being what it is I feel that I should enter into some form of safeguard for myself for the future, at the same time.

When I was in New York recently I was asked by Gibson Danes, the Dean of Fine Arts at New York State University, if I would be interested enough to put myself forward for the job of Director of a large new museum which Philip Johnson is building for New York State University at a new campus, given up to the fine arts, just outside New York City [now the Neuberger Museum of Art]. There will be three or four theatres, three or four concert halls, very important new schools of music, drama, choreography and dance, and the fine arts in general. At this museum, I would build up a permanent collection of modern art and put on large temporary exhibitions. Really it would be like Whitechapel on a bigger and better endowed scale. And, of course, for the first time in my life, there would be a decent salary. Lastly, it would mean that I should not at all be turning my back on England as there would be lengthy university vacations, and I should retain my house in London.

Sir Kenneth Clark, Henry Moore, Francis Watson (Wallace Collection and one of the Whitechapel trustees) are all giving me references, but a few words from you as Chairman of the Arts Council, which has been so closely connected with Whitechapel, would be invaluable. I shall be most grateful for your help.

If I get the job, it would not start until next summer: the museum itself will not be ready until the summer of 1971.

With kind greetings, etc.

[3] Letter to Hugh Willatt, Secretary-General of the Arts Council (dated 29 October 1969)

Dear Hugh,

You will remember that it was left to me, after our lunch together some time back, to write to you with an approximate programme of the ways in which I might be of service to the Council in an advisory role. Since then, two things have happened which clear the air completely: first, my appointment has been confirmed as Director of the new Museum which Philip Johnson is building (for the State University of New York); and, very shortly afterwards, Robin Campbell's succession as Director of Art [at the Arts Council] was settled.

The decision regarding Robin delights me: I have a high regard for him, and we get on well together. I have already written him a long letter containing, among other matters, proposals for certain exhibitions which I believe are worthy projects: one in particular, concerning Bridget Riley, needs urgent attention because the factors surrounding this exhibition are already established and the Council's participation, if forthcoming, has to be resolved quickly.

If you can find time, could you glance at the facts outlined in that letter? It is important, I'm certain, in this instance to co-ordinate with the initiative shown on the Continent: from the point of view of the prestige of English art abroad, the earning capacity abroad of a major English artist (for economically England alone cannot support artists of this calibre) and as part of the English move toward closer ties with Europe. I know that you work, very arduously, at a higher level than mere 'exhibitions policy'; but if there are any complications over the Bridget Riley plan (though I cannot envisage any) could you and Robin and myself have a brief talk together before the project is turned over to Panel discussion? There are many highly relevant aspects of the Riley show which cannot be compressed into a letter.

Now for my main purpose in writing to you. The job in America is unique and at the highest level: I have had to wait so long for a decision because the competition was phenomenal: there were hordes of applications from all over the academic world in the States, as well as from the Museum of Modern Art and the Metropolitan. I shall be Director of the Museum, with a great collection from which to build, as well as the task of organizing about two very spectacular shows each year. Nelson Rockefeller is giving his collection to the Museum and they expect to get the Jacques Lipchitz collection of antiquities and primitive art.

I have also been given the status of full Professorship: so that I can play an effective part in inter-departmental decisions as well as conduct an occasional seminar with graduate or undergraduate students: but this side of the job will be minimal. I shall also be expected to travel and keep in touch with Europe: and of course the University vacations mean that I shall retain my house in London and spend long periods here annually. As I think I explained, the Museum is part of a new complex devoted to the arts on a scale that is quite without precedent, anywhere: around the Museum will be four theatres, three concert halls, and Schools of music, drama, and ballet. The Fine Arts faculty is divided between art history studies, like our Courtauld, and studios and workshops for painters and sculptors. The equipment and technology involved, and the overall budget, are all phenomenal. Pierre Boulez is to be the first resident composer: Robert Motherwell, the first resident artist. I shall have to pay some visits to America from April onward: but I do not completely take up the post until next October.

This means that I could fulfill the advisory role with the Council to quite a reasonable extent for a year, from now until October of 1970. From then on, I firmly believe that it would be in the interests of the Council to have direct contact with an Englishman in America as centrally placed as I shall be: with access to all the official and unofficial thinking and planning in the art world. I am certain that this liaison, however the role is described, would be invaluable for both sides, as it were; and I know that the Americans strongly welcome the possibility. I am certain that many economies could be effected, and certain acts of co-ordination; whilst very relevant insights and practical information could be freely exchanged, bearing in mind that my context will involve all the arts, as well as museum and exhibition policy throughout the States.

As I am deeply committed to British art, I shall spend enough time here and be in sufficient touch generally to know what the issues and problems are in England. My concern will be constant.

Until I move over to America, I should like to prepare reports on a regular basis, and offer practical advice regarding any matters which present problems. There is general policy to consider as well as individual facets. I am absolutely independent of any faction in the art world (and have always struggled to maintain this freedom): and knowing of the general concern over the work of the Council on the art side, which is shared by many sectors of opinion, I believe that I could also offer something really constructive with regard to your issues that have developed so rapidly in the last year or two.

I shall spend a certain amount of time on the Continent, on and off, during the next few months: the Italian government has asked me to prepare an exhibition of Italian Style in the post-war period, ranging from architecture and industrial design through to fine art, stage design, bards, typewriters, clothes. This means that I shall be very well informed about personnel over a very wide field in addition to the art world. All this information, as a file or dossier, would be useful to the Council. There are many other things.

In general, I should like also to report on the needs, occasionally, of particular artists who might be having a hard time economically, working along difficult lines in new areas of classification: suggest exhibitions or other schemes which might benefit the public as well as the artists: help discretely with public relations (there is too widespread a feeling that Council officials are for ever sealed off inside HQ and do not put in appearances where they are due): and report back with information from wherever my work and interests take me. There is much else, but I do not want to weary you with a longer letter.

I should like a decent retainer for the current year, and the appointment should be formally phrased and announced. This would give my role a reasonable degree of stability, and would please quite a lot of people as well as clearing the air generally. I must stress that I have no thought whatever of committing the Council to anything, anywhere, appearing in any confusing light of 'interpreter' for the Council's art policy: or acting in any way without reference to yourself or Robin. I should simply be engaged in reporting to the Council on matters which would seem either urgent or relevant as long term considerations.

In America, I would like to sustain the link which would then require another dimension. I could become nominal or could be restricted to occasional (and limited) expenses. Any other remuneration could be based on specific reports, or periods of practical work achieved back here in London. Over all this is the fact that Robin, yourself, and your other relevant colleagues, would not be committed to any action as a result of my advice, though I would hope always for its serious consideration. As much as anything, I should like to build up a large file of concrete facts, references, and the functions and usefulness (or otherwise) of personnel, as well as plans and projects.

I have written to Arnold Goodman, who liked this plan very much when last we spoke together; but have explained to him that as my last contact was with you, the onus was left with me to report back to you with a rough programme. I have now done so – and shared with him the details. But before a decision is reached I should be grateful if you and I and Robin could have a discussion.

The Ghikas are back at last from Greece and I shall be hopefully arranging that long promised meeting soon. But apart from their absence abroad, I have felt inhibited about social contact with you and Evelyn until now because of all kinds of vague intangibilities to do with professional life – now all happily removed.

With best regards, etc.

Bryan explained the situation further in a letter to an official at the State University of New York (dated 11 June 1969), elucidating the fact that he was being pulled in conflicting directions. He wrote:

But the pressure here from a large number of artists who want me to stay and work in England, and probing from officialdom at a high level (Lord Goodman, Chairman of our national Arts Council) as to whether I really want to go and work in America as opposed to declaring myself for a key position with the Council (Director of Art) has been intensive. As you sensed, it became increasingly difficult for me to hedge indefinitely; especially with no firm ground beneath me regarding America to provide the answer. And an explicit answer has been required: the set-up here is too complex for me to flirt with the Council as a possible secondary consideration to coming to Purchase. It has been an all-or-nothing series of enquiries, including breakfast meetings with Goodman, a hard-worked man with fingers in many aspects of national life (legal adviser to government) and he doesn't do this unless seriously concerned with a particular issue. All this is to explain my sudden s.o.s. and to hope that nobody has been irritated by it.

He concluded:

Your letter tells me all I can possibly expect to hear at this stage. I shall deal with the Arts Council in the way that I really wanted to, anyway, by suggesting an advisory role for about a year. I badly need a fair amount of time for the completion of writing commitments so this will suit me ideally. There is no question of being hung up: I have to fight for free time as it is! But I could not wait until the end of the month to declare myself in this way because too much is involved at a public appointment level.

At much the same time, Bryan was writing to Ellsworth Kelly, a letter full of admiration which was also a kind of discreet notice of being 'Open for Business' – in terms of writing about Kelly or putting on a show of his work, either in England or in the USA. At this juncture, Bryan seemed to be keen to keep as many irons in the fire as possible. Certainly he was marshalling considerable support for his future career plans. Francis Watson, Director of the Wallace Collection, had been one of Bryan's Whitechapel trustees, and was also a referee for his application to Purchase, along with Rothko, Moore, K Clark and Arnold Goodman. Heavy guns indeed.

Adventures in the USA: the Neuberger Museum, 1970–1975

Bryan took up his post as Director of the Neuberger Museum at Purchase College, State University of New York, on 1 July 1970, with an annual salary of $20,000. I do not propose to write at any length about Bryan's

years at Purchase: the job was the wrong one for a man of his gifts and administrative confusions, and he got on the wrong side of his hosts. Paul Huxley described the situation:

He didn't really stick up for himself. He wasn't politically tough. That was one of the problems of arriving at a new campus when he came to New York with all the infighting of the academic world. It's highly competitive, and there he was, parachuted in, never been part of any organisation other than the Whitechapel which he had been head of. Feuding academics would have made mincemeat of him. There are aspects of America which are curious. In many respects they warm immensely to the British and see us as friends, are charmed by our accents and see us as part of their origins. But there's another side to the coin. A sort of anger at the memory of their history, and they can be very vengeful about it. And that, I'm sure, would have come out quite a bit in battles and intrigues at the university. But he fought for his side and I think he did marvellously within his ability. He was appointed before the museum was built.

There was no museum to run and in which to install beautiful exhibitions. There was a collection to build up, but not always the funds to pay for it. Bryan often found himself in the awkward position of asking for money, or asking for gifts of art. At the Whitechapel he had been able to dispense patronage by offering artists one-person exhibitions. He was good at giving in this way, just as he was a generous host. Going around with a begging bowl was not in his nature, yet his position compelled him to do it.

Anthony Caro's widow, Sheila, commented during an interview in April 2014:

I think he would have been too English in a way to have gone down terribly well in America. He wasn't really intellectual enough – or perhaps tough enough. I would have said he was very English – with the sense of humour, he didn't take things too seriously. Americans get very serious. I think his sense of humour wouldn't have gone down so well. I think Bob Motherwell liked him very much because Bob was very English/European.

Ken Draper recalled Bryan's Purchase years:

I don't think he was happy with the American period at all. I met him there, and he introduced me to so many people – Frankenthaler and Jasper Johns, Lee Krasner, who he was a great friend with, and the architect Philip Johnson – and they all adored him. But I think the new people he was meeting – I can remember being at a show at MOMA with him – didn't seem to understand his humour.

I remember Bryan saying to me: 'It's very strange: when you're in America and you get back to London, you suddenly feel like a European. You're no longer English, you're European, and you realise just how different the Americans are from the Europeans.' I think that kind of wonderful understatement that he had, used to get lost on the Americans. Then he was miles from anywhere and the museum was still being built, and he had this tiny flat in New York (literally a little bed-sit) and travelling was very difficult for him, just getting from A to B. He was not good on trains, he was used to jumping in a cab. I felt really sad for him. I was there for two weeks with him in New York before I went off round the West Coast, and then I saw him again when I got back before I came back to London.

John Hubbard recalled two of Bryan's most loyal American supporters.

Elaine Malsin and her husband Ray became friends of Bryan's in the 1970s when he was at Purchase New York, running the Neuberger Museum. He needed friends: it was a fraught time for him. Ray Malsin had been a very successful New York businessman and she had been a showgirl, so to my eyes they were very like a couple out of a comic strip by Peter Arno. She was very tall and handsome and he was short and bald, with a big nose, and rich. Very nice and very clever. They saw that Bryan was splendid, they were very beguiled by his humour and fun, and when he got into hot water – and he was like someone permanently poised on the edge of a hot bath – he needed help and they came to his assistance because they loved him and admired him. They gave their collection of sculpture to the Purchase when Bryan was Director there. And when he stopped being Director they continued to be great friends.

He was fun in New York too. He was staying in a flat way up-town on the West side and that's when he introduced us to the artist Cleve Gray, with whom he became good friends, and his wife Francine du Plessix Gray [the writer and literary critic]. They were two of his best American friends. He needed support then because his time at the Neuberger was difficult.

Paul Huxley recalled:

Jeanne Thayer was one of Bryan's ladies in New York – very old but very beautiful. Her husband was an immensely wealthy man in publishing. She was very supportive of Bryan and desperate to think of ways to help him. She may have been one of the anonymous donors who helped him out in later years. Bryan on one occasion after his American adventure got a letter from a lawyer saying that someone who wants to remain anonymous wishes to make a gift to you of £20,000, or whatever it was. It was just what Bryan needed, but come what may, he couldn't discover who it was. He once joked to me that because he couldn't find out who it was he'd have to be nice to everyone from now on! I think it could have been Jeanne Thayer. It had to be someone who knew him well and loved him and knew his circumstances and had enough money to give away. It helped him enormously, and probably added five years to his life.

Bryan left Purchase in 1975 and once again there were various rumours of financial irregularities. One situation that was not easily resolved emerged after Bryan had decided to purchase a significant Hepworth for the museum's collection. She was very pleased about this, and reduced the price. But in fact the sculpture was never bought, for the money simply wasn't available. Apparently, it was one of a number of cases in which he'd promised to buy something, and then been unable to follow through. In a sense, his enthusiasm had betrayed him. Bryan suggested that Hepworth give the work to the museum, but this was not a popular alternative after the thought of a sale had taken root. Hepworth could be generous. She had given Bryan a beautiful wood-carving after the first show of her work he put on at the Whitechapel. Later he sold it, being characteristically short of money, but unsurprisingly this did not go down well with the artist. A great survivor in what was predominantly a man's world, she had a tough streak and she wanted the sale to be confirmed or the sculpture to be shipped back to her. This must have been awkward and embarrassing for Robertson, and it was still not resolved by the time of Hepworth's death in 1975. Certainly, it soured the last years of their friendship, and it didn't help his wider reputation. The stigma of unreliability grew darker around his name.

The following excerpt is taken from a letter of Bryan's to Kenneth Clark from New York (dated 2 November 1974), and gives some indication of his troubled state of mind:

Your advice and possibly help are sorely needed at what is a crossroads in my life. I know which way to turn but I need, badly, a little encouragement or at least a reaction, and a realistic one. I have been caught here in waiting so long for the museum to open (or be allowed to be opened), and now it is, and I've done a very good job with it (from nothing, I may say, and with no help, only terrible obstacles) and I want, within a year, to move out and return to England. I shall have done, *have* already done, what I came over to do.

The simple thing is, that I miss English art and artists dreadfully, and miss my English involvement more than I can say. I worry about it all and wonder what is happening, all the time. I only came here because there seemed nothing for me to do in England, and I believed that I could be *useful* to English art *here*. I can't: the situation is insular and there's no interest whatever. Arnold Goodman (prodded by a letter with many artists' signatures) tried to persuade me to put myself forward for Director of Art at the Arts Council, saying he and Jennie Lee would back me as well. I declined, because I thought Robin Campbell should have it (he did), among other reasons – all sensible at the time – but now I hear – though I'm not *sure* – that Robin Campbell is retiring in about a year, and I want to see if there's a chance of my having that job now – or, rather, when it's vacant, when Robin retires. Should I write to Robin, or Hugh Willatt?

I want to leave my present death-trap within this coming year; above all, I want to return and *work for English artists*, in England. The last four years have been a degrading experience – too many people want to run the museum, I'm not allowed the right kind of 'status' or staff etc – but I've learned a lot: one always does. What I badly need is your comments on how you react to my Arts Council idea; or whether you *might*, at the right time, maybe put in a word for me at the right place, also – I imagine with Lord Esher, who I don't know, met him, once. The Arts Council would also have the immense advantage of providing me with the kind of already-formed administrative structure that Whitechapel never could, and which is equally impossible here because they 'got me on the cheap' and want to keep all power centralized. I was kept without even a secretary for over 2 years. Now I just have a young 'trainee' assistant, which is hopeless. Nothing can change the structure. I'm not even provided a professional governing body.

In some symbolic way I've never really unpacked here: some inner disbelief prevented it, apart from the real horrors of life spent in trying to open a museum within a context that doesn't really want a museum at all, and delayed its opening so ruthlessly that we nearly lost the collections that I'd gathered together.

The Australian job, 1975

As the position of Director of the Neuberger Museum became increasingly untenable for Robertson, he looked around for a suitable job elsewhere. Australia had long exerted a strong grip on his affections – as a source of light and colour and hedonism, as well as for its art. He had friends and connections there, and he was highly regarded in the museum world. His championship of Australian art at the Whitechapel had made him popular with at least some of the artists, even if the home-grown critics liked to take issue with his judgements. So when the directorship of the National Gallery of Victoria in Melbourne was up for grabs, Bryan was very seriously tempted, and wheeled in his trusted referees and advisers. The following excerpt from a letter from Kenneth Clark to Sir Murray Porter, Australian politician and agent-general for Victoria in London (dated 21 July 1975), demonstrates K's good opinion:

For about fifteen years Bryan Robertson was in charge of the Whitechapel Art Gallery, and during that time he gave a series of exhibitions of modern painting which were much the most important and influential to be shown in England. It was amusing to see rows of expensive cars standing outside the Whitechapel Gallery during the time that he was Director. Everybody who cared for art had to go there.

'In Australia you find a deeply sophisticated landscape, in parts, like a head-on collision between Fantin-Latour and Redon, or nature "presented" to us, as it is on a Japanese screen.'

He has not only introduced the leading painters of the New York school but he discovered relatively unknown talent in this country. He has a genuine understanding of artists as well as of their work, and became friends with them. He is an intelligent man with a passionate love of art, and personally I should like to have seen him made Director of the Tate Gallery, but he is not naturally an administrator, although he seems to have run the Whitechapel quite well, and he also suffers from asthma, which occasionally knocks him out for a day or two.

All things considered I would say that he is the most gifted gallery director (next to Sir John Pope Hennessy) who has been produced in England since the war, and I think Melbourne will be very fortunate to have him, especially if his associate director took charge of the administrative side.

Although he had virtually decided to accept the Australian job, Robertson panicked at the last moment. In essence he couldn't bear the thought of being so far away from London and his friends, as this letter from Bryan to K (dated 5 September 1975) makes explicit:

You haven't heard from me before, though I should have so enjoyed the briefest meeting, because I've been plunged in an ocean of indecision over going to Australia. You know all this, because I know how deeply and recklessly kind you've been in, as it were, backing me both ways. And this I also know to have been doubly kind because you are, however imaginative, a most scrupulously *exact* man intellectually and my dither must have seemed both sloppy and protracted. All over now, I've chosen to stay in England and do the very best work that I'm capable of, and it will be a pleasure to try to excell [*sic*] at being constructive in order to give expression to the joy I feel at having such a good and kind friend as yourself.

At least be assured that I have written very decent letters to all the relevant Australians and, in passing, have made it clear that you, and any others they may have contacted, firmly believed that I was off, imminently, to Australia – as, indeed, I did myself. I have put forward 'long-term anxiety about possible health in relation to climate' as a reason for not going because I didn't want to offend edgy Australian pride. As it is, they'll be vexed but I believe it will pass away and I've stressed my great admiration for the Nat Gallery and hope to help in any way *here* – and I think they'll also know what a fearfully hard decision it has been, at this moment. More when we meet, which will be soon ...

I really love you and Jane, I've hated being away, and am so thankful to be back – however hard the times.

As ever, Bryan

Mark Hudson

The art critic of the *Daily Telegraph*, Mark Hudson, had this to report, by email in March 2017, recalling his own student days and a fleeting visit from a great man:

Robertson came to give a lecture at Winchester School of Art, when I was a student there, circa 1978. In contrast to the rather messy, shambolic character of the place, he seemed a regal and imposing figure, who brought a sense of the grandeur of important places: standing centre stage, very upright in a smart grey suit, silver hair swept back, surveying the grungy looking mass of students and staff – with people wandering in late – obviously very unimpressed. He said this was clearly a slovenly school. He'd looked round the studios, the work was very poor, only one student's work was worth considering, who he named – a rather intense, hard-working girl in the first year. He then launched into a soliloquy on the essentially sensual nature of art, citing Pollock's *Blue Poles*, the Spring frescos in Pompeii and a very long Chinese painting on silk. Becoming exasperated at people still arriving late, he said he'd fine any other latecomers. At which point the painter Graham Crowley, then looking like a twelve-year-old punk rocker, wandered in.

Robertson: 'You're late! Twenty pence!'

Crowley: 'I am actually a lecturer.'

Robertson: 'I knew this was a slovenly school.'

Kenneth Draper

The sculptor Kenneth Draper (born 1944), who has himself been the victim of chronic ill health, remembers how Bryan used to refer to his own 'dodgy' periods of poor health. He recounts, in his own inimitable email style, his memories and impressions of his friend.

From an email of 15 November 2012:

Bryan was one of the most incredible spirits I have ever met and was hugely inspirational to me – we had fantastic times together over decades since I first met him in 1966 with Bryan Kneale when we were hanging Bryan's sculpture show at the Whitechapel – I next met him in my 2nd year at the Royal College when he was visiting the studios there – he remembered me and while talking about my work which I was making – he bought a sculpture!!! – the first I had ever sold – while hanging it in his house in Islington he invited John Hoyland over for the evening and it was the first time I had met John – unforgettable!!!

I think what I will do is instead of trying to write a 'rounded piece' for you about Bryan – I will keep sending you small very personal pieces about different key times we had together over the years and various often mad events which took place – I'll just do it in 'note form' which I am sure you will get the drift of –

And later, 13 April 2017, by email:

we immediately became friends and I saw him often over three decades until I left London to live in Menorca in 1994 – always had a few dinners with him when over for exhibitions etc – and always wonderful – although I'm sure he never quite forgave me for leaving the country!!!!!!!! – he liked his friends 'available' he used to joke with me!!!!!

Severe health problems prevented Draper from taking part in the extended email correspondence he had anticipated, and we finally conducted a long-distance telephone interview in May 2017.

I always remember Bryan saying: 'The two things that are most interesting to oneself and the most boring to everyone else are one's illnesses and one's holidays.' After one trip to Rhodes he said to me: 'I'm not getting on terribly well with my memoirs and I'm feeling very guilty about it. I need to do it for all my friends!' I mentioned this to John Hoyland and John said: 'We've had it then!' I've kind of come to understand this a lot better, seeing as I've gone through a lot of this. His health was always very strange and it's the kind of tiredness and weariness that sets in – the mind is wanting to be doing things and the body is too tired. Thinking about him at that time, he'd have incredibly good intentions and great ideas and ring up about something, 'I'm going to do such and such,' and go on about it at length, then three weeks later I'd say, 'How's that project?' and he'd go, 'Yes, well, you know'. It was so sad: the mind was still there but the energy just let him down a lot. That was happening with him most of his life, I think.

But what an amazing man! I was twenty-two years old when I first met him and I'll never forget it as long as I live. He was already a legend at that time – it was 1966 – and he'd made the Whitechapel into the total place where new art was going on. *He* was known – it was the Bryan Robertson Whitechapel. At the time I didn't know who ran the Tate or the National Gallery, but I knew about Bryan. Extraordinary. He had a profound effect on me when I was so young. I mean he had a big thing about invention. He would say all art is about invention and making. That's why he hated anything to do with conceptualism – you had to do it, you had to make it. And about trusting yourself. He was such an amazing communicator. When I think of him – which I do still, often – I think of his generosity and warmth. The thing was he loved sharing things. If he went to a movie he'd ring everyone up the next day and say: 'You must go, immediately. Drop everything you're doing! Get to the West End and see such-and-such now, and I'll ring you tomorrow to see what you think about it.' And it was never an ego thing, it was a genuine kind of passion to share something that he found exciting.

The Whitechapel Gallery was instrumental in my going to London, because most students at Chesterfield went to Sheffield Art School to carry on into the next stage. But when I was seventeen, a friend at the art school had an American pal in London who rang him and said he must get down to see the Mark Rothko exhibition at the Whitechapel Gallery. I'd never heard of Mark Rothko or the Whitechapel Gallery. I'd only been to London once when I was about thirteen, but a few of us decided we'd go and I can remember taking the tube round to Whitechapel and getting out thinking 'Bloody Hell! Is this London? It's scruffier than Sheffield!' This weird street and market stalls, and it was a dull grey day and we walked along and then suddenly we walked in off the street into this amazing white space, this huge white space and these massive paintings. At the time I'd never painted anything bigger than two foot by one foot. The paintings were twice the size of any room in my little house back in Yorkshire. And this white ethereal space. It was such an epiphany moment, and going back on the train I said to my friends: 'That's it – I'm going to London, I'm not going to Sheffield. I want more of this.'

And when I got down to London in 1962, all the shows that were really important were happening at the Whitechapel. The Caro exhibition, the Rauschenberg, and then of course the brilliant *New Generation* exhibitions, which made Bryan a kind of legend, I think, at that time. As everyone knows, they were an absolute store of genius, and nothing had been seen like that kind of work. Just amazing! What an inspiration he was.

Meeting him was one of the scariest days of my life. I'd worshipped him and the shows from afar and I'd seen him occasionally in the Whitechapel in one of his lovely suits, and he gave a lecture once at the Royal College. Then I was working as assistant to Bryan Kneale for his 1966 Whitechapel exhibition. All the work was sent off and I knew I'd be meeting Bryan [Robertson]. I couldn't sleep that night – I'm dead serious – there was no one I wanted to meet as much as Bryan. We arrived in the morning and were setting up the show and Bryan was wafting around giving orders, and Bryan Kneale introduced me to him. 'Oh hello,' he said. 'I hear you're at the Royal College. Are you still doing lots of life modelling?' 'No, actually, I make constructions.' 'Oh yes, you were a painter, weren't you? Bryan's told me. Yes, yes, yes. We must talk about it.' Then he went off, and that was the last I saw of him that day.

Next day I was standing outside on the street, covered in oil, and I suddenly looked behind me and Robertson was there, smoking a cigarette in an absolutely beautiful white suit, looking absolutely immaculate. He suddenly said, 'Have you seen Tim Scott's exhibition, at Waddington's?' I said I had and he said, 'What did you think of it?' So I said, 'Well, I liked it very much actually. I'm interested in the colour and the ziggurat, but in many ways I think they're very related to Hoyland's ziggurat paintings and Huxley.' So he said, 'Hmm, hmm. Do you like Huxley's work?' 'Yeah,' I said, 'but I prefer Hoyland'. He asked why. 'I think they're more raw. I prefer the rawness. I think Paul's are slightly more sophisticated.' He kind of looked me up and down – me covered in grease and him in his white suit, and he said: 'There's nothing wrong with a bit of sophistication, you know!' swung on his heel, and walked back into the gallery, leaving me thinking 'Fuck! I absolutely fucked that one!' And for the next four or five days he never spoke to me while we were setting up the show. He totally ignored me. I thought I'd buggered everything up.

Then the day of the opening we were all going for lunch at an Italian restaurant very near the Whitechapel. We all walked in and I didn't know anybody apart from Bryan [Kneale] and he was being whisked ahead with various people. And I'm walking in at the back and not quite sure what to do or really whether I should be there, and suddenly Bryan Robertson turned round and saw me. He was in the middle of a table and shouted, 'Ken, Ken, come and sit with me'. I went and sat with him. 'Shall I order for you? I know all this food and you won't.' I said that would be wonderful. So he ordered the entire meal and talked to me for about an hour and a half about art and sculpture. He was absolutely so generous and so wonderful and I'll never forget it, it was just a joy, absolutely amazing. So he'd obviously been slightly playing games with me, I think! He knew all about me. Then the next time I saw him he came into the sculpture department of the Royal College, saw a very early piece of mine and bought it. 'I love it,' he said. It was absolutely wonderful – the first sculpture I'd ever sold. That was pretty bloody amazing. He also bought a piece from Nigel [Hall] the same day.

After that I saw a massive amount of him. It was just an absolute joy to have known him through all those decades. I was lucky because I lived in the Barbican. I always used to joke with people that you always see people who live near to you. So from the eighties I saw a lot of Hoyland, a lot of Nigel and a lot of Bryan. Bryan would often ring and say he'd got tickets for Sadler's Wells and would Jean [Macalpine, Ken's partner and later wife] mind if I came. I went to so many concerts, movies, theatre with him. Again the great communicator. He'd talk about dance for two hours afterwards: 'Did you notice what happened when those two bodies came together and that movement of the leg?' I was absolutely enthralled listening to him talk about dance, with just the same kind of excitement he'd talk about a picture.

I'll tell you a very funny story. We were at Sadler's Wells, and after the show everyone went off to a party somewhere. During the evening this young dancer was totally chatting me up, which I didn't know quite how to handle. I noticed Bryan across the room giving me little smiles and nods. Anyway, I managed eventually to convince this young dancer that I wasn't interested, that I didn't bat for that side. Just as we were leaving, Bryan said to me, 'I noticed little Jeremy was chatting you up'. 'Yes,' I said, 'it was a bit difficult'. 'I know,' he said, 'I told him you'd just got out of prison and that you'd been sent down for two years for mucking around with young lads on Clapham Common'. I promise you! And he'd done things like that with other people ... He was a total wind-up merchant.

When I'd been away in New York, he'd ring me and say, 'It's a good thing you're back. Ugly things have been happening in the Barbican, wild parties while you've been away. Jean has been really having a good time.' And he'd go on and on and on. Bless him! I do miss him terribly. The weird thing is that he became such a good friend, and we saw a lot of each other until I left London [in 1994] – and he never forgave me for coming to Menorca, because I was a thousand miles away instead of ten minutes away – that I had to kind of remind myself what he'd done and how important he was. Because he never played the 'I was this, and I did that' role ... he was very modest and he got quieter as he got older.

Draper recalled Bryan's unease at being permanently in America:

Bill Pye remembers Bryan saying that conceptual art was 'a sort of spiritual anorexia nervosa'.

Later that year, I think July 1971, he came back to London for the summer and he was suddenly like the old Bryan again – he was so happy. He was a real Londoner: he loved Islington and he loved his house and his dinner parties. It was amazing seeing him again. Then he went back to New York but didn't stay long. I remember him saying he'd been offered a massive job in Australia and he was thinking about it for a few days and then he rang me up one night very late and said, 'I can't go. It's too bloody far'. He went on: 'Do you realise that when you've got to San Francisco, having flown for many, many hours, you're only halfway there?' I think it was just too far emotionally for him. He loved London and he loved his friends. And his friends loved him too.

The other thing which depressed him quite a bit in the seventies was that he didn't like the art that was happening. He hated conceptual art with a vengeance and wasn't writing anything then, but I used to have these amazing evenings with him when he'd go on and on. And I'd say, 'Bryan – you've got to write this somewhere! Somebody's got to listen to this!' He'd got that way of suddenly mixing humour with being serious, so he'd go into one of his rampages about something, and you'd wonder if he was being serious or wisecracking. I remember him saying that all artists feel very guilty at having holidays, and not being in the studio. But if you're a conceptual artist you can go walkabout for two weeks through the Highlands somewhere and pretend you're working! So funny.

In the seventies he had a tricky time, I think, and probably sold a few of the paintings and sculptures he'd been given over the years. He seemed to be moving from crisis to crisis. I actually tried to get him some teaching, just to earn a bit of money, but it was such an effort getting him anywhere. I'd arrange a day at Camberwell and pick him up in the morning and get him down there. He'd walk into the sculpture department and say, 'It's so filthy in here! Don't they ever clean up?' And I had the job of babysitting him. Paul de Monchaux was Head of Fine Art then and he asked me to look after him for the day. I'd get a student for him to see on the hour every hour. The students were terrified because they knew about the Whitechapel and the sixties and were all very nervous about meeting this legend. I'd introduce him to a student and leave them, and five minutes later Bryan would wander back in and say, 'Who am I seeing now? I've done that one.'

I'll never forget walking into the Life Room with him and there was this boy there doing a full-size life figure of this very old man. I thought, 'This is going to be interesting – I'm going to stay and watch this!' Bryan walked around the figure and walked around the sculpture that this student was making and did what I'd always dreamed of doing when I was sent out to Manchester and the Outer Hebrides on a day's teaching when they used to get the most difficult students for you to see. He stood back and said, 'Don't let me disturb you. Do carry on!' Swung on his heel and walked out. By 12.30 he had seen all the students he was down to see and it was, 'What do we do now?' It was so funny and wonderful seeing him in places like that. He did an amazing talk at the Central to a group of students. He had a look round the sculpture department and no one was using colour. So he tore up this bit of paper with his notes on and decided to talk to them about colour in sculpture. He gave this amazing talk about Rauschenberg and Caro and the St Martin's artists, and the students just sat there with their mouths open. He did this for about one and a half hours non-stop and was brilliant.

Then in the eighties he got the Warwick Arts Trust, and that was like a new lease of life for him. He needed outlets, Bryan, he needed places to demonstrate or do something. I think that was brilliant for him for about two years, and then he started to lose faith in it. He wasn't sure about it all and pulled out, I think. He did some rather beautiful, incredible shows there. I remember for Prunella's show he painted an entire wall black. Prunella said, 'I'm not really sure about what Bryan's doing'. He wouldn't let the artists anywhere near – he'd hang the exhibitions himself. He used to throw me out in the garden with a drink. He said, 'Artists should never hang their own exhibitions,' which I'm not sure about. With Bryan in that mood, you didn't argue. But he was amazing and very unexpected. He'd suddenly put a drawing quite low to the floor. I can remember him doing very curious juxtapositions of pieces in a way that I'd never have dreamed of doing. The Whitechapel shows were like that. They were always hung in

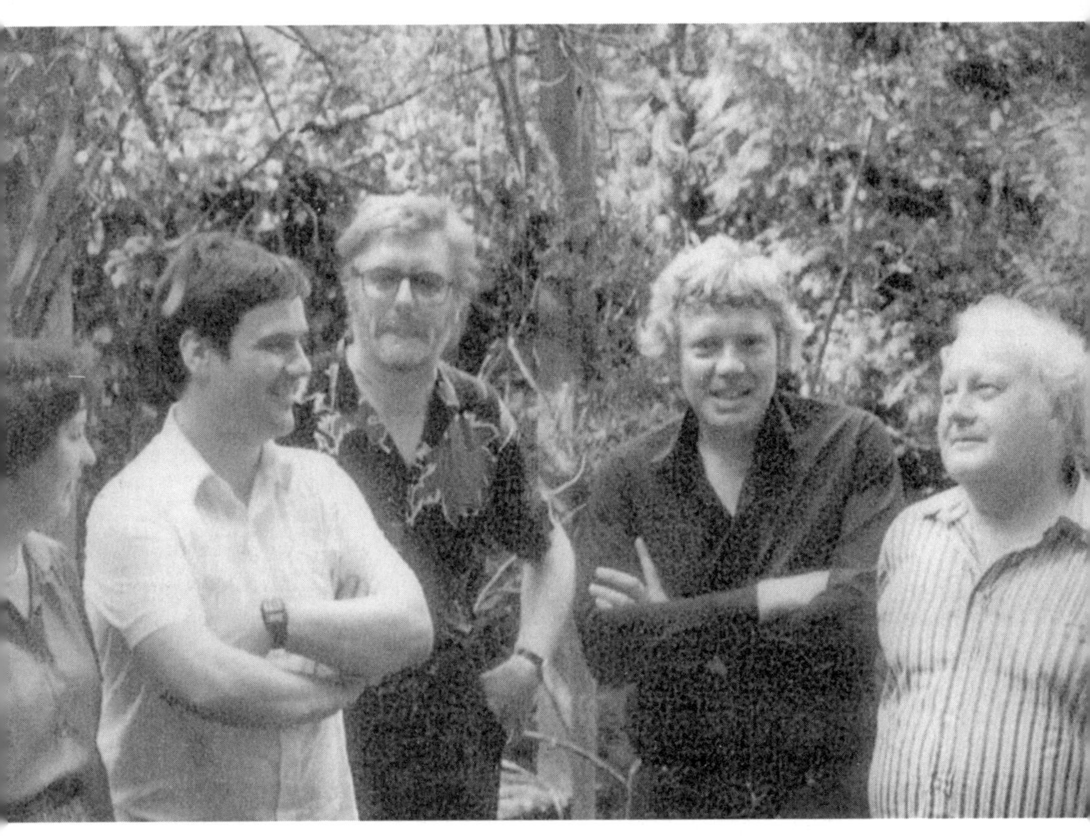

23 Group including John Hoyland (with glasses) and BR (right), with Kenneth Draper between them, taken in the 1980s in the Oxfordshire (Shipton-under-Wychwood) garden of Milton Grundy, Director of the Warwick Arts Trust
Photograph by Denis Conti, Whitechapel Gallery Archive

rather extraordinary ways. I'll never forget walking into *The New Generation* painting show, and then about a year later *The New Generation* sculpture exhibition. I can't remember ever having been moved quite so much, certainly through that whole period of time, by anything. It was just like you'd gone to Heaven or something. It was all so unearthly and incredible and fantastic.

As an indication of Bryan's very particular sense of humour, Ken read out the text from a postcard sent by Bryan to him in hospital after Ken had had his first heart problems in 1991:

Dearest Ken,

Your palpitations have triggered off the most terrible and awesome sight in recorded history in the London art world. Nigel Hall has bought an exercise bike, new chest expanders, running gear, spiked shoes for rock climbing and a silk set of sports knickers. John Hoyland has been glimpsed puffing wearily round and round Charterhouse Square at 6am in old football shorts, purple-faced with exhaustion but sporting the whitest pair of legs in EC1.

John Carter has sworn off all meat and drink, shaved his head, started to wear a rough woollen habit and chants mantras for hours each morning. Even yours truly is now down to a mere seventeen stone and hasn't eaten pudding for a day and a half. The entire staff of your terrified gallery has taken out a subscription to the Whispering Glades Memorial Rest Home. The British Council have withdrawn every work by Gilbert & George on show in Europe and Anthony d'Offay has even begun to pay some of his artists. Where will it end? Terror stalks the streets. The Milk Marketing Board has gone bankrupt. Is it true that they are inserting pacemakers these days from some very peculiar apertures to avoid surgery? Dear Ken, I didn't intend my letter to have such a dramatic effect on you. Loving thoughts, leave the nurses alone and leave yourself alone. Is it true Jean is spending all your money with Alister Warman?' [Ken notes that Bryan had this fantasy that all the girls ran off with the charming arts administrator Alister Warman.]

John Carter

The artist John Carter (born 1942) was in *The New Generation 1966* exhibition, and met Bryan for the first time that year. He recalled the event in a telephone conversation in May 2017:

I was working for Bryan Kneale on his Whitechapel exhibition in 1966, and Bryan Robertson appeared at the forge and I met him there. I think at the time he was hunting for people for the next *New Generation* show. In a way, although he knew all the people in the two shows before, my feeling is that he got a bit stuck to know who to ask, and felt perhaps not quite so in touch with the younger people. So the Central School, where that nice painter who came from Bath, and great friend of Bryan's, Thelma Hulbert, taught, meant there were an awful lot of Central students in *The New Generation* [1966]. In fact I later heard that it was regarded as their degree show!

At some stage he wanted to come and see my work, which was quite a thing because I was living in what was basically a bed-sitter in Blackheath. Anyway I met up with him somewhere, and we had to go and see Irene Worth first. She was another of his ladies. So we went there first by taxi and later out to Blackheath. She was a terrific character, very sophisticated and a powerful personality. He was very close to her. They fell out, John Spurling told me, but then he fell out with everybody at certain times and then they tended to come back again. I know Ken Draper's theory is that Bryan knew so many people he had to fall out with a few now and again to cut the numbers down. I fell out with him and could never quite understand why.

I know the moment because he was just starting the book about John Hoyland that Mel Gooding took over. He said he was writing about John and I said, 'Oh that's good', and then I tried to find out what sort of book it

'To confuse Johns's work at any level with pop art would be equivalent to considering the innovatory work of Degas in the same light as those paintings by Tissot or other Salon artists in Paris who might, coincidentally, have recorded theatrical and racecourse scenes in the same period.'

was going to be. Whether it was going to be a paperback or what. I couldn't think how to put that. I was always slightly frightened of Bryan because of his sophistication and everything and so I unfortunately said, 'Will it be a sort of coffee-table book?' I just saw this as a big glossy book – the way to describe a large art book – but he absolutely froze. 'Well, one hopes not,' he said. 'Well, I really must get on now,' and he put the phone down.

I sometimes sent him postcards if I was abroad. The thing was, if you knew him, it was terribly difficult to get hold of him. For me to phone Bryan was always a very loaded thing to do somehow. It was a bit like phoning Nick Serota, that sort of thing. Bryan was a very potent figure in the art world then. That was the sort of intimidating quality phoning him had – not that he was the least intimidating in person. He was on the whole fantastically amusing. To phone him, you'd have to brace yourself and charge yourself up to do it. Then you would phone and there'd be no reply, and you'd have to go through the whole process again. You could be trying to phone him for a week. Sometimes it would be engaged and sometimes it just rang and rang. It was all quite unnerving doing it.

So he came to see my work and then asked me if I'd like to take part in the show, which was like absolute heaven – unbelievable. He also invited me out quite a bit after that. So I might go to the theatre with him one night. Sometimes I would be taken out to dinner – all of which was very nice and very enjoyable. He was a good companion, but one could never really get a word in edgeways. The moment one started to speak he would immediately interrupt.

I went to America in 1972 when he'd been appointed at Purchase and hoped Bryan would put me up as he had put other people up, but at that stage things were going really seriously wrong for him. He'd actually lost his flat and was staying in rooms in New York. We drove out to Purchase. He was driving at that time which was terrifying. Those big American cars, air-conditioned and completely soundproof. We'd be sailing up Amsterdam Avenue: 'Oh dear, was that a red light?'

(On another occasion John recounted a visit to Jasper Johns at his house called the Bank. He went with Bryan and it was the only time he saw him overwhelmed and put in his place. Every time Bryan tried to tell a story, Jasper squashed it, and talked over him. 'Bryan ended up looking pretty beleaguered while Jasper insisted his guests play backgammon.')

I was at a small private party a long time ago for Princess Margaret. I was approached to go and speak to her. I had met her before at the opening of the *New Generation* show I was in. Bryan was in quite well with that circle. So I was introduced by Bryan at the Whitechapel: 'This is John Carter – he's just discovered gin!' There was a gin cocktail at the opening and I was trying to stop people putting glasses on my sculpture. I think Princess Margaret was very fond of Bryan and knew him surprisingly well, actually. She told me something that amazed me. You know he got the job as head of the National Gallery in Australia? And he went out there and whilst there [she told me] he phoned her quite late at night and said, 'I just don't know what to do. I've just got this job and I just can't face it. I can't face having an entirely new life in Australia with new people that I don't know, and I'm thinking of resigning.' That's what he did, in fact. But of course he was a big hero in Australia, because he'd introduced Australian art to England.

When he got back from America, Bryan proposed organising a series of exhibitions at the Warwick Arts Trust, independently and without interference. Milton Grundy, who owned the building, agreed and Bryan set out to do it. That was wonderful because it enabled him to do the other thing that he did at the Whitechapel – other than the big American shows, a lot of which were on European tours anyway and he got a lot more credit for than he was due – which was to put on big exhibitions of contemporary British artists. He gave retrospectives to people: Jack Smith, Prunella Clough, John Hoyland ... He fulfilled something that nobody else did. It was absolutely marvellous, and ever since he left there, there's been an absolute dearth of anybody doing anything like that. It's appalling, and I think the Tate has behaved disgracefully.

A very bad effect that Bryan had on me was about money because he was tremendously generous with it and also liked to behave in quite a grand way about it, based on Kenneth Clark, I think. I remember him quoting me Thomas Beecham going to some great industrialist to get some money for an orchestra. The chap said, 'No, I can't do that,' and Beecham said, 'Of course you can, why not?' And that was very much Bryan's attitude, that everything must be devoted to art, and that you sacrificed everything for it. That's what he did, and that's how, trying to live like this, I ended up in incredibly bad debt for about ten years.

Gary Wragg

The abstract painter Gary Wragg (born 1946) recalled his close friendship with Robertson, another relationship that began with art and deepened into an easy companionship. The following comes from a conversation at the artist's London home in May 2015:

Bryan came to my 1976 Acme show, eight years after he gave me a prize when I was a student at Camberwell, and from then on, all his life he backed me. That's when he started inviting me to his house for dinner. I used to be there quite a lot. If I got a little bit depressed he'd invite me over for a drink. He'd sit me down with a whisky and get me to put my feet up on his Eames chair, sit back and listen to Billie Holiday. And then we just had wonderful discussions. He'd tell me what he was working on, who had been there. I used to stay there – he had a pull-out bed. One morning he said, 'Did you sleep well? Were you comfy?' I said yeah. He said, 'Well you should be, Helen Frankenthaler slept in the same bed.'

He had a lovely collection – Hoyland, Phillip King, Lee Krasner. Bryan bought three paintings for himself from my second show in 1979. In his will he donated all three to the Fitzwilliam. And it was through him that Pontus Hulten bought a painting of mine for the Beaubourg and Duncan Robinson bought one for the Fitzwilliam. Bryan preferred Pollock to de Kooning, and we had endless discussions about everything Pollock did, and about Lee Krasner. He told me this story about Pollock and Krasner. Lee had the studio upstairs and he had the one downstairs and she was working one afternoon when she heard this banging and crashing downstairs. She ran down to see what it was. Pollock had this big Picasso book which he was throwing from one end of the studio to the other. She asked him what was wrong and he replied, 'Every time I think of something new to do I look at this book, and he's done it!'

Bryan was by nature a procrastinator, not particularly focused and much given to displacement activities, so he liked to have friends around to distract him. Wragg visited him maybe once or twice every other week. He said: 'Like Baudelaire, he didn't like to be alone.' Wragg also used to house-sit when Bryan went abroad. 'His day was maybe dispersed,' recalls Wragg;

He liked to potter around the house and while he was working he also liked to go out in the garden to tend the flowers, or go to a shop or do some cooking. Or get on the telephone and talk about something else completely. He was very good on the phone and did spend quite a lot of time on it. He didn't like practical matters much – he was hopeless at that. But he taught me how to make a really good tomato salad.

He had a lot of style. He would cook and he would be gesturing and talking about something that was mind-blowing at the same time. He didn't like to sit still unless he had a cigarette. Conversation sparked him to take off at a tangent, quite often into something he was really interested in. He was a great eccentric. If I was with him and we had to leave the house to go and see something, you had to go back three or four times. He could never just leave the house. He'd always forget something. It was a compulsion.

There was another evening when Hoyland came to supper and we decided to levitate him. It was something I had just learned in T'ai Chi. So Bryan and I sat him down on a chair and tried to pick him up under his thighs. Of course he was heavy and we couldn't pick him up. Then I did this little thing of how to make people light. Bryan was sceptical, he didn't think anything was going to happen, he was giggling. I said we can only use two fingers, one each. I said lift, and up John went. He got a shock. From then on Bryan always talked about it.

Bryan could be very snappy, and impatient. He didn't suffer fools gladly. If he took against you that was probably it. He was lavish. He left the Whitechapel completely bankrupt because he was just so extravagant. If he had to get something done, he'd get it done and think about the money afterwards. He was out on a limb. He'd always be behind with work and the books would be piled up everywhere. He'd make appointments and not turn up. People would come round and he'd not be ready.

But Bryan did visit Wragg's studio often and was prepared to offer constructive criticism:

He did respond to the work, but he was always critical as well, always tough. He had a fantastic eye. Bryan was definitely one of the most important figures in my life.

He was very disappointed with what was happening in the art world. He hated a lot of the conceptual work, for not being life-enhancing enough. He was very aware of people who were ignored or out of it and would try to include them at dinner-parties. He was sympathetic to people's troubles as well. He was a good listener. But he liked to educate you as well. We went to Covent Garden sometimes, Sadler's Wells, good restaurants. He knew you didn't have access to this because you didn't have the money. But he had the clout and he would introduce you to things. He was so interested in people and what they were doing. He was also game for things. When I had a studio at Martello Street in the 1970s, opposite was one of the best Reggae clubs in London, the All Nations Club, with lots of different rooms for restaurants and bars and dancing. It didn't start until midnight, so I'd work at the studio and then Bryan would come over and we'd go to the All Nations Club, where he could get a hot Jamaican patty. He wanted to dance. I made the mistake of asking him to look after my wallet once, and during the evening it was pinched. But there wasn't much in it in any case.

I never really knew any partners of Bryan's. He was always very respectful – the fact that I wasn't gay he totally understood. I don't think he was very active – in fact, I think he got lonely sometimes. He wasn't particularly camp. When I was at the Slade, Keith Vaughan was like that – just like Bryan. I used to take girlfriends around and Bryan would get on so well with them and be totally understanding. He wouldn't be judgemental. In every kind of way he was amazing – as a person, as a human being, he had compassion. He loved cats – he liked strays and would look after them. They would come and go. If he saw a cat he would always try and talk to it and pick it up. And going down the street he would suddenly talk to somebody – he'd say that he liked their shoes or something. That usually went down well because he was humorous and good-natured and well meaning. So he often got a really good response. He wasn't shy – he would suddenly be in the moment and do what he needed to do in that moment. He was totally himself.

Wragg dedicated the second volume of his comprehensive catalogue of paintings, published in 2014, to Robertson (the first volume is dedicated to his family). Hilary Spurling, who provided the first and most illuminating text in this ambitious two-volume compilation, firmly locates and identifies Robertson's importance for Wragg, quoting him in the first paragraph of her essay, and returning to him throughout. Spurling quotes Wragg who quotes Robertson's story of visiting Rothko in his studio in downtown New York. Rothko explained his daily routine of driving to the studio, sweeping the floor, putting on some music (Mozart or Gabrieli) and lying down on a single bed in the corner of the room. 'While I'm in the studio, I haven't failed,' was the punchline of Rothko's disquisition.

This assessment is taken from Bryan's catalogue essay for Wragg's 1997 Flowers East exhibition:

Gary Wragg's powerfully composed and in terms of colour richly orchestrated paintings are a pleasure to describe, but their content does not give itself so readily to straightforward explanation. As the paintings are clearly abstract, purists might well object at this point to even the suggestion of 'content', now rather an old-fashioned or redundant word, and prefer to allow the paintings to exist solely within the bounds of their strongly abstract character, looking and conjecturing no further. But I have known Gary Wragg's work for the past twenty years, living with beautiful examples. I believe him to be one of the most remarkable artists working now in England, a formidably gifted painter with special gifts which are utterly personal, and as the peculiar nature of these paintings can present problems, in my experience, to some viewers or at least set up an admittedly exotic and beautiful barrier, however slight, to their full enjoyment, I want to try to define the special identity of Wragg's best work.

I say 'best' work because Wragg is sometimes uneven and perhaps rather more inclined to be hit or miss in his approach than other abstract painters who carefully deploy a circumscribed and only too familiar formal vocabulary. Wragg's work, in contrast, is at risk all the time: he skates dangerously close to surfeit and a kind of congestion or excessive density, he is totally unconcerned with aesthetic decorum or whatever the prevailing conceptual aesthetic may be. His best work is transcendentally original and 'right' in terms of mood, light, texture, brushwork, placement, incident and overall structure. If my qualifications sound too much like strictures, I intend them only to define a highly personal working process in which Wragg is never

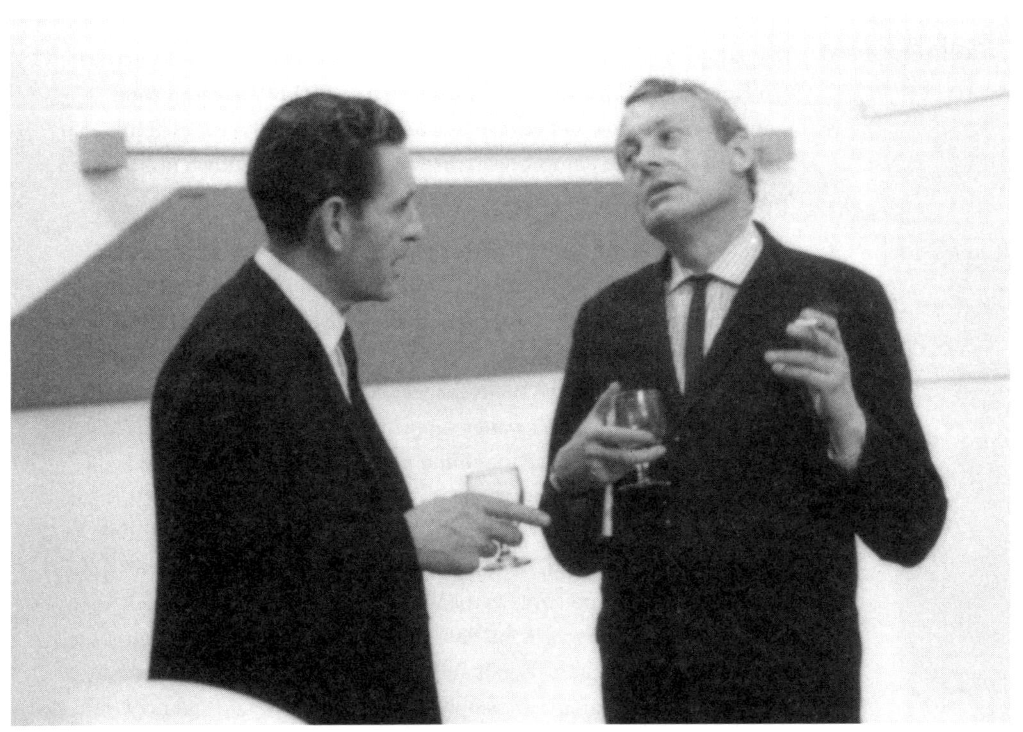

24 BR at *The New Generation: 1968 Interim* exhibition opening at the Whitechapel
Whitechapel Gallery Archive

afraid to risk everything and occasionally, perhaps, even to risk making a fool of himself. In my book, this is a great attribute which secures all my respect: it can be applied also to the paintings of John Hoyland or the sculptures of Phillip King or Anthony Caro, for example.

Before we dig any deeper into the possibilities of identity and content in Wragg's work, there is one last proviso – and a crucial factor for the viewer. In my experience, Wragg's paintings do not reveal themselves at first glance: they not only repay prolonged study, they demand it. They very often look confused initially, seeming to lack focus or convincing structure, or they can look ill-composed, unconvincing, messy. But if you return to whichever painting you find unconvincing or opaque, you will find it transformed after you have exposed your eye and your imaginative response to other works by Wragg. Given time, a real act of disclosure amounting to transformation takes place. Wragg's special world of form and colour takes time to establish itself, to arouse something vital in that imaginative response which alone can stimulate disclosure. Time and patience will secure great rewards. What emerges apart from great beauty is an absolute rightness, a feeling of physical resolution in each canvas with everything in the exact place.

John Hubbard

The painter John Hubbard (1931–2017) recounted the joys and frustrations of a Robertson friendship. He and his wife Caryl both had very fond memories – mingled with exasperation – of Bryan. John recalled this characteristic mix in an enjoyably discursive interview over lunch in a London brasserie in November 2012:

We met Bryan in the 1960s. Caryl knew him when she was working at the New Art Centre and Bryan used to come in, and she liked him very much. So she talked about him. I remember that we gave a drinks party at my brother-in-law's house in Chiswick. Bryan came and I was very wary of him as he was then running the Whitechapel and I was rather in awe of the whole Whitechapel thing. I didn't want to appear to be desperately anxious to make an impression, so Caryl had to remind me during the party to go and talk to him. I remember one day when I was teaching at Camberwell that Bryan came to see Robert Medley. He said he had a wonderful show of, I think, Bob Motherwell. He said, 'Why don't you get all the artists out of this dreary place? Cheer them up – come to the Whitechapel!' We all went, Frank Auerbach included, Bryan was in full flow and gave us the most marvellous time. From then on we became friends and saw him a lot. We had so many mutual artist friends, beginning with people like Prunella [Clough] and Liz Frink. He used to like coming to visit us down in Dorset.

He was an excellent guest. The only thing was rather a tendency to walk off with books. We knew he did it: sometimes one noticed his suitcase was much heavier ... but it was always quite a small suitcase. I got very cross with him because he took away a book I was very fond of – the poems of Seferis, translated by two people that we knew, Philip Sherrard and Edmund Keeley. It was an edition that I particularly liked and I *knew* he'd taken it, and finally I said, 'Bryan, you've got my book'. He denied it for a very long time. Then about two or three years before he died he suddenly relented. I think he'd done a housecleaning and come across it. By that time he'd also given me a replacement copy, not as good, a different edition. So now I've got them both – I've got my own one back. But that's a minor thing – he was fun to have to stay. Sometimes he'd bring people and stay in our cottage – Stephen Chambers or his sister. He would entertain down there sometimes.

Bryan was quite interested in what I did. I know he didn't like my work very much in the early days. Then I had a show in 1968 at the New Art Centre – ten years of charcoal drawings. And he really liked it. He'd never seen my drawings before and he got very excited about them and bought one for himself. He paid for it, which was equally extraordinary. And he wrote a lot about my work. He also organised that little retrospective of my work at the Warwick Arts Trust. Bryan used to ask questions and then answer them himself. He'd ask a long and complicated question, often in five or six separate parts, and if you hesitated for a second, he'd then answer himself. When I got to know him very well I'd tell him to shut up. The worst expression of this was after he came back from America when he'd theoretically bought some of my pictures for the Neuberger. He said, 'I've been thinking about your work and I want to write a piece about you. I'm doing a long piece and it's about you and Lee Krasner' – whom I'd met and liked very much but I couldn't see any connection at all – 'and when it's done I want you to come to dinner and I'm going to read it to you or you can read it yourself'. The time came – he actually did complete it – and he produced this wad of paper. Prunella Clough had come to dinner as well. Bryan left us to read it and Prunella said, 'John, do you know about this thing? It makes no sense, absolutely no sense at all, you won't like it. My advice is, don't read it. It's not really about Lee Krasner or you.' So I never read it.

He did do an interview with me for *Modern Painters*. One of the things that Bryan liked to do in an interview was trace all your artistic antecedents as he imagined them. Sometimes they were plausible but at other times they weren't. The trouble is that critics reading such a piece quoting twenty antecedents, ranging from Fra Angelico up to Jackson Pollock, would make fun of you. So it had a bad effect of deflecting their attention from the work in hand. One knew he did this. The truth is, one forgave Bryan. I had bad times with Bryan but they were always overshadowed by the good times.

A typical bad time happened in the early seventies when I was doing my Moroccan paintings, about 1972, and Bryan said, 'I'd love to see them – I'd like to do a piece about them – but I can't come down to Dorset, what shall we do?' I said I'd send them up to the gallery one weekend. The New Art Centre [in London] said they'd take down their exhibition, hang my pictures, and Bryan could come and see them on a Saturday or Sunday. I went up to London and hung them. There they all were on Saturday at 10 o'clock. No sign of Bryan who was supposed to be coming in about 11. I phoned at 12. Not Bryan's voice, a youngish man, who said Bryan was in Palermo – he'd gone to Sicily. So I was pretty upset, I didn't know what to do. I rang, in an act of desperation, John and Hilary Spurling and Kenneth Clark. I explained what had happened. They all knew Bryan, they were all sufficiently generous and friendly, and they all came round. We actually had rather a nice time, so the day ended happily. Bryan and I never discussed it – he simply said he'd forgotten.

I'm afraid the last piece he wrote [about Hubbard] for *Modern Painters* was a disaster. Everything went wrong – his writing was not very good, it wasn't focused at all. That was disappointing. One always forgave him – he was so adorable. What Bryan was marvellous at was he'd come to the studio and look at work and he always had wonderful perceptive things to say. Perceptive things, not flattery or destructive. If there was something he couldn't take or was worried by or something that really didn't work, he would say. But he'd say it in such a way that you could follow the point he was making and either agree or not agree. He was very good at that, and never failed. People knew this. Victoria Miro wanted Bryan to come to Peter Doig's show because his powers of perception were so good. But Bryan never came. A lot of this was due to ill health and bad management.

He was interested in ideas rather than detail. He was always marvellous to be with – a very lovable man. He was not physically forward, and I remember when Bridget [Riley] gave a party for him, it was probably his sixtieth birthday, it was a surprise party and Bryan was very moved by it. I remember at the end of the party I kissed him on the cheek to say goodbye, and he was incredibly embarrassed, he shrank. He wasn't expecting that. He would kiss ladies, but not that. He was English. It was also intriguing to have his sister stay with him – they were so different – with her son, Marcus. Peggy was very sensible, very down to earth, plain-spoken. She loved Bryan and always explained any of his more outré things with common sense, saying 'It's just him.'

At his best he was good as a writer. He needed editing. I'm sure that in his earlier writing days, editorial control was better. When he did the catalogue for the Dufy exhibition at the Hayward – which was a phenomenal success – Joanna Drew [Director of Art, Arts Council of Great Britain, and thus in overall charge of Hayward exhibitions] was driven to distraction. At one point they had the catalogue printed and he insisted on changing one paragraph. In the British Library or somewhere he'd seen manuscripts of poems by Wordsworth or Shelley, with the main bit in the middle and additions all around the edges. Bryan liked that, and copied it in his own writing. I've got a marvellous letter. It was when he was just starting at Purchase, and he came to my studio. It's a list of my paintings with stars indicating their rating and his plans for buying them. So I sent off three or four paintings to Purchase, and then they came back again. Obviously the purchase hadn't been okayed by the powers that be.

But he dared to do things – and it was that spirit and that attitude which was part of the success of the Whitechapel. He dared to take the initiative. Hardly anybody now does that. England opened its doors to Europe and America through the Whitechapel. Bryan made it possible for the Norman Rosenthals of this world to function later. Writing was not his strong suit. His strong suit was insight, perceptions of work of all sorts, and his ability to present it in a way which showed it to its best. The only other person who was even remotely near him was Lawrence Gowing. Bryan was supreme. He was better, I think, than David Sylvester.

Bryan loved all things French and spoke very good French. He made Caryl and I go to see an absolutely awful Lurçat show in Luxembourg. He loved Lurçat. He liked the French élan. One of his happy times was working with Artcurial in Paris – he did several shows with them. He said triumphantly: 'You won't believe it – I've introduced Adrian Heath to the French and they adore him!'

John and Caryl didn't go to dinner as often as they might, not being Londoners.

The dinner parties were always fraught with drama because you were never quite sure whether there would be any food. And there was a lot to drink. He was a very good cook, and fish was his special thing. I remember one dinner which was very high-powered. Philip Roth was there with Claire Bloom and the Dean of Dance from Purchase. I remember the Dean of Dance was sitting between me and Philip Roth, and at one point I turned to find he was gone. I asked Philip, 'Has the Dean left?' He was under the table, drunk. Bryan did like to drink, but he held his drink. He had a very good head. His sense of humour was so delightful. He had frequent financial crises and one particular one, five or six years before he died. He went away to Paris and when he came back I said how did you get there? He said, 'I borrowed some money because I had a credit.' What was that? He said, 'Well, I got a cheque for $10,000 the day I was leaving for Paris and there was no time to cash it so I put it in the ice-cube tray in my fridge. When I got back there it was – one of my first assets.'

Bryan was good on the phone. One of the things that he adored was the opening of the Italian gallery up near him – the Estorick. He loved it because it was Italian. He didn't like Lucian Freud, Frank Auerbach – he didn't respond to struggle art. Not only did he let fresh air into the art world, he also (as I wish could occasionally be remembered by curators of exhibitions today) didn't just follow what looked good on paper and accord with the taste of the time. He was very keen on women artists of all sorts. He was very good at doing unexpected things. He asked me to lunch at the Connaught and I wondered what had happened. Had he come into a lot of money? Had he sold a painting or done a book deal? He loved Burra and had wanted to do a book on him – it never happened. So we had a delicious lunch and I said Bryan why are we here. 'I wanted to tell you,' he said. 'I've asked Helen Frankenthaler to marry me. And I think she's going to say yes.' I don't think she did. That was the excuse for a very expensive lunch. He was elated by this idea and wanted to share it with someone.

His passion for Bridget Riley reached its peak in Australia, apparently. It became very embarrassing. It went very wrong. Helen was on the other side of the ocean, but Bridget was much closer, and they were together in Australia. Colin MacInnes played an enormous part in his life, and I think there must have been a romantic element to it. Bryan was in love with Patrick Procktor. He loved people like Paul Huxley, for example. He loved quite a few people. He didn't love Patrick Caulfield, Patrick worried him because of his drinking, but he admired him. He loved Hoyland – and didn't worry about his drinking, but then it wasn't as bad. But I think his intellectual make-up was very influenced by Colin MacInnes – his taste in literature etc. I thought Colin was a dark man and I found him worrying. I couldn't relate Bryan to him at all. Bryan's own taste was very much his own, very wide-ranging and very interesting. He enabled everyone to see Dufy [in the 1983 exhibition], for instance.

Among Robertson's papers in the Tate Archive is this delightful spoof of a letter, from John Hubbard, typical of the letters and postcards these two friends exchanged:

STINGHAMS BUNCOMBE *Seminary and Training School for Art Critics*
Blackmoor Vale, Dorset

Oct 20 '65

Dear Sir,

We have been so impressed with your ROBERT MOTHERWELL v. American and European Culture article in the *Times* of yesterday that we have decided to offer you the post of Warden of our seminary in recognition thereof, a recognition, it may be added, that implies no need of any further passive training or instruction on your part. On the contrary it is evident that such proficiency in sheer, creative, lyrical self-expression as your article displays can only have been acquired in a rival training establishment and it is these methods which we would like you to use (assuming you accept the proffered appointment – at a salary of three Green Shield stamps per month) on our trainees.

We feel it very fortunate indeed that the post of Warden here has just fallen vacant. For spontaneous creation of verbal matter, for a display of self-generating, multi-proliferating, crapulous, pyrotechnical-polysyllabic free-fall we consider you have absolutely no rival. Even the inevitable (and scandalously libellous) comparison with Mozart was there. 'now Pollock brings Mozart to mind'. Whose mind? Not even Lord Bootboy's mind works quite as abysmally as that.

Trusting to receive a favourable reply from you in due course.

Yours very appreciatively,
George Ampersand
Bursar and Acting Warden

The following excerpt is taken from Bryan Robertson's essay in John Hubbard's 1981 Warwick Arts Trust exhibition catalogue:

In 1962, Hubbard felt the first resistance to a gestural expression of landscape when he experienced the totally individual light and terrain of the Greek mainland and islands. He had his first sense of a different structure in landscape for which gestural handling was not applicable. It is perhaps from this moment that Hubbard began, slowly, to discover himself as a painter: when the landscape began to answer back in different terms.

Certain things in Hubbard's work are constant. There is a deep and obsessive concern for place, ranging from Dorset itself, to Greece as a recurrent point of departure, to Africa ... Drawing plays a constant part in the give and take between perception and imaginative response through the way in which a pencil line or brush stroke is placed so 'openly' as to be atmospheric and abstract as well as descriptive.

In painting, there is a reconciliation between the eccentricities of place and specific visual circumstances with the demands of the painting as a separate entity which embraces those characteristics whilst extending into other and less predictable, certainly less descriptive, areas of abstract construction. Hubbard wants to make allusion as concrete and exact as straightforward description might be. With the gradual, bitterly self-critical and slow advent of confidence and freedom in painting terms slowly won throughout the sixties, Hubbard has still gone through concentrated phases of drawing straight from nature.

Caryl Hubbard

John Hubbard's wife, Caryl, remembered Bryan from the early days of the New Art Centre (of which she was a founder and director) in the mid-1950s, and here recalled his character in an affectionate interview which took place in her London flat in October 2015:

He loved artists and didn't really like galleries. He liked the informality of working with an artist, and loved the way artists thought and acted. A lot of his great friends were artists. He liked educating them. He knew an amazing amount about films and books and theatre. He always used to say: 'The trouble with artists – they're so ignorant! They don't know a thing!' In certain ways he was a cultural critic rather than an art critic, always appearing on *Critics' Forum*, *The Critics*. He loved that – he was perfectly confident about discussing any book or any play. He was a man of strong opinions, definitely, but not narrow.

I think he probably did think he was always right. He didn't always listen terribly hard to what other people were saying. He always had something else to say himself. He didn't so much disregard others, but he was always bubbling, so no one else had a chance to get a word in. He wasn't a brilliant listener, though I think he did listen to artists. He was a brilliant interpreter – he understood what artists were about. He was extremely unreliable in things like coming to appointments.

According to Caryl, Bryan would cancel, postpone or simply forget a studio visit four or five times before an artist would get fed up and want to give up on the whole idea, at which point Bryan would turn up. And his response would be so perceptive and encouraging that they forgave him and fell in love with him.

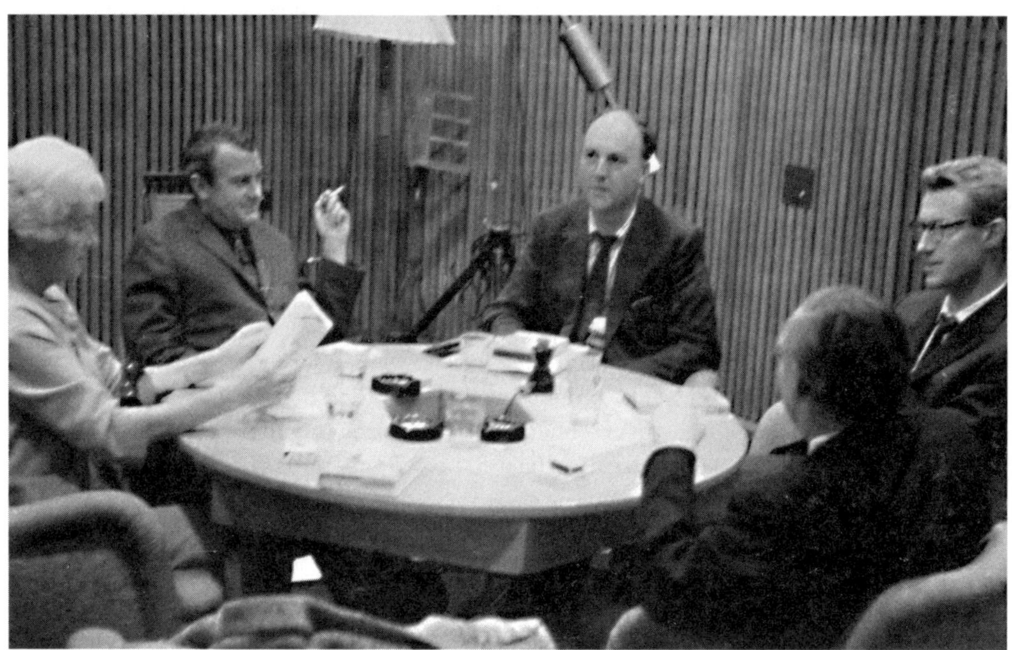

25 BR in the broadcasting studio for the BBC Radio programme *The Critics*, *c.*1969.

He did just have that ability to hone in on what an artist was trying to do, and that's very rare. He just could do it – he was born with it, and that's why artists respected him so much. He'd make constructive comments, which not many people would do, with real and genuine enthusiasm. When Bryan left you'd feel uplifted. I think that was his great gift really.

Bryan's ability to actually get something done – like even a simple review – was not good. He never got things done on time, never. That's why, in a sense, he had such a tough time. Apart from his session at the Whitechapel, which was wonderful, you couldn't employ him to do anything much, as it would never really happen. So many people say what a tragedy it was he was never director of the Tate, but of course it was never a possibility, he wasn't that sort of person. If he had been that sort of person he wouldn't have been Bryan. He didn't think like that.

One of the reasons why Bryan was very good at the Whitechapel was because he was very confident in what he liked. He didn't have any problem about showing the Bridget Rileys, the Hoylands, the rest of the *New Generation*, but he also showed Mary Potter, Thelma Hulbert and all sorts of other people. A lot of people wouldn't do that because they'd think you can't like both these things. If Bryan liked something and knew it was good then he showed it. His taste was very personal. Those Whitechapel shows were wonderful: so beautifully put on, everything looking perfect, and there would be Bryan in the middle, laughing at something, an impresario really. He was good at presiding. He wasn't a shy man, but he was perhaps a little less extrovert than he may have seemed.

I still miss him, he was a big presence. I counted him as a very close friend, but he didn't like talking about himself at all and he would not like you to ask him personal questions. Absolutely not at all. He didn't volunteer it and he didn't want to talk about it. He was quite inhibited, I think from childhood, about himself and his relationships, and I don't think he'd have wanted you to talk about yours either. You'd go to Bryan if you were feeling awful and you wanted cheering up. By himself he'd cheer you up, by telling you what he'd seen, or funny stories about somebody. But he was quite personally inhibited.

I think he was a kind man. I never heard him being bitchy about an artist, but he wasn't very keen on the art establishment. I remember him once saying to me, 'You're getting far too friendly with Nick Serota. It's not at all good for you.' I think there was always one bit of him that felt that he had been ignored by the establishment, which in a sense he had. He was not an establishment figure. He wasn't a conformist at all. He was an outsider and that's why he was so wonderful. He wasn't really a bitter person, but from time to time I think he thought, 'why am I struggling on?' No money, etc. etc. If I could choose who should hang a show for an artist – and I like the way Serota hangs – I think I'd go for Bryan as he had the greatest intuition, about how the paintings should look. Not much art history would come into it.

Occasionally he made mistakes, getting an artist slightly wrong. He knew how we loved Prunella Clough and her work, and he said once, 'I want to bring Prunella to stay with you'. I said I didn't think it was a very good idea as she was a very private person and quite shy. But he wouldn't listen. He arrived with Prunella, who didn't look terribly happy – quite nervous – and we showed her round. Anyway we had supper which went all right, and then we went to bed, and in the morning she'd gone. She'd driven off. I said, 'There you are, Bryan – what did I tell you?' She couldn't stand it. Bryan was pretty amazed that she'd gone. His enthusiasm overcame his sense of what would work. But he didn't often make mistakes like that – he usually knew people sufficiently well.

I think he had an open mind, actually. He wasn't frivolous at all, really. He was a complicated character and very direct in a funny way. You always trusted him. Which was surprising when you heard him carrying on about this and that – you would think what is this guy all about? Somehow there was something running through that was very true and you trusted it, which is interesting.

Caryl Hubbard's assessment helps to account for what Bryan achieved – it gives him credibility in the face of his incurable incompetence. Caryl said that Bryan was not a figure you felt sorry for in later life:

You didn't feel you had to pity him, though it was a pity he never did anything else here after the Whitechapel. I think he would have done the Serpentine rather well with a free hand and back-up.

Actually, I didn't think he was a terrifically good writer. But in conversation he could be very funny and he had wonderful jokes. Sometimes they were funny stories about people, sometimes just straight jokes. This is rather poignant. When he was very ill, I rang him up to say I was going away, but I'd be back in a week and would like to come and see him in hospital. I said, 'How are you, Bryan?' And he said, 'So far, so good'. I laughed and he said, 'I'll tell you a joke about that. There was a man looking out of the window in a skyscraper in New York, forty-two storeys up, and he saw the window cleaner who he'd known for years, falling past his window. He waved to him and said "Hi Bert, how are things?" The window-cleaner replied, "So far, so good," as he hurtled to the ground.' Bryan just adored that. The poignant bit is that when I got back and rang up, he'd died that morning. What was so touching was that a week from death, and feeling pretty ghastly, he could still tell that story, and still laugh at it.

Madeleine Bessborough

Madeleine Bessborough was the other founder (with Caryl Hubbard) of the New Art Centre, which she still directs. Here she remembered Robertson in an interview in October 2015 at Roche Court, the Wiltshire sculpture park to which the New Art Centre relocated:

I met Bryan through my mother, who had worked for Henry Morris after she left Cambridge. She taught in the 'Village College', which was a great movement in the 1920s to rebuild the schools in Cambridgeshire for the whole population, not just children. They were created by Henry Morris to serve the whole community and to teach parents to read and write in the evenings, and the children in the day, and were to be at the centre of the towns and have all sorts of facilities. My mother thought this was such an exciting idea. When I grew up and had the idea of starting the gallery, Henry said that the one person I must meet was his friend Bryan Robertson, who had just got a gallery in Heffer's. I remember having lunch with Bryan and Henry Morris and my mother, and Bryan said the gallery was a good idea. He was rather frightening: I was nineteen and he was almost ten years older than me and very sophisticated.

He didn't help very much, in fact, but always remained a close friend, and all my gallery life he was always there. He liked all the artists we showed, like Mary Potter, and came to all the exhibitions. He suggested we show Elisabeth Vellacott, who had known Bryan since those early Cambridge years, because her father was the Master of Peterhouse. She was very much a Cambridge artist. She adored Bryan – the nearest thing to being in love with him.

The tragedy with Bryan was that he was a brilliant showman who put on the most wonderful shows. He had no sense of money at all and people like John Sainsbury, who backed him a lot with various projects, got exasperated with Bryan over money. He shouldn't have had to worry about money. He was a total impresario who should have had a great patron, a patron with an endless pocket, who realised they were on to a gem with somebody like Bryan, who had this incredible eye and incredible enthusiasm and intelligence, but shouldn't have to worry about paying the bills.

He was a good raconteur but I don't think he was a very good listener. A lovely performer. He had a wonderful sense of humour. Not a sense of the absurd, just incredibly funny about human foibles and the pomposity of things. But then he also went along with it – a number of his friends were very grand. He loved going to Covent Garden. I think it was just the whole extraordinary 'all the world's a stage and has a thousand people on it' and he liked them all. To a certain extent. He was very funny and you can get away with an awful lot of things if you're funny and relaxed. He was fantastically good company. He loved life and didn't really care about what other people thought. He was completely entertaining and very interesting.

Later 1970s

Back in London in 1975 after the debacle of Purchase and his decision not to go to Australia, Bryan cast around for new projects. The art book publisher Phaidon decided to inaugurate a series of paperback monographs on contemporary artists, and commissioned Bryan to write one on Edward Burra. Then they wrote in September 1977 cancelling his original contract, suggesting that a smaller book might do instead, and asking optimistically where the manuscript was. Not surprisingly, nothing ever came of this venture. The next month Bryan sent a letter summarising the projects they'd already discussed to the literary agent Pat Kavanagh, with a view to her taking him on.

1. New edition of Pollock.

2. Burra book for Phaidon.

3. Hoyland monograph.

4. Art Memoirs – K has volunteered to write a preface.

5. A Concise History of Australian art in the 20th Century.

6. A long interview on film with Sutherland part of a projected series of films on old and redoubtable people such as Rebecca West, Enid Bagnold, Moore, Gielgud, Peggy Ashcroft, Joseph Needham,

William Walton, Michael Tippett, Graham Greene. If the series were Anglo-American he'd include Balanchine, Martha Graham, Noguchi, Buckminster Fuller, de Kooning. If of a more European caste, then Jean Renoir, Luis Bunuel, Sonia Delaunay.

In November 1977 Bryan drafted a letter to Norman Rosenthal, then the Exhibitions Secretary of the Royal Academy, proposing three exhibitions of artists in the Diploma Galleries (now the Sackler Galleries): John Hubbard, Nigel Hall and Gary Wragg.

From 1979 there is correspondence with Graham Sutherland about the possibility of Bryan writing a text for an Italian publication on him. Sutherland generously offered to underwrite any shortfall of the fee Bryan might ask, writing, 'good of you to do it at all. One can have no one but the best – perhaps the only critic in England'. They also discussed the possibility of Sutherland designing a ballet on the work of Matthias Grünewald. 'At any rate let us meet and talk,' wrote Sutherland, 'and please make us both *laugh* as you always do'.

Remembering this period Bryan Kneale commented: 'There were spates when I saw a lot of him and spates when I didn't see him at all. He wouldn't reply to letters and had a reputation for not keeping appointments, and I told him that. He was extremely cross with me for telling him. It didn't go down very well.' Kneale, who John Spurling refers to as one of the 'top discoveries' of Robertson's Whitechapel, had joined the Royal Academy as their first abstract artist. He did so on condition that he was allowed to choose and curate a sculpture show there, which he duly did in 1972. Then he had the idea for a follow-up exhibition of painting, to be curated by Bryan. The main problem was that Bryan was now in America, and very difficult to keep tabs on. Kneale described the difficulties:

He wanted the exhibition to start in 1890, though I wanted all the artists to be alive. He started to get obsessed with particular pictures and how he would hang the show. He was talking about borrowing stuff from The Louvre, but he wouldn't necessarily hang it if it didn't fit in. Fundraising had started, but in the end Casson [Sir Hugh Casson was President of the RA] lost his rag and said: 'Enough!' and paid Bryan to forget it. Out of that came Norman Rosenthal.

In an article entitled 'The Whitechapel's Future' (*Evening Standard*, 27 January 1972), the art critic Richard Cork examined the post-Robertson state of play at the gallery. He began by announcing a full-scale Leon Kossoff retrospective there at a time when the gallery had been faced with possible closure for many months. Cork wrote:

For one thing at least is clear: the Whitechapel *can* continue to function, albeit with funds considerably more modest than its last director – Mark Glazebrook – thought necessary. Not that shortage of cash was the only reason why he resigned. Another, equally complex question centred on the very identity of the gallery itself, caught uneasily between the greater resources of nationally subsidised institutions on the one hand and powerful commercial dealers on the other.

Cork went on to identify the unusual position of the Whitechapel in the art world:

A uniquely independent constitution ensures that it becomes whatever its director wants it to be: and, under the ebullient leadership of Bryan Robertson, it managed for many years to mount trail-blazing shows which were instrumental in dragging English artists out of their post-war provincialism ... For more than a decade Robertson made his gallery into a prime source for everything provocative and challenging ... But by the time he left in 1969, this sense of consistent excitement had dwindled.

The role of the Whitechapel, as Cork saw it, was two-fold: to offer artists in mid-career the chance to show their work, and to be an open house for young cutting-edge artists (thus suggesting that at least two aspects of Robertson's exhibition strategy should be adopted):

It cannot be stressed too often that the Whitechapel's principal room remains the finest display area in the city, providing an unlikely blend of monumentality and warmth which the aggressive pyrotechnics of the Hayward so conspicuously lack. While the one invites, the other bullies: space at the Whitechapel becomes a source of expansion and relief, whereas at the Hayward it is used as a threat, an arid desert which paradoxically clamps down on everything placed within its clinical walls ... the Whitechapel should always be regarded as a space which any artist is privileged to find at his disposal.

Michael Heath

Bryan was always on the lookout for alternative sources of revenue rather than writing, one of which for a time became the renting-out of his basement in Barnsbury Street as a small self-contained flat. Later he even contemplated selling it. One of Bryan's tenants in the 1970s was the *Spectator* cartoonist Michael Heath (born 1935), who lived there for about six months. In a telephone interview of December 2017 he recalled:

I was living in Brighton at the time and I needed somewhere to crash in London sometimes in the evenings. Bryan was around the *Spectator*, as I was – I suppose he was arts editor – and he was a flamboyant, interesting, funny old thing. It was a horrible two-roomed flat, I don't remember what I paid for it – very little, I'm sure – but I remember his art collection upstairs which I was very impressed with. He had some good things and some things that weren't thought good then, Rauschenberg and stuff like that. He seemed to be very easy-going about it all. But his private life was a bit odd I thought, inasmuch as it was very difficult to sleep because of the noise going on upstairs. I remember being woken up one morning by a young man at my basement door, saying 'You've got to help me! Get me out of here or hide me or something!' He'd been upstairs, so I think it was all rather racy. I think there was a steady partner, someone who was there and put up with his philandering – that sort of easy-going relationship. I don't suppose it was drugs in those days, just straight booze. We were all boozed – everyone in the *Spectator* was drunk, as they were everywhere. Wonderful!

Heath was never invited upstairs for parties.

No – I wasn't rough trade or anything like that. And there's a big difference between sophisticated friends and artists and *cartoonists*! We got on, but Bryan thought what I did wasn't art. I left the flat – things were being stolen, though there wasn't much in there anyway, radios and things like that. I was a bit frightened of the place, to tell you the truth. I had a girlfriend at the time and I was playing away and all that nonsense. I was happy and in love and crazy and drunk – something you don't realise will go away one day. It was around the corner from her flat. I loved that area – it seemed fun at the time, romantic. But no, I didn't meet anybody with him particularly, and he seemed to be away a lot. I've a very bad memory – drunken cartoonist who can't remember too clearly what went on. I was more likely to be with Jeffrey Bernard.

Peter Adam

Peter Adam is a British filmmaker and author born in Berlin, and was a close friend of the designer Eileen Gray who was Prunella Clough's aunt. Bryan admired John Berger as a writer but was completely at odds with him over art and its purposes. Adam, a close friend of both Prunella Clough and Keith Vaughan, reminds us in his autobiography *Not Drowning but Waving* (1995) that both Robertson and Berger were friends of Prunella, and both could be encountered at her kitchen table over dinner. Adam also writes of giving his own dinner parties when he lived in London.

I was not afraid of mixing people up, always hoping that the sparkle of the conversation would make up for the blandness of the food. Once I remember Bryan Robertson and Irene Worth getting in such a huff over the music of Aaron Copland that Bryan stormed out, leaving me alone with an actress I much admired but hardly knew, both covering up our embarrassment with unhealthy helpings of *apfelstrudel*.

Adam, himself a sophisticated European intellectual, remembered Bryan as 'cultivated and cosmopolitan':

With his open-mindedness and many-sided interests he had turned the [Whitechapel] Gallery into the most interesting place in London to see art and to meet people. Bryan was also the most ingenious and generous host, although he never seemed to have any money, as people of his diverse talent are notoriously badly paid in a country where art is not a priority. In his house one would meet an array of different people. He had the wit and imagination to mix the filmmaker Antonioni, Princess Margaret and new young painters such as Derek Jarman and Paul Huxley.

Adam was also high in his praise of the first *New Generation* exhibition, saying that the opening was 'a very jolly affair', and noting the prices: 'for £65 you could buy a Patrick Caulfield, for £100 a Riley, a David Hockney oil was priced at £225.'

Nigel Hall

The sculptor Nigel Hall (born 1943) met Robertson while still a student at the Royal College of Art, when Bryan was being conducted round the sculpture school by its Professor, Bernard Meadows. The Professor was uncomplimentary about Hall's life figure in plaster, which the sculptor defended. Undoubtedly, Robertson would have been impressed by the young artist's determination to make his own decisions, for he not only bought a sculpture by Hall at this juncture, an important early piece entitled *Freeze 1* (1965), but the two swiftly became friends. When Hall was graduating from the Royal College in 1967, Bryan encouraged him to apply for the Harkness Fellowship, which resulted in a fruitful period when Hall was based in Los Angeles and travelled across America. Hall and Robertson met up later in New York in the 1970s, and in 1980 Bryan selected and wrote the catalogue for Hall's Warwick Arts Trust exhibition.

Hall told me in a phone interview in March 2018 that Bryan had been keen to write a monograph on Jackson Pollock, but was thwarted in this by Pollock's widow, Lee Krasner, who for some reason objected to him writing it, perhaps because he was British. Then at a New York party she overheard him talking about his love for Pollock's work and became convinced that he should write it. That's how it came about, and how he also became a great friend of Krasner. Hall recalled that Bryan lived with a large and beautiful painting by her in his Barnsbury house. Hall's political views didn't always coincide with Robertson's left-wing ones, but this

never threatened their close friendship. Hall says: 'Despite his unreliability to turn up for a dinner party, even ones he was hosting, his joyful presence was so rewarding when he did show, that one quickly forgave these lapses.'

Hall continued:

In May 1971, I was in New York for an exhibition at the Robert Elkon Gallery. Bryan had lent me his apartment there while he was in New York State. It was during his time while Director of the Neuberger gallery at Purchase, not his happiest time. I went to meet him at his 'Betsy Trotwood Cottage' on the Stuyvesant Estate where he had felt marooned over the winter, because he wasn't driving at that time. He was keen to get out and about, but before we left, I remember the large figure of Robert Motherwell framed in the doorway. Two of my heroes and the day had just begun! Next step was to choose the car for the day. In a huge barn – rows of cars to chose from: Cadillacs, Mercedes ... there must have been twenty cars in this garage belonging to the Stuyvesant Estate, all the keys there, ready to go. We played it safe and took a Volvo, setting out to visit the neighbours. These included James Thrall Soby, the one-time curator at MOMA, and Alfred Barr, ex-Director of MOMA, both of whom were welcoming and happy to show us their impressive collections. We then went on to the famous Glass House in New Canaan, Connecticut, to spend the day with its architect, Philip Johnson, and his partner, the curator and gallerist David Whitney. As well as the beautiful house, we were shown his exceptional collections of paintings and sculpture, in their separate galleries. Lunch and dinner appeared as if by magic, silently and beautifully arriving from somewhere. I recall his comment that the expense wasn't the house but the wallpaper – namely buying the surrounding land. Ironically, despite his magnificent collection, he lived in the Glass House with one classical landscape only – a Poussin [*The Funeral of Phocion*, *c.*1648]. A memorable day, recorded in the slim volume [*Johnson House, New Canaan, Connecticut, 1949*, published 1972] edited and photographed by Yukio Futagawa, with text by Bryan. It was published by ADA Edita in Tokyo in the Global Architecture series.

What a wonderful friendship I enjoyed with Bryan from when we first met at the RCA in 1965 until his death. Over those years we had countless meals together, often in his Barnsbury Street house. These dinner parties were extraordinary gatherings of friends from all walks of life – painters, musicians, actors, writers. Among those I met through Bryan were Colin Davis, Claire Bloom (with Philip Roth), Beatrice Monti with her husband Gregor von Rezzori, Michael Frayn and Claire Tomalin. We would be gathered around his big elliptical table chatting, while Bryan cooked in the adjoining kitchen, most often venison with an abundance of juniper berries. He would burst in with 'Never mind all that – now listen to me!' And all these luminaries would shut up and giggle.

This quotation is taken from Bryan Robertson's introduction to the catalogue of Hall's 1980 Warwick Arts Trust show:

This exhibition has been planned to demonstrate the evolution, in a necessarily truncated way, of an exceptionally gifted English sculptor. At thirty-six, Nigel Hall is well known internationally for sculpture of extreme refinement in which the traditional functions of space, mass and volume have become so inverted through a use of slender rods, of variable thickness, colour and tonality, that the space disclosed by each work is equivalent to constantly changing volumes or planes, by implication. At the same time, these planes and volumes alter through the angle of viewing as much as they are transformed, through different perspectives, by the linear construction that contains them.

The introductory text that follows is the result of questions put to the artist by myself, and if it may seem incorrect to put my own name to a text that would appear to have been written by the artist, I should explain that far more questions were put to Nigel Hall than appear here, and the transcription of his patient replies is a synthesis between his direct answers and my insistence on extreme simplicity of language. In other words, although substantially dictated by the artist, the text that follows may be fairly described as a combined venture with the artist's final approval.

In the following excerpts from *Art and Australia* (vol.22, no.3, autumn 1985), Robertson focuses on Hall's early work:

He is genuinely wholly absorbed by landscape and by particular convergences of skyline, scale, wind pressure, stillness, distance and flatness, shadow and substance, light and density. But it would be absurd to imagine that he is a disguised or sublimated nature poet or in any way dependent upon landscape for his initial formal impulse. He is trying, successfully in my view, to reverse the entire concept of sculpture, so that the space trapped and disclosed or flowing around his slender coloured rods is itself the sculpture, with the rods almost serving as negative voids, or positive conduits.

If Hall is not in my sense a frustrated landscape artist, he is not a romantic constructivist either: the principles of Constructivism would be alien to this artist with his essentially surrealist sense of space. But in the mid-1960s the beginnings of Minimalism were also stirring in London, fed by the examples of Donald Judd and Robert Morris, and there is no doubt that the avoidance of either flesh or filigree in Hall's work for so many years comes from his own personal distillation of ends and means.

Robertson the writer

Bryan had an enviable articulateness that bordered occasionally on verbosity. His writing had some of the pace and informality of conversation, but sometimes also a scatter-gun approach to distributing words

over a wide area in the hope of hitting at least some targets. He could become almost paralysed by having to prepare too much in advance – to think about what he wanted to say. This somewhat random, rather indiscriminate, manner worked well when Bryan was talking informally – perhaps to students or over the radio. It did not adapt so well to the page. His informal, conversational style – with one thing leading to another – was difficult to stop or interrupt because his mind was running on ahead, and was so well stocked with information and opinions to share. Even close friends sometimes found this difficult. Prunella Clough, for instance, complained (in an undated letter) that Bryan didn't let her get a word in edge-ways. He was well aware of his tendency to get carried away. Elsewhere, in another draft document, he writes: 'But I'm launching into a tedious lecture, and I apologize. I don't really always carry on like a Mahler symphony – it's just that sometimes there's a lot to say. I'll be brief.' Perhaps this garrulousness stemmed from a Celtic ancestry. He certainly claimed in a letter to John Craxton that he was not English, but had Irish Scots blood.

Bryan was not a great one for the structure of a piece of writing; he was less interested in the niceties of construction than in the headlong rush of ideas and enthusiasm that bubbled out of his teeming brain. As a consequence his articles and essays often end abruptly after a grand series of images or perceptions, rather than with any conclusion. He breaks off almost in mid-sentence, certainly in mid-conversation. Thus his best writing has the spontaneity and invention of spoken speech. Occasionally, he would turn in a slack piece of writing, repetitive and poorly punctuated, such as the introduction to the Whitechapel Rauschenberg catalogue of 1964, no doubt grappled together at the last moment when he was not at his best. Sometimes working with a savage deadline can bring out the best in a writer, and sometimes it worked for Bryan. But not always, and there are too many careless pieces in his bibliography.

All his writing was done in longhand in a very distinctive script. There were constant digressions, revisions and interpolations, and a Robertson manuscript quite often looked more like a wackily illuminated manuscript than a cogently argued review. The job of deciphering his words was given to a secretary, or more properly a typist, though these tended not to last long as Bryan was not the easiest of employers. In the late 1970s the woman next door typed for him and did secretarial work for a while, but he rarely had much continuity in this. He would have benefited hugely from a loyal part-time assistant who could cope with him, such as he found at the Whitechapel. The one that most people remember is Tejas Englesmith, who was Bryan's assistant in the 1960s. Hilary Spurling pointed out that Tejas had constantly to cover for Bryan – as indeed she herself had done, when arts editor of the *Spectator* – because he would periodically remove himself, not answer phone calls or the door, and suffer his asthma in silence. She said that Bryan hated to be pitied and didn't want to be seen when he was feeling below par. This was part of his desire always to give and not to take. Paul Huxley remembered Tejas (or 'Con-tejas' – contagious – as John Hoyland used to call him) was 'a very nice young man, very sociable. He mixed and chatted with the artists and I met him when he was Bryan's sidekick on *The New Generation*. It can't have been an easy job. He was a tireless supporter of Bryan's, and a good organiser.'

If he would have benefited from the ministrations of an able assistant, Bryan could also have done with a full-time editor to curb his wildest excesses and keep him to deadlines. Considering his lack of self-discipline, it's amazing that he got anything done at all, but inevitably what did emerge from his pen was of very variable quality.

Bryan used the words 'artist', 'painting' and 'sculpture' freely and frequently. He wasn't so keen on the word 'art'. When used, it often seemed to indicate a rebuke, or a lowering of the spirits, especially when coupled with the words 'world' or 'market'. It is as if it represented a false or synthetic construct, as opposed to the genuine activity of creation. He was equally certain about other preferences. For instance he always preferred the term 'English' to 'British'. He explains his antipathy to the latter in a letter to Philip Roth. 'I loath and detest the word "British", a politician's invention, usually invoked to signal a new piece of chicanery. You do not ask in the butchers for a joint of "British" beef or a leg of "British" lamb – and we do not study in our universities "The history of British literature" or "British poetry".'

When it came to punctuation, Bryan made extensive use of the colon, as he endeavoured to clarify or amplify a point. Also dashes – a hangover perhaps from his method of making notes. However, he doesn't much use hyphens in words, as in low-key or still-life, preferring the run-on, however odd it might look: lowkey, for instance, or threedimensionally. (Of course, this may be the fault of the poor typist instructed to decipher Robertson's much-annotated scrawl.) Semi-colons also abound, and commas were scattered in a rather indiscriminate and inconsistent way. This latter may again be down to the typist, of course.

Sentences wind round and round, or rather, slither sinuously along, subordinate phrases slipping in, as he wrestled to get the exact meaning he wanted into words. Sometimes one almost feels that words are not his natural way of expressing himself. He scorns to use just one word when several, heaped together, might do the job more thoroughly. Fortunately, he usually takes the reader with him, such is the power of his enthusiasm, and the sentences most of the time end on a high note rather than a dying one. Favourite words include radiant, extraordinary, self-conscious (and its opposite), integrated, lived-in, sensation, feeling. Bryan didn't often make use of quotations in his writing.

Bryan's first book was devoted to Jackson Pollock, which he said he spent 'two years sweating away on', and was written with the help of Pollock's widow, Lee Krasner. Published in 1960, two years after Pollock's Whitechapel show, it was a hugely distinguished monograph on one of the legends of contemporary art and published when the author was the relatively youthful age of thirty-five. After it appeared, everyone who was anyone wanted a book by Bryan Robertson (and, of course, an exhibition at the Whitechapel). Robert Motherwell, with whom Robertson was close friends, was supposed to be the next subject, and although Bryan took copious notes over the following few years, and stayed often with Bob, *and* gave him an exhibition at the Whitechapel (in 1966), the long-awaited Robertson-Motherwell monograph never appeared.

Bryan sent a typically half-boastful, half-self-deprecating letter to Kenneth Clark on 22 September 1960:

> My Pollock book comes out in mid-November, and I long to get hold of it. I shall be quite insufferable, with my first book, re-reading it all, avidly, and sitting demurely on buses and trains with a copy nonchalantly on my lap. It's full of weird ideas, half of which I now want badly to add to, and expand fully. No doubt the reviewers, if any, will point to them.

One at least was to refer to Robertson's 'high purple prose' and to take exception to his flights of lyrical description.

Thames & Hudson did an excellent production job on *Jackson Pollock*: the book is beautiful, printed on thick stock with superb colour reproductions individually tipped-in on black cartridge-paper backgrounds. Drawings and paintings are reproduced: there are 169 illustrations, 36 of which are in full colour. This was deluxe treatment for the beginning of the 1960s. In fact, some people maintain that there's never been visually a better book on Pollock than this. (The dealer and collector John Kasmin recently bought another copy of Robertson's monograph, as he believes that no other Pollock book can hold a candle to the quality of its reproductions.) Bryan's Pollock book was not only published in London and New York, but there were also German and Italian editions. The first edition appeared in 1960, with a second impression in 1968. Later there was talk of a revised edition, but typically Bryan never managed to finish the required work on it. The first edition has to stand on its own.

The text begins baldly – Bryan leaps straight in bravely, but doesn't attempt any chronology until over halfway through the book. The writing is shot through with intriguing ideas and arresting perceptions, but it is not well organised. Too often, Bryan allows his prose to get bogged down in generalisations and abstract speculations. But there is still plenty of

good material here, to accompany the splendid reproductions. This first excerpt is the book's opening paragraph:

As a man, Pollock was taciturn and contemplative by nature, though he was drawn to violence by fatality and, at last in his death, by its finality. He was absorbed all through his life by the structure of violence: an essentially twentieth-century speculation. The inner springs and tensions of violent action or a dramatic situation moved him and aroused his imagination rather than the violence itself as an emotional display.

The discussion and analysis of individual paintings is exhaustive; here is a single paragraph about a key image, evoking its new attitude to space and the way this engages the viewer:

The impact of *Blue Poles* comes also from its scale. Delacroix's requirement of a picture that 'it must be a feast for the eye' here shares equal ground with another basic necessity: that a picture should always make a world, self-contained and utterly convincing, which the spectator should feel able to enter, explore, and move about in. This painting is seven feet high and sixteen feet long. It is roughly the size of a wall. A man moving in front of the picture is enmeshed in its movement and engulfed by its space. The space, described by colour and the density of movement, is frontal, aggressive, and thrusts outwards from the picture plane towards the spectator. We are confronted by a new conception of pictorial space. There is practically no recession, though there are resting-places for the eye on the poles and in the areas of white which drift like clouds across the surface, diagonally from right to left, in a descending and stabilizing movement.

This final excerpt is taken from the ultimate two paragraphs of the book which summarise what Robertson felt about his subject:

The act of painting in itself had become for Pollock a semi-religious activity. Everything he felt and experienced was unleashed into it. He reaffirmed the essentially primitive nature of painting and completely dispensed with the present-day corruption of that nature, in which exercises in taste and empty picture-making disguise a paucity of true feeling or genuine creative instinct. He saw art as an inadequate vehicle for expressing the impact of life on himself, as an individual, but he did everything that it is possible for one man to do with the existing conventions of art. He used them and finally dispensed with them. In so doing, he made painting advance both in what it could suggest and in the means that might be taken to expand its basic language rather than its mere vocabulary. De Stael had already made us conscious of a formal displacement of space through showing us the residue of form, reunified with a space that was itself reorganized, on equal terms with that residue, into a Cubist conception of space. Pollock showed us an entirely new space enlivened and quickened by the traceries of his subconscious imagination after it had run the gamut of formal speculation.

For Pollock to draw continually from his subconscious was not a denial of the artist's responsibility but an added and terrible burden, an increased and optimistic acceptance of the potentialities of painting as an expression of life. His last act of affirmation in painting *Scent* has tragic undertones, for he died in the following year. The search was ended, the great gesture was made, and the exorcism was complete. The effort killed him.

Undoubtedly, Robertson's book was much read and much admired. It was also heavily plundered by artists in search of inspiration or a role model, and by writers in search of material. The popular picture book *Pollock*, in the Hamlyn Twentieth-Century Masters series, with a short essay by Alberto Busignani, appeared in 1971, cribbed most extravagantly from Robertson's book. In fact, Busignani's entire text seems to be a dialogue with Robertson, quoting extensively from his book, a dialogue by no means uncritical, much of it carried on in ludicrously long footnotes. Bryan's book remains a pleasure to handle and consult.

Although Robertson did not live up to expectations and write any more books with the ambition and scope of *Jackson Pollock*, he did subsequently contribute essays of varying lengths to a number of jointly authored books. A letter to K Clark (dated 17 July 1977) mentions his long preface to a new monograph on Robert Motherwell by H.H. Arnason (1977), which apparently the artist said was 'the most acute essay on his life and work ever written'. Bryan comments: 'I aim to write with the "force, lucidity and ease" of [Edmund] Wilson, though I'm miles short.' Apart from the books about Australian artists (see pp.154–6) there were other publications, chief amongst which is *David Carr: The Discovery of an Artist* (1987). This monograph, for which Bryan wrote the principal (but still not extensive) text, contains some of his most relaxed and enjoyable writing, including evocative description and cleverly worked-in autobiography. For these reasons, I have quoted from it extensively.

The reality and purpose of life for David now was painting. His early work is clearly affected by Cedric Morris's example: sharp contours, clearly delineated forms, a slightly naïf treatment of figures, quite thickly if smoothly painted surfaces, decorative rather than analytically simplified shapes and a narrowly restricted palette. His subjects were wholly figurative: landscape, still life, and figures, fellow students or himself…

I met David Carr for the first time early in 1948, in London, at the Lefevre Gallery in its New Bond Street phase. It was the year of Dubuffet's great North African watercolours, when Peter Brook's magnificent production of *Boris Godunov* appeared at Covent Garden with sets and costumes by Georges Wakhevitch and Paolo Silveri singing the great role, when Katherine Dunham's so-called Caribbean dancers arrived with such impact in London for the first time, Mae West was seen on stage in her own weird production of *Diamond Lil*, and Cocteau's film of *Orphée* was screened.

The occasion for meeting David was a 'between shows' mixed group at the Lefevre of small paintings by Keith Vaughan, boats and beaches, lowkeyed, rather turgid and distantly Braque-influenced; one or two strong paintings by Robert Colquhoun and Robert MacBryde, Italian puppet figures by Colquhoun and stilllife pictures by MacBryde; some vividly coloured ink-and-watercolour Mediterranean scenes by John Minton made about the same time as his Corsican travels with Alan Ross; two or three abstract gouaches by John Tunnard; a wooden carving with painted colour by Hepworth and two or three small, jaunty semi-abstract still-life paintings by Nicholson of St Ives motifs: a typical house show of the period. While I was living and studying in Paris for a year, in 1947, I had been invited by Duncan Macdonald, the lively and irascible director of the Lefevre, to start work in the gallery when I returned to London and I had accepted his offer. The Lefevre in 1948 was not only famous for nineteenth- and twentieth-century French painting, as it is still, but also represented through Macdonald's taste and enthusiasm some of the best artists working in England at that time. As well as Hepworth, Nicholson and Burra, with the two isolated figures of Lowry and Tunnard, the younger Lefevre artists, Colquhoun, MacBryde, Minton and Vaughan formed the major part of that English neo-romanticism which had come into being in the isolated, insular war years and included John Craxton and Michael Ayrton. The prevailing mood had been encouraged by Geoffrey Grigson's revelation of Samuel Palmer and affected also by the disparate examples of Sutherland, Lewis and the Picasso-derived style of Jankel Adler, the gifted emigré Polish artist, who had spent time in Scotland as a refugee and got to know the two Roberts, Colquhoun and MacBryde ...

Starston [Carr's home in Harleston, Norfolk] was a revelation. As the director of a public gallery [the Whitechapel] forever in quest of works of art for exhibitions, I had been a weekend guest in many of the great country homes in England, but I had never seen a country home before that had been kept in such perfect and wholly unpretentious eighteenth- or early nineteenth-century country-house style. It was high summer; the deceptively small-seeming, rectangular house, so roomy inside, completely engulfed by deep green and gold country, ploughed fields and crops, grasslands full of flowers, woods and copses, a rolling landscape right up to the plain front door, without even the flattery of a flight of steps or grand portico, was part of the landscape. A stone-flagged hall, drawing room to the left, dining room to the right, bare wooden floors, a few rugs, fine period furniture – and flowers everywhere, on tables, on shelves, on window ledges, mixed garden flowers, beautifully flung together and wild flowers. Many tables in the two main rooms were covered with small precious objects: pictures, photos, enamel boxes, stones, jewels, mementoes, toys, clocks, musical boxes. Starston was Barbara's special creation, it was plain to see. A countrywoman from birth, and not, as in David's case, by adoption, she adored children, dogs, horses and her painting but had little interest in conventional domestic pursuits, or in cooking. David had always done all the cooking, which he enjoyed, and he looked after the hard side of things, digging, sawing, or repairing the house. The taste everywhere, which was the finest and most delicate imaginable – and very much an artist's fine taste – was wholly Barbara's and managed to incorporate the paintings by Freud, Lowry, Colquhoun, Bauchant, Clough, Vaughan, Hillier, Bonnard (a lithograph), Jack Smith, Morris, Millares, Saura, Tàpies and Appel – and a small portrait of Cedric Morris by Freud that he gave to Barbara as a student. The paintings were placed on the walls in an almost casual way, the house was an untidy, unglossy family home, but the elegance and unselfconscious prettiness were unforgettable. The feeling of being outside the time-flux was very strong, also, as if the hall and the two main rooms were a foil for characters drawn by Dickie Doyle – one expected to see chairs round the wall, ready for a dance, as in a novel by Thackeray or Dickens. The atmosphere was entirely unselfconscious and accentuated, I suppose, by the lamps placed in each room and by Barbara's extraordinary mélange of tiny games, toys and bibelots of all kinds placed around the rooms, precious, delicate, full of colour and light …

David's earlier paintings, completed at Starston, are very different in their domestic themes or portraits of grim-faced, black-shawled Irish peasants or Lowestoft fishermen and net scenes, but their extreme simplification, compression and use of strong contours make a loose connection with the man-and-machine images which followed them. These early paintings show the influences of Cedric Morris in the simplification of form, dense use of creamily opaque pigment and obsessive focus on edgy still-life sequences; Lowry in the whites of sea and sky, black horizon lines and cold blues, reds and grey-green; and Freud, marginally, in the big, staring, close-ups of heads and graphic delineation of features. The early works have an intense charge of their own, in which domesticity has a loaded stillness and the peasants or fishing folk have the tough simplicity in structure of pub signs or primitive art.

Bryan as essayist

Besides lecturing at art schools and universities, and broadcasting extensively on radio and television, Bryan contributed occasional art criticism to the *Cambridge Review*, the *Spectator*, the *New Statesman*, the *Listener* and the *Sunday Times*. He also wrote rather longer (and sometimes more considered) articles for exhibition catalogues, mostly in support of those artists he had already decided to back. Occasionally there was an exception. Here follows a short selection of passages from catalogue essays to give a flavour of what Robertson wrote in the 1970s after leaving the Whitechapel.

ANTHONY GREEN *Rochdale Art Gallery & touring, 1978*
Anthony Green is an independent artist who has found the perfect pictorial means with which to express his idea of the universe or, more exactly his own life and times. It is a sophisticatedly deadpan but loving view of everyday family life, and adds up to a celebration of the manners and tribal customs of a fairly knowing branch of the bourgeoisie that combines in its steely disconnections the tenacious eye of a Mauriac with something scattier – as if Woody Allen had decided to re-make a Jacques Tati film. Lurking behind the cycle shed or lying prone beneath the dining room table (shot? stoned? bored? just resting?) is something like the baleful but also affectionately satirical eye that illuminates Raymond Chandler's map of suburbia, so that when we are introduced in a drawing room to a nice lady in a black dress with pearls we wonder if perhaps she is taking time off from her frequently raided gambling club.

If this doesn't sound like painting, then think of the edgily particularized and caparisoned world of Clouet and Corneille de Lyon, of the relished, earthy detail in Flemish and French Books of Hours, the white and bulbous nudes of Lucas Cranach, and that bossily informative, wholly convinced world of posters and pub signs when advertising and street signs were in the hands of real artists – Les Frères Lissac (relatives of the Anglo-French Green) for spectacles, for instance, or other advertisements in France and England in the thirties and forties – before the delights of advertising were undermined by dreary photographic journalism – which so often presented elaborately detailed scenes from everyday life disrupted and transfigured by a surrealist dislocation of detail or combination of circumstance.

Green's work for the past fifteen years must have given pause to those who see painting only in tightly prescribed lines which follow, in varying degrees of personal inflection, the recommended attitudes of international style. I refer of course mostly to method. This narrowness and shallowness, both of focus and expression, is because art criticism and its attendant promotion has been taken too seriously by too many artists eager for the comforting precincts of an accepted style – and partly because art schools, everywhere, have changed from schools of basic instruction into culture factories. The really compelling abstract art of this century, the art of Klee, Mondrian and Miró, for example, came from deep personal and organic roots of feeling and response to life as well as to geography and tradition, and was not at all concerned with reproductions in art magazines, the chic or otherwise of current exhibitions, or any kind of established market. Least of all did artists of this calibre resort, in picture-making, to the kindergarten exercises of basic design as abstract conclusions in their own right.

Figurative or representational art has had to fend for itself as a kind of intermittently welcomed poor relation of abstract art, in the face of much snobbism. But the arrival of Johns with his Flags, and Targets, and Maps, and Rauschenberg with his Dante drawings alone, removed forever that tired and confused old 'literary' tag that was so often applied, dismissively, to good figurative art.

ELISABETH VELLACOTT *New Art Centre, London, 1972*

Earlier in the 1970s, Bryan had suggested to the New Art Centre that they look at the work of his old friend Elisabeth Vellacott. The result was Vellacott's first exhibition in London, from November to December 1972. The following excerpt comes from Bryan's essay in the catalogue:

The paintings and drawings of Elisabeth Vellacott have the unforced authority and concentration of scriptures describing the casually monumental phenomena of everyday living: indoors, in the garden, through the orchard, and beyond. Completely themselves, they reflect the seductive unpredictability, the abrasive allure, of truth itself. Free of formal mannerism, they have allegiance only to the essential nature of each occasion in terms of an imaginative identity. The paintings, however, become oddly stylized in their emotional tone, achieved through the consistency of a prevailing atmosphere which is calm, still, detached, but also grand and ceremonious in the way each painting celebrates, and so extends, the existential eloquence and the under-lying ritual of apparently inconsequential human gesture. Equally, the supposedly ordinary and familiar aspects of a domesticated landscape become subjects for conjecture, for they are seen with such unstartled but extra-ordinary freshness that an element of mystery enters the scene. It is like picking up a volume labelled Balzac and finding yourself reading Flaubert or Stendhal.

In more exactly equivalent terms of painting, the sensation is also rather like that happy revelation in which Persian or Chinese art suddenly seems able to embody within its decorative fragility something of the earthiness as well as the tender poetry of Brueghel. The paintings, and certain drawings, have at least one other essential characteristic: a resonance achieved through the way in which certain shapes or particular figures that might seem almost gauche, certainly somewhat primitive, in their first simple disclosure, suddenly reveal themselves as sophisticated ikons, loaded with imaginative implication and potential life.

This artist creates her images very slowly, after prolonged contemplation of nature; and it is a modest and precise use of language to say that there are many, many years of devoted study and application behind all the work in the present exhibition. I cannot think of any other artist in recent years in England who has waited with such patience for a first one-man show in London: waited, that is, for the middle years of complete maturity of vision and the full development of a totally personal authority in handling colour and form before presenting her paintings and drawings to the public. It is yet another paradox of Elisabeth Vellacott's work that the visual sophistication which illuminates this composure finds expression in such apparently straightforward inventions: there is no rhetoric here, no straining after effect, and no regard whatever for fashion or for superficial bravura display.

The colour in Elisabeth Vellacott's work is peculiar to her and deserves special attention. It has the 'inhabited', 'lived-in' quality, with all its richness and purity, that we find in Bokhara rugs or woven fabrics, and that off-key tonal suggestiveness that we find also in African or Indian materials. Basically, the colour is nearer the sharp or soft vibrancy of vegetable dyes. It is unexpected colour, always decorative but perfectly calculated for the psychological as well as the physical timbre of each painting. It is an immensely seductive murmur, never a shout.

The way in which this artist builds up an illusion – for the work has little to do with realism as we normally encounter it – of foliage in her drawings of trees, from hundreds of minute, delicate, strokes of pencil or chalk (so near Persian art and the deceptively tenuous drawings of Bonnard) finds its counterpart in the weightless, really very abstract, distribution of figures and landscape features in her paintings. A rhythmically slow-moving almost musically counterpointed synthesis is brought about between figures and landscape. The earliest paintings of Stanley Spencer, notably the series of Christ in the Wilderness, had something of this peculiar state of innocence and grace: but Elisabeth Vellacott's work has a sharper, more astringent resolution.

JASPER JOHNS *Hayward Gallery, 1978*

Johns was an artist that Bryan showed at the Whitechapel, so it was a logical decision on the part of the Hayward Gallery organising committee to commission Bryan to write a text for the exhibition leaflet when the Whitney Museum of New York's show came to the UK.

I know how irritating it can be to consult catalogue material which, through expressed intention, promises straight answers to sensible questions, only to find preliminary excursions in the text that instantly construct a barrage of stated difficulties, disclaimers, hazards of interpretation. If I appear here to be guilty of delaying tactics of this kind, my provisos from here on are aimed at an eventual clarification of Johns's identity as an artist – which is both forthright and exceedingly subtle. With this in mind I'm bound to say at a deliberately loaded tangent that any attempt to describe on the page – without the immediate physical presence to point to Johns's art and its consistent iconography, its subjects if you like, with absolute simplicity of language and clarity of definition – is rather like trying to explain Buster Keaton's face to somebody who has never been inside a cinema, let alone watched the great man on film – the face which, in the reserves of its alertly sensitive impassivity, speaks with mute eloquence for everyone trying to get to grips with life and survive in the first half of the twentieth century: in the same way as the archaic smile of the Apollo of Veii, exultantly cheerful and heartless, says something forever about the Etruscans.

Johns's attitude to art has been invigorated from his earliest beginnings with the spirit of the dandy, if you'll accept for a moment my idea of a dandy in art as a highly self-conscious man who knows very well the rules of the game and bends them not only in order to win but also to hold up the game for fresh scrutiny – sometimes even isolating the rules, one by one, as a kind of game in themselves to re-examine and thus analyse their inherent potential within the 'game' as a whole.

John McEwen and Alister Warman: A dialogue

I interviewed these two old friends of Bryan over lunch in a North London pub in August 2015. Although in a sense on opposite sides of the fence (McEwen the art critic, Warman the arts administrator), both independently formed lasting ties of friendship with Bryan and were delighted to get together and talk about him. In fact, the dialogue was their joint suggestion. Their affectionate reminiscences lie at the heart of this celebration of a remarkable man.

AW His legacy in terms of the written word is not representative of his genius really. I think he was much more comfortable talking than writing.

JM He was very lucid, wasn't he? Lucid and elusive. He was elusive – I had to get copy out of him for *Studio International*. (I was the office bell-boy. I forget what the title was – editorial assistant? That's when I first met Bryan.) I'd have to go up to Islington in the end and bang on his door.

AW I think the problem with Bryan was that he had an amazing photographic memory, so he had no editing facility because he had total recall. And that gets in the way of written words somehow. He was so ahead of his pen. He'd always fire off four or five adjectives in the hope that two would stick. He wasn't worried that there were three entirely beside the point. Usually under pressure of deadline. To some extent he was a reactive person in the sense that he needed the stimulus of an interlocutor. He very much saw himself as a cavalier of colour in opposition to the duns and browns and greys and drabs of the Euston Road palette and the Bombergian school.

JM I really got to know him at the *Spectator*. He was the arts editor. The Spurlings got him in there, I think, in the late 1970s. It was when he wasn't doing very much. Because he was away in America in the early seventies, which he hated; 'the melancholy of the suburbs', he said. Bryan famously got the chop from Purchase for letting the budget run away with him – by mistake on purpose, I think, he was quite keen to leave – but it was the shipping in of mature weeping willow trees to act as a proper background for a Barbara Hepworth sculpture that finally did the trick. Must have cost a fortune!

AW Bryan's opposition to puritanism included money. I remember the Finance Department of the Arts Council, if they knew that Bryan was involved in an exhibition, would put their toughest policeman on the night watch, but even then he would outwit them. Taking artists out to lunch, you went to the best restaurants and sent the bill to the Arts Council and didn't expect questions to be asked. This was the time of the austerity brought in by Roy Shaw, when budgets were tightened and wine for arts committee lunches was banned. In protest Lawrence Gowing had two bottles of whisky. He thought it was outrageous that the Arts Council would invite people to volunteer their time without adequate hospitality.

JM Bryan did ride the wave, didn't he? The fifties and early sixties – he timed his entry perfectly. The post-war surge. He went out on a crescendo as the whole thing collapsed.

AW And then he struggled.

JM Hence his being arts editor of the *Spectator*. Though I should imagine that just kept him in a few lunches. He wasn't there long at all. Three or four years? When I first met him at the *Spectator*, he came swanning in with his chest out to meet me. I was sitting in the outside office and he came sweeping past saying, 'Where is he? Where is he?' We got on really well so that was fine. He was no bother at all. In fact he was very sweet. One of my brothers died while I was at the *Spectator* and I was immediately despatched on Bryan's orders to Paris, which was a very nice idea. I vaguely reviewed some show… It was purely a gesture of support. And we got Patrick [Caulfield] and all sorts of people to do covers. Then there was a classic moment, very typical of Bryan's generosity, when he went to enormous effort to get a cover of the *Spectator* to salute Henry Moore's eightieth birthday [1978]. He got a drawing of a pair of hands that had never been seen before, which would duly appear upon the cover. I did a review of Moore's eightieth birthday exhibition at the Serpentine, the title of which was 'Bone Idle', and that was the gist of it [the review] too. It was a sort of attack on Henry Moore, and Bryan didn't mind at all. I always liked what Bruce Bernard said of Henry Moore's sculptures: 'suburban cavemen'. It was the suburban bit. But they all felt the same about Barbara Hepworth and called her Dame Gracie, after Gracie Fields.

AW The younger sculptors that Bryan championed are very much the ones who worked in colour.

JM And Michael Sandle. The Arts Council, in the late sixties I imagine, said to Bryan that they'd like him to make a selection of three to six small works by young artists of his choice. So Bryan homed in on the word small, went round to Michael Sandle and got him to build the biggest sculpture he'd done. *Gesualdo* – one of those enormous, very good pieces. And that was it – the Arts Council had to lump it.

JM The only person Bryan never got a good review from throughout his time at the Whitechapel was David Sylvester. You were very much either a Bryan or a Sylvester man. David Sylvester was much more the art historian. And David was a tremendous fixer. He was famous for saying, 'I have a price, but I don't know what it is'.

AW I remember Bryan saying it always astounded him how David would somehow leave with the most attractive woman at the party. He always failed to comprehend exactly what was David's charm or power when it came to women. He couldn't see it.

JM David was the most tremendous flatterer. He got into trouble in New York because he told about ten critics that they were the best critic in the world. He really laid it on. David hitched his wagon to the stars, but Bryan made them. Bryan actually made artists do things they wouldn't have thought they'd do. For instance, he gave Mary Potter a show at the Whitechapel and he told her to paint big pictures for it. She'd never painted anything big before. And she did. John Hoyland used to say that not all Bryan's shows at the Whitechapel were absolutely top-notch, but obviously a lot of them were.

AW Bryan would occasionally come to the Byam Shaw [the art school where Warman was Principal 1991–2011] to give a talk and there was always a problem about slides, and I suspect there never were any slides at all. There might be a call in the morning saying he would be a little late because he couldn't find his slides. Anyway, he arrived to give a talk on Brancusi without any support at all, and there was a full house, as you might expect. He talked for about an hour and a half recalling his visits to Brancusi's studio, and it was quite an astonishing performance as he could recollect every detail, every sculpture he saw, he could describe the space, the light, what Brancusi was wearing, how he sat. And he kept students who were not bothered at all to disguise their boredom (if they were bored they would walk out of the lecture), he kept them rapt for an hour and a half, without a single image. And usually what art students like is to look at lots of things on the wall. He didn't flag in the slightest, in fact he gathered momentum the more his memory came ... This would extend to sets for opera and dance: he could describe what he'd seen many years after the event. This is where I think his photographic memory was a handicap as well. It was marvellous if he was talking, because the speed of talking kept pace with his recalling, but if it was writing, the two were out of sync, and so he lost it.

JM He was a dandy. I remember he appeared at the *Spectator* party once with a blue rinse – rather too strong – a Royal blue colour. He always said that middle age was the worst time for an artist, apart from old age. And at the Warwick Arts Trust he made a real point of resuscitating people like Ivor Abrahams and Nigel Hall. It was a very noble and very interesting thing to do. The Tate was just totally uninterested, which he abhorred. He said they pick these people up and they just don't support them.

AW He was generous with his taste, just as he was with his own money and other people's – especially the Arts Council's. Sometimes generous to a fault – there were some dud shows at the Whitechapel, and he championed, in my view, some not very good artists. But then that's what's so unusual ...

JM I don't think he picked up people because they were underdogs, he just kept with them out of loyalty even though they down-turned. De Staël he put on. That was a huge, fantastic influence on British art. That really ripped through everybody. That was like the Picasso/Matisse show of 1946. That was the great thing about him – he was not provincial at all.

AW No, and he wasn't at all predictable, either. I first met him through the Arts Council. I don't remember him being on the Arts Advisory Panel as such, but he was very much around, and always a friendly presence. Rather later I went to a couple of dinner parties. I can remember when he was going through a hard time financially, one of his American patrons who knew that he was rather up against it sent him a very large dollar cheque, and Bryan for a long time lost it. It was really rather an important source of income, and two years on he discovered it in the fridge, and it was still just about presentable to the bank. During the interval it had appreciated quite considerably in value ... He was a big risk-taker and he knew some things were not going to fly. And pretty much totally impractical. But he was a marvellous cook and a very good host, and dinners were always extremely stylish.

JM Jeanne Thayer was one of his American ladies. She was married to Walter Thayer, one of those super-rich Americans, not Rockefeller but more or less. I think she probably sent Bryan the cheque. She was on the board of MOMA and stuff. She met Bryan somewhere and he switched her on to art. She became a very good friend of his. Bryan was very good at fixing one up with people to stay with, and I remember once I went to New York in the mid-seventies and he fixed me up with Jeanne. Her husband wasn't so keen on this fixing up. But I went and it was actually a very grand part of New York. One day I was in their sitting room wondering what to do when the telephone rings. There's no one else there so I pick it up. [strong Scottish accent] 'This is Hamish Fulton's brother! I'm absolutely disgusted with what you've written about my brother, Hamish Fulton, it's revolting. I'm going to take you to the courts about it.' This of course was Bryan ringing up for a chat. He loved practical jokes. I was absolutely poleaxed.

AW I can remember him telephoning me at the Serpentine and pretending to be outraged of Hounslow or whatever. He had a huge sense of fun.

JM He was Mr Mischief.

AW Bryan led, he didn't follow.

AW I remember John Hoyland saying he went with Bryan to Italy once, and he'd be waking up with a hangover to hear Bryan crashing back from having tried to seduce the local youth in the city walls. I think the repartee John and Bryan enjoyed was of a very high level.

JM There was a great Hoyland set piece about them sharing a bedroom and Bryan saying, 'Are you feeling lonely?' And then John said, 'No'. And Bryan said, 'Well, would you like me to come over and see you?' And John said, 'You're not one of those people my mother told me not to have anything to do with, are you?' And that was the end of that ... They were both quite old at the time ... But there wasn't a lover, I don't think.

AW Bryan's relationship to being gay was complex, I think. I don't think he liked being gay very much. I wouldn't say he was camp, but he was flamboyant – in what used to be called the euphemistic way.

JM I had a great friend called Alberto de Lacerda who was a Portuguese poet and was in the same areas as Bryan. They were the same age, they were both gay, and Alberto was very keen to meet him as he'd seen all Bryan's shows but didn't know him. We tried to get them off, but it didn't work.

AW But you never felt Bryan was lonely.

JM I think he telephoned a lot of people. He knew a lot of people and he kept his fronts open on all sorts of levels.

AW He had invitations to dinner here, there and everywhere. He had his favourite restaurants where he'd run up enormous bills.

JM He had a very noble disregard for money. I think a lot of the time he was flying on empty.

AW Rather like the *bella figura* in Italy – you can live in a tiny little room but when you go out on the street, you are well turned out. Bryan was never less than soigné. He was very proud in that respect – his public presentation.

JM He could be penniless but he would never say, 'I'm a bit short, let's go for a pizza'. No, no. 'Let's go to the Ritz!' He was a superb example to us all, there's no question.

[At this point, I asked them both what they thought was Bryan's greatest strength.]

JM Director of the Whitechapel. A creative curator, a creative director.

AW I would say he was unusual in having been an aesthete with quite a profound moral sense, and you don't necessarily get the two together – with generosity. He cared about people and was sensitive to aspirations and feelings. He was led by aesthetic considerations without being forgetful of moral considerations. I think Bryan was making a new world.

JM You felt that when Bryan was a friend, he'd be there.

AW He was a critical friend too. I can't remember precisely what it was, but I can remember thinking this was an intelligent question to be asking and it has an edge to it.

JM I remember I blacked out somewhere and he said, 'Oh John, you must take care of yourself, and go for a walk every day'. He was really concerned.

AW I think I'm right in recalling Nick Serota at Joanna [Drew]'s memorial event saying the three influential people in his formative years in the art world would have been David for curating exhibitions, Joanna for organising exhibitions and Bryan was the third – though I forget what it was he was celebrated for.

JM To have David and Bryan on the same list is pushing it ... If one wrote something and Bryan agreed with it he'd ring up. He criticised Richard Hamilton once [in public] and he said he never forgot that lugubrious face looking at him across the room. He was so much better known for supporting [than criticising].

AW The hardest collaborative project I did with Bryan was an exhibition called *Recalling the Fifties* [Serpentine Gallery, 1985]. Of course it was rather a ridiculous show to do in so small a space, especially for someone with a huge, omniscient memory. It was partly dictated by who was prepared to lend. There were some rather good paintings that have rarely been shown since, but in no way could it hope to be an account of the period, though it had a flavour [the artists shown included Burra, Nolan and Bacon]. One of the aims was to tempt all sorts of people from the fifties out of the woodwork. I remember Kingsley Amis came to the opening, saying as he was leaving, 'Hated it all'. I don't think he had a visual bone in his body.

JM Bryan loathed him.

AW The theatre, opera and ballet were all very important to him. He would have learned that in Paris. I remember him saying he was surprised how so many artists that knew him were totally ignorant of other art forms.

JM He put on people like Derek Hill that were surprising and quite good. Talking of Paris, he was mad on the Luxembourg Gardens, and he particularly liked that bit where they have a fruit garden, with all those apples and pears in hair-nets.

AW That is a very Bryan detail.

JM That Dufy show he did [at the Hayward, 1983–4] was absolutely superb. But wasn't it a fill-in? Had to be done at short notice? That was the making of it, of course. Bryan was not given too much time to change his mind. It was really Bryan's last great show.

AW It's very indicative of Bryan's slightly oblique position on things that he'd zoom in on something being overlooked. And a good example of the Hayward's versatility as an exhibition venue.

JM I remember when he was dying I went round to see him with Michael Sandle and he said, 'You look like a couple of undertakers!' It was rather disappointing to hear. Michael always wears black, of course, but I think it was more to do with our lugubrious expressions.

AW Bryan was never part of the establishment – that's vitally important. He always made sure of that. He would work with it but keep his distance.

JM I remember him saying, 'They'll never accept me, the establishment – however much you think they will'. Which I think is true, actually. If you're not a member already. But he liked being a maverick – it was part of the fun, wasn't it?

From the Editor of the *Spectator*, Alexander Chancellor (dated 19 August 1977)

Dear Bryan,

I have tried to telephone you in the hope of seeing you before I go away tomorrow, as I suddenly realised that you would be gone on your holiday before I get back from Egypt in September. But I have been unable to get hold of you.

The reason is that I have very regretfully decided to abolish the job of Arts Editor. We are obliged to make economies, and, in such a small company as this, there are none I can make which are not painful. I feel that now we have a good collection of regular contributors to the arts pages, and this is very largely due to your efforts. But I think that with only four pages to fill, we do not really require a special Editor, however brilliant and distinguished, simply to select a weekly feature or two in addition to the regular contributions. I am sure that you yourself must find the situation rather limiting. As, I gather, you are going away again for the whole of September, it seems sensible that you should effectively relinquish your duties at the end of this month. We will pay you up till then and I enclose a cheque for £300 in lieu of notice, thinking that you might find it handy on your holiday.

I would like to emphasise how grateful I am to you for the notable improvement you have brought about in our coverage of all the arts and that I very much hope you will go on writing for us from time to time. Above all, I am very keen that we should keep in touch, for we would all miss you if you were to disappear altogether from our office.

Bryan gives advice

TO KEITH VAUGHAN

From an undated draft letter on Whitechapel paper, probably 1950s: 'You must go into the country more and look at landscape; trust your emotions more and love people very much, with no reservations. You have it in you to be a very great artist and these doubts of yours only confuse the true issue.'

THE ARTIST JANE DIXON

During the decade that I knew Bryan our relationship was a professional one, certainly, in that he was the most loyal, insightful and earliest supporter of my work, but it also became a personal friendship in which we could have a lot of fun. An aspect of this seemed to be the freedom Bryan felt to give me lengthy and not entirely appropriate advice (usually over dinner, Bryan was very generous in his hospitality) about vitamin regimes I should be taking (he was a devotee, quite evangelical) and most amusingly, who I should and shouldn't be going out with … I never showed any willingness to act on this advice (obviously), but this didn't seem to deter him. Bryan was personally often very kind, having been ill for long periods as a child he was often able to empathise and offer support when persistent health issues complicated my career.

STEPHEN CHAMBERS
He'd give you very firm advice – some of it completely useless. How to treat a woman is to buy her perfume, etc.

TO CECIL COLLINS *from a draft letter (dated 26 August 1952)*
First, you should not continue to live in Cambridge. By doing so, you will, I am quite positive, lose all chance of making a real reputation for yourself and you will completely fail to make that sure place in English art which, dear Cecil, is waiting for you. The implications of this are that you will be personally miserable; Elisabeth will fret and worry, and your work will suffer and decline. It is absolutely inevitable.

Second – The main reason for leaving Cambridge. In Cambridge one paints in a vacuum. I am sure you will agree. It is no exaggeration. And a true artist, with great gifts such as yourself, cannot paint in a vacuum. If he tries to, he will kill his talent. And that is what is happening to you. Furthermore, apart from the vacuum element, there is the fatal current of amateurish-come-dilitantiism [*sic*] which is at its strongest in Cambridge. That current is insidious and paralyzing.

Now if you lived in London, continued to teach at the Central, fought like a trooper to get an additional day's teaching for the money and to make a worthwhile job, you would not have to bother about such things [as inviting people to his studio]. You would spend your main time in painting (as you do now, but in a quite different mental climate – physical too: you and Elisabeth would feel much better in London, I assure you – Cambridge is debilitating) and the second part of your time in teaching. Clear cut and simple. What was left of your time would be spent in KEEPING IN TOUCH WITH THE LEICESTER (a weekly visit with smile and handshake – v. important), looking at shows, seeing the artists and critics, making contact with the buyers and generally keeping in the swim. It is so simple.

TO ANDREW LAMBIRTH
'Read Paul Durcan!' An exhortation on a train back to London after visiting Tate Liverpool to review an exhibition, AL for the *Independent*, Bryan and Tim Marlow for *Kaleidoscope*.

TO CECIL COLLINS AGAIN *(dated 5 May 1961)*
The work is splendid and very highly charged and better and better in painting. You should extend and add to your content and what you are

painting about. This is not criticism of what exists but constructive suggestion for what might exist, so don't be affronted.

Your work has its public, and this can be added to, but your work also has an intimacy and a preciousness which keeps it away from the bombastic interior decorating poster work that nowadays wins prizes and gets sent to Biennales. Your limitations are also your strengths, so don't be disheartened or feel any envy for noisier performances.

Don't let yourself get stale or too cut away from sources of inspiration. Think hard about a time in Greece or Italy – not less than three months. Ideas cannot come for visual expression only from thought, belief, contemplating poetry or music. Visual expression feeds primarily on visual stimulation, no matter what kind of interior vision animates the work. You are making pictures, not poems.

TO NAN YOUNGMAN *on how to make time for her painting*
Mary Kessell is my ideal for a tough and determined painter: she behaves with complete selfishness and implacability whenever she has any working time and it's useless to ring her or talk to her or anything at all – obviously one just cannot behave like that in the life that one lives, but I can see her point.

To go with his advice, Bryan also liked to give presents, perhaps of a book or a bottle of perfume. Bryan Kneale confirms that Robertson was always doing or saying things to cheer people up. 'He said to me: "You ought to have a nice gold lighter from Dunhill. I'll get you one." I'm still waiting for it.'

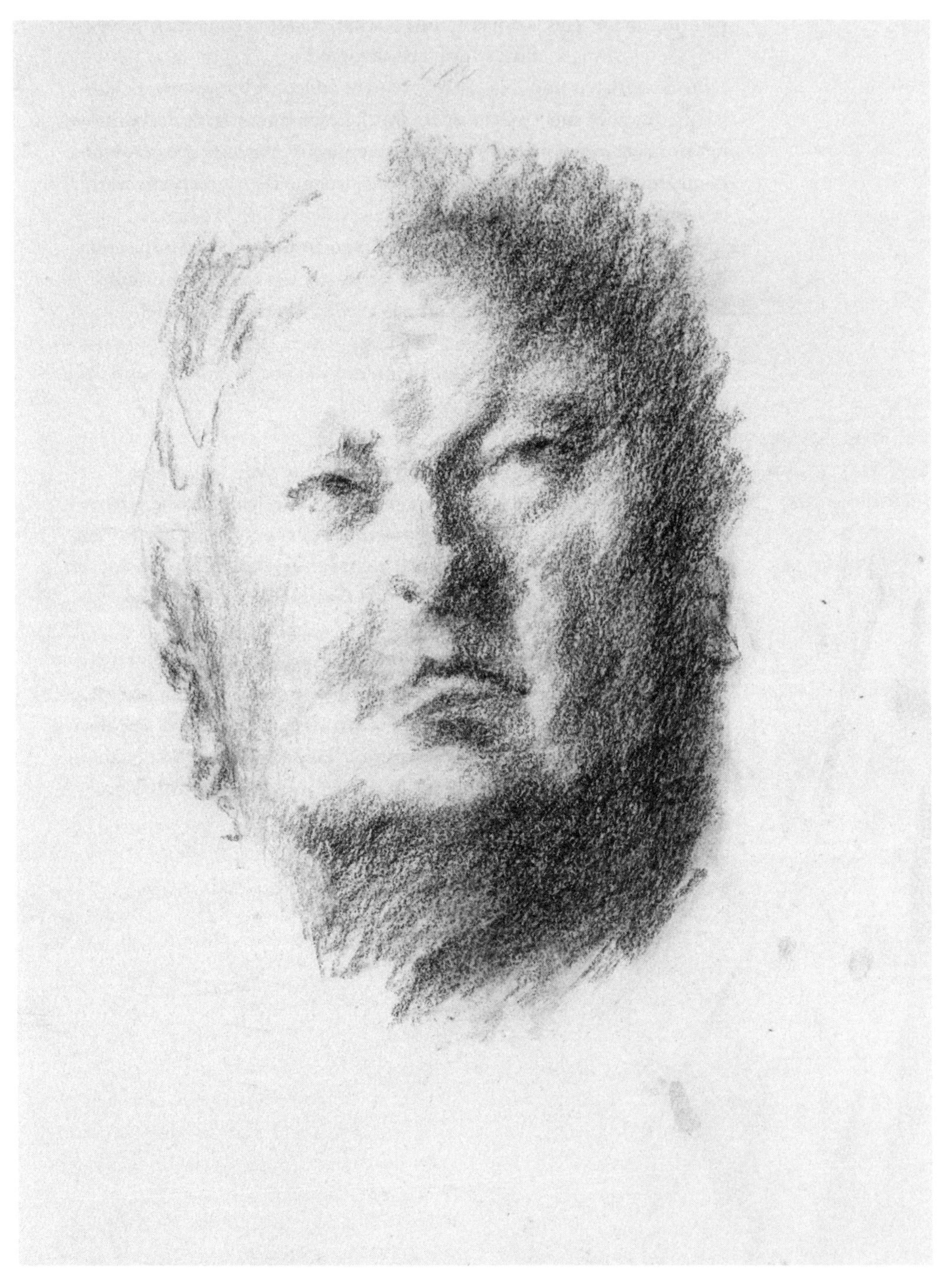

26 Bridget Riley, *Bryan Robertson*, early 1980s, 50.1 × 33.6 cm, black Conté crayon on paper

The 1980s and 1990s

Back in London, Bryan devoted himself to freelance writing and exhibition curating, but – with the notable exception of the hugely successful Raoul Dufy show at the Hayward in 1983–4 – his talents were never really used to their full. He was considered something of a maverick, a difficult man to handle, and because no institution would take the risk of employing him on a regular basis, the world lost out on a series of Robertson extravaganzas which could have lit up the exhibition horizon in Europe.

Proposal for 'S.W. Hayter: An Autobiography' with Bryan Robertson

Bryan regularly proposed ideas for books – he often thought he wanted to write them, rather than just earning some money – and the John Hoyland monograph he eventually abandoned to Mel Gooding (published by Lund Humphries in 1990) was just one of a list. A book with S.W. Hayter must have sounded attractive (not so much work as a straight monograph, perhaps), especially as he already knew the man and the work rather well. The proposal was for approximately 60,000 words of text, with between 6 and 8 colour plates and 60 to 65 black-and-white illustrations, of which one-third were to be actuality photos of Hayter with well-known figures in the art world, studio interiors with craftsmen and artists at the Atelier 17, Hayter at work, and Paris life – café and art gallery scenes; the other two-thirds of the illustrations would reproduce etchings, drawings and paintings. Hayter died in France in May 1988, so this proposal must date from before then, perhaps the early or mid-1980s.

Bryan wrote in the proposal:

Hayter has for many decades been acknowledged as the greatest living printmaker, a pioneer and inventor of new techniques and processes in engraving. He has taught most of the famous artists of the twentieth century the principles of engraving and lithography, contributing also to the visual language of this century through his own original paintings and engravings. Hayter has been honoured at the Venice Biennale, where he represented England in 1958; by a retrospective exhibition of paintings and engravings at the Whitechapel Gallery in 1957 and a retrospective exhibition of prints at the Victoria and Albert Museum in 1970. Not essentially an academic, Hayter was Professor of Fine Art at Brooklyn College, New York, 1948–9, and is the author of a standard work, *New Ways of Gravure* (Routledge) in 1949.

The autobiography will trace Hayter's life and times – he was born in Hackney, London, in 1901 – through the early years in Persia working for the Anglo-Iranian Oil Company – Hayter had taken a degree in chemistry at King's College – to the decision to become a professional artist in 1926 and move to Paris; the establishment of the internationally famous Atelier 17 in Paris in 1927 and life in Paris through the twenties and thirties, friendships with Calder, Matisse, Picasso, Miro, Brancusi, Giacometti, Breton, Eluard (whose books Hayter illustrated) and others, as well as his role as a participating organiser of the Surrealist Exhibition in London in 1936 – Hayter was a close friend of Roland Penrose and his wife Lee Miller, Herbert Read and all the other figures involved in the movement.

In 1940 Hayter moved the Atelier 17 to New York and continued to work in the US. He was close to de Kooning, Motherwell, Matta and the other European emigré artists in New York at this time. Pollock, among others, made his first engravings under Hayter's tutelage, and Hayter took part in a crucial series of seminars at the Californian School of Fine Arts, San Francisco, with Mark Tobey, Morris Graves and Mark Rothko. The text will cover Hayter's relationships with these and other celebrated artists as well as his role in contributing to the basic initial precepts of abstract expressionism. In 1946, Hayter returned to Paris, and re-opened the Atelier 17.

Hayter has gradually been absorbed by the French establishment into their own culture and has been granted a role in the École de Paris – but his achievement is greatly honoured internationally with important groups of his work in museums throughout the world.

The book will cover Hayter's close friendships with particular artists like Alexander Calder, the inventor of coloured mobile sculpture. Hayter remembers calling in to see Calder in his Paris studio on the morning that his first son, Augy, was born. 'Calder boomed congratulations, poured out some Cognac for both of us, picked up a thin sheet of metal, went on talking about the joys and tribulations of family life, fed the sheet of metal into a machine without once glancing at it, moved it around, pulled it out, folded over two curved shapes and – regarding it for the first time – handed it to me. It was a perfect child's chair, for Augy.' Many other artists, writers, critics and famous collectors are vividly recalled by the artist.

Bryan Robertson, who is working closely with Hayter on the text, has been a friend and supporter of the artist for thirty years, when he presented Hayter's first retrospective exhibition in London. Robertson remembers a walk in the West End with Hayter in the fifties and Hayter standing still to stare at the art deco lighting design over the façade of the old Studio One cinema in Oxford Street. 'That's what I've always wanted,' said Hayter – 'a building, to decorate all over with neon. They've never asked an abstract artist to decorate a building … I could use neon colour as it's never been used before.'

Needless to say, the Hayter collaborative autobiography was never written, though Bryan took masses of notes towards it (most of which seem to have gone missing, or perhaps been thrown away). But Bryan did contribute to a posthumous book on the artist, *The Renaissance of Gravure: The Art of S.W. Hayter*, edited by P.M.S. Hacker and published in 1988. The following is extracted from his text on his old friend's paintings:

The art of S.W. Hayter soars like a fantastic bird across the general context of English art in the twentieth century: powerful, unpredictable, and finally too exotic and glittering for national assimilation, a brilliantly coloured and shaped parakeet or iridescent humming bird, incongruous in the company of thrushes and owls. The analogy is not far fetched. Hayter's art does tend to seem foreign, like something from a hotter climate, when set beside the typical English art of any decade since the twenties – although, lamentably, his work also tends to be omitted altogether from official surveys of English art in the twentieth century assembled in England. He has worked abroad too long: the ranks close. Educated memories are in short supply. But in its obvious stature, Hayter's achievement since 1926, when he first settled in Paris, has to be assessed at the same level as those of his fellow Englishmen and near contemporaries – Moore, Burra, Pasmore, and Sutherland, for instance – if he is to be seen at all within an English spectrum. His original contribution to the international Surrealist movement in the thirties and his equally personal discoveries as a distinct forerunner of the Abstract Expressionism which found itself in the US in the forties and fifties have immense consequence in the evolutionary complexity of English art.

Robertson's ladies

Bryan liked women and spent a lot of time with them, and also expended a great deal of energy in promoting women artists. As Sheila Caro observed:

He was very good with women, very kind to them. We met Prunella Clough at his house, Bridget Riley, Claire Bloom. He came up to my studio and said 'This is the best painting I've seen in London' – it was lovely. He put me in touch with the John Moores and tried to help. It was as though he had some special sympathy with women painters – as if they weren't getting their full share.

John Hubbard recalled the sensitivity of one of Bryan's female admirers:

Elisabeth Vellacott was a great friend who just adored Bryan. She looked at him like a Labrador. She had a rather Labrador face and she looked at him with moist eyes, and stared at him in absolute admiration, which he enjoyed but it also irritated him. She was very high-minded, a marvellous person, one of the people I knew who spoke reverentially of Tonks at the Slade. She had one particular story when she was staying with Bryan in our cottage. She was very hungry, we all were very hungry. Bryan was a good cook. He said we're going to have chicken for dinner. Time passed and at about quarter past eight there was no sign of it and we couldn't smell cooking at all. Bryan suddenly said 'Ooh' and opened the fridge and produced a chicken which he put in the oven. Elisabeth burst into tears and rushed out.

It seems clear from all accounts that Vellacott (1905–2002) loved Bryan in a more intense way than ordinary friendship, and always kept a photo of him with her. He was a great supporter of her work and a close friend, but whether their relationship was any more intimate than that must be a matter for speculation.

It's certainly possible that Bryan had occasional sexual encounters with women, and he seems to have boasted of such. John Hoyland used with great relish to tell various slightly risqué stories about Bryan. Typically scabrous was Hoyland's account of going on holiday with Bryan who would disappear into the dark and return with grass stains on his knees. One of the more decorous stories recounted an occasion in Italy:

We went to a party given by Agnelli, the head of Fiat. Everybody was moving about and talking and Bryan disappeared and I was just drinking champagne and admiring the scenery. When we get back in the car, he's giggling, so I ask him what's funny. And he pulled out a pair of black lace women's knickers, as though he'd had it off somewhere. I never knew the answer to that.

In Prunella Clough's memorial address Bryan spoke with authority of the 'fluidity' of her sexual relationships, implying a bisexuality that he may himself have shared. What is certain is that Bryan from time to time asked women to marry him. More than one of his friends recalled his plans to marry Bridget Riley, and John Hubbard remembered a special lunch at the Connaught when Bryan delightedly announced his intended marriage to Helen Frankenthaler. Beatrice Monti, founder in 1955 of the Galleria dell'Ariete in Milan, one of the first European galleries to show the new American art, wife of the late novelist Gregor von Rezzori, and now running a writers' retreat in Tuscany, recalled: 'Bryan always told me – I don't know whether it's true or not – that he had an affair with Helen Frankenthaler. He said, "It was very good because I had the reputation of being gay, so she could go out with me and nobody could believe we were lovers".'

Despite Bryan's lifelong determination to keep some parts of his life in separate boxes, there was the occasional suggestion of a male lover. Bryan was friendly with Bill Hayter's widow Désirée, for instance, taking her to Le Caprice for lunch in October 1989. She in turn offered him her flat

in Paris for a couple of weeks in May the following year, writing to him in August: 'I hope you are well and wicked.' Later, in 1999, she asked in another letter, 'What happens with your affair and is it still actual?' This supports Maggi Hambling's recollection of a relationship that Bryan mentioned with a young Turkish man.

Bryan was interested in women, he was funny, he was good company, and he felt strongly that women artists had been unfairly treated. He championed Hepworth, Clough, Riley and many more, and his support made a real difference to their careers and reputations. John Hoyland, as usual with his own slant on his old friend, commented:

In Paris, Bryan dated Juliette Gréco's sister and met Marlene Dietrich. Don't forget it was *tabu* to be gay. He always tried to play the thing that he liked [sexually] both women and men. I think he liked women as friends, and he was very aware of how a lot of women's art had been neglected. That was another hobby-horse of his.

In 1955, Vellacott was a founder member of the Cambridge Society of Painters and Sculptors, along with Cecil and Elisabeth Collins, Charles Howard, Gwen Raverat, Nan Youngman and Betty Rea. (Youngman was the prime mover behind the Society.) Robertson was to be supportive of the work of all these artists – with the exception of Gwen Raverat, whose paintings he disliked. He did however respect Raverat's integrity and honesty, while describing her, according to her biographer Frances Spalding, as looking 'like some benevolent hospital almoner or cook, while always being as dignified as it was possible to be'.

Bryan spoke to Caryl Hubbard and Madeleine Bessborough about the possibility of showing Vellacott's work at the New Art Centre, and in 1972 this came about, with her first solo exhibition in London. After that she showed with the NAC every three years or so, and had a retrospective at Kettle's Yard, Cambridge, and the Warwick Arts Trust, London, in 1981, the latter organised by Bryan. Bryan spent the best part of a week with Elisabeth preparing the catalogue for that show and extracting from her the requisite information for a chronology of her career. Amazingly, the catalogue was the first publication on this seventy-five-year-old artist, and Bryan also wrote a substantial appreciation of her work from which the following passage is taken:

It is tempting to relate in some way the world created in Elisabeth Vellacott's paintings and drawings to other worlds created by some English novelists, notably our gutsy women novelists, although it is undoubtedly foolhardy to try to do so with any accuracy. Her paintings are really not at all literary, but an atmosphere or mood builds up and one wants to define it. Partly, this mood comes from a very quietly stated comedy of manners. *Women*

Arriving celebrates the rather self-consciously disruptive appearance of a stylishly garbed (one hesitates to say 'dressed') woman, tall and seemingly important, in a large room in which several other people are quietly at table. One of them gets up to greet her. It is extraordinary how this act of mildly comic social aggression stays in the mind, best explained, doubtless, by the interplay of colour and sharp contour in the painting. And yet for all the very strong abstract qualities in Vellacott's best paintings, her figures are never anonymous or impersonal ciphers, or mere shapes. A glance at the richly expressive silhouettes of the figures deployed – and they are deployed – in *The Concert* 1977, reproduced in the catalogue, should dispel that notion. They are abstractly satisfying, but they are also highly suggestive in their individual structure. If I had to mention any writer with whom Elisabeth Vellacott's work has often seemed to me to have a tenuous but real relationship it would be Iris Murdoch, whose characters play out their part in highly formalized myths within a domestic location, and whose psychological and symbolic insights have always been matched by a vividly memorable, if only sparsely indulged, visual sense. There are odd lines of description in Murdoch's novels which haunt the memory and they have the same artful simplicity and de-materialized physicality as some aspects of Vellacott's scenes.

And the other side of the coin: this is from an undated letter to Bryan from Elisabeth Vellacott: 'Don't think of writing to apologise for having gone off to America when I was supposed to be having dinner with you – it was just rather funny, and I wouldn't have mentioned it if I minded at all.'

A substantial catalogue accompanied the *Elisabeth Vellacott Memorial Exhibition* at the Redfern Gallery in 2003. The main text was by Quentin Stevenson, who frequently quoted from Bryan's writings on the friend he first met in 1949. Stevenson writes of Bryan's support of Vellacott:

For the first time Elisabeth was to have a champion, a young tyro whose eye, and brain, she could trust, a promoter and a friend who would do everything he could to place her pictures and assist her career. He gave her the attention she needed, and the encouragement that her work was not only exciting to him but a constant surprise to him. She gave him much in return.

Stevenson then quotes Bryan writing to Vellacott in 1964:

I so often think of those lunches and dinners you gave me for so long, and so much else: comfort, sympathy, great intelligence, loyalty, sound advice – and so much greatly treasured affection and understanding. As an artist I believe you've made an extraordinary and absolutely personal statement, with absolute authority, and one day that truth will establish itself. It's a heroic achievement.

In his address at Vellacott's funeral Stevenson quoted a letter written by Bryan to her in the 1950s:

This is a time of despondency, *petits riens*, anxiety, impoverished paint quality, inept drawing, insignificant content, and the complete abnegation and disintegration of the great tradition. Pictures today are skimped in every conceivable way. You have the gift with which to combat all this. I enclose two pieces of ship's canvas: the wrapping round food parcels we received this Christmas from Australia. You may be able to use them in some way for pictures. If not, throw away.

John McEwen, art critic of the *Daily Telegraph*, writing on 18 July 1998 in a review of a Mary Potter exhibition and biography, had this to say:

The best curators are critics, and the best critic is one who opens an artist's eyes. This is what Bryan Robertson, when director at the Whitechapel Art Gallery in London, did for the painter Mary Potter, confirmed by her son Julian Potter's newly published biography, *Mary Potter, A Life of Painting* (Scolar Press, £20) and the exhibition *Mary Potter (1900–1981)* at the Fine Art Society, 148 New Bond Street, W1 (until July 26).

In 1962 Robertson wrote to Potter, then a respected but still struggling artist, proposing a retrospective in the wide white spaces of the Whitechapel. 'My own feeling, quite simply, is that you have never had a real chance with your work. You have only been able to exhibit it inside a very restricted and dull framework, and this kind of thing does not present the right kind of opportunity or stimulating challenge to an artist. I believe, absolutely, that your work has an immense potentiality which is not yet realised. You are eminently capable of realising it and I look forward to the time when your painting really takes off, as they say.

'In good measure you have an original vision: an extraordinarily sensitive feeling for paint or matière in general, and a highly personal and inventive feeling for colour. It would be tragic, with all these gifts, for you to be condemned to producing small cabinet pictures – which are lovely, but are in danger of becoming too easy and thoughtless, I feel.'

Potter was no country mouse. She was the divorced wife of writer Stephen Potter (of Gamesmanship fame), had been an early member of the pre-war Seven and Five Society, famous today for nurturing progressive talents such as Moore, Hepworth and Hitchens, and was a close friend of Benjamin Britten and Kenneth Clark; but Robertson's letter changed her life. She rose to the challenge, had the show and from then on became one of the most interesting and individual of English twentieth-century painters.

This is clearly demonstrated by the small show at the Fine Art Society, which has works from 1921 until 1979. Potter's precise way with pale tones, her delicate use of apricot, lilac, plum, powder grey, jade, brown (or 'cow pat' as she resolutely called it) is consistent, also her selective eye for subject-matter. But it is only after Robertson's challenge that she throws caution to the winds and lets colour, shape, texture and pattern exist more or less independent of a subject.

Until she was sixty her paintings could be by one of a dozen distinguished English post-School-of-Paris artists with a local take on Vuillard, Bonnard or Braque; afterwards she is Mary Potter. Not that she ever became completely abstract, as her titles (*Evening Window*, *Sun & Tree*, etc.) emphasise, but she hovers on the edge of non-depiction. *Evening Light on Pine Branches* is among the finest of the late works in this chronological display; a range of buff and dun tones which are touched here and there with foxy linear suggestions of trees and branches, acting as rhythmic promptings.

Upstairs there is a stock show which includes some paintings of a similar sensibility by Sutherland, William Scott and Prunella Clough, today painting better than at any time in a long and distinguished career.

An important exhibition could be made of this particular strain of quiet but never quaint painting – sensual, passionately committed and puritanically restrained – which runs in British art from Gwen John to the present. Who better to curate it than Bryan Robertson?

And here is the veteran artist and educator Nan Youngman, a friend of Bryan's from the early Cambridge days, writing a letter from her home in Waterbeach, a village on the edge of the Fens (dated 16 March 1990):

Dear old Bryan,

I've tried your telephone, but you obviously leave the receiver off all the time. Just to say what a lovely addition you wrote to the Jane Grigson obituary. You at your very best. She has been one of my mentors for years, and I never knew that she was the Jane you had at Heffer's. You evoke her as only you can. And of course I am so pleased to be mentioned. Bless you. Elisabeth is being very philosophical – on the telephone anyway – about Lucy. Bless her too.

No need to reply. I would probably die of shock if you did.

Love from the old bag.

In 1997 it was time to reassess Nan Youngman's work with an exhibition two years after her death, at the Morley Gallery in London. The accompanying publication contained an evocative text by Robertson about a 1948 self-portrait by Youngman. But even more significant is this extract from a letter from Bryan to Nan, dated 21 December 1951, about her quandary in being torn between two careers, as artist and art educator:

I must say that if things had been different, I should want to do *exactly* what you do and I admire your work, and all its ramifications and implications, more than I can say. It is a quandary, your work and your painting, and anybody can see how very difficult it is either to choose between them or to effect a working compromise. All I feel is that you don't ever appear to set enough store by your painting, which is – to use an appalling cliché – vitally important, and very fine indeed. Potentially, extremely exciting. You are unique in your job all right, partly because you have the feelings and intuitive qualities and passion of a painter, and partly because you know human beings and how to handle them.

Robertson wrote about many other women artists and actively championed several. Chief among these was Thelma Hulbert (1913–95), a painter of landscape and still life now almost entirely forgotten. The following extract is from Bryan's preface to the catalogue for Hulbert's Whitechapel exhibition (1962):

The work itself, I would suggest, shows the steady technical development of a very considerable artist, from tentative and modest beginnings to the present effulgence of light and colour; and the equally steady process of recognition – increasingly positive and defined – of an extraordinary personal vision. All this has been fought out over a period of some fifteen to twenty years against a background, familiar to so many dedicated artists, of great material difficulty. It is not easy to conserve physical or imaginative energy for the complex processes of painting when working for a living for almost the whole of each week. And it is not always easy to keep faith in a vision when the official world of exhibitions, sponsorship and promotion is remote. Miss Hulbert's comparative isolation from the main scene of events in the London art world has been self-engendered, and she has a markedly composed and amiable self-sufficiency, but this does not make her solitary accomplishment any less remarkable …

A capacity for abstract construction in terms of light and space is becoming more and more clear; for the marginal beauties of her paintings are always more arresting and engrossing than the actual object portrayed in each picture. Even so, she has brought great freshness and originality to bear upon subjects which are traditional, and now often debased. This is both life enhancing and indicative of the large measure of originality contained so quietly and unostentatiously in her values as an artist and her touch as a painter.

The catalogue also contained an essay by Colin MacInnes from which the following is taken: 'It now seems to me that of all the painters working at Euston Road, her development has been the most remarkable; and also that she is the artist who has most fully transcended the limitations of the Euston Road manner, and created a visual world of power, beauty and originality.' MacInnes had himself been a student at the Euston Road

School, and perhaps his partiality to Hulbert's work had some influence over Robertson's championing of this particular artist.

Gertrude Hermes (1901–83), the wood-engraver, printmaker and sculptor, was an old friend of Bryan, and in 1967 he gave her a solo show at the Whitechapel. The following 'Note on the Artist' is taken from that catalogue:

The question of style, here so highly individual, brings me to the most consistent characteristic of the whole range of this artist's work: its benign severity. There is no sentimentality in anything made by Gertrude Hermes, in sculpture or in graphic work, and she has brought the same clear-cut ruthlessness to bear on her more explicitly decorative projects. The design and the imagery certainly do not lack feeling, but their warmth and flair are the by-products of visual intelligence and formal discipline, not rhetoric. Her best work is tough, concentrated, and has a certain air of minimal tactile or formal expenditure, almost abruptness. This notion may amuse the innumerable friends of the artist who are as aware as I am of the engaging lengths, and depths, of her generosity as a person; but her professional energies are more economically deployed.

An American member of the Robertson's Ladies team was Betty Parsons, a hugely influential gallery owner who was also an artist in her own right. Giving her a solo show at the Whitechapel in 1968 was something of a risk, but just the kind of gesture that appealed to Bryan, as he explains in the catalogue:

I first met Betty Parsons in 1958 when I was in New York to do research for my monograph on Jackson Pollock. Her close contact with this artist during the 1940s made it important for me to study her correspondence files and go through catalogues and photographic material. Everything was opened up for me, including a coincidentally touching insight into the particular nature of Mrs Parsons' activities as a dealer throughout the early years not only of Pollock but so many other fine artists in America. Betty Parsons didn't consistently make very great sales for them, though she managed always to raise a basic income for her artists; what she did achieve, however, as it emerged from her files, was something of far greater consequence: she gradually got their work and ideas appreciated by a wide range of museum officials, critics, and some influential collectors. The work of her artists was gradually accepted by juries planning important exhibitions; shows travelling at museum level also, slowly, began to include work by artists from her gallery; articles were written by intelligent critics. Gradually, the process of acceptance infiltrated through to general consciousness …

This exhibition may bring its qualities more directly into the open and serve, in passing, as a tribute to a creative entrepreneur who has always put

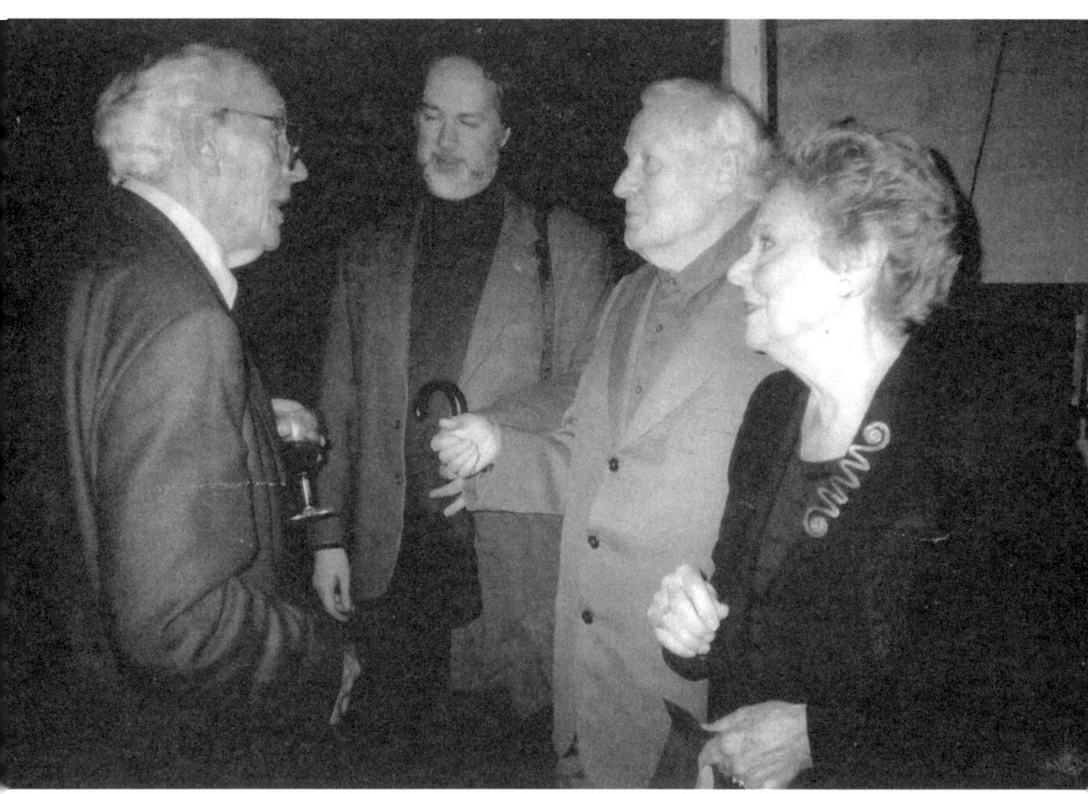

27 BR with Paul Scofield (left), Richard Alston and Irene Worth at the Almeida Theatre, Islington, 2001

the needs of others ahead of herself – but who could not have accomplished what she has, as an entrepreneur, without working in the way that she has as a painter. The life and work of Betty Parsons are one, in a very particular and mutually enriching way.

Irene Worth (1916–2002) was an American stage and screen actress who spent much of her time in England, joining the Old Vic Company in 1951, the RSC in 1962 and the National Theatre in 1968. She spent most of the 1970s in America. She also gave a number of dramatic readings or recitals, often with John Gielgud in the 1960s, and concluding with a one-person show based on the life and writings of Edith Wharton in the mid-1990s. Cecil Beaton was very attached to her, but was well aware of how difficult she could sometimes be. He recorded in his diary an evening in 1970 when he invited John Gielgud to dinner after a long period of *froideur* between them. He also invited Irene Worth and the English actress Cathleen Nesbitt. Worth had just returned from a successful run as Hedda Gabler in Canada, but no one in England seemed prepared to offer her a part. This made for much tension over dinner, with Beaton noting that she was not only 'strident' but lashed out 'in all directions'.

Bryan first met Worth on Long Island during a trip to America in the 1960s. In a letter to K he refers to her as 'your charming friend'. Worth was a girlfriend of Clark's, and she coached him for his TV performances. She saw him regularly and was enough of a friend to stay at Saltwood Castle for Christmas. Clark's biographer, James Stourton, wrote: 'The actress Irene Worth was another faithful adorer, but their association became too much for her, and a period of estrangement followed.' Later there was a rapprochement, and in the early 1970s Beaton took Worth to lunch at the Garden House on the Clarks' estate, while after Jane Clark's death Worth (among others) rallied round to console K and keep him busy. Although it would be wrong to think of Bryan as a satellite of Clark, they did share some of the same tastes and certainly had friends in common. And both were somewhat difficult and demanding men. Compare the following two extracts from correspondence between Worth and Bryan.

In January 1970 Worth wrote: 'What an angel you are ... I am always touched by your extraordinary qualities of goodness ... It was a lovely evening – I adored seeing all the sweet people I love and sharing it with you.' Then in a letter of June 1993 she comments: 'Thank you so much for your very elegant letter and kind thoughts and I look forward to a renewal of our friendship which, having cooled off for a bit, is I daresay all the better for it.' Bryan often had fallings out with friends. As Ken Draper has suggested, it was the only way he could cope with so many friends – by resting them every now and again after a good row.

Paul Huxley recalled meeting her:

Bryan often would sell people to other people. I remember him saying, 'You must meet Irene Worth, she's wonderful'. I met her, we had dinner together and she was great fun. He said later, 'She's terrific and not in the least bit theatrical. She's not actressy.' But of course she was! She was very actressy. Nothing against her, but he was blind to that. He knew her qualities, her stage-craft and deep knowledge of things, and failed to notice that she was in real life very much an actress. He took her to exhibitions and introduced her to all his artist friends and she became very converted by his enthusiasm, and shared it. She became friends with the Hubbards, for instance. She bought a painting of mine.

I remember once driving – in those days Bryan couldn't drive, Irene couldn't drive – in my tin-pot little Mini from London to Chilcombe [in Dorset] to visit the Hubbards. I had the car radio on and there was a piece of music playing and they were saying to each other 'Who is this? Is it...?' and they'd mention a name I'd never heard. 'No ... is it ...?' And I was thinking, it's Mozart, surely. I'm sure it's Mozart. But I didn't dare say that. It ended up that what they were trying to identify was the conductor, not the composer or musician. And I thought 'Thank God I didn't speak up!' But that was the level of their conversation. She had that level of sophistication.

The American supporters club

In addition to close woman friends in the art world, Bryan had a group of wealthy lady supporters he had met when in America, mostly when fundraising for Purchase. A number of these rich enthusiasts remained persistently loyal to Bryan, and kept him going in later years, with welcome cheques when he was at a particularly low ebb. One of the most devoted was Jeanne Thayer, who wrote to me in May 2012, when she was ninety-four, from Santa Barbara, California:

I met Bryan in 1967, and was with him, or corresponded or spoke by phone and letter; as well as travelled with him, in New England and in Greece and England, until his last illness. I am greatly in favor of a good book that would reveal to a larger audience all that Bryan was, what he did that changed or improved the public's vision of art, music, theatre. His sharp eye, depth of knowledge, desire to add dimension to others' perceptions through a unique and exhilarating sense of humor is unmatched still.

Through Bryan, Thayer met and made friends with Hilary and John Spurling, Caryl and John Hubbard, John and Jill McEwen, and also Irene Worth, who became one of her closest friends, as well as many artists. Stephen Chambers described his friendships with American patrons:

When he went off to America he had to find money for the museum. He did that by going to talk to the local billionaires. He was very good at that because he wasn't scared of money. He never had any but he certainly didn't respect it. He was just charming, especially to the widows who adored him and kept him afloat, bankrolling him later. Actually, he was a financial car-crash.

New recruits

Bryan loved to be with young people, drawing on their energy, matching their enthusiasm, so to discover young artists of promise was an important activity for him, from the beginning of his career to the end. Here three of the artists he encouraged and championed in later years – Christopher Le Brun, Jane Dixon and Stephen Chambers – offer their recollections of him.

Christopher Le Brun

The artist Christopher Le Brun was greatly encouraged by Robertson from an early stage of his career. Wanting to capitalise on Robertson's enthusiastic support he asked him to write a text for the first monograph on his work. The ensuing saga, as Bryan pondered but did not write the expected essay, was enough to try the patience of a saint – let alone a

struggling artist. Le Brun talked candidly in his South London studio, in April 2015, about the experience:

I met him when I was first showing with Nigel Greenwood in about 1979–80. Nigel and Bryan were good friends. He came to the gallery, then he would have come to the studio, and the relationship developed quite quickly because he used to ask us to his dinner parties. The first dinner party I went to, I went with Charlotte and we were quite late. He introduced us to the guests (Philip Roth & Claire Bloom were there) and then said, 'This is Christopher – he's an experimental dancer'. Everybody took a step back and I must have blushed. He'd guessed it was my least favourite nightmare dream horror. Then he said 'No, no, no – Christopher's a wonderful painter!' And I was looking at them thinking 'They don't believe the second statement'. It was a fantastic evening but that was always happening with Bryan.

He was *the* most exasperating man. When Charlotte and I tried to organise a return match for the dinner party, nothing at all as grand as Bryan's, not having quite the same range of guests, he would call about 20 minutes before and say 'I've got a little bit of a cold' and cancel. (Charlotte would have slaved over the meal.) He did that again and again and again. Once the upsets had washed through, you just got used to how Bryan behaved.

Another dinner party we went to at his house, we arrived on the steps just as Prunella Clough arrived. We rang and rang on the doorbell and nothing happened and it was dark. Prunella said: 'This is very odd, but it's also very Bryan. I wonder what's happened.' We carried on ringing and eventually a light went on on the landing and he came down in his silk dressing gown with bare legs and bare feet. He said: 'Oh, hello!' We all said: 'Bryan – are we on the right day?' 'Oh! Do come in. Let me fix you a drink.' So we went in for a massive gin and tonic or Campari and soda and he said 'Now – what have I got in the fridge?' At which point we said it probably wasn't a good idea and we should come back another day, and Prunella and Charlotte and I went round the corner and got a pizza on the main road.

I think it was just the way he was. He always seemed to be a slight victim of health problems. The fact is that I admired him a lot and to be honest with you I was a young artist and he was a senior figure and if I'm waiting in my studio and he doesn't arrive for two hours, I can hardly call him and say 'Look Bryan, this is intolerable'. I just suffer. Because when he did come to the studio it was just wonderful. He'd always have the same reaction. He'd come in: 'How are you? How's your child bride in Farmyard Avenue or whatever terrible dump you're living?' (He always regarded Charlotte as about sixteen and that I'd eloped with her.) Then he'd come into the studio and he'd look at me and say 'How marvellous! Christopher, you're on such good form!' One would glow – it was wonderful. What was nice for me as a painter was that he was a French modernist; colour, sunshine, exuberance, the good life – the pleasure of art, celebration. Also the French link to American abstract expressionism. That for me was a wonderful pedigree that I felt very connected with, and still do.

The fact that he knew Rothko and could in bits and pieces tell me what he was like as a man was enormously helpful because one hangs on to these tiny little snippets. He would convey an atmosphere. We used to talk about Helen Frankenthaler and there was an implication that he had an affair with her. He did describe her as she was in the fur coat, the grand lady in silk stockings, in a very convincing way, which contrasts to the sort of grunge that English painters get used to having as a badge of honour. If you look at the School of London, it heads pretty rapidly in that direction – Paddington back streets and terraces. I'm thinking 'She sounds rather wonderful – I like the sound of that!' Because it returns you to a sense of art as a wonderful imaginative enterprise. He'd talk about people like Helen and introduce me to wonderful people like Helen, John Hubbard and Patrick Caulfield. John Hoyland was often there at supper. I'd known John because he was one of my teachers at the Slade, although not in a conventional sense. All the tutorials happened in the pub and you'd need at least three pints before you got anywhere. One day at dinner John said [to Patrick Caulfield]: 'Patrick, what are you doing? You look just like a scoutmaster!' He was wearing a sort of safari jacket. But it didn't put Patrick off, he just went on wearing his scoutmaster's outfit.

We planned the monograph some years before, but Bryan would never deliver text. He was commissioned to write the book but what we ended up doing was a major interview with Bryan, with another introduction by Charles Saumarez Smith and a further piece by Norbert Lynton. We packed it with different voices in order to make the book, but it was driving us absolutely crazy because we couldn't get him to produce the text. Eventually the only thing to do was for me to go to Rhodes with him. In the book there's a photograph of the two of us sitting outside. He had this most wonderful sea captain's house, ancient and decorated with shells, with a very Middle Eastern feeling. I must have spent about five or six days there in the late nineties and we did the interview. But even doing the interview was difficult! Eventually after breakfast and a bit of shopping we'd end up in his study at about a quarter to twelve to sit down and do it. And he'd start off by telling me his own story, and finally we'd get to little me. It was all immensely frustrating. I think it's quite a good interview, but the questions aren't questions where he steps back. It's a dialogue and he says quite a lot on his views about painting which is very helpful. That was the way we got the text eventually from him.

We had a wonderful time on the island and went all over and ate well, but everything at a very gentle pace. He used to call shopping marketing.

I'm the worst shopper in the world with the patience of a gnat. Bryan would stroll around and spend ages discussing this and that. This was the late nineties and he said 'I think you're looking a bit peaky, Christopher. What I'd like to do is give you some money (he didn't have any money) so you can go off somewhere warm and just have a sabbatical.' I said: 'Well, that's incredibly generous, Bryan, but I am married with several children.' 'I'm sure Charlotte your child bride would agree – it's in your best interests as an artist.' Actually I think he was right, but the fact is we're embedded in the real world and the way we are. And probably I was looking a little peaky because I was stressed with Bryan! Anyway it was very generous and I think that suggestion ended up in the Bryan Robertson Trust and the awards they give. He was very keen on who's looking after the Middle Generation artists.

All I was thinking was that here's this man who's been the director of the Whitechapel Gallery, knew the great American painters, has a wonderful eye, writes beautifully and is interested in my work. It was never about introducing me to people, though he would put you in a milieu where there was that possibility and leave it up to you. The slight issue for me, if I'm candid about it, was having Bryan as a supporter, unworldly, hopeless with money, with my dealer at the time, Nigel Greenwood, unworldly, hopeless with money. A fantastic double act! Both were focused entirely on art and not much good for helping me launch myself on New York, for instance. It's a tough world, the art world. I'm not complaining but just to put Bryan in context.

Another thing I want to say is that some of his writing on my work is the most generous I've ever experienced. Bryan would say things like: 'This is some of the most splendid and effulgent and wonderful painting I've seen in my lifetime.' No one says that – that's quite a serious thing to say. I was aware that he wasn't really interested in fashion, and therefore when fashion moved away from my work, he stayed. He stayed with the artists he believed in and supported. Bridget [Riley], John [Hoyland], Patrick [Caulfield] – I was really on the edge of that. He was looking at art in a way that was consistent with pleasure and joy and ranking that as highly as toughness and ethics and struggle. As a young painter I was faced with various choices and one of the directions was the School of London, which felt more moral or ethical. Bryan wasn't really interested in all that.

Bryan could be quite sharp. Did Le Brun ever fall out with him?

I don't think so, but don't forget that I was that much younger. I was very respectful of Bryan. I couldn't take the sort of risks that would allow you to have a row. And I carried on seeing him till within a few days of his death. I saw him in the Chelsea and Westminster when he was really in quite some distress and he was on morphine and was hardly there at all the last time. The time before, he was lying in bed and at the end of the bed was this terrible rubbishy painting. 'And look what's happened! All this – a lifetime spent thinking about art and then this crummy painting!' Of course the nurses didn't get it. He couldn't just swap it for another painting. He saw the irony of it, with as much humour as he could.

He was an aesthete who loved the good things in life and was prepared to indulge them, which I think was behind his lack of punctuality as he was always inclined to say 'Oh, let's not bother'. He'd say this about appointments. 'Have another drink.' He was always like that. And for a moment time ceased to expand. Somewhere there's a collision happening elsewhere.

I asked Le Brun whether he thought Bryan was fundamentally lazy.

The word I'm thinking about is self-indulgent. If you want to think about your feelings and your reactions to things all the time, and your life depends on shades of feeling about colour and so on, you do need to be rather self-indulgent, because you've got to give yourself time to know what to think. Bryan's life was devoted to the eye.

Bryan said: 'You know Howard Hodgkin had an affair with David Sylvester?' I said no. He said: 'Can you imagine two rhinoceroses in bed together?' Bryan used to tease. That does absolutely give the flavour of it. But I wonder if there was something [uneasy] about homosexuality because I remember a conversation at one of those dinner parties. I think Leslie Waddington – who could be quite outspoken – said, across the table, something like: 'Oh Bryan, but we know something about your sort of man.' And Bryan really flashed back at that. He said: 'What do you mean?', very sharply, and then proceeded to justify himself and I think he even mentioned Helen Frankenthaler. It was a horrible thing to say and it got under his guard. I know what Leslie meant, and it was meant in a teasing way, but it really misfired. Because it wasn't ever spoken about [that Bryan was gay] and so I just wonder whether he was distancing himself from situations where that was the milieu. He liked handsome young men, and there was a sense of that. I'd been out with him to restaurants on Rhodes, and he would flirt. But it was pretty harmless.

Bryan was a pretty good critic of the work – if he didn't like something he didn't really talk about it. He didn't like to be negative. But the type of art world that developed in my time wasn't quite Bryan's, so he found himself not oppositional but as an alternative voice with a hinterland of people that were fond of him. But he didn't have any position. A man independent – and respected for that – but because of his independence rather disenfranchised. But it did enable him to say exactly what he thought. When Nick [Serota] asked me to be a trustee of the Tate in 1990, Bryan was concerned about me [being taken away from the studio]. He said 'All institutions are corrupt,

Christopher, be very careful.' And they're not, actually. I think it says something about Bryan's relationship with them. He did say that and it lingered in my mind.

In the sumptuous Le Brun monograph of 2001, which was originally intended to be written solely by Robertson, is reprinted the article that Bryan wrote originally for *Burlington Magazine* in July 1983 entitled 'A New Safety Curtain for Covent Garden by Christopher Le Brun'. The following quotation is taken from that article, in which Robertson summarises Le Brun's figurative and mythological work:

This feeling for imagery and mood is caught in paintings which are broadly expressionist in their sumptuous handling of paint, with large and visible brushstrokes, complex glazes and variable impasto. The paintings have a spirit which is partly a bravura variant on abstract expressionism at the service of figuration – in handling, not unlike Philip Guston in the early sixties – and partly a neo-romantic extension of the grand manner, replete with sympathetic glances at Rubens, Delacroix and Moreau. The paintings are remarkable for the way in which a specific late-afternoon mood of isolation, stoicism, fatality and other characteristics of the romantic agony is brilliantly trapped in a series of which each element has all the supercharged freshness of a vast sketch.

When Robertson proved incapable of delivering a complete new text for the book, it was decided that he conduct an interview with Le Brun that could be taped and transcribed. (It was subsequently edited and rewritten.) The interview took place in Lindos, Rhodes, on two separate occasions, in April 1997 and January 1998, at the house to which Robertson retreated in later years, supposedly to write his memoirs. Though wide-ranging and usefully contextual, it takes up a mere eight pages, and offers rather thin fare as the central text of a major new examination of an artist's work. Some writers choose to do an interview as a means of avoiding writing enthusiastically about an artist when they're not sure of the value of the work. There's no suggestion that Robertson felt this – rather the reverse. It seems that he was simply incapable of the application required to produce a substantial text, whether for the Le Brun monograph or for his own memoirs.

Of course, being a Robertson excursus, there were many fine things in the interview, even if several are in the nature of digressions or asides. For instance at one point he commented acutely on the blurring between the various techniques:

I'm thinking, for instance, of my irritation years ago when the critics excitedly praised the way in which Sutherland's actual brushstrokes or chalk marks from his original designs had been faithfully reproduced on an enlarged scale on the tapestry of Christ in Majesty for Coventry Cathedral. This seemed a vulgar confusion of media. When Dufy made some of the greatest designs of the century for silk materials made by the Bianchini-Férier Company in Lyons (1911–22), they were quite different to the designs he made for cotton or for linen. I think the proprieties in the treatment of different substances should be maintained. Tapestries are woven from wool and the great tapestry designs are formalised in terms of stitching with threads.

Jane Dixon

The artist Jane Dixon counted Bryan as one of her earliest supporters and something of a mentor. Here, in an email of September 2015, she traces their friendship:

I met Bryan in 1991 when I was a scholar in printmaking at the British School at Rome. He visited the school whilst he was in Rome to give a lecture in the city on Stanley William Hayter. He seemed particularly interested in my work and after a long conversation in the studio he gave me his contact details and suggested I should get in touch when I returned to London. I had just left the RCA and had gone straight to Rome. At the time I knew nobody in the art world and so Bryan's generous gesture was very important, not only because it was a validation of the work I was doing from such a significant figure but also personally; he was very open and interested and that meant a lot to me at such an early stage in my career. Later, in London, he introduced me to many of his friends, some of whom gradually became my valued supporters, colleagues and occasionally friends too, in particular Prunella Clough, Deanna Petherbridge and Stephen Chambers.

My first solo show in a public space was at London's Café Gallery [in Southwark] in 1992, the year after I returned from Rome. For the invitation, Bryan wrote a beautiful brief introduction to my work which reflected ideas we had talked about in Rome and later at my studio in London. In 1995, Bryan selected me as his *Artist of the Day* at Flowers East, when the gallery invited him, along with other critics, to each curate a one-day show. Although the show was a good experience for me the thing I remember most about it was the photo session for the catalogue … Bryan arrived at my studio in what was then the industrial wastes of Stratford (now the Olympic Park) in customary grand style by taxi, which he kept 'on the meter' for over two hours. (I didn't know this until the driver somehow found his way through the factory building to my studio door to ask would Bryan ever be coming back.) Bryan was having fun 'advising' the photographer about potential poses, his (and my) 'best side', lighting etc. The resulting photo has Bryan somewhat looming over me in one of his flamboyant shirt and waistcoat ensembles looking far more serious than reflects what had been going on, whilst I seem to look a bit glazed ... possibly as I had lost count of the number of pictures that had been taken by then. I don't think the gallery was thrilled with the taxi bill either.

In 1997 Bryan was influential in my receiving an award from the Mark Rothko Memorial Trust for travel to the US. The wonderful thing about the award was that it came with total freedom (something Bryan held dear), and it could be spent in any way I chose, so long as it was in America. There were no conditions attached that I should explain or evaluate my use of the award when I returned, just the stipulation that it should be used to enhance my life and work. An extraordinary luxury and unimaginable in our current climate. It enabled my longed-for first visit to the States and whilst I spent most of the two months I was there in New York, I did also visit Washington, D.C., and Chicago. It was an experience which transformed my work and inspired me on a personal level to the point that I thought of some aspect of the trip daily, for many years. It has a resonance for me even now, almost twenty years later.

In 1999, Bryan included a painting of mine from that year, *Untitled (Green Tunic)*, from my Armour Series, in his exhibition *'45–'99: A Personal View of British Painting and Sculpture*, held at Kettle's Yard, Cambridge. I would be awarded the Kettle's Yard Fellowship in 2000–1. After his death, I was a recipient (2006) of the annual award given by the Bryan Robertson Trust to an artist to support their career. Once more this was a quite life-transforming help to me. It enabled me to have a year solely in the studio to develop a new body of work and was the start of my Regeneration Project which I produced between 2006 and 2010.

Stephen Chambers

Stephen Chambers was privileged to know Bryan particularly well because they were near-neighbours in Islington. Whenever at a loose end or in need of a companion for dinner, cinema or theatre, he could call on Stephen with the likelihood of finding him working in the studio, but usually prepared to be interrupted. Chambers was a good listener and the two became close friends, so much so that Bryan appointed him his executor (along with John Spurling).

Bryan was extremely good company, he told and liked a good joke, he was irreverent, he could be a bit waspish, he could be very wrong. I knew him pretty well by the end and I worked something out quite quickly when I met him. I was very young, slightly overawed and tongue-tied. I was doing a postgraduate at Chelsea, and I vaguely knew his reputation. I received some correspondence from the Warwick Arts Trust where he was director saying there was going to be a show called something along the lines of *Artists of Fame & Promise*. As Bryan didn't like to make things too hard work if they didn't have to be, the show was Christopher Le Brun and Gary Wragg, punctuated with young artists like me. I was recommended by Gary Wragg who had been a tutor at St Martin's. I got a call from Bryan saying could he come and see my work. This was 1983 and I was living in a squat near Islington which turned out to be about 400 metres from where he lived. I had just left Chelsea so the paintings I had made there were in the front room of the tumbledown house. He'd never seen them before. He came round and I would have been quite nervous. He knocked on the door and he introduced himself and he said, 'I've brought some biscuits'. Then he looked at the packet and said, 'Oh, I seem to have eaten them all'. They were fig rolls, and I was rather grateful as I'm not a fan of the fig roll. He said all the right nice things. I was very timid.

In the end Christopher Le Brun didn't take part and he was probably advised by Nigel Greenwood that his career was going too fast for this type of thing. But Gary Wragg did, and I should think about ten others, including me. I was really thrilled to be in the show but rather tongue-tied. Bryan was incredibly sophisticated (especially compared to me). He was self-taught, inquisitive, very bright, and particularly able to make up his own mind. And that gives a lot of liberty: if you know what you think, you don't have the anxiety as to whether that's right or wrong. I don't think you really mind what other people say. And his vision was eclectic.

My paintings at that time were figurative, narrative, slightly naive arguably. My self-doubt said that this guy had to put a show together and I was only in there because there was some space to fill. That was my default setting. But somebody I went to the opening with overheard him saying (possibly to Caryl Hubbard), 'I think this person's got something'. I then went off to Rome for a year. And I was not confident enough to be in touch with him on my return. I wasn't in touch for at least two years, when I did a residency at Winchester School of Art and had the first exhibition in Winchester. There was a little catalogue produced, and I posted it through his door, and he phoned me up within about half-an-hour and said, 'I love these'. I had a studio in Robinson Road at this point and he just really loved those paintings.

He began to invite me to his house and we'd have dinner or go out to a restaurant. He was clearly talking to other people about me, but he never wrote anything – he was too lazy. He wrote one very inadequate thing once upon a time. I did recognise very early – which has probably got quite a lot to do with why our friendship endured – that he was very unreliable, and that if I ever asked him to do anything I would get so wound up at his unreliability that I would become irascible and it would break down our friendship. So I never asked him for anything. I worked that out.

I was extremely fond of him and he was extremely generous. He was a very constant friend. Because I was local and because he was so unreliable, he would quite often phone me and say, 'Let's have dinner tonight' and I would say, 'Great!', and then three hours later it would be cancelled, or sometimes ten minutes before I was supposed to go round. It wasn't a problem because he was just down the road. He would say, 'I've got gastro-enteritis' but I think he was just tired, didn't feel like cooking. He was extremely changeable like that as he got older. Certainly the restaurants of Islington were hit when he died.

I guess I listened to him. I remember one conversation. He said, 'What have you been to see?' I said I'd been to a Tony Cragg exhibition and he said something like, 'I don't suppose that was very interesting'. He was quite dismissive of it. I said that actually I thought Cragg was a very good artist. And we'd have a little conversation about it. Then three months later we'd be sitting round the dinner table and Tony Cragg's name would come up and Bryan would extol his work. I think sometimes I gave him my opinion as opposed to what a lot of people do, which was give him the opinion they thought he might want to hear. I wasn't a yes man, but I did listen. I remember when he died I said to someone I never knew why we were such good friends. That person said, 'Because you listened'.

He was a great raconteur and he was very good at putting people together (at dinner parties, sitting you next to someone you'd never otherwise encounter) and I think he did it with consideration. Those dinner parties were fun, they were excessive. The living room was on the first floor and the kitchen was on the ground floor. You'd walk in and see bags of ingredients sitting in the kitchen and know he hadn't even started cooking. You'd ascend upstairs and maybe there was Prunella Clough, Tim Marlow, Harrison Ford once upon a time, and you'd be given a Negroni and he'd go off and cook and then bring you another one, and another one. Eventually about 10 o'clock you might sit down. In a traditional Elizabeth David type of way he was a very good cook. He liked his food. He did say to me: 'Stephen, one of the reasons I like you so much is that you're the only person who drinks as much as me.'

Chambers visited Lindos a couple of times with Robertson. 'The only time that he was supposed to be writing something about me – a big feature for something like *Modern Painters*, which ended up being a hopeless one-column description of my family life – I'd gone out there and he was supposed to be interviewing me and writing this article, and we just went to restaurants.' Clearly Chambers was quite tolerant of him. 'I think I was. I remember once or twice being driven round the bend.' But he always remembered the upside because Bryan was worth it.

He didn't like being teased very much. I remember standing looking at a blue sky as a jet plane went across in the evening leaving vapour trail and

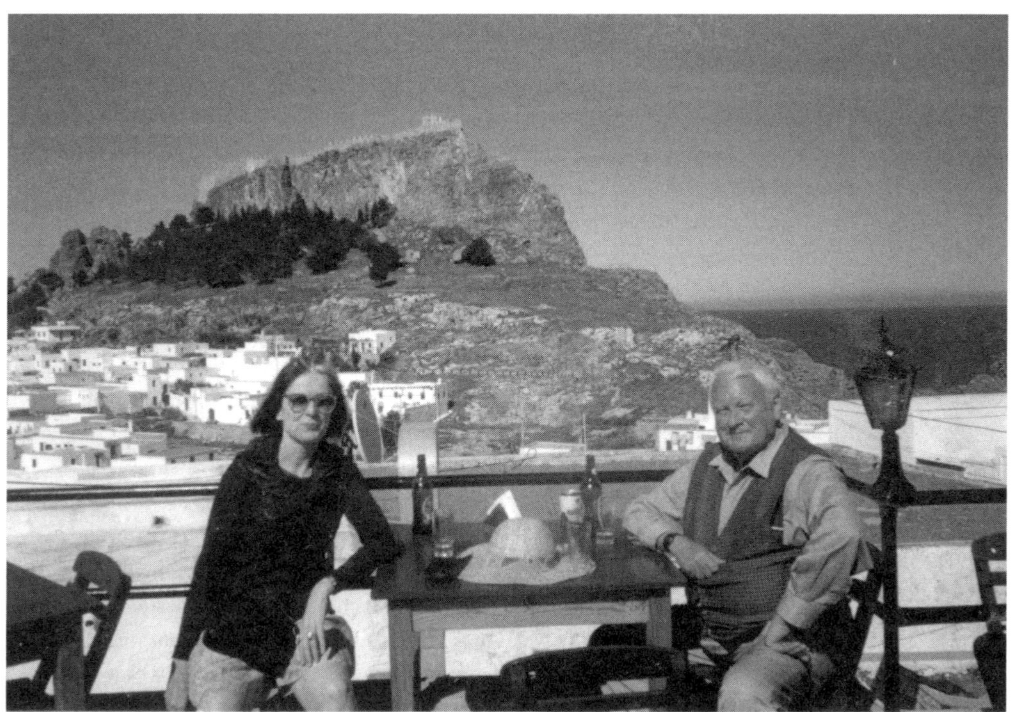

28 BR with friend, Lindos, Rhodes, 1990s.

him saying, 'Ah, Barney Newman!' I said, 'Mmm, it's a bit more interesting than a Barney Newman'. He thought that was quite funny. He liked a good joke and he was very, very funny. I remember certain anecdotes he told, they weren't lewd or risqué but they were funny, as he recalled conversations that he'd had with people. He could be quite rude about people.

I think he could be touchy. I was aware, particularly as he got older and got ill, that nearly everyone that had got close to him had had a falling out with him. I remember him showing me (in hospital, a few weeks before he died) a letter from Bridget Riley, with whom he'd been very close, and of whom he always spoke with huge respect. They'd had this massive bust-up and not spoken for years. She had written him a letter which he asked me to read. He asked me what he should do. The letter was really a building of bridges, a reconciliation, so I said just answer it, this is a conciliatory letter. And I believe he did. And when I came across such things that he had taken as a slight, they seemed to me rather small.

Having him as a champion probably did quite a lot of indirect good. I think it was known that Bryan was supporting me. He said he contacted Annely Juda, who came to the studio a couple of times, perhaps one or two other people. What he loved was those early slightly naive paintings. He really liked abstract painting. With figurative work, he was noticeably on the naive end of figuration. Or the idiosyncratic might be a more interesting word to use. Edward Burra he adored. He did a show of Mary Potter. But no interest in Lucian Freud, Frank Auerbach, etc. Hockney he had a huge amount of respect for. So he could fall out with people and still like their work a lot.

He didn't come to the studio frequently – I was aware he wasn't that interested in what I went on to do as he was in the beginning ... It was very frustrating. When I had an exhibition he'd come to it but sometimes you'd have to strap him to the roof of the car and drive him there. He'd often come late and all that sort of stuff. He was lazy and terribly disorganised. He had art which he would sell in moments of desperation. When I first knew him there was a Lee Krasner, which I remember him selling for a fairly healthy six-figure sum. I should think that lasted him about six months or a year. He sent me a thousand pounds, which to me was an absolute fortune. I was extremely embarrassed by it, and didn't know what to do. I was really touched.

Because he could make up his own mind, he wasn't afraid to champion people that were not fashionable. He adored John Hoyland and Prunella Clough. He loved the Hubbards, both John and Caryl, but I think Caryl was particularly important because she was one of the few people that told him off – that he'd gone too far – and he would listen to her. He liked women, but he said he found men more interesting. I was always surprised he said that because I thought women to him were very important. I think his friendships with Caryl Hubbard and Prunella Clough in particular were really important to him. He was really fond of Prunella.

He went off to live the winters in Greece, and I remember him telling me about a Greek that had come to interview him for an article. 'And do you know, Stephen,' he said, 'we were at it on the staircase!' That was unusual. Mostly he would intimate about relationships in his earlier life, but that was the only moment in the twenty-five years that I knew him that he referred to an encounter. I think he was quite optimistic about it, I think he saw it as the beginning of a relationship. That when he was in Rhodes he could go and visit this man in Athens, where he had his clothes made. Bryan loved clothes – I don't think he approved of my casualness of dress. He thought clothes were a type of art form. And I think he held the Greek as something more than a brief encounter. I don't know what happened, but I don't think it went very far.

I think he referred to Colin MacInnes as the love of his life. He also told me that he'd been engaged to Bridget Riley, which I think must have raised a few eyebrows certainly. I never met anybody as a partner of Bryan's, but he was capable of having circles of friends who didn't necessarily overlap. I lived close and was useful to him. I had a car and could transport him places. I fixed his boiler. We went to the theatre together. I remember he invited me to dinner on a day that happened to be Valentine's Day, and

I think one or two people thought 'Aye, Aye!' but I never thought that for a moment and I don't think he did either. He probably hadn't realised.

We went out for dinner every couple of weeks. We went to see films. I introduced him to Tarkovsky, which I think was a revelation to him. I took him to see *Andrei Rublev* which I subsequently heard him describe as the greatest film he'd ever seen. He liked comedy – we'd go and see Alan Ayckbourn. I recognised that I couldn't really reciprocate in any of these ways and anyway he liked to be the giver. I never invited him to dinner. I once or twice went to houses where he was a guest and I could see he was much more comfortable as the host than the guest. And he was an extremely good host – really the best.

I remember going to see *Babette's Feast* with him, which was OK as it was all about food. We used to go to a restaurant in Islington in the late eighties and early nineties, called The Crazy Crepe, which was run by an Egyptian chef and his Israeli wife. He was a great cook, very cheap. 'Ah, flat food!' said Bryan, fed up with plates being sculpted. The chef came running out: 'Who said that?' 'I did.' 'Thank you – you noticed!' I remember going to an Indian restaurant called Parvi and he'd order huge amounts. He had an old-fashioned enjoyment of good manners and good service. He took me to L'Escargot which was really stylish.

He wasn't camp, though you would have probably guessed he was gay. He was quite open about his preferences. He liked buying perfume for his friends. As well as him not coming to my house for dinner I used to go to see him alone – Denise did not join me. He said to me, 'I prefer people on their own'. He didn't like dealing with couples. He was a kind of nightmare and kind of wonderful and I think some people found him unreliable but endearing. Bryan was very susceptible to fawning and the compliment – he loved it. The attention. He was very excited by fame. He was susceptible to beauty. He liked a little bit of celebrity – he liked fame and being with famous people.

He would become enraptured by certain things – for instance, a certain writer – and then all his friends would be given a copy of the book, like *My Name is Red* [by Orhan Pamuk]. He gave this book to many people, but I wasn't sure he'd read it. I suspect he read the first chapter and the last chapter and got the gist. Bryan was much more sophisticated than I was so could introduce me to interesting people and interesting situations, theatre and films and so forth, and ways of behaving. I think he was a good friend, and an unusual friend largely because of the age gap. Of all the people who were his good friends, I think that I and possibly Prunella Clough were the only ones who never had a fall out with him. He had bust-ups with everybody at some point.

Bryan had a big two-and-a-half-metre long rosewood Saarinen tulip table, oval, one-and-a-half-metres wide, a really beautiful table.

He subsequently left it to me but it was too big for my house and I sold it. It was in remarkably good condition. He gave me loads of books, and left me the first choice of his entire library. I ended up as his executor with John Spurling. I was quite diligent. John was really fond of Bryan. He and I don't see eye to eye on everything but that's probably quite good.

He liked performing – radio, for example. I think he was better on the radio than he was writing. That would be left to the last minute. He was good with a microphone. He could improvise, he was eloquent and enthusiastic, whereas writing involved sitting down and working. I remember saying something moderately disparaging about David Hockney and he pulled me up short on that. I don't think Hockney by that time was a good friend, but they must have known one another in the sixties. He wasn't uncompetitive even though he was undisciplined. I don't think he had huge respect for David Sylvester, but he recognised that Sylvester was more disciplined than he was, and that he would be carrying on working when Bryan was in a restaurant in Islington.

Round the dinner table I met Claire Bloom, Irene Worth, various directors of this and that. I remember once a car coming round and he remembered he was supposed to have lunch with Princess Margaret. He said, 'Go and tell them I'm not here'. He'd forgotten all about it. He did pretty much what he wanted to do. There were times when I'd go round to dinner and he'd forgotten that I was coming. But it didn't matter because I could just walk back down the road. If I said to Denise, 'I'm having dinner with Bryan tonight', she'd answer, 'Well, maybe'. And it would be maybe.

He liked young people doing things and he was – to some extent – interested in what was going on now. He got a kick that I came from a different generation. I was quite useful at keeping him up to date with what was going on, but he was not that concerned with current developments. But every now and then he would find something really interesting. He always had an opinion. Sometimes the opinion was wrong, but he had it, and that's quite important.

Later catalogue texts and essays

Bryan was often asked to write essays and catalogue introductions for exhibitions, mostly, one suspects, by the artists concerned, because they knew how perceptive and enlightening he could be. The publishers and gallery administrators may not have been so keen, for Robertson would frequently be hit by writers' block, and be unable to produce to deadline. Unfortunately, this became the norm as he grew older (though deadlines were a lifelong problem), and there are many tales of his dictating an essay at the last minute over the telephone.

CERI RICHARDS *Tate Gallery, 1981*

Robertson curated a memorable Ceri Richards retrospective at the Whitechapel in 1960, which was deemed a considerable success, and marked what Bryan described in the show's catalogue as 'the beginning of a generally more expansive phase in Ceri's career: he signed a contract with Marlborough Fine Art at that time, which must have held out the possibility that his work would be exhibited abroad, and he was selected to represent England at the Venice Biennale in 1962'. In 1981 he worked with Mel Gooding, Richards' son-in-law, on a major Tate exhibition surveying the extent of the artist's achievement. In the catalogue Robertson summed up: 'In my view his work should be considered at the same level of radical achievement in British art as the sculptures of Moore and Hepworth or the paintings of Sutherland, Nicholson, Hitchens and Bacon.'

Earlier in his essay in the 1981 catalogue he had written vividly of the artist:

Ceri Richards seemed always to live entirely within his work or to exist self-sufficiently behind the protective shield of his family. I was first stirred and elated by his paintings of pianists in interiors in the late nineteen-forties and the cheerful Trafalgar Square series of paintings in 1951, painted to celebrate the Festival of Britain. Ceri was already middle aged when I first met him a year or two later in the early nineteen-fifties, a man of medium height, thick-set but not flabby, rather powerfully built and with a strong, oddly restrained but alert and listening presence as if he were considering something, some factor, outside and beyond the boundaries of the conversation. He was a distinguished and good looking man, rather like a more conventionally handsome Picasso and, apart from his greying hair, he did not seem to change much over the years. With this curiously intent presence, at once watchful and withdrawn, there came also a strong impression of a fundamentally innocent man: not silly by any means and even quite reasonably worldly-wise, but still a man without the usual barriers of artifice or self-preservation.

WILLIAM HENDERSON *Arnolfini, Bristol, 1983*

Often in his catalogue texts Bryan would wax lyrical about movements in the history of art, or specific developments he had observed, leaving the detail about the artist under discussion for a few lines at beginning, middle or end. His introduction to the work of the abstract painter William Henderson is a case in point:

When Degas was asked by a friend for his opinion of Odilon Redon, the work, the man, everything, Degas replied 'He is a hermit, but he knows the train schedules'. Paradoxes and apparently irreconcilable oppositions are deliberately deployed and synthesized in Henderson's paintings, but I am not of course comparing his work to Redon's, or to Degas's nice equation between holiness and sophistication, except to suggest a comparable degree of sophistication, great refinement, and a head-on clash, magisterially held, locked and revolved, between adamant physicality and the further reaches of something, some kind of condition, or light, or state of being, that is quite metaphysical. A two-way action, in fact. It is as if the mysterious essences and fine calligraphy of, say, Mark Tobey, were superimposed and galvanized into a new and startling life by the emphatic energy, the bristling dynamism of a Leger.

I have never seen an abstract painting in my life which seemed to me to be wholly abstract, totally without feeling, merely a mark, or a balancing act, or an equilibrium, or a space, or an absolute, say a blank square. The wholly abstract painting doesn't exist, and never did. I do not mean that I see faces in Malevich or Mondrian, Albers or Rothko or Pollock or Riley, or clouds, or any sort of buried imagery or surrogate landscape references or sunsets or sunrises. But I am aware of strong feeling in the work of all these artists and in each individual and distinct case, a situation with its own original aesthetic, structural drama.

For me, the exact position of that small intense red square in a black and white Mondrian grid in relation to a slightly larger blue rectangle is as tense, loaded and taut – as dramatic – as the human relationships and confrontations in that hypothetical Ibsen drama. Rothko's paintings are excursions into the Sublime as well as an effort to reach a condition of light, colour and space that can move emotionally between the sombre depths of a Rembrandt and the elation of a Matisse, or the domesticated sensuousness of a Bonnard. In any case, Rothko disliked being referred to as a colourist, which he rightly saw as a restricting and patronizing label, and was essentially concerned with an almost mystical obsession with proportions that sprang from his great love for Greek temples, their columns, steps and ground plans, once briefly experienced on a holiday and never forgotten.

ELISABETH FRINK *Sculpture: Catalogue Raisonné, 1984*

In 1984, Bryan wrote the critical essay for the first catalogue raisonné of Elisabeth Frink's work, and in June 1993 he narrated a South Bank Show for London Weekend Television in tribute to her. When Edward Lucie-Smith was compiling his book on her, *Frink: A Portrait* (1994), the artist admitted that Robertson and Lucie-Smith were the only art critics she'd ever talked to seriously. Robertson said of her work: 'All her figures, although so unhistrionic and contained in their calm muscular energy, have a special sense of survival, of endurance and alertness.' The following is from his 1984 catalogue raisonné essay:

Frink's subjects are basic, familiar to us all, and could not be simpler: man, men, birds, dogs and horses. These are the subjects that she understands as part of her living experience. It is a measure of her artistic and imaginative integrity, in which an exceptional purity of spirit is the bedrock, that for all the constant accessibility of her sculptures and the ease with which all kinds of people can comprehend and enjoy them, there is never any recourse in their formal realization to academic mannerism or cliché. An occasional personal mannerism of an obsessive kind creeps in – not often – but this could be said of the work of any strong painter or sculptor throughout history: it is after all how we recognize their work.

Bryan also contributed a dialogue with the artist, from which the following comments about Brancusi and Giacometti derive:

I am surprised that you did not respond more to Brancusi. I visited his studio many times in 1947 and from then until his death in 1955. For me he is the supreme innovator of the century in sculpture, the antithesis of Rodin and a very great artist. So far as your art is concerned I should have thought that Brancusi's immaculate and classical sense of being outside the time flux, untouched by the normal pressures of time and circumstance, would have moved you more than Giacometti's time-worn shapes and surfaces in which the attrition of time, space and the ageing process, or decay, seem to govern the form.

I believe myself that Giacometti's finest work was made before the war; later he became very mannered and repetitive, I believe, and somewhat academic in his drawings. Apart from the rather numbing repetition in those skinny figures and etiolated drawings, the awful inner pressures of his ravaging illness had an effect on his sense of form so that everything was suffering from attrition and emaciation. A noble artist, but best when young, I believe.

HANS TISDALL *Albemarle Gallery, London, 1990*

Painting the broader picture, Bryan would often deviate from his ostensible subject, though the text would nearly always circle back towards the artist in question. Here he eloquently conjured up the benefits brought to England by the influx of emigré artists during the early part of the twentieth century.

For sixty years, Hans Tisdall has lived and worked in England, made extremely beautiful paintings with a number of distinguished public decorations and, coincidentally but very importantly, he has helped to civilise us. Tisdall is a painter, first and foremost, of considerable power and refinement whose ability to make a compact, glowing abstract ikon from something seen in nature – sea, cliffs, boats, landscape, flowers – has never stood still, never become dated in any one aspect of the successive formal resolutions of this century and most refreshingly, makes the ikon work convincingly in quite abstract terms whilst retaining the gleam and scent and presence, the essential spirit in some odd way, of the thing first apprehended in nature. His best work has all these elements working together in absolute calm and harmony. He is concerned with essences and each distillation is made with the illusion of great ease.

What we owe in England to our foreign residents can hardly be calculated. Where would our publishing world be without Victor Gollancz, Frederick Muller, the Neurath family, André Deutsch, George Weidenfeld and a number of other contemporaries? Where would our knowledge and taste have been if the Gimpel brothers, Erica Brausen, Annely Juda and the Fischer family had not arrived in England to instruct us? The only detailed assessment of English architecture was initiated and completed, volume by volume, by Dr Nikolaus Pevsner. And where would English painting be without Freud and Auerbach – or, in the huge area of commercial design, the pioneering work of F.K. Henrion? Some of our politicians wonder about England entering Europe. Perhaps someone should inform them that it is already here, making things work very well. Hans Tisdall's contribution to our culture is a vital one and deserves the kind of celebration that he has always offered to us.

ALAN REYNOLDS *Annely Juda, London 1991*

After a hugely successful early career as a modern romantic figurative artist, painting the teasels and hop fields of southern England, Alan Reynolds – like Victor Pasmore before him – underwent a conversion to abstraction. Robertson, unlike many of Reynolds' erstwhile supporters, preferred his radical abstract work to his former romanticism.

Reynolds has explored a new and quite monumental calm in these reliefs, notably in the compositions in which horizontal rectangles predominate. In others, small squares appear to be trapped or securely contained, at one side or the other, by these grand horizontal areas, to be released or to exist within an open space at the opposite side of the white relief. All the reliefs have a majestic equilibrium of their own, an extraordinary, loaded simplicity of formal means and a fresh spaciousness. They are beautiful contemplative objects and give out the sense, the feeling of a distillation of knowledge, an extreme concentration of aesthetic experience.

When considered one after another, the reliefs also remind me yet again of the way in which highly gifted artists are wasted in this country. For surely Reynolds should have been commissioned by now to make a relief mural for a public building? If money and site can be found for a big Richard Serra minimal sculpture at the new Broadgate development, for instance, why cannot a suitable wall be found for Reynolds in one of the new buildings? There are of course other sites elsewhere, both in London and in England as a whole, and certainly other artists deserving of public patronage. But the art of Alan Reynolds could illuminate and give a coherence to a public space in a unique way.

Reynolds had fond memories of Bryan, and knew, for instance, that after the Second World War Bryan not only went to Paris, but also made 'a sort of tour of Germany, visiting Munich and so on, which was very unusual then'. He thought Bryan very well informed, and perceptive about the processes of making art. 'I was in the last wave of artists who moved from a figurative background and training, to a non-figurative one,' remarked Reynolds in a telephone interview in June 2013. 'Robertson took that in his stride: he was 100% supportive of my move to abstraction. But although he was a great supporter of the work, and a good friend, we never saw much of each other.'

When Bryan visited Reynolds in preparation for writing the catalogue essay excerpted above, he was very impressed with the artist's workroom, which he loved. Reynolds gave Bryan lunch and served him fresh pineapple for pudding, and he long remembered Bryan's unfeigned enjoyment of the fruit – 'he was just like a kid!' Reynolds enjoyed Bryan's sense of humour and his loyalty, and felt that 'What he did at Whitechapel fully justified him taking the Tate, but he fell foul of the wrong people'.

LAND OF THE FREE, HOME OF THE BRAVE: ARTIST IMMIGRANTS IN AMERICA IN THE TWENTIETH CENTURY

Crane Kalman Gallery, London, 2000

When Andrew Kalman put together an exhibition of twentieth-century artist immigrants in America, from Rothko to Louise Bourgeois, it was an inspiration to ask Bryan to write the preface to the catalogue, which turned out to be the publication's only text. Here he reflected upon the very particular character of American art:

American art was received more generously and with greater comprehension in London from the mid-nineteen-fifties onward than in any European city. But today, nearly fifty years later, the fact remains that in England, we still hardly know American art in all its great richness and diversity. This is not because of the comparative dearth of American exhibitions in London during the past couple of decades compared with the many great occasions of the 1950s, sixties and seventies. The truth is that even then we were only shown, on the whole, what the Museum of Modern Art in New York wanted us to see in work from various artists exemplifying Abstract Expressionism, Pop Art, Colour Field painting or Minimalism. But this restricted our view to the work of those artists who reached maturity and celebrity around mid-century. And such a version of events, although bringing to our attention some works of undisputed originality, and sometimes genius, also cut out a great deal of work by other very remarkable artists who came to maturity earlier in the century. Names mean nothing without visible example but the London public has yet to see an exhibition which presents the work of, say, Marsden Hartley, John Marin, Max Weber, Yasuo Kuniyoshi, Arthur Dove, Ralston Crawford, Lyonel Feininger, Charles Sheeler, Charles Demuth, Charles Burchfield or Loren MacIver among a good many others.

It was quite right to focus on Rothko and Pollock, Johns and Rauschenberg at the time of the first broad recognition in Europe of American art because these were among the great originators of their time, but in honouring them so much else was missed out, notably the ground swell in American art from around 1900 on, to be felt strongly in some of the work of the twenties, thirties and forties, and still largely unknown to us.

RICHARD SMITH ***Flowers Central & Flowers East, London, 2001***

Richard Smith was an artist of great originality, closely associated with the pop art movement, but whose work embraced the formal values of abstraction to a far greater extent than most op artists. Bryan was deeply interested in his work and, besides including him in the group exhibition *British Painting in the Sixties* (1963), gave him a solo show at the Whitechapel in 1966. In this 2001 catalogue essay Robertson analysed his particular genius:

Given his consistently high level of invention, the dominant characteristic of Richard Smith's work over five decades in various media is the way in which his art touches on the most radiant, purely enjoyable and stress-free aspects of twentieth-century style as we find it in certain kinds of painting, design, architecture, and even in the sharper and wittier forms of commercial packaging or advertising. Smith's art has nothing to do with Andy Warhol, who was a highly original and fastidious embalmer, entranced by death, and hardly anything to do with the rest of pop art as we see it in, for instance, the magnificent declamations of Robert Indiana or the crafty art games of Roy Lichtenstein. If we look at the peripheries of pop art, Smith relates more to Jasper Johns or Ed Ruscha and the world of ideas, devices, stylistic double-takes.

Smith's art, stress-free, radiant and enjoyable, does not even touch upon the pleasurable bourgeois hedonism of Matisse or Bonnard, or the sportif wit and gaiety of Dufy with his flag-fluttering regattas, but rather something which exists as pure gleaming spirit somewhere between the delectably deadpan formality of Juan Gris, and the lean, dry brightness of Ellsworth Kelly. Free of sentimentality, devoid of nostalgia in the best twentieth-century tradition, utterly without stress or struggle, the creative spirit in Smith's work can also be found in those syncopated hymns of the twentieth century, the short, sharp, lyrical melodies of Gershwin. Free of the past, mordantly optimistic about the future, buoyant and rooted in the man-made city.

As an artist and as a designer, Smith loves and is endlessly preoccupied by delicate but steely oppositions and culminations, or formal resolutions: open and shut, dry and wet, hard and soft, a grid-like structure against which soft amorphous shapes are splayed in semi-rhythmical formation like splodgy shadows – irresistible, to me; liquid and solid, knots as a formal device, hinges. Smith makes a new world of his own from corners, angles and grids; finely articulated mesh counterpointing soft cloud shapes; shadow and substance. He enjoys an almost Japanese austerity of rich colour balance, structure and linear infrastructure, notably in his big two-part inventions, like formally abstract diptychs. He touches also, and rather differently, on something quite glamorous in his silky, fluttering painted surfaces and in his very personal use of colour: like cosmetic colour, lipstick shades of red, pink and orange, mascara tones of mauve, green and silver, other colour like the fathomless and frontal colour of printer's inks.

Beatrice Monti

Baronessa Beatrice Monti della Corte von Rezzori is, according to one journalist, 'an impatient, charismatic, preternaturally controlling woman', but I found her charming to interview (in her London hotel in April 2015), full of insights and with a deep love for Bryan. Santa Maddalena, her writers' retreat in Tuscany, is her home, converted into a retreat after the death of her husband, the novelist Gregor von Rezzori, in 1998. Writers come to stay for six weeks at a time, and Bryan was frequently a treasured guest.

Aged twenty-five, after the Second World War, Beatrice founded one of the first European galleries to show new American art, the Galleria dell'Ariete in Milan, where she exhibited works by Cy Twombly and 'that beautiful, brilliant couple', Robert Rauschenberg and Jasper Johns. She met Bryan when he was running the Whitechapel.

He was very well known at that time – he was around and about everywhere. He came to see me in Milan, and I had a big show of Rauschenberg that he very much wanted to have. So this was the first thing in a working situation with him. He was delightful. Very disorganised, totally charming, a genius. He knew every discipline you can imagine. After we became intimate friends he would come to Milan and stay with me. He was a voracious reader and that made him so extraordinary and cultivated in every possible way. I had a house in Rhodes, in Lindos, and he went there for many years in the winter. He didn't have asthma there. It's a very beautiful spot but not at all comfortable – it was very much a summer house. He was adored by the people of the village and he took trips in Turkey during the winter with the owner of a local restaurant.

I think his brain was bizarre – I think he was sort of self-made in a way. It was his intelligence and his eye. He was gifted, and in what he liked he was very deep. He had great authority. I saw him a lot in America. [He put on exhibitions of Motherwell and Frankenthaler there.] Enormous sense of humour, very witty. The conversation was always a delight, I never had a moment of boredom.

He was not an ambitious man. He was also an *amateur* in many other things – his connoisseurship for music, ballet as well as art. He was not a gallerist – although he could have had a job if he wanted to. I think he wanted to do other things. He had an acute intelligence, this is what I remember, plus the cheerfulness, he was very endearing. But he could do terrible things. [In the days of her gallery when she had pull in Milan he suggested an exhibition put on by a distinguished foreigner which would be Italy presented to the Italians by a foreigner.] It was an amusing idea. So I got the go-ahead to do it and suggested Bryan as the curator. He said yes, yes, and disappeared. He was supposed to come and speak to those people who were putting up the money. He forgot or got lost. He disappeared for a month – perhaps he was in love? – we didn't know where he was. He was like that – sometimes he could be bizarre. I was very upset for some time. I was very cross for a moment. He wasn't always reliable. He was a free man – let's put it that way. You can't be director of the Tate and a free man.

He was chaotic (I am the same). It's very difficult to sit down and do one thing, it's easier to do two other things. He was very unorthodox – which was his great genius. 'Regularly' is not a word to be applied to Bryan, but he came a lot to my house in Tuscany. He loved the place very much and when he was very sick I went to see him at the hospital, and he was always making fun of himself, but he had a moment of emotion and said, 'One of the sad things is that I won't be able to come and stay in the tower'. And I said, 'Listen, we are both very unconventional. What do you think of the idea of coming in another format there?' And he said, 'Would you do that?' And I said, 'Yes, I would, of course I would,' and he kissed my hand.

So when he died Hilary Spurling arranged for Bryan's ashes to be sent over to Italy and he is buried in Beatrice's garden with Gregor and the family. 'I feel very close to him always, you know. He was so able to understand the quality in a being, in an object, a landscape. I miss him. He was always able to surprise you, never be boring. I remember his voice and his laughter and his big blue eyes.'

1980s In 1981 Bryan assisted the National Gallery of Australia in Canberra to acquire Léger's *Les Trapezistes*, for which he was paid a fee of more than US$3,000. The same year a letter arrived from the Athenaeum Club in Pall Mall politely asking Bryan to pay his subscription, which was considerably in arrears. His life seemed to oscillate between these kind of extremes, with a dash of idealism thrown in somewhere along the way. He felt very strongly about the anti-apartheid cause, and in 1982 tried to enlist Francis Bacon's help in donating a picture to be sold as part of the Art Appeal to raise funds for the International Defence and Aid Fund (for Southern Africa), but in this case without success. Among the sponsors for the Art Appeal were Edward Bond, Peter Brook, Sir Hugh Casson, R.B. Kitaj, Iris Murdoch and Tom Stoppard. Bryan was at least in good company.

The Warwick Arts Trust, a privately funded exhibition space in Pimlico, offered Bryan the chance to put on exhibitions of those he particularly admired. This he did for a short period in the early 1980s, beginning with a retrospective of Nigel Hall's early drawings and sculptures in May 1980, and continuing with shows of John Maine, John Hubbard, Ken Draper, Elisabeth Vellacott, Ivor Abrahams and F.E. McWilliam. Caryl Hubbard recalled what a good space it was, but that Bryan's extravagance once again rather sabotaged the project. He commissioned beautifully printed catalogues for each exhibition, all produced to the highest standards on the best paper with top-quality photography and design. Far too many were printed and a storeroom was filled with unsold copies. As Caryl said: 'Bryan never thought about such things. It just didn't occur to him. If he was putting on a show of Paul Huxley or whoever, he wanted it to be the best show it could possibly be. If the walls needed repainting, even if they'd been painted recently, then they were repainted. That was how it had to be.'

The writer and journalist Judith Flanders wrote about Robertson's Dufy show in 1983–4 at the Hayward on her blog in 2011:

> I met him in the early 1980s, when he was preparing his great Dufy show … This was a revelation – not only an artistic one. It was a revelation because I had thought I knew what I thought about Dufy, but through the care and love and sheer blazing intelligence that Robertson gave to the show, I realized that I knew nothing. It was a revelation, too, because it took away that adolescent sense of certainty and made me see that aged twenty (or thirty, or forty, or fifty), there is always space for rethinking. That was Robertson's gift. And he taught me, too, that you can have fun while you do it. He would talk about Dufy, and then leave messages on my grandmother's answering-machine, claiming to be the Scotland Yard vice squad (all of it,

I assume): 'We have been watching for days, and we've seen thirty-seven young men going into your flat, and all coming out exhausted. And we just want you to know that we think it's disgusting.' (She was amused and more than a tiny bit thrilled.)

The Dufy exhibition was Bryan's last great public act of curating, and a great triumph, but it occurred twenty years before he died. He should have done others like it, but he was considered too unreliable, too much of a risk. He was his own worst enemy in this respect but, besides himself, the ones to suffer most have been us – his potential public. What magnificent spectacles we might have seen. I still remember the Dufy exhibition with something approaching awe. Instead, Bryan was reduced to writing catalogue essays for dealers' shows (not quite as challenging or engaging) – or at least for those who could tolerate his extreme dilatoriness. David Juda, managing director of the Annely Juda Gallery in London's Mayfair, insisted that Bryan's Dufy exhibition had completely changed the way he thought about that artist. He also said what a nightmare Bryan was when it came to delivering text. On one occasion the gallery was right up against the wire on a printer's deadline for an exhibition catalogue and it was clear that Bryan still hadn't written a thing. At the very last minute he dictated his essay over the phone to a secretary, ad-libbing like mad. Fortunately, it was brilliant, David said.

By nature, Bryan was more of a constructive critic than a destructive one. Generally speaking, he preferred to praise rather than censure, but there were occasions when his disapproval got the better of him. Curator Richard Riley mentions one occasion when he was publicly dismissive of Richard Long's work (see page 270 below), and another instance arose at a Tate discussion on Richard Hamilton, in the presence of the artist. According to Richard Morphet, who curated the Hamilton exhibition, Robertson had previously attacked Hamilton in print in no uncertain terms, but subsequently refused to be drawn on a public platform. In an email of March 2018 Morphet wrote:

I think the Tate thought it would be a good idea to have one or more public events in connection with Richard's retrospective. The exhibition was a great box-office success and was on the whole well received critically. But his work had roused controversy from time to time, so it was felt that a public discussion in which Richard was able to discuss hostile criticisms of his work with their author would be enlivening and illuminating.

Richard proposed a discussion between himself and Bryan Robertson, who in earlier years, in public print, had been critical of Richard's work, and who Richard felt had also, at other times, rather glaringly demeaned the status of Richard's work by omitting mention of it in pieces intended to tell readers what, of interest, was on display in London. Richard also resented the fact that (as reported by Richard, and no doubt checkable in the cuttings) Bryan had omitted mention of Richard when reviewing the major survey exhibition *Pop Art Redefined* at the Hayward Gallery in 1969, in which Richard's work was prominent.

It was my awkward fate to be the moderator of this discussion, which was held in front of a large audience in the first big, long gallery on the left after you enter what is now Tate Britain. I have found my speaking notes for this event, but cannot, of course, be certain how much of them I spoke.

My notes show (and I am sure these particular details are accurate) that Bryan's published critical writing in relation to Hamilton, from dates before 1970, had included the following propositions:

— Hamilton was, in his work, too concerned with admass.

— Admass material is always boring.

— Admass subjects are lethal to art.

— Hamilton's work is too aware of art, and too little aware of life.

— It shows an excessive identification with process at the expense of image.

My notes suggest that Bryan had also written, before 1970, that 'Duchamp was always an academic practitioner' and that Duchamp's *Nude Descending a Staircase* was 'plainly a retrogressive portmanteau work', and that I quoted these views, too, at the event.

I don't know how the audience felt about the evening. I don't remember any complaints, but personally I found it excruciating. With all these hostile opinions of Bryan's on Richard's work being on the record, I felt sure the evening would be an occasion of lively dispute, about real issues. But whenever I quoted to Bryan (and to the audience) any of his negative comments on Richard's work he refused either to acknowledge the views I had quoted or to discuss them. He did not, of course, disavow what he had written, but just airily brushed each quote aside and deflected discussion. The result, as I recall it, was that the tenor of the event was affable, light-hearted and substantially content-free.

And Morphet concludes: 'If that memory is correct, it seems to me to have been a bizarre state of affairs!'

Bryan recalled Hamilton in later years writing (in a letter to John McEwen), 'I cannot help smiling at memories of that glum, bashed in potato face looking gloomily at me across the room in parties over the years'.

In turn, not everyone approved of Bryan, or thought he had much left to offer by the 1980s. The contrarian critic Peter Fuller quoted with approval the opinion of the *Daily Telegraph*'s art critic Terence Mullaly of Bryan as a 'poor, old, spent force', when reviewing the 1983 Hayward

Annual Sculpture Show in *Art Monthly*. Meanwhile, Bryan was protesting about the Hayward and the Arts Council. He wrote to Marghanita Laski, who was vice-chairwoman of the Arts Council, on 21 October 1983:

You may recall lunching with me last autumn to discuss the Hayward Gallery and the fears expressed to me by the Art Panel, of which I am a member, and the Exhibitions Sub-Committee, of which I am chairman, over the Gallery's future. There was a general feeling that possibly Council did not fully appreciate the role the Hayward played in serving as a storage and servicing centre for exhibitions created to travel round the Country as well as serving as the main 'official' exhibition centre for London. It is our only equivalent to the Grand Palais in Paris for shows arranged with foreign governments. I pointed also to the way in which the Hayward served as a vehicle for important exhibitions which evolved from an idealistic and independent policy, democratically formulated, which was clear of the vagaries of fashion or the demands of money that has seemed quite often recently to shape exhibitions policy at the RA or at the Tate.

I submitted a short list of reasons for the Hayward's importance to the British public and to the Arts Council, and you were sympathetic in the main to my reasons. We both agreed that the Hayward was not the most sympathetic building that we could conceive of, for art, but it was all that we had and it could be improved, with care.

My meeting with you was the result not only of anxiety expressed by Panel and Committee colleagues but came during a very long and arduous series of meetings, often running until late at night, convened in what everyone felt to be an emergency, caused by financial pressure, the need to cut exhibition expenditure and postpone the Romanesque exhibition and, what seemed then, the threat to the gallery. We all worked tremendously hard. Since then, a number of us have been working even harder, with Denys Lasdun and others, to draw up concrete plans for improvements to the Gallery. Roy Strong, our new Chairman, is a model of sense and enlightenment in this aspect of our work, as indeed in all others.

You may imagine, with this background of worry, work, and hope – and real effort by so many good people – how everyone felt when the *Sunday Telegraph* back in the summer holiday period, published an account of how the Hayward Gallery was in fact disposed of by Sir William Rees Mogg last year. I visited Sir William in his shop last autumn to put to him the views of my colleagues, to express concern and to present all the reasons for the Hayward's importance for this country, as I had already done with you. I was assured by Sir William that the Hayward was quite safe for the foreseeable future.

In a draft letter to Lord Gowrie, then Minister for the Arts Council (dated 23 December 1983), Bryan expressed his shock at what he termed the 'unethical, unconstitutional and ruthlessly complacent and contemptuous

behaviour on the part of administration at the top level, at the Arts Council'. In the light of this, he felt he must return his OBE, 'awarded me for services to art twenty-seven years ago, and which gave pleasure to my parents'. He no longer wanted to be connected in any way with 'official' honours relating to government, although this move distressed him. He wrote additionally: 'I want to try, separately, to improve the bad situation at the Arts Council, and not resign.'

Letter to America

Bryan was a great reader and admirer of novels, having himself once nurtured aspirations in that direction. Here follows a draft letter to Philip Roth (dated 14 January 1988), a friend and frequent dinner guest with his then wife Claire Bloom at Robertson's Islington home. In the letter Bryan discussed Roth's novel *Counterlife*, and his hopes that the writer would not cut himself off entirely from England. The letter is every bit as supportive and enthusiastic as any of his missives to visual artists.

Dear Philip –

Counterlife is a book without precedent in my experience, a marvellous invention, and I'm very happy that you've had just recognition. The novel-of-ideas is now a bit alien to the English, so perhaps it's been seen less clearly here although friends of mine across a wide spectrum relish it keenly. Your presence here for a part of each year is precious to us all. Your work is really loved here, and so are you as a man, an extraordinary identity, and I hope you know, properly know and feel, the great depth of affection and regard there is for you in London.

God knows, it cannot be easy. Intellectual life has more bite and force in the US, arguments for and against positions are fiercer, alignments are sharper and very personal. Here, the contours seem softer or more blurred, and there is a *gemütlich* sort of faintly vapid amiability. And much ignorance.

But I know from experience of both cities, and others, Paris and Rome, that all cities have their provincial side, their parochial self-absorption – and embarrassing chauvinisms. New York can be amazingly closed-in, and a bit self-pleased. The way to be is [an] old-fashioned *citoyen du monde*, and that is what you have become. Don't retreat to the US. I write because I hear that you feel you've 'had' London and want to stay away. Obviously, you must do what is right for you as a writer, for your ease and well-being – or for your stimulation. But don't forget that there is a tremendous great pool of love and admiration for you here; and that for an artist, London can be like wearing an old and comfortable glove ...

The thing is, though, that we don't see you as a foreigner. You are our much loved Philip. So don't change everything too drastically: there are benign bonds of affection.

As for me, I love and revere what you write and what you have in your spiritual identity, more than I can say. Your work and what you stand for, humanely and in our western civilisation, has more than once brought tears to my eyes. I have laughed so much at many things in your books, but the serious side, the absolute commitment to truth and kindness and real love is very affecting to me. And your overwhelming and unswerving love for literature and passion and concern for its integrity. It moves me as Mann and Kafka and Joyce move me. I treasure our friendship, love and admire what you do and create, and hope you'll keep a big foot in England.

Much love, dear Philip; as they say, be of good heart. Bryan

The younger generation

In later life, Bryan had a beneficial influence on a younger generation of writers and museum directors-in-waiting, who have now come into their maturity and are holding positions of power and influence themselves in the art world. I interviewed four of them (Marlow in June 2015; Riley in July the same year; Farquharson and Groom by phone in August 2016), and their memories and appreciation of Bryan appear below. Tim Marlow, having worked extensively as a broadcaster on radio and TV, edited *Tate* magazine and been a director of White Cube Gallery, is currently Artistic Director of the Royal Academy of Arts. Richard Riley was Head of Exhibitions for the Visual Arts at the British Council until he resigned in 2015; he has worked as a freelance exhibition curator since then. Alex Farquharson is Director of Tate Britain. Simon Groom is Director of the Scottish National Gallery of Modern Art.

Tim Marlow

Bryan was my greatest mentor really. It was in 1986 or 7, I was doing an MA at the Courtauld, and my thesis, which became a Ph.D., never finished, was on *New Generation* sculpture. Chris Green, my tutor, sent me to see Tim Hilton, who was writing a book about St Martin's (never published) and said I ought to go and see Bryan Robertson. I found Bryan in the phone book and telephoned him. He asked me round to lunch and was legendarily about two hours late with lunch, with me drinking Martini cocktails before and then a bottle of wine. He was so entertaining and engaging that we never quite got down to what I wanted to talk about. Then I made a more formal appointment to go and see him and he gave me access to his papers – stuff he'd not sorted for years at the Whitechapel – bin-liners full of it. And then he opened up doors to meet artists. He invited me to dinner with Tony (Caro), and John Hoyland and Patrick Caulfield were there, and suddenly this world opened up really. But it was research to begin with.

Sometimes you'd get a phone call in the middle of the afternoon: 'I know you're coming to dinner tonight, but I've got a bit of a cold, and I'm not really feeling up to it.' That was much better than making excuses or lying.

I think I did once turn up to dinner when he wasn't expecting me, but he still rustled up something rather marvellous. No, in the main, I'd say I had about a 70% hit rate with dinner parties with him, which is higher than most, I think. But I think about 99% entertainment value. The dinner parties were unbelievable – I met all sorts of fascinating people: Bridget Riley for the first time, and to see the Hoyland/Caulfield double act in action as I did at Bryan's was pretty good actually. And the art that he had. I remember talking to him about the Krasner on the wall, the Kenneth Draper sculpture on the chair, the Phillip King *Twilight* piece upstairs, the beautiful Bridget Riley in the hall, the Hoylands he had. It was a wonderfully eye-opening thing.

I always felt that Bryan was under-used. I think I made this point in the memorial for Bryan at the Tate. David Sylvester was properly revered and properly used in his later life, but Bryan wasn't. Although Bryan may not have been 'the best director the Tate never had' because of administrative disinterest, I can't understand why he wasn't used as a curator. I don't think his taste was always impeccable – look at David Sylvester's art historical taste, David always backed winners – but Bryan remained loyal forever, in the unfashionable middle years or whatever. That's to his absolute credit. I learned many things from Bryan, but that idea – if you start to follow an artist, you're with them for life unless they really go off the rails – I like that about him. And he was more prepared to take risks than David.

He was an excellent broadcaster and he got me into that. There's a fantastic beginning of a *Monitor* film [a BBC TV series] about Robert Rauschenberg and it starts with Bryan. There's a close crop on him and he starts to talk. He knows what he wants to say but he's ad-libbing in that beautiful way and the camera slowly pans out to show Bryan standing in front of a combine with a slightly sheepish-looking Robert Rauschenberg who's had to stand there for five minutes while Bryan extemporises. Then he asks Bob a question. A minute or two later, Bryan feels in his pocket while he's listening to the answer and gets out a packet of cigarettes and lights up. Puffing away and wafting his cigarette broadly in the direction of the combine. On no level would you get away with that now.

Bryan got me involved in radio. He was the one who said, 'What are you going to do now?' after my thesis was delivered. Bryan said, 'Maybe you could talk – the BBC are looking for young people'. Then somebody rang me from the BBC and I started doing some reviewing and then presenting. The first review was of Tony Cragg. I thanked Bryan effusively and told him about it. 'Marvellous, marvellous.' I said, 'Did you hear it?' 'No, no but I bet it was marvellous!' Just for a moment I thought he'd actually heard it.

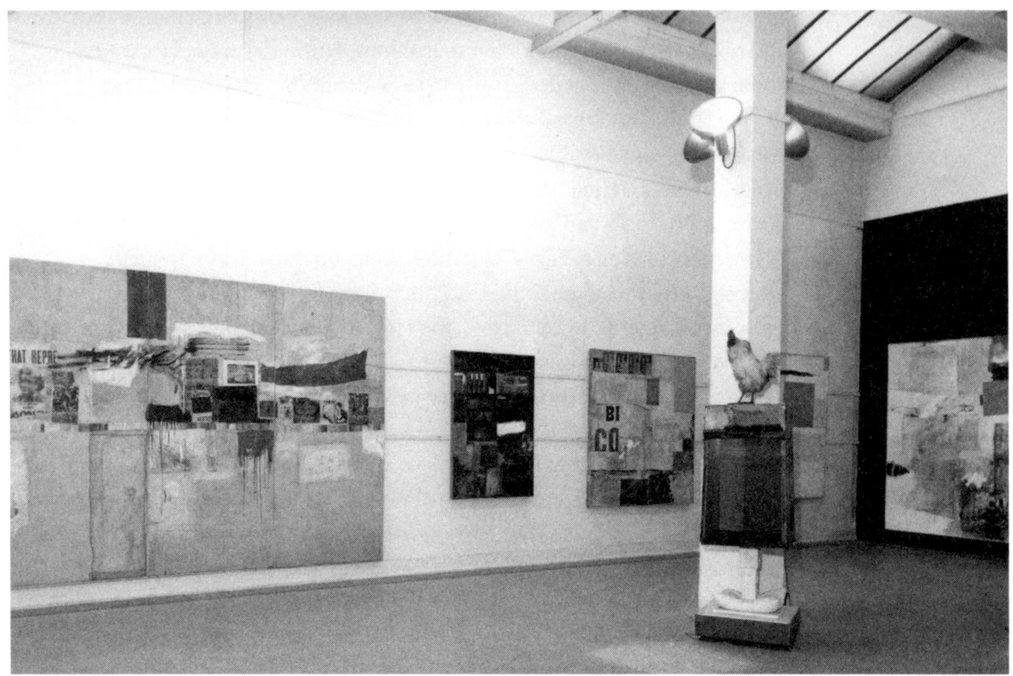

29 Installation view of the Robert Rauschenberg exhibition at the Whitechapel Gallery, 1964

Marlow and Robertson subsequently worked together often on radio:

There are two great moments that I remember most with Bryan in the studio. One was when he was reviewing a Calder show. We'd been to see it together and then he was reviewing it live in the studio. He loved the chaos of the studio with live bands and all of that. He was going off on a brilliantly Bryan-esque tangent about Calder, and the producer in my headphones said 'This is great stuff, but can we just get back to the show?' So I described a work and how it looked in the space and then threw it back to Bryan who said: 'Yes, yes, all of that, but anyway as I was saying ...' and just went straight off again. The other thing was when a troupe of bagpipers were the introduction to the show. They came in and Bryan's face was a joy to behold. Later in the show, the producer came in and asked us to applaud their next performance. Bryan said: 'Certainly not – I'd like to kick them into the middle of Kingdom Come!' In the same programme, someone was talking about *The Simpsons* – nothing to do with Bryan – and he suddenly started waving, and I said 'I think Bryan Robertson has something to say'. 'Yes, I'm a big fan of *The Simpsons*', apropos of absolutely nothing, and on the discussion went.

He was very broadly cultured, Bryan. He didn't know a little about a lot of things, he knew much more about many things than he often let on. But equally he had certain tropes, certain ideas ... Lazy is not the word. He'd have too much on, he'd be too much cornered by the three reviews or books that were outstanding, and there was a certain default mode of writing. Invariably Mark Tobey would be referred to ... There's a great catalogue – is it for Colquhoun & MacBryde? – in which he starts going on about someone's 'disparate great uncle' in the essay. You can almost see him sitting at his typewriter thinking 'Crikey, I've got another 5,000 words to do' and bashing off any old thing, but God it was entertaining and well written. He spoke and wrote – he had a beautiful timbre or style to what he did and said. He was mischievous and could be twinkly-eyed in prose, but God he could go off at tangents ...

There was a rumour that when it was the final, final deadline, he was talented enough to say 'Yes, yes, I've written it out, but I can't send it through to you, the fax machine's not working, so I'll dictate it'. Basically he'd be making it up over the phone. He spoke in pretty well-formed paragraphs. If you look at some of the essays he wrote when he was at the Whitechapel, under the kind of pressure that running an institution might have given him, the writing was more focused. As a freelance he didn't say no to commissions because he needed the money, being extravagant.

I lived in Islington and saw him regularly. I could stagger home late at night. He used to have piles of post. I remember John Boundy, who used to edit *Critics' Forum* and became Head of Arts at BBC Radio, just after the end of *Kaleidoscope* saying to Bryan: 'These are all contracts from the BBC, you have to sign all these and send them back.' Bryan thought they were demands or something. I remember telling John, who said he'd sort it out. They went back three or four years – and I think Bryan was owed a couple of thousand quid. Letters were often demands, so nothing ever got opened.

I visited him in hospital. To begin with it was 'I don't want you to see me in this state', but I did visit. And he was still making me laugh. Bryan never really talked about his sexuality and I remember once towards the end trying to give him a massive hug – it was more me that needed it, he was never tactile with me. I think he sensed that I was a bit choked up and he said 'Oh, don't be so soppy', and virtually pushed me off. He wasn't predatory, he was the mentor. We went on a trip to New York together to see Jasper Johns for an interview with *Tate* magazine. Although it was the most chaotic thing to do, it turns out that it was probably one of the most historical documents there. It was Bryan interviewing Jasper but they insisted that I join in, so it became a three-way conversation.

When I arrived, as I stepped through the door of Jasper's house, full of reverence for this great artist, Bryan said: 'Jasper, let me introduce you to Whiplash Willie, he spends a lot of leisure time dressed up in rubber.' Jasper looked amazed, and then I realised I'd been talking to Bryan about my surfing obsession and the wet suit, so it got off to an odd start. Then coffee arrived, and I was nervous or slightly in awe and I put the coffee cup and saucer down, and as I did so Bryan went 'No!' and I realised I'd put it down on an Andy Warhol Brillo box.

In New York, Bryan had arranged for me to stay in the flat of Pauline Kael, the great *New York Times* film critic, while she was out of town, while he stayed with another friend. Every morning he'd ring me up to arrange what we were going to do that day. It was something different every day – 'Come out with your hands up, the building's surrounded!' – all that kind of stuff. That twinkle. Once Bryan was reviewing a monograph on his architect friend Denys Lasdun for *Tate* magazine. It was typed up by the editorial assistant, Michelle Ogundehin, now editor of *Elle Decoration*, who left a note on it saying that it wasn't a review so much as a rant against what had happened to the National Theatre. I didn't notice this, delivered the text to Bryan's house and then went round next morning to check it with him. 'Who is Michelle Ogundehin?,' he said. 'I will not rest until she's selling matches on the streets outside the Strand Palace Hotel.' Of course he'd read her note to me. But he didn't take offence, he just laughed and then we went through the details of it all. She was right, but equally it was a great thing to publish.

I didn't know him when he was younger, but I got a feeling that when he was Director of the Whitechapel, I'm sure he was chaotic, but he had deadlines, he had a team backing him up, he was inspired, his writing was more focused, the broadcasting was done – the busier you are, the more you fit it in. I think once he became fully freelance, and probably did have to hustle, to a certain extent – though the fact that he never cashed any of the damn cheques shows that he found another way through – [the chaos] became a kind of defence mechanism to try to protect himself from taking on too much that was disparate. But I think he deep down knew what mattered. A lot of the things that he didn't fully finish, perhaps didn't matter fully to him. He'd done a lot of what mattered to him in his life, and he was very loyal to friends.

I didn't get a sense of a life unfulfilled from him and yet I always feel it wasn't a career that was as fulfilled as it might have been. He did say that he went to New York and then realised that wasn't the life he wanted. He was offered a major job in Australia – I think he accepted it and then pulled out because he said he could see himself just taking elderly women to the opera and being an escort. It was the loneliness, he said – being away from home and his friends and his family.

I would say that in the post-war period to now, he is one of the top three museum directors Britain has produced. That's a hell of a thing. Maybe top five. I think Serota and Neil MacGregor are the giants, but Bryan in some ways was far more visionary. I know the climate allowed that but the range and extent and ambition – and his intuition. He was self-taught! There was a brilliant lecture he gave at the Tate during the *Paris Post War: Art and*

Existentialism 1945–55 show [1993] – he talked all about his education in the 'flesh-pots of Paris'. While others of his generation were in university, he was in Giacometti's studio or visiting de Staël. Another thing at the Tate was the evening event with Joanna Drew and David Sylvester and Bryan. They were like two unruly schoolboys and she gave up trying to control them. Bryan was actually trying to be quite placatory because David was in one of his curmudgeonly moods. There was one brilliant moment when Bryan tried to change the subject and said something about natural light in galleries. 'David – you've always been a big fan of natural light in galleries – as have I – but the general public often want a more consistent light.' And David turned to the audience and said 'Well, the general public can just fuck off!'

When I saw Bryan the next day and told him how marvellous he was, he said 'It was ridiculous! It was like feeding buns to a gorilla!' But also that night David was swearing now and again, and then Bryan said 'Bugger'. Bryan said: 'There you are, David: you've been fucking all night, and I've started buggering!' He then asked David about Francis Bacon. Bryan said: 'I never really got on with Bacon. We met once, when I went to visit him in Menton. But it was odd – we never quite got on. Which was odd, given that we shared certain characteristics.' He looked at the audience in a wry way, and everyone started giggling, then said with perfect timing: 'Yes, we were both chronic asthmatics!'

He did tell me that he once tried to buy a Bacon. It was about a year's salary and he knew it was worth buying, but he couldn't get the money together. It would have set him up for life. I said no regrets – but that was a regret. I think he lived in the moment, odd for someone with such a deep historical understanding. Art, even historic art, was something for him that became a living thing in his hands, or his eye or his mind. That's how he made shows. I don't think he hung a show anywhere near as beautifully as David Sylvester, it was never as classical as that. He was pragmatic whereas David was a kind of obsessive perfectionist.

Richard Riley

I joined the British Council in December 1989, and one of the first things I had to work on was a Stanley Hayter show which was going to be in Rome. It was organised by Désirée Moorhead, who became Désirée Hayter, and she had commissioned Bryan to write an essay for the catalogue on Hayter's paintings. I didn't really know much about Bryan. It was 1990 and he had dropped off the radar a bit – a lot of people had forgotten him. This was a commission he wanted, but he was the world's worst at keeping deadlines. My job was to go up and extricate this essay from him. I used to phone him up. The phone just rang and rang – he didn't have an answer machine, no doubt for the very good reason he'd probably get so much abuse on it.

Eventually he answered and we made a day for me to collect his essay. I got to the house, and there he was pootling around in the front, looking slightly Pickwickian, very smiley. Straightaway he was fun. He started talking about the plants in the front garden and he knew all their Latin names, then we went in and he offered me a drink. I said I'd love a cup of tea as it was about 4 o'clock, but he said 'Oh no, no, no', and we had Campari soda because I didn't know what else to have. I probably stayed about an hour, chatting and enjoying his company, then said I really ought to go. So he gave me an envelope and off I went. On the bus back I opened it and realised this wasn't the full essay, only about the first two-thirds of it. The book was about to go to print, and we did finally get the last bit, but it took forever.

Then I got to know him a bit. I'd become friends with Tim Marlow, and Tim was a protégé of Bryan's. (He was always very good at spotting people.) I was working on an exhibition for the Council (*Out of Print: British Printmaking 1946–1976*) and I asked Bryan to write the essay because he had known a lot of the artists involved. But I made the all-time schoolboy error of not giving him a very strict deadline. It was a Collection exhibition that was planned for long-term touring and he was unbelievably late. He wasn't answering his phone so I wrote to him saying I'd have to go ahead without him. Then I got a postcard from him in the fabulous left-handed scrawl, falling off the page, sort of apologetic, and then he did produce it. I just re-read the essay and it's good. He has his own way of writing which is very him and you smile because you can hear his voice as you read it.

I loved hanging out with him and we travelled together a couple of times for Tony Caro shows. Tony was very close to him. Bryan had helped Tony's career enormously and Tony was devoted to Bryan. Bryan was very, very good with Tony, because Tony could get quite agitated and he was quite difficult to manage then. Bryan used to be able to calm him down, like no other. In 1995 we travelled to Japan together – Bryan, Tim Marlow, Paul Moorhouse and myself all flew out together. Bryan was fantastic on that trip, he'd never been to Japan before, he loved Japan. He was hilariously funny, slightly confused but made light of everything. Tony Caro was quite agitated, worried about the installation, but Bryan came up to him and said, 'Tony, it's the greatest exhibition of sculpture I've ever seen.' And from then on he was absolutely fine.

Bryan was very taken with the museum and loved Japan. The Japanese loved him – here was a slightly eccentric very English gentleman. He'd been living on Lindos and he'd lost quite a lot of weight and he'd had all these suits made and he was looking quite the dandy again, as he had when he was younger. He was back in his prime and pretty energetic. Then we went to Greece together, in 1997, again for a Tony Caro show – the opening of the Trojan War sculptures exhibition at the National Gallery in Athens. Bryan arrived and again was great with Tony, and very canny at avoiding people who might be a nuisance. We held a press conference for the show, and it was the day after New Labour got in and Chris Smith had announced that the Elgin Marbles were to stay in London. The audience was very hostile to Caro. Bryan said the Marbles should definitely come back to Greece. I think Colin MacInnes had said this years before, but the press didn't listen to Bryan – they were gunning for poor Tony.

The whole Japanese trip was slightly surreal. There's a famous artists' club in downtown Tokyo, run by Yuko Shiraishi's mother, so David Juda had an in and organised an evening there. It was by far the best night of the trip. You sit on the floor and eat out of rustic pots – the food's fantastic and the atmosphere's great. Bryan was being very impish and he got those hand wipes (like white towels) on a plate and started throwing them around at people, these wet towels. Then we started collecting them – he hadn't realised this – and when he stood up to go everyone pelted him at the same time. There was never a dull moment. He was very mischievous and very funny at taking the mickey out of people as well. Ian Barker was rather his target on that trip. He also made us laugh a lot about Roy Strong who he really didn't like. They'd both been on committees together and he was very funny about him.

He adored Patrick Caulfield. Patrick told a story about when he was living in a bedsit when Bryan came to see him about the *New Generation* show. Patrick said, 'I'd never met anybody like that before'. He was really quite nervous about it. Bryan came in and sat on the bed. Patrick said, 'I was very uncomfortable about this. I was worried that somebody would come in and see me in the room with Bryan and think we were up to no good. I was really uncomfortable about it.' Patrick was quite conservative in that kind of way.

When Caulfield was to have his major Hayward show, Bryan was mooted for the catalogue but thought too risky to write an essay. Instead he was commissioned to compile a chronology. What he handed in stopped in 1980, twenty years short. 'Only Bryan would do that,' commented Riley.

Bryan was very non-predatory (as a gay), he was just tremendous fun. My memory of him is that he was very warm and incredibly generous – even when he had no money. Bryan talking about the things he'd worked on in the past was fantastically interesting and engaging. I saw a few lectures. He gave a talk at the old Tate when they did that *Paris Post War* exhibition. He was hilarious. He was brilliant on stage because he was a performer. He did this very funny thing – he was talking about somebody who was a curator, an Englishman, but he wanted to be all things Germanic and he even affected a sort of 've haf vays' of speaking. Bryan did that on stage which was very funny. It was very engaging. He did another one at the old Tate with David Sylvester. It was supposedly chaired by Joanna Drew. It should have been great, but the problem was that Joanna was being slightly patronised by both of them. David was very gloomy, while Bryan was like a sort of butterfly flittering about. But it was a slightly missed opportunity because Bryan started going on about artists he didn't like, like Richard Long. He just didn't get Richard. He said he was like an Edwardian lady pressing flowers in a book. And he said this publicly. It wasn't the right moment. For those of us who knew him, it was fine.

I suppose when I met him he was pretty much in the doldrums, but then in the 1990s he came back and Nick Serota was very supportive of Bryan. They hosted his seventieth birthday party at the Tate and I think Nick was very respectful of this former Whitechapel great. Bryan's era is the one. I once asked Sylvester about Bryan and after one of those long silences he said 'He's a very good committee man'. It wasn't exactly what Bryan would have wanted to hear – but he probably was. But David was probably slightly jealous of Bryan in a way, because Bryan had helped make the careers of those younger artists. He really helped Tony, and Tony always felt that show at the Whitechapel was the moment, the springboard really, for the second phase of his career. Then there was John Hoyland and Tim Scott. I mean he didn't get them all right – Jack Smith, for example, fell by the wayside – but Bryan was a pretty big deal.

Alex Farquharson

I first met Bryan when I was doing an MA at City University in Arts Criticism in the early nineties. That turned out to be very useful to me because through that experience I understood what I wanted to do. It was considering all arts forms from the discipline of arts criticism, from contemporary visual arts to opera, though it was very loose and un-rigorous. I'd studied English and Art at university (the Art being my own art) and decided I didn't want to be an artist. Bryan was the Visiting Lecturer handling the visual arts. I was about twenty-two, twenty-three, and I'd not heard of Bryan, which reflected my short history. He was in his late sixties and I think he was doing this to pay the bills. There were one or two times when he forgot to show up, I remember, and we were left looking at each other. Bryan's classes often took the form of visits, to galleries, museums and artists' studios, which I really appreciated doing. For example, not coming from a very gallery-going background, I'd never been to the Wallace Collection, and it was also my first experience of a studio visit. It was that kind of thing – immersing you in different situations, what a curator does.

I think the fact that I didn't know who he was has something to do with a crossroads in art history which he was very much on one side of. By the late sixties you have this watershed of conceptual art, and to some extent minimalism before it, which became the backdrop to postmodern tendencies in the eighties. And these are tendencies that I think Bryan didn't relate to, or if he sometimes did it was on different terms. Also it was a crossroads in wider culture – the counterculture, and the sort of values that came with and after it. I suspect Bryan had a certain relationship with some of that, but at a distance. I remember him referring to hanging out at the Factory, but not partaking of all that was to be partook of there. He was very public-minded but not a political radical. He wasn't a hippy, didn't have that world view, but I think enjoyed a certain kind of different bohemianism.

I think he was an aesthete fundamentally, and his philosophy of art is not a conceptual one, it's not a theory-driven one. My first response to Bryan was he seemed a dyed-in-the-wool traditionalist, and represented a certain kind of modernism that my generation and the previous generation had moved beyond. That's what I mean by the other side of the crossroads. To begin with I was perhaps a little resistant and a little bit cocky – I'd begun trying to get my head around theory during my undergraduate studies. The situation was that we were an oddball group of a dozen or so, generally young, from all art forms – from a literary route, music route and so on. There were just a couple of us who were primarily interested in the visual arts. One of us became an artist and I suppose I was the more bookish of the two. It was probably natural that Bryan and I keyed into each other.

All this is really to say that very quickly I began understanding, through the references Bryan was making, his outstanding importance to the British art scene post-war, and quite what his curatorial achievement had been at the Whitechapel, which I had known nothing about. Quite rapidly I came to respect him and his achievement, but also his eloquence when it came to talking about art, and although there was much he wasn't interested in, I was always impressed by the breadth of his artistic purview. It would always open up in ways I hadn't quite expected. I also got to know him personally: he invited me to dinner at his house in Barnsbury. There would be good people there. I always felt quite young, and he was very generous at introducing me to people. At that point the next-youngest person he'd supported and got close to was Tim Marlow, who it seemed to me was already firing on all cylinders.

It was a Georgian three-storey house in Barnsbury, elegant but quite small spaces, but within it you had very big art. There was an amazing Lee Krasner which I think was the outstanding piece in his collection, and a wonderful Phillip King cone piece. That would always be in the corner, not quite with a teacup on it, but somehow so close to his life that it must have been quite difficult to maintain that separation.

I think it was in a seminar, which were quite free-form really, and I think he was talking about his time in New York and an anecdote about a beached whale in Coney Island. (This was early on in my encounters with Bryan and I hadn't got the measure of him.) He said something like: 'I took three artists to see that whale: Mark Rothko, Barnett Newman and Andy Warhol.' To a twenty-two-year-old who only knew of these people as icons in art-history books, not individuals you could hope to personally encounter, this degree of separation by one was deeply impressive. It was in moments like that that I began to understand the import of Bryan's lifelong relationship with art.

Simon Groom

I met Bryan in Italy at the house of Beatrice Monti. I was doing an MA and my research led me to her door in 1994. He wasn't there the first time, but I got on very well with her and her husband, Gregor von Rizzori the writer, and I spent the whole of the summer of 1995 with them cataloguing their collections. That's when I met Bryan, along with all the other glamorous people who used to come through that house. It was extraordinary – you never knew who would turn up because they were so well connected. Bruce Chatwin was the one they always used to talk about, but there were museum directors and actors and writers, and one of them was Bryan.

I was very young and I knew nothing about the art world. I had no thoughts about what I wanted to do. I was doing a Ph.D. [on the post-war art of France, Japan and Italy] because I got funding for it, and I still wanted to go off into letters and writing, literature. I don't think I'd even been to the Whitechapel, but Bryan had such a funny way of telling stories that you were rocking with laughter, even if you didn't know who all these characters were. I didn't. I just found him intensely engaging and very curious. I think I'd given him the first chapter of my Ph.D., or my MA or something, and he'd taken it to bed one night and come down the next morning and he quoted at me my very first line, which contained the word 'problematise' and that of course set him off on this huge kind of demolition job, but done so well, so brilliantly, that I didn't take any umbrage at all. I just thought that actually he was so right.

By picking out that word he kind of nailed the way I was making problems for myself. 'What do you mean exactly by "problematise"?' Rather than make me offended, I really warmed to him. He was much more human in his values. It wasn't intellect for intellect's sake, it was attached to a complete belief in something. There was always a warmth there, even when he was being – as he could be – very cutting about people. It was still said with a kind of affection. He wasn't quite a Falstaff, though there's a kind of rotundity there … he was just one of these kind of eccentric characters – there was a parade of them – through that house in Italy.

I met Bryan a couple of times in Italy. He'd been staying at Lindos, in Beatrice's Greek summer house, where the running joke always was that he was there to write his memoirs, and of course he never got round to writing his memoirs. Or if he did, nobody found them.

Simon Groom does however have two dossiers of writing by Bryan that were returned from Lindos to Beatrice, mostly of correspondence concerning the Brett Whiteley book:

It's just so funny – there is such miscommunication. He's always pleading his position. Bryan must have been notorious in always getting in his manuscript late, always in illegible handwriting. There's a sense of absolute certainty from where he sits that the world radiates out around from him. That these are playthings for him. Sample letter to Barry Pearce: 'Dear Barry, Do you ever respond to faxes? They're meant to be faster than ordinary mail, but not if you ignore them.' This is part of a really long negotiation in which Bryan had already not responded to a letter from Barry months before. He then writes to him as if Barry should have known that of course he was away for the whole month of August! Another quote: 'May I please have the fee straightaway? As I said, it is more helpful to me here in Greece living away from home than later in London. The old strategy of being required to wait until publication in September won't wash with me. If you order coal from a coal merchant in June to burn in November, the coal merchant quite reasonably expects to be paid on delivery, not in November.'

Bryan was very good to me and I've never quite known why. Maybe because Beatrice really liked me and when she took me under her wing, Bryan felt the same impulse to do so. But when I was back in London and trying to find somewhere to live and get this Ph.D. written, we found a place in Hackney and he was so nice – he actually came round when we moved in. He came round with two casserole dishes, which must have cost a fortune. He was always so generous to me. I still use those dishes and every time I use them I think of him. Just little touches like that. And he'd invite me round to dinner. I'd arrive at the time he said to arrive, and he'd be getting out of the bath or something, and he'd wave me in and start talking, asking me whether I'd read this or read that. Always I felt it was kind of like an exam. I felt terribly ignorant in his company. Then the doorbell would go and it would be Prunella Clough, Patrick Caulfield, Anthony Caro – and to me it was like the gods coming in. It was just amazing generosity in having someone like me sit amongst them. I've always been really amazed by it. Then the whole evening disappears because you're so drunk before you even start eating ... They were magical, magical, magical times and I've always felt very grateful to him.

Then for me what was outstanding was that I had finished my Ph.D., I didn't know what I wanted to do, but a job came up at Kettle's Yard and I applied for it, was shortlisted and had an interview. Bryan was just in the process then of putting together his selection for an exhibition there and I can't help but think that he put in a good word for me with Michael Harrison, the director, who took a punt on me. I'd never curated anything, I'd never hung anything, then I got the job of exhibitions organiser, and I'm pretty sure it was Bryan who must have soothed any nerves or vouched for me. It felt like a real benediction in a way.

He was never patronising and he always treated you as an equal which I was always amazed by. I remember one thing that really impressed me and has really stayed with me was some kind of public talk somewhere. Bryan was up on the podium. I think it was Tim Marlow who was slightly dismissive about a painter like Lowry. I remember Bryan almost quivering with anger – which I'd never seen before – absolutely passionate that artists like Lowry shouldn't be looked down upon and that they are absolutely part of the living currency of what art was. It was about the power of education which for him was the motivating force. Art had to communicate at all different levels. Education was what he thought was the real key, that it had a wider broader life and that it was part of all our responsibilities to be open rather than closed. I think that was him in the end – he was always open, always generous, always giving.

I loved his very cavalier attitude to money. He probably worried about it, but it just seemed to come and go. The more that I have learned about the impact he had, the more phenomenal his achievements really are. In a sense you could say that it was Bryan who opened up Britain both to its past (Turner, etc.), and to contemporary international art.

Nick Serota pays tribute

Nick Serota, who ran the Whitechapel Gallery from 1976 until 1988, and was then Director of the Tate for nearly thirty years, was a sincere admirer of Bryan's work in the art world, and outlines below his assessment of his achievement.

I think the first show I saw at the Whitechapel was the Franz Kline show in 1964 and then I was a regular visitor – to Phillip King and other shows Bryan did in the late sixties before he left. I only came to know Bryan after he came back from America, in the early eighties. It didn't work out for him. I understood better why he had gone – or at least what the impact of him being there was – when I once visited Purchase and saw the Robertson hand at work in the collection. He had a good hand. The intriguing thing about Bryan is that he was actually very catholic in his interests and taste, more so than most people. When you look at the shows he did at the Whitechapel, and then the shows he did at the Warwick Arts Trust, I am always deeply impressed by his independence of view and his willingness to champion artists who other people didn't have a high regard for. It might be Thelma Hulbert, Ken Draper, Prunella Clough, Charles Howard. Many of the figures that he championed are largely forgotten, but they're also not insignificant artists in the least.

I think his programme at the Whitechapel – especially once I'd got there – impressed me more and more. It's easy to be impressed by *The New Generation*, impressed by snapping up Jasper Johns, Rothko, Rauschenberg,

Guston, etc., and I know that those shows were snapped up, often they were done at six weeks' notice, amazingly. It's difficult to believe. Many of them were shows being sent by American institutions abroad and they were looking for a London venue and the Tate wasn't very receptive, and there was no Hayward, no ICA. So once Bryan had identified the Whitechapel, or anyway built on Hugh Scrutton's achievement after the war, once he'd identified it as his venue, things were naturally offered to him. But he still made choices. I don't think he ever planned more than a year ahead. I'm sure he had ideas of shows he'd like to do at some point, but I'm certain he hadn't got round to putting them into a schedule.

I think he always left decisions to the last minute, and I think it was ultimately the reason he left the Whitechapel – as far as I know. He ran up debts and people just got tired of running in that way. And perhaps he sensed a wind of change. The Tate was beginning to do its own shows, the Hayward was just opening, the ICA moving to The Mall, and one of the difficulties the Whitechapel had over the following ten years was persuading people that there was any need for a Whitechapel any longer. You had four directors in eight years – that can't be good for anywhere. It was always a struggle. Mark [Glazebrook] was very bold and took over responsibility for the upper gallery. Everyone forgets that in the whole of Bryan's time at the Whitechapel he didn't have the upper gallery, it was only the lower gallery. The upper was let out to the ILEA and they used it for arts classes and schools programmes. Mark left and Jenny Stein, who'd been his assistant, struggled to make it work and tried to reconnect it with the area. She left in '74, then Jasia [Reichardt] ran it for two years and then she gave up and I came.

There was a legacy of ambition, really, to do those major shows. If you looked at installation photographs you could see great and beautiful shows in a very beautiful space. I remember Bryan coming in one day and asking about the installation of a show, who had done the installation. I said that I did it with the artist. And he said: 'With the artist, Nick? You mean you let the artist in while you were hanging the show?' It told me everything about a change of generation. He had some interesting blind spots. He always avoided St Ives – apart from Hepworth. He never showed any of the St Ives painters. He never showed William Turnbull, which you might have expected him to do.

By the time I was at the Whitechapel, Bryan was back in England and occasionally reviewing for *The Critics*. He wasn't writing a great deal, so he would come padding in on a Tuesday afternoon, just ahead of John Spurling or someone. He was pretty friendly. He didn't become an instant friend. I came to know him better actually after I grew up a bit. He stopped seeing me as this young person who was doing the job that he would do better. Once I got to the Tate I saw him probably more often, after he'd done the Warwick Arts Trust. We could probably have a more interesting conversation.

I really didn't have many reservations about Bryan. He had had an enormous influence on the British art world in that period. It's difficult now to remember just how important the Contemporary Art Society (CAS) was from about 1965 to '85, and the taste of the CAS was really fashioned by Bryan, and by John Sainsbury, Caryl Hubbard, Madeleine Bessborough and the New Art Centre. Bryan was very influential on the New Art Centre – the programme there was highly influenced by him. The Stuyvesant Collection would not have happened but for Bryan. There were prizes like the Marzotto Prize which came to London through him. It's really difficult now to fully comprehend just how powerful a figure he was. A lot was going on behind the scenes. You can understand why he wasn't made Director of the Tate in '64, but he would have been brilliant. And actually he would probably have been brilliant with Norman Reid as his deputy. Though I think Norman surprised people when he became Director, as to just how good he was. He was a brilliant director.

The thing about Bryan was that he was not patronising, he just assumed that people would come to his level. You saw it in his writing, you saw it in his broadcasting. He undoubtedly wrote fewer books than he should have done. I'd put him in the top five curators of the post-war period in England, definitely. Who would they be? David Sylvester, Bryan, Lawrence Alloway (until he went to America), Gowing, Bowness (in the '50s and '60s he was key). I wouldn't put him number one, but two or three really. He did a great Riley show at the Hayward in '71.

Missed opportunities

The art critic William Feaver claimed that one of Bryan's failings was not recognising the value of Kurt Schwitters' work when the artist's girlfriend, Edith Thomas (aka Wantee), took a bag of his collages into the Heffer Gallery and Bryan turned down the chance of exhibiting them. A young man's mistake? Bryan's career was in fact more notable for the talents he recognised and boosted, than those he missed, which is why it is intriguing to examine a few of the ones who got away.

One of the first and most tantalising of 'might-have-beens' in Robertson's Whitechapel was a Picasso retrospective planned for autumn 1953. Although Kenneth Clark counselled against it, Bryan pushed ahead, using all his charm and diplomacy and calling upon such contacts made in his Parisian period as the great Gertrude Stein, who did indeed offer to help. Bryan enlisted the support of Douglas Cooper, the capricious cubist scholar, collector and friend of Picasso. Sadly the idea had to be abandoned when Daniel-Henry Kahnweiler, the artist's dealer, insisted that the exhibition be confined to works in English collections. And there were worries in London about the mounting expense of the projected

show, as well as Picasso's communism. None of this was Bryan's fault, and there was much support for his proposal. Another idea which didn't reach fruition was an exhibition of Julio González's sculpture, which Bryan was rash enough to announce in his catalogue preface to the 1955 Michael Ayrton show. González at the Whitechapel had to wait until 1990, when an excellent exhibition was finally staged there.

Edward Burra was an artist Bryan deeply admired and even became friendly with but, although he was represented by a watercolour in the 1954 group show *British Painting and Sculpture* at the Whitechapel, to his regret Bryan 'never got around to presenting a full scale show of his work.' There is but one reference to Bryan in *Well Dearie! The Letters of Edward Burra* (1985): 'Gerald sent me a copy of the Spectator and in it was a peice [*sic*] by Bryan Robertson, I didn't think he cared much for Burra but I was wrong it seems.' This was written in 1969 and shows how all-too-sensitive artists can easily get hold of the wrong end of the stick. Apart from reviews, Bryan did write a catalogue essay for a two-hander exhibition of Burra and Paul Nash at the Grey Art Gallery and Study Center of New York University in 1982, entitled *A Sense of Place*. His essay was on Burra, Andrew Causey's on Nash, but Bryan's was (typically) a near disaster. The director of the Lefevre Gallery, Burra's dealers, sent Bryan a telegram on 21 January 1982: 'YOUR BURRA TEXT NOT RECEIVED IN NEW YORK. CATALOGUE NOW IN JEOPARDY. PLEASE PROVIDE COPY I WILL SEND BY COURIER URGENT DESMOND CORCORAN.'

The following is taken from the catalogue essay – delivered at the eleventh hour:

> Like an exotic and conceivably poisonous flower thrusting its way through the middle of a bed of daisies, Edward Burra's paintings have been specially cherished and admired by English artists for half a century, beginning in the early thirties when Burra began to make his mark. A small number of painters and sculptors in England were making honourable contributions to the modern movement: Nicholson and Hepworth abstractly and Moore, Nash and Sutherland among the semi-figurative artists with others whose work is not yet known much abroad. Prestige and financial success at that time was fairly tepid and the end of the thirties saw the emergence, backed by the establishment, of the Euston Road painters whose refined academicism, reinforced by social commitment, was quite untouched by abstraction, surrealism, or any of the other advances in form and structure that had been pioneered so many years earlier.
>
> Burra's art continued to look very good to artists in England in all the successive decades: sharp and astringent against the low-keyed neo-romantic art of the wartime forties, brilliantly clear and incisive in the muddy-toned and not always coherently painted era of the 'kitchen sink'

neo-realist art of the fifties, dazzlingly accomplished and full of fantasy in the brightly coloured sixties when Burra seemed to be right on the button, looking like a full bottle of gin behind the holy water in the more or less conceptual or minimal seventies when painting lost confidence …

Nobody has ever used watercolour with such splendour, so richly and so sonorously: these paintings do not look like the work of a chronically weak man who was almost continually ill or exhausted by illness.

One artist Robertson might have been expected to show at the Whitechapel was the lyrical New Zealand painter of landscape and still life Frances Hodgkins, who lived in England for much of her life. Her work was considered advanced – she was a member of the Seven and Five Society along with Ben Nicholson, Hepworth and Moore – was colourful and original, and yet Robertson seems to have overlooked her. In the review below, published in the *Spectator* (17 January 1970), he writes that her work would have been most interesting to exhibit in the mid-1950s, but that 'nobody bothered to bring her work forward at that moment, when it would have aroused the keenest sympathy and recognition'. Who better placed than Robertson himself to show her work at the Whitechapel? And yet it didn't happen. At least he celebrated her later, but what an exhibition he could have made.

The Commonwealth Institute in Kensington has an excellent gallery almost continually filled with a flow of exhibitions that receive scant critical attention mostly, perhaps, because critics have a slight feeling that these are 'duty' exhibitions in which artistic standards may be subordinate to socio-political motives, however humane these may be. All the more reason, then, to welcome the retrospective exhibition devoted to Frances Hodgkins (1869–1947), a true artist, who was also a New Zealander, and one hopes the pride of her country, but spent most of her life in Europe and gradually settled into England. This was fortunate for us, for she was one of the best painters working in England in the twenties, thirties and forties; in fact her contribution to the art of the period was at a level that can only be described as surprising for its time and remains, even from the vantage point of today, considerably ahead of many of her better known contemporaries.

Why has this artist's work passed from public attention? And if one cannot go on paying attention indefinitely to an artist's qualities when, after death, they are bound by the static condition of a known body of work, then why does work by Frances Hodgkins not appear in official résumés of art of the period; why is her work never referred to and why is it unknown to a younger generation? The answers are, first that there has been for some while a fairly stiff resistance to the painting (and writing and everything else) of the 1940s, and this kind of attitude to the zeitgeist cannot be shifted:

it is best left for the time being. Second, Frances Hodgkins' extraordinary achievement, particularly in her late work, would really have been most interesting in the mid 'fifties, when artists were very conscious of a fresh emphasis on gestural spontaneity, of abstract expressionism, in fact – nobody bothered to bring her work forward at that moment, when it would have aroused the keenest sympathy and recognition, and now the possibility has passed because art is concerned with different issues.

Frances Hodgkins was not heavily productive, her scale was the scale in which everyone worked at that time and therefore modest (a three foot by four foot painting is big, for her), and most of her supporters in the commercial art world are now dead. Her paintings stay alive as treasured possessions in private collections, or a few public galleries, but no one is really actively engaged, it seems, with her reputation. Eric Newton wrote of her work with special warmth and belief, and one of the most beautifully written and exact appreciations of her work I can recall was the essay by Myfanwy Piper for the Frances Hodgkins paperback in the old Penguin Modern Painters series, now out of print.

Landscape through her eyes is given the intimacy and particularity of still life but still retains the gleam and flash of the outdoors. The sense of lovingly observed detail, as obvious in her drawings as the swelling arabesques which unify them, is translated in her paintings into floating vignettes of barn, picket fence, cows, roof tops, fields and ponds. Her colour is unique and unforgettable: chocolate bluish-brown, coloured whites, riverweed greens, French blue and mauve-grey. The paint is always silky, and bland in surface: the actual marks and brush strokes alive, pointed, and meaningfully beautiful in themselves. This artist really had a vision, and caught it.

Another painter of independence and originality was Craigie Aitchison (1926–2009), a superb colourist whose work would have looked well at the Whitechapel, but who had not perhaps produced a large enough body of work at the point when Robertson was director of the gallery. As I am aware from personal experience, Craigie bore a grudge against Bryan, for supposedly writing a disobliging review of his first exhibition in the *Times*, when such articles were unsigned. Bryan always denied authorship of the offending piece, but Craigie chose to believe it was by him. Apparently, they subsequently had a huffy stand-off on this very subject at one of the *Spectator* summer parties. However, in Robertson's review of Aitchison's show at the Beaux Arts gallery in London below, published in the *New Statesman* (10 December 1960), he is almost enthusiastic, and the year before, as a buyer for the Contemporary Art Society, Robertson had been responsible for purchasing Aitchison's large *Triptych*, which was subsequently given to the South African National Gallery. This must be counted as real support.

Craigie Aitchison's second show at the Beaux Arts gallery is very good. It sustains the promise and the gentle radiance of his first appearance at this gallery nearly two years ago. He is from Scotland, in his early thirties, and came late to painting. The work is still a shade immature, sometimes possibly too slight in conception, but his vision is in itself so fragile and thin that those limitations may well turn out to be part of the nature of his gift: not immaturity after all, but innocence. We are confronted by some flower pieces and small landscapes in which sheep may very safely graze: soft green grass, a vast looming mountain with light diffusing its skyline, a cluster of flowers in the foreground. A doll's house Nativity with tiny pink angels flying through the starlit sky. Calvary with the three tall crosses almost floating in a great blue-green space with what seem to be pyramids in the distant haze. Awkward, twittery trees like dry sticks push up against a hedge and a horizon; one's gaze wanders along a tidily mapped and symmetrical garden path, glowing in the late afternoon light. The paint is thin, anonymous and unremarkable. Somewhere lurks the charming gaucherie of the pavement artist. But give these pictures time and much more is revealed. Do not be put off by my description or the fact that this kind of painting could so easily be coy, whimsical and pretty excruciating on all counts. Mr Aitchison's spiritual integrity will see you through your first sight of his pictures. He has something sweet and true to offer us.

A further article in the *New Statesman* (17 February 1961) focused on the Scottish CoBrA artist William Gear (1915–97). Here was an abstract painter he was able to enthuse about (there are echoes in Gear's work of Merlyn Evans, whom he knew, and Gear exhibited with Jackson Pollock in New York), and yet he ends his encouraging review with the question 'Who is cherishing him?' The answer might have been Bryan Robertson, but it was not to be.

Why on earth don't we use our artists? If the public in general, with the exception of a narrow minority, considers that a lot of modern art is remote from life and sometimes incomprehensible, then it might follow that this same public never gets the chance to live with it or see it in use. Modern art in England is only encountered inside the artificial and somewhat clinical conditions of temporary exhibitions. Artists are condemned to 'shows' every two or three years, like a season in cabaret; with luck they may get at some time a large show of a retrospective kind covering a couple of decades; sometimes a show with a 'theme' is organised, and even then the results are fed back into other galleries – but where do you go to see all this work in public places?

The answer is nowhere. I've almost given up going to Covent Garden because the standard in sets and costumes for both ballet and opera is so dispiriting; Christmas card gentility or hack poster modernity. Has nobody heard of Richards, Nolan, Nicholson, Evans, Vaughan, Davie, Boyd or Collins? The list could be much longer. Our department stores could do with a face lift: plenty of artists here could make a couple of floors look like 1960 instead of 1934; and these new, bleak and poker-faced buildings are going up without a vestige of colour or decoration to humanize them – heaven forbid with murals, which hardly ever work, but some big paintings in lobbies and entrances would do no harm and could always be changed around. But nothing happens.

This old despairing war cry – which could be amplified – was prompted by visiting William Gear's small retrospective at Gimpel Fils. Gear is a highly gifted Scot, middle-aged, energetic and very experienced: a veteran abstract painter both in his consistency and in his consciousness, since early youth, of European painting in a broad sense. He was working hard in Paris at the end of the war, in an idiom quite new to this country, and a handful of paintings from that period in this present show stand up to the test of time. (Gear should be represented in the Tate by a couple of works, showing development, but has nothing there.)

Since then he has kept up a remarkable drive and momentum. Most of his richly coloured and robustly designed work comes from nature: vibrations of light and colour over foliage or the play of light on water; and it has that tough simplicity which usually only the French dare attempt. Other paintings may bring in wing- or blade-shaped sculptural forms and are less evenly distributed in terms of mass and volume. There is an early debt to Picasso, and Gear has been influenced by other artists. But who hasn't? He has still kept an essential character of his own. Sometimes this becomes a shade wooden, a rather dour Scots puritanism takes over, noticeably in recent work, but at his liveliest he is very good indeed, an artist to enjoy and cherish. Who is cherishing him?

Of course Bryan did not please everyone – only a fence-sitting mediocrity may do that. Lucian Freud, for instance, disapproved, saying of Bryan, 'He had an unerring eye for the second-rate'. (This emerged during a conversation I had with Freud's biographer, William Feaver, in Stockwell, 20 September 2016.) Perhaps Freud was influenced by the fact that his erstwhile chum John Craxton was given the full Whitechapel treatment, with a lavish retrospective and catalogue in 1967, and he was not. Bryan never did seem to favour the School of London realists, but then neither did he much like the St Ives School (with the notable exception of Hepworth). This latter was all the more surprising, given his love of colour and abstraction (Heron, Frost), and his positively appraising comments on both Peter Lanyon and Roger Hilton in his book *Private View*. In fact, it emerges from various surviving letters that Robertson was

at one point seriously contemplating an exhibition of Lanyon's work at the Whitechapel.

He wrote to Lanyon in the most enthusiastic of terms:

> I should like quite simply to say that in all ways you seem to me to be the only landscape painter that England has produced since Turner. There is no one else. I think you're a great painter; and you've added immeasurably to the landscape idea by humanising it and not only pushed the tradition several miles further but bust it up and put it together again. That takes genius.

Robertson concluded his letter: 'So, you see, your exhibition here is something very dear to my heart and an immensely important event to me – and it will be to everyone else when it occurs. I want to present it in the same way as the Pollock show: differently, of course, but with that weight.'

Lanyon must have thought he'd hit the jackpot, but very soon doubts began to dispel any euphoria. In a letter to Alan Bowness (dated 4 July 1960), he was touchingly enthusiastic: 'Bryan Robertson has proposed to me! A retrospective in October next. I would like you to have a bash at the blurb.' At the end of September, Robertson wrote to Lanyon confirming the idea of a retrospective 'in the early part of 1962'. But clearly there were delays – not an unusual situation for the Robertson administration. On 19 February 1961, Lanyon wrote to Bowness: 'If you ever see Bryan Robertson could you find out *whether* he intends to have the retrospective in 1962?' Later that year, in another letter to Bowness (dated 30 August 1961) Lanyon comments: 'I have not seen Bryan since our recording sessions on Monday. I imagine he is dancing around in a Bikini on Porthmeor Beach.' Then at the end of the letter: 'I can't get any firm date for a Whitechapel show yet but if Gimpel play, it may happen in 1963.'

This mention of 'recording sessions' refers to a Lanyon talk first proposed by the British Council in 1960, to be conducted between Robertson and the artist. Clearly, from Lanyon's comments, the recording was at least begun in 1961, but not completed. (A familiar story.) Bryan pulled out in May 1962, pleading a hectically busy schedule. At this point Alan Bowness took over and the talk was recorded in the autumn to serve as a ready-made public lecture that could be given at any of the British Council's outposts around the world. The tape was sent with a box of slides. Perhaps Robertson at the same time abdicated his interest in showing Lanyon. Certainly nothing further was said, and the proposal for exhibiting the work of 'the only landscape painter that England has produced since Turner' (splendidly typical Robertson hyperbole) was quietly shelved.

Bryan was an influential champion of British sculpture, promoting the major figures such as Moore, Hepworth and Caro, as well as the New

Generation. He also refocused attention on the slightly overlooked but extremely interesting sculptor F.E. McWilliam (1909–92), to whom he gave a retrospective (concentrating on the early work) in the summer of 1982 at the Warwick Arts Trust. But one of his longest-cherished dreams was to inaugurate a permanent sculpture park in the capital. In 1999, Bryan wrote in the catalogue for the exhibition *The Shape of the Century: 100 Years of Sculpture in Britain*, at Salisbury Cathedral and the New Art Centre at Roche Court: 'I am hoping to establish, with absolute optimism, the first national sculpture park in London with the permanent siting of a handful of masterworks, to be added to, over the years.' To this end, he wrote long enthusiastic letters to English Heritage and the Arts Council, but did not live to see his pet scheme inaugurated. We are waiting yet.

Testimony

This lengthy section brings together artists, writers and curators who knew or worked with Bryan, and whose experience of him spans more than a particular period.

Allen Jones

As Allen Jones pointed out in an interview in his London studio in July 2014, you didn't feel with Bryan that he had a particular axe to grind or that he was influenced by the thought of his career. He just responded to the work in front of him. Jones recalled the impact of the Whitechapel shows:

Our generation was at the tail end of what would have been a classic nineteenth-century art school academic education. I remember seeing the big Pollock show and saying to Ken Kiff (who I'd been at Hornsey with), 'You know, we ought to be able to sue the art school. What have we been doing for 5 years? There was no hint of this.' The only man who did give you an idea of the avant-garde was Allin Braund, a lithographer who taught stained glass. By the time we got to the college [RCA] it was plain to me that Modern Art was a march to abstraction. The formal language had hit the buffers, but there was no reason why we shouldn't try to make a new figuration so long as it was relevant.

The first time I was aware of Bryan in a personal way was when he included me in *The New Generation* [1964], having spotted me in the *Young Contemporaries* [in 1960, at the Suffolk Street galleries in St James's]. Figuration was not his interest, unless the pictorial language was something he could relate to, or, rather, related to his world, as mine did. I had no idea of a career path. In those days it was just a staggering idea to be in shows in which you didn't see William Scott or Keith Vaughan. Those were the big artists then. And the idea was that you had to work for years to achieve that sort of status.

Bryan opened my show in Liverpool [at the Walker Art Gallery in 1979, curated by Marco Livingstone]. I was very pleased about that but totally nonplussed by his speech, even though I had been round the block by then. I suppose it went down really well except that it wasn't the ringing endorsement that one wanted to have. He pooh-poohed all that. He stood up and said, 'Old ladies should go home! Lock up your daughters! Are you ashamed of what you see about you? Are you worried about this? Should you be worried? Should your daughters be here?' Afterwards I thought, is he drunk or something? In fact I was not pleased. There were Leslie Waddington and [Alex] Bernstein, etc. there. And afterwards we had to come home together on the train and Bryan was very combative. He took on everybody. I suppose my work was a challenge to him. He was getting very garrulous and drunk and he took on Bernstein, saying more or less, 'It's all right for the rich and the wealthy ...' Then, as the train got nearer to London, he steered the conversation round, saying 'I'm sure you've all got your limos taking you home, and your drivers waiting'. So of course Bernstein said to his driver (rather sourly), 'Take him home'. And I thought – that's how you do it.

This is Marco Livingstone's version of the same event:

In March 1979 Bryan was asked to open the Allen Jones retrospective that I curated at the Walker Art Gallery in Liverpool. It was, curiously, a midweek afternoon affair with blue-rinsed ladies in attendance. Bryan gave a hilarious impromptu speech in which he said, among more serious art historical things, 'There came a time when I realised that girls could be more than just friends. And there came a time, too, when I realised that boys could be more than just friends, but that's another matter,' or something to that effect. The poor director of the gallery, Timothy Stevens, was on the edge of his seat, wringing his hands nervously at what Bryan might say next.

Allen Jones concluded:

The last occasion I remember him having anything to do with me was when he was an adviser to the Ballet Rambert and he had arranged for artists he had some regard for to work with Rambert. John [Hoyland] had done something and so had Patrick [Caulfield]. That was terrific, I must say. Then Hodgkin did something. Anyway, I was up for it, and did Satie's *Cinéma*. That was 1987. I suppose Bryan was not a huge supporter of my work, nor were we that close. But his influence on me and my career was immeasurable, because you can do something which has repercussions for the person involved without necessarily having been (literally) in bed with each other!

Bryan's introductory essay for *Allen Jones: New Sculpture* (1988), although commissioned by Waddington's to accompany a selling exhibition, does not read like a commercial catalogue essay. Beginning with a lengthy

history of polychrome sculpture, it is more like a museum catalogue essay, though the writing has Bryan's very particular tone of voice, engaging with spoken rhythms and inflexions. The following extracts give something of its distinctive flavour:

My first sight of that elusive complicity between abstract and figurative elements which so consistently distinguishes the paintings and, more recently the sculpture of Allen Jones in the last twenty-eight years was in 1960 in the annual *Young Contemporaries* exhibition at the Suffolk Street galleries. Even then, it was an alert and edgy complicity rather than a tacit alliance. There was little attempt to synthesise the opposing elements of figuration and abstraction which were, instead, set out as equal events, interdependent but separate, with explicitly uncertain boundaries. His painting then and often since reminded me of Kandinsky through the way in which hotly coloured form and space seemed to move across the canvas and set up a tension obliquely, on the diagonal. I featured Jones' work in the 1964 *New Generation* show at the Whitechapel Gallery.

Paintings of such demonstrative precocity and sophistication are rare. The sophistication was in the formal handling of the imagery, not in the subject matter: a clothed hermaphrodite figure or a packed but airy composition of rectangular lozenge shapes with fluttery edges which turned out to be buses. The paintings bristled with paradoxes which still characterise Jones' subsequent work including the more recent painted sculptures created from 1981 on. His work then, as now, seemed both ambiguous in concept and crystal clear in structure and delineation: delicately thin in painted surface but robust, almost raucous, in colour. Radiant with light and yet peculiarly cool in execution, it still celebrates in sculpture or painting a formidable balancing act between compacted, sinewy force and repose, like filmed sequences of fast action replayed in slow motion …

These sculptures give off a strong whiff of joy. Can it be so, in the art of 1988, with anti-modernity calling itself post-modernism, vacuum cleaners on plinths presented as sculptures and the Pont Neuf only lately concealed in polythene? The very word 'joy' seems to belong to another era, to Matisse's *Jazz* perhaps in the forties, but joy is what Jones' work contains, joy as it was still experienced by really good Charleston dancers of the twenties or formation dancers doing *The Madison* in the sixties and which continues to be felt by a few thousand every now and then at rock concerts, the Olympic Games or listening to Mozart. There isn't much joy in recent art, at least not since the death of Calder in 1976.

Mel Gooding

Mel Gooding is married to Rhiannon, daughter of Ceri and Frances Richards, and a distinguished writer on modern art. He has written a number of monographs, including two on John Hoyland, the first of which (published in 1990) was supposed to have been written by Bryan,

who failed to deliver. Mel recalled, in a telephone interview of November 2016: 'A bit later, word came that Bryan had relinquished his option on the book and was happy for me to do it. He never said anything to me about it.' A few years earlier, they worked together on a Ceri Richards exhibition at the Tate.

Bryan was a great champion of Ceri Richards, putting on the Whitechapel show in 1960. In those days a major showing was much rarer than today. Artists had to wait longer for acclaim. The Whitechapel made a great difference to Ceri. Bryan arranged for Merlyn Evans' wife, Marjorie Few, a concert pianist, to play in the gallery. He brought in a grand piano on a rostrum and she gave a concert of the Debussy preludes, which the paintings referred to. That was typical of Bryan's flair. He meant a great deal to Ceri and to Frances, who had enormous affection for him as well as respect. I didn't meet Bryan until I worked with him on the Ceri Tate show in 1982.

Bryan was a complete nightmare – this is the other side of him. I loved working with someone of that stature – I hadn't even written anything at that time of any note, except the little catalogue on Ceri's graphics. Bryan did the selection, he knew where a lot of the stuff was. He would come to the house and we would work in what was then a very tiny study upstairs, side by side at the desk, looking through pictures, talking, saying we must have this, must have that. He was wonderfully relaxed and insouciant about the whole thing. Finally the selection was made and I said I would write a life [of Ceri] for the catalogue, and Bryan would write the main text. Came the deadline for Bryan – no essay. It went on for three weeks. By this time Ruth [Rattenbury, the exhibition organiser] was absolutely tearing her hair out.

I went in on a Thursday and she said, 'Bryan's essay still hasn't come'. I said, 'Well, look, if it hasn't come tomorrow – because that was the absolute deadline for the catalogue – I'll write an essay over the weekend, so there will be something'. You know, this is for a Tate catalogue, with a retrospective looming in about three weeks' time. Well, on Friday she rang and said, 'The essay has come'. It's very interesting: if you know Bryan, you can see how it was done. Desperately he finally had sat down. The first sentence reads something like, 'Before we can consider the art we must consider the man'. You can imagine him sitting down and writing that sentence in the fervid hope that it will lead to the next thing. He was a man of wonderful clarity of intelligence. You know how you build a thing up when you've got nothing – where do I start? You can see him sitting down and starting this essay in a kind of funk.

It's in two parts, it's quite short and it's very generalised. But it was sufficient. One of the things Bryan did say to me which I think is very interesting, and certainly made me think, and I've many many times thought of it since, he said, 'Nobody reads what you write. The publishers only want it because it gives a bit of bottom to the book.' I think he has a point. He was quite adamant about that in relation to book texts – he wasn't talking about catalogues so much. Of course he only wrote in longhand, almost illegible, and he had a lady who could type it because she knew his handwriting. One imagines if she wasn't well, then it couldn't be done. It was very primitive in that way. He could be a beautiful writer, but he was lazy. He scribbled and hoped. A lot of the writing is incredibly slapdash.

Working with him on the exhibition was interesting because it was done so intuitively. I learned a lot really because I realised that it was a good show. His knowledge and skill and knowledge of people [owners, etc.] was very important. I wasn't disposed to argue with him – he knew so much more about the work and about everything than I did. I was happy to go along and learn from it really. It was quite an experience to see how makeshift the process was. If you're outside you think everything is done and ordered, that people know what they're doing. He probably ran the Whitechapel like that – ramshackle and without any regard for finances. So he ran the Whitechapel into terrible debt. But he was indulged, because he was so brilliant. He was a brilliant, brilliant person, and acutely intelligent. Witty, which is always the sign of intelligence, and wonderfully clear about what was going on in art. Marvellously generous and open-hearted as well as open-minded about work. Also an enthusiast for the smaller talent, which was in marked contrast, shall we say, to the other panjandrum (with a reputation totally undeserved, I think) – David Sylvester.

You must realise that I didn't know Bryan very well. Rhiannon and I went to dinner a couple of times with him in Islington and had nice evenings with him. He always cooked when you were there and often appeared to be cooking something he hadn't thought about. You had the impression of him in the kitchen space picking various things up as if he wasn't quite sure what he was going to do with them, then cooking the whole thing while you were there. It was performance. He was a great performer. Wonderfully comic and funny.

When Frances [Richards] died in 1985 – this is typical Bryan – he was going to come to the funeral, which went from our house in Castelnau [London SW13]. I remember holding things back and holding things back – Bryan isn't here yet, we must wait for Bryan. Bryan's presence was important. Of course he never turned up. I don't think there was ever a word of explanation, we just took it for granted. I don't know why we expected him to turn up, we knew what he was like. It was our folly, not his.

Paul de Monchaux

Paul de Monchaux first met Bryan in the late 1970s when he was running the sculpture department at Camberwell School of Arts and Crafts, and there was an annual prize-giving for the sculpture students in the South London Gallery.

I invited Bryan to adjudicate the prize. He came along and did it very well. I was very struck by the guy. He seemed to have a really generous enthusiasm for sculpture of all kinds, quite unaffected in any way by fashions in thinking. I had him back from time to time to go round the studios and talk to the students. He would also come to the degree shows and more than once he quietly bought a piece of work from a student. He didn't tell me about it, but I heard about it eventually. I got on with him very well. He was good friends with one of the staff, Ken Draper, and Nigel Hall was also a friend, though not on the staff. Both of them were very close to Bryan from student days, so I'd known about him for some time and heard about him from those guys.

At that time there had been huge changes in the art schools in the early sixties, and one of the things that most of them packed in was life drawing and modelling. We kept that going at Camberwell and Bryan was very supportive. That was so unusual at that particular time that I was very heartened. Altogether, he was very good to have around. Also he was completely unimpressed by the hard-line division between art and design. He was interested in everything, I think, and one of the things about the school in those days was that it was the Camberwell School of Arts and Crafts, and that is exactly what it was. So there was a more than average mix between the design course and the fine art course and that was the way the place worked. He supported that and this was very good as it was by no means a common attitude at that time. He took the trouble to insist on coming to my studio and that kind of thing.

The next time we encountered each other was to do with *The Sculpture Show* in 1983, when Bryan was Chairman of the Arts Council Exhibition Committee. They were discussing the Hayward Annual and he proposed having a major sculpture show that would use not only the Hayward but the Serpentine and the surroundings of each gallery, so there was to be work outside as well as inside the galleries. Very ambitious. Quite out of the blue the Arts Council got in touch with me and invited me to be one of the selectors. To start with there were two of us – myself and Stuart Morgan, the critic. Very early on, for reasons not quite clear to me, Stuart dropped out. Two more selectors were very quickly assembled: Fenella Crighton, a writer, and Kate Blacker, a former student of mine who had not long been out of the college. The three of us visited studios and there was also an open submission. It was very interesting and I saw a lot of work I wouldn't otherwise have seen. Then we presented a slide show of the people we were thinking about to this committee. Bryan was more than just a referee then. They were a pretty high ego bunch, that committee, and they were very opinionated and pressing very hard. If anyone started laughing or joking about the slides, saying something silly, Bryan was in there like a shot, defending his selectors and the seriousness of the work. Whether he approved of it or not, he didn't put up with any facetious nonsense. I remember that quite vividly and I thought, 'Well, this guy's all right,' because he kept the thing going.

Once he had proposed the exhibition and the committee had agreed, he was very much in the background but *not* – if you know what I mean. He knew what was going on. So it proceeded and the show was put on. He evidently was hoping that some of the artists he had been promoting would find their way into this show, but for one reason or another they didn't. He was charming. He took me out to dinner to a posh restaurant near the Warwick Arts Trust. We had this very pleasant dinner and he went through the list and very mildly and ruefully mentioned that I had missed out on some major figures. I admitted that was true, but that had been the way the selection went. He was fine, really, but I know that he was a bit disappointed. He obviously had a vision for this show where his protégés and lots of younger people would all come together, but it didn't quite work out that way. Most of the chosen artists were quite young and unknown to the general public at that stage, and though quite a few of them have now become household names (Tony Cragg, Richard Deacon, Antony Gormley, Anish Kapoor, Richard Long, Bill Woodrow), they weren't then. In retrospect, *The Sculpture Show* is generally seen as quite a significant event.

In another world Bryan would have been a big-time entrepreneur, a super businessman. He kept all these things going – so many things that no ordinary person could keep up with it. Anyway the exhibition came off, though probably disappointingly for him and certainly for the Arts Council it wasn't well received by the critics at the time. I didn't feel that was a particularly intelligent response. However, it was a big success with the public and had very good attendance. And I happen to know that for many of the artists taking part it was a very important show. Other shows came out of it, commissions came out of it and it was notorious for the vandalism to a huge piece of sculpture by David Mach [a submarine made of tyres]. There was a catalogue produced with an interview between myself, Kate and Fenella, with Bryan asking the questions. The subject was art education generally, how you get to be a sculptor. It was very awkward: we went to Bryan's house and he was charming as always. He asked these questions and there was a certain amount of tension – not on my part, but on the part of the other selectors. Personally I got some quite good feedback on that from various people – critics and people who knew art-school business. Bryan was very supportive: he understood how important it was to have an art school somewhere in the background to arrive at any sort of position as an artist.

I didn't see him very much after that, but I did visit his exhibitions at the Warwick Arts Trust, which were quite inventive because he used to have concerts and that sort of thing which wasn't particularly common in those days. I know it is more so now, and certainly always has been in places like Germany. They were very good exhibitions. Nigel Hall had one and Prunella Clough, and one of my former tutors, F.E. McWilliam. That was good because when I was a student he had a very substantial reputation, but by the early eighties he was certainly not to the forefront any longer. Bryan actually ignored that kind of thing. He would very confidently support people who were not being supported, and I liked that about him. He would talk about artists you weren't hearing about anymore. I really liked the guy, and I think he has been a bit marginalised as a figure within the art scene of those days. He took the students very seriously and treated them absolutely as equals. He was very helpful to me at Camberwell. We were, I have to say, the kind of antithesis of St Martin's at the time, and that was often not such a straightforward position to maintain with the people running the system. But we did keep going with drawing and modelling and so on, and here was someone coming along with a big reputation for introducing new art into the public view, he came along and said out loud that he was supporting this 100% which made quite a difference. Also he left money for bursaries for artists – how many people do that? That's admirable and one only knows about it because one's known of people who've benefited from it.

The following excerpts are from Bryan's catalogue text for *The Sculpture Show* (1983):

I am sceptical, as ever, of a system in which the training of artists is geared to a quasi-university level, with essential standards in other subjects. Artists are usually well educated, but on their own terms and in their own time. Artists read books at times in their lives when they need to read them, and not for an exam. I fear that within the present system perhaps Picasso, or Brancusi or many others would not have got enough O levels and not gained a place.

There was also the competitive empire-building in the 1960s and 1970s in art schools over prestige, space, equipment and personnel, all linked to the discovery of higher degree course funding. The system also accounts for our mistrust of art on its own terms, and the apparent respectability of art for the English if it is dressed up in other ways. I believe that art students need more than anything, a good space, materials, life classes, technical instruction and some intelligent contact with a few other artists. The apprentice system had a lot going for it.

My other great worry is over the rejection of the art of the past, even the fear of it.

Quite a lot of artists now teaching were themselves taught at a time when a 'basic design' course – much simplified and in many ways distorted from the Bauhaus principles established by Klee – reduced abstract art at art schools to little more than pattern making or playing around with elementary shapes and processes. Those teachers who were formed by 'basic design' tend to evade the complexity of history as irrelevant, which means that a very large number of students for nearly two decades now don't go instinctively to the British Museum or the National Gallery to study. They feel no curiosity, and if anything think of the art of the past as a dead weight and keep clear of any entanglement. But history is our heritage, and the art of the past is alive, not dead. It didn't bother Picasso ...

By the entrance of the new university museum in the United States that I directed for its first five years, I had two small plaques placed. One read simply 'The eye is the first circle', which is Emerson's opening sentence in his marvellous essay called *Circles*, and which seemed as good a way as any other of getting across to student visitors that before you have conceptual ideas in art, there is perception of visual reality and art therefore does not come directly from metaphysics or mathematics but only indirectly, after direct observation of the physical world. And that everything, finally, of course, is in the eye of the beholder.

The other read: 'All I want to say is that the only possible teacher except torture is fine art,' and was said by George Bernard Shaw. To me it's a profoundly important observation because it says it all: if you study art properly and in serious depth you will inevitably learn all about the history of princes and the history of serfs, of astronomy and astrology, of mathematics and magic, topography, agriculture, architecture, clothes and manners, animals and birds, saints and martyrs, religions and philosophies. How else could you comprehend Giovanni di Pisano, or Piero, or Van Eyck or Stubbs?

Maggi Hambling

When Hambling got to know Robertson in the 1990s, they dined together amidst much laughter, and Bryan sent her off-puttingly intellectual-looking books which remained unread on her shelves. Characteristically she dictated the following statement to me in May 2016 and subsequently edited it.

For a Camberwell art student in the 1960s, the Whitechapel was a place of pilgrimage. Bryan Robertson brought us the American greats: Rothko, Rauschenberg and the abstract expressionists. Our eyes were opened. The touch of paint on such a grand scale was completely new to me.

At Robert Medley's parties I was in awe of this sparkling, elegant, exotic and clearly witty creature. Suddenly in 1994, out of the blue, the distant god telephoned me. He had been to the Barbican and come across my exhibition of *Laugh* paintings. He told me he loved the madness of trying to paint the laugh because it was a completely impossible thing to do. He wanted to know what I was up to and came to look. I had begun my first little bronze sculptures, and he told me I must finally have a dealer, having previously remained stubbornly independent. He asked which one I would like and then arranged for Marlborough Fine Art to visit the studio. My first show at the gallery was in 1996, and Bryan wrote the catalogue introduction.

When he came to my house he looked intently at everything and was the only person to notice and delight in a linocut by my art teacher at school, the painter Yvonne Drewry, entitled *Wild Summer Garden*. That was typical of his spontaneity and conviction about surprising things. He was the reverse of conventional.

Bryan Robertson and David Sylvester were still the presiding *éminences grises* in the 1990s, and whereas David would take a good twenty minutes to get his thoughts together in answer to the simplest question, Bryan was like quicksilver. Of course physically they were poles apart: David lugubrious prize bull, and Bryan a darting dragonfly.

At a Sunday lunch with the writer Paul Bailey (Pearl Barley to his friends), Bryan and he were trying to out-queen each other at either end of the long table, telling stories simultaneously. Silence only occurred on the rare occasions when Alan Bennett interjected and everyone listened in awe. As the playwright was driving north to see his mother, collecting some Marks & Spencer's food en route, he alone was being abstemious.

Bryan was a compelling mixture of wisdom and wit. He told me the only thing I must never forget was that 'between disaster and ruin, there is always time for another glass of champagne'. I have not forgotten.

Goodness knows his corpse must have stopped off for a snifter or three on the way to his funeral, for as with his catalogue essays or any other bits of writing, delivery was always late. Bryan was a perceptive and loyal friend, fruitily camp and a truly passionate lover of art. And he had an intuitive understanding of artists, taking great pleasure in helping them.

The following extract is taken from the beginning of Robertson's catalogue essay on Hambling for her 1996 Marlborough Fine Art exhibition:

These delightfully expansive, generous spirited and rather grand, almost operatic scenes and situations, the first series of sculptures in bronze by Maggi Hambling, all have an odd, built-in tension between playfulness and grandeur which gives them an arresting presence but also a questioning identity. To speak of an arresting presence and a questioning identity sounds a bit like scenes in a police station or bumping into the artist herself at a party. But I am serious here: we are on the spot in this exhibition rather more than the works themselves. They question us: how much do you *care* – rather than what do you know, recognise, remember. Above all, what do you feel?

For thirty years or so, much contemporary art has been concerned, often quite brilliantly, with sensation. By contrast, all Hambling's work from start to finish is to do with feeling, unsentimental and laconically expressed but always there, from sharp portraits to effulgent sunrises and sunsets, from the savaged bull to the death of the artist's mother or the bravura of an old entertainer at the end of his life. And these sculptures in a rather different and new way have also a button-holing but majestic intimacy through the way in which they project themes of life and death, pain, endurance and survival, the tragi-comedy of being an artist, the business of carrying on, getting on with it, the eternal balancing act of existing with some sort of grace or humour confronted by disintegration and the blank unknown.

Ken Cranham

Like the choreographer Richard Alston, actor Ken Cranham early on felt that he had to choose between visual art and a career in the performing arts, but also like Alston he has retained his original interest and enthusiasm for painting and sculpture. Later, when he had begun to do well on TV, he used to go with his best RADA friend, Roger Lloyd Pack, to auctions. Cranham now collects Scottish art and good drawings. Maggi Hambling, who already knew Cranham, arranged for Ken to meet Bryan in the mid-1990s when she realised that they lived only 300 yards from each other and that Bryan had long admired Ken's acting. Coincidentally, I was also a guest at the dinner party where they met for the first time. Ken recalled that evening and his friendship with Bryan in a telephone interview in February 2017:

Bryan talked about some of the things I'd done and it was so perceptive. That particular evening the widow of Kenneth MacMillan, the choreographer, was there as well. And he was a fan of mine from the Royal Court years. I was so bowled over – you don't really know who's seeing what you're doing or who's paying attention to it. You just get on and do it. But Bryan would talk about my performances and say things like: 'That was very good what you did because you haven't done much of that.' And we had a series of evenings at his house …

One of Bryan's great qualities was that he was very erudite but he never punished you with it. Those people are very valuable in your life if you haven't come from an artistic background. He always enriched my imagination, and whenever I spent time with him I was given a relish for something that I was going to seek out. To create curiosity and relish is a fantastic gift.

What Bryan did was organise evenings – dinner parties – that he would cook for, and there would only be me and one other there. This happened twice: once with Claire Bloom, and once with Irene Worth. These are serious contenders. The fact that he thought that *I* had enough to entertain these people when he was doing the cooking was very flattering and encouraging. Actually when you do that, you really talk to people. Those evenings were very special. He would always tell me about things I didn't know about. One of the stock questions when you're interviewed is, 'What's your dream dinner party?' I feel like reeling off that one and saying – 'And I was there!' I mean, you couldn't make it up! To meet Bryan like that and then for us to forge a friendship that was quite vivid but for such a short space of time. But what happened in that stretch of time … I met Patrick Caulfield and John Hoyland, a whole bunch of painters. Honestly, painters are worse than actors! Actors actually get on rather well …

Bryan was always telling me what books to read or films to see. 'You won't be my friend if you don't enjoy x, y or z.' He was also very switched into everything in Islington and what the fishmongers [Steve Hatt] was like. He regarded umbrellas as common property – you shouldn't worry about them, just take one from wherever you are, you shouldn't pay any heed to the ownership of them. I think that the bit of his life that I knew him in was better than had I known him younger, because I think he would have chased me round the kitchen table.

When I last saw Bryan in hospital his eyes were empty, and that made me very angry at the injustice of it. I just thought 'Oh no, please don't go', because I'd discovered the value of a rich warm friendship which had such potential, for each of us. Because he really liked what I did and I really liked everything that he could tell me and knew about. I did get to speak about him later at the Tate [at his memorial]. I talked about the last time I saw him, on his deathbed practically, really concerned about the choice of my next job. My life was important to a man who was losing his: it was terribly moving. I brought him a book about Esther Williams, the swimming star, a ridiculous book but I thought it might amuse him …

We just had a very rich friendship, based on things I knew nothing of, but he was seeing me do things as an actor that really had reached him. That's marvellous and rare. I think the great difference between people is not whether they're rich or poor, but whether they have love in their lives. I think that's the great thing to have. And Bryan seemed to have that in abundance. He was very good at giving. He gave you texture, and you linked many things up because of him.

Norman Rosenthal

Often known as 'Storming Norman', Rosenthal has had a chequered and often controversial career in arts administration. He met Bryan early in his rise to fame and influence, at which point they seem to have got along well enough, though later this was far from the case, as Rosenthal recounted in a telephone interview in March 2016:

I met him quite late on in his life, around 1969, 70, through a young friend of mine, John Carl Bowen, who was gay mafia basically, and took me into the world of art. It was the kind of world of London subcultures which he [Bryan] wasn't really part of but always on the fringe of. I would go for tea at his house a few times, I was just an art-world hanger-on in those days. I think it was after I'd done the show at Brighton Museum called *Follies and Fantasies* [1971]. I remember at Bryan's house in Barnsbury meeting the rather effete Graham Sutherland. Then after Brighton I struck lucky with the ICA. After that, in the seventies, Bryan allowed me to write some articles in the *Spectator*, of which he was at that time the Arts Editor, and amongst the articles I wrote was one on the Royal Academy. As a result of that article about what I called the potential of the Royal Academy, I got a letter from Hugh Casson saying what an interesting article and that he was going to send copies of it to every member of the Academy to read. A few months later I was in the job [of exhibitions secretary at the RA]. So in a sense I owe a lot to Bryan, but then of course I betrayed him.

He was violently against *A New Spirit in Painting* [Rosenthal's RA show in 1981], he was horrified. All that generation believed ultimately in abstraction – maybe they allowed for pop art – but they believed in the Sacred Order of Abstract Expressionism. Bryan was part of the gang who tried to boot me out of the Royal Academy, but I must say that it was the conservatives at the Royal Academy – Hugh and Roger de Grey – who protected me. It was the so-called radicals, the Paolozzis and the John Hoylands, who were against me. They wanted me out. And this was the exhibition that not only put Baselitz on the map, but Richter and Polke and Cucchi and Schnabel and late Picasso too. It's the most important show I did. If you do a show like that once in a lifetime, you're lucky. In a way it was maybe more important in terms of changing the world of art than Roger Fry's Post-Impressionist shows. Bryan turned furiously against me. We didn't really have a reconciliation after that. The art world is a very fickle world and art has many mansions. I went against what he stood for. Bryan was a wonderful person and I owe him a huge amount, but in the end he only believed in his glorious days with abstract expressionism and its spin-off in England, and that's not enough. The reality is something else.

Critics' Forum and Paul Bailey

Derek Malcolm in his obituary of the great film critic Philip French (*Guardian*, 27 October 2015) wrote about the BBC Radio programme *Critics' Forum*:

Much of his knowledge of the arts was amassed during his time as producer of *The Critics*, on BBC Radio. Those selected for the panel were expected to see a film, go to the theatre, read a book and visit an art exhibition. French, of course, went along too. The programme, the predecessor of *Critics' Forum* and now *Saturday Review*, was transmitted with only a bit of editing after we had all eaten lunch at Portland Place. It was not an especially good meal but there was enough wine to loosen our tongues in time for the broadcast. One of us was the chairman, but sometimes French himself would lead the discussions, without a hint of the stutter he had for the rest of the time. He could not explain why this was the case. But it was, and he ruled us with a rod of iron, though never without sympathy for any person who could not quite manage to say something coherent about one or other of the subjects on hand.

Bryan was a regular contributor to both *The Critics* and *Critics' Forum*, but somewhat difficult to stop when in full flight, as the novelist Paul Bailey recalled in an interview over lunch at Quo Vadis in August 2015:

I first met Bryan on *Critics' Forum* and the producer was Philip French. Philip said to me: 'The thing about Bryan is that once he starts talking, he never stops.' And I remember when I was chairman on the programme trying to get Bryan to stop talking was almost impossible. I ended up doing gymnastics, leaning under the microphone and semaphoring him to stop. I couldn't say it, because it would go out live. He was always very interesting but he'd forget that there were three other people on the programme who also had to say something. When we were on subjects that he knew a lot about, he would take over – but in the nicest possible way. He was the greatest name-dropper I've ever met. He would come out with things like: 'As Peggy Guggenheim said to me ...' And you thought, 'Well, yes – he did know Peggy Guggenheim'. It wasn't a kind of posturing thing at all. He knew these people – Mark Rothko, Jackson Pollock. He was always very circumspect. He didn't criticise people who would have been considered in another sphere his rivals. He never said anything derogatory, in my hearing anyway, about David Sylvester, for instance. It just wasn't his style. And I think he had a much better eye than Sylvester – he could see quality. He was amazingly well read, not just the classic books, but he liked to keep up with what was going on in literature. I remember he would make comparisons with writers. He'd say, 'Oh the novels are all right, but it's the short stories you should read'. He did have a discerning critical faculty which I must say greatly impressed me. He also had a great sense of humour.

People had said that if you invite Bryan to dinner, he will either turn up very late or he will phone the day after and say, 'I'm awfully sorry, I've just looked in my diary and I should have been with you yesterday!' This was a constant. I remember sitting at Bryan's funeral at St James's Piccadilly and the coffin wasn't there. He was late for his own funeral. The pianist – who was playing wonderful music, Bach, Schubert and so on – got through his whole repertoire. Then there was a pause and then he started again from the beginning.

When my friend Jane Grigson was dying [this must have been in 1989] she said she'd love to see Bryan again. She had been his assistant at the Heffer Gallery in Cambridge. She was mad about him. He was older than she was and she always had this thing about older men. Then she suddenly realised one day that Bryan was gay, but it didn't in any way stop her from admiring him – in fact worshipping him. She thought he had exquisite taste and knowledge. Anyway, he came to Sunday lunch with Jane, and it was one of the happiest afternoons. Arriving in Shepherd's Bush he looked around and said, 'This is what Mae West would have called *the purlieus*'. The other guest was Alan Bennett, with whom I'd been doing a tour of Russia. Alan was on his way to Leeds, and left early. Bryan and Jane stayed till about six o'clock, and they were just falling over each other with mutual admiration. It was so touching. The affection between them was completely genuine. They talked about people, painters that they'd met. Bryan was a great admirer of [Jane's husband] Geoffrey's art criticism.

I think Bryan suffered from that terminal disease of people who ought to be great writers – he talked too much. I think that's the saddest thing about him. His speech was brilliant, so well informed, and he was a great anecdotalist, mainly because his anecdotes were so casually expressed – he wasn't there to impress you. It was like a stream of consciousness.

Bailey, at the end of his novel *Chapman's Odyssey* (2011), placed a list of some seventy names on a page by themselves, a column of dead friends, the people who mattered. Bryan Robertson was among them.

Peter Murray

Bryan wrote an impassioned but clearly argued account of the crying need for sculpture parks in the UK in the *Spectator* (23 September 1978), entitled 'Sculpture in the Air'. It was a cause he was to take up again later, but for now he confined himself to a witty description of the public lack of response to public sculpture:

For most people sculpture is a kind of decorative garden furniture, glimpsed in the distance against the formal hedges of a rather grand estate open to the public in the summer months, and the glimpse recognises some sort of cheerful or strenuous aspect of classical mythology, comfortably removed to the remote past. For others, sculpture is merely a landmark looming up through the trees to tell them that they're sauntering in the right direction across a public park.

As he pointed out, the public lack of knowledge and enthusiasm about sculpture was even more dispiriting given the plethora of talented sculptors then working in England. Robertson pointed to the Kröller-Müller Museum, in the Hoge Veluwe National Park in the Netherlands, as a contemporary example of what could be done in the way of siting

sculpture in extensive parkland, describing it as 'the most important collection of modern sculpture in Europe, delightfully and unselfconsciously distributed'. In the second half of his article, he eventually got round to the Yorkshire Sculpture Park (YSP), open now for just over a year, and 'off to a flying start', with an exhibition of work by the first 'resident sculptor', John Maine. As Peter Murray, the Director of the Park, recalled in a telephone interview in May 2017, that was really the first serious coverage for the YSP and, as such, hugely valuable and much appreciated.

I think I first met Bryan in 1978. Obviously I knew about him from the Whitechapel days and I'd read his essay in the Silver Jubilee Battersea Park catalogue [for a sculpture exhibition in 1977], but I hadn't realised he'd been out of the country for some time. We appointed John Maine as an artist-in-residence and it was through John that I met Bryan. We had an opening for John, and Bryan came up for that. I got some money from Sotheby's to make a little publication of our first exhibition at the YSP and Bryan agreed to write an essay for that. It was a nightmare trying to get it out of him. (I can't now remember which came first – this commission or John Maine.) Sotheby's in those days had a charity arm and they were ever so nice to deal with, and very professional, and they kept phoning me to ask, 'Where's this essay?' I'd phone Bryan, and he'd say, 'Oh, it's getting typed in the other room as we speak'. And of course I believed him, as I didn't really know him. But eventually it came and it was lovely. I loved the way he wrote. His writing was always exciting, it went on at such a pace. His observations and what he had to say about artists was terrific. He had a terrific memory.

He became a big supporter of YSP for a period of time. He decided we were the best thing since sliced bread – he'd been waiting for something like this forever. When he came here and saw the potential and we met properly, he immediately said he would get in touch with Henry Moore, and of course I took that with a pinch of salt, really. But no, two or three days later he phoned me and said that he'd arranged to take me to see Moore, so I met him in London and we set off to Perry Green [the hamlet in Hertfordshire where Moore lived]. Henry was very welcoming and incredibly warm and friendly towards Bryan. Obviously they had a pretty good relationship. Bryan had given him a major show at the Whitechapel but he'd also given him a show at Cambridge before that. So he knew Henry from way back. I remember Henry saying to Bryan, 'We were at the theatre the other night in London and we drove past your place to see if you were in, but you weren't there'. So obviously they were more than just colleagues, they were very affectionate, and as a result of that Henry gave me a huge amount of time. And then, again as a result of that, Henry Moore came to visit the

Sculpture Park with Mary, and they spent a day here. Later he came back a couple of times.

So Bryan was very helpful. What was interesting about the Sculpture Park was that we didn't have any money – we still don't! – but as a result of Henry coming here he gave us £5,000 immediately, which in those days seemed a huge amount of money. It was immensely useful. Then he said he would be the patron of the Sculpture Park and he would loan a piece of work. All of that came about through Bryan. Then Bryan decided he was really going to help us and that the best way to do that would be to have a series of lectures, which he would kick off and then get David Sylvester to do one, and so on and so forth. People would pay to attend and the lecturers wouldn't get a fee, so all the money would come to the Sculpture Park. That was a bit of a disaster, actually, because Bryan kept forgetting to ask these people, and then he came to give a lecture himself.

I went to Wakefield Station to meet him and he arrived in his slippers. He had a suit on but no shirt – he had a V-necked sweater, and in those days that was not cool. And he had a dog on a lead. He gave me the story that he'd just got this dog – it was a stray he'd found and decided to look after, and it was the craziest dog you've ever met in your life. He said he'd taken the dog for a walk before he was due to catch his train, and locked himself out of his house and left all his slides and all his notes there, but thought he'd better jump on the train and come. So he arrived with absolutely nothing – no slides, no notes, this mad dog, no clothes, and stayed here for about three days. He gave this lecture in the evening and it was not one of his best performances. This was a college and it had a beautiful music salon with a big grand piano, and that's where he was giving the lecture. We tried to hold on to the dog in the audience while Bryan was lecturing, but the dog was so upset with not having Bryan, it leapt on the stage and was chasing Bryan round the stage. So in the end, Bryan tied the dog to the leg of the grand piano and continued giving his lecture. The dog was dragging the piano across the stage. It was so funny it was unbelievable.

But Bryan absolutely loved it here, and kept coming back, and brought people, and so on and so forth. He suggested artists we should be looking at. He said we should be looking at David Smith, but Tony Caro was also saying we should be looking at Smith as well. Bryan thought that we should have a big clump of Henry Moore bronzes here, and he was very, very keen on us pursuing Hepworth

One or two people advised me not to ask Bryan to become a Trustee – to have him as a friend and supporter but not as a Trustee because he was a bit unreliable. Which in my experience was certainly true. The other person that Bryan introduced me to, who was a great friend of his, was Rudi Oxenaar, the Director of the Kröller-Müller in Holland. (He was the one who really established the sculpture garden there, and he had a great interest in British art.) Bryan wrote to Rudi and as a result of that I went over to the Kröller-Müller and spent a couple of days shadowing him and I really learned a huge amount from that. That was terrific actually. And Rudi became a Trustee as well. So I had two incredibly powerful trustees, Alan Bowness and Rudi Oxenaar, and Henry Moore was our Patron.

To a certain extent Bryan's involvement dwindled after that, but I think he was a bit like that. He was madly in love with us for a period of time and then he disappeared for a bit, but he did come back. It wasn't that we fell out – but he literally disappeared. I remember he once brought for the weekend a lady from Australia who was an art adviser. Basically he wanted her to invite me to go to Australia so that I could organise an exhibition of contemporary Australian sculpture. That didn't materialise – I didn't want to do it anyway, and had too many other things on my mind. That may have cooled him down a bit. Then he came back when we were putting Henry Moores in the country park, and he also came back for Phillip King. We did a beautiful Phillip King exhibition, and later organised a King retrospective for Forte di Belvedere. That was a terrific show.

I saw him from time to time. I saw him at Tony Caro's studio quite a few times and we talked about various projects. Bryan was a big supporter of Nigel [Hall] and we had some lovely drunken evenings with Benden [a collector and arts benefactor]. We didn't do anything together after that, but he was always very friendly and supportive. I think that without him it would have been really quite difficult in the early days. To get his enthusiasm and to be introduced to some of the people he knew ... He was very active in the early days in terms of trying to introduce me to people and keeping my enthusiasm going and keeping me entertained – a very important thing to do – but what I enjoyed about him, apart from the fact that he was great fun, was his perceptive view of art. I thought he was incredibly perceptive in the way that he could look at something and come up with a statement very quickly, which quite often in my view summed up the quality or the character or the significance of that painting or sculpture. I think that's extremely rare. David Sylvester could do it, but was a bit slower and more ponderous.

Interlude: Introducing Peter Potworowski

In 1999, the Mayfair dealers Connaught Brown staged an exhibition of the work of Peter Potworowski (1898–1962), a Polish painter of rare and lyrical talent, who came to live in England during the 1940s and 1950s. The show was accompanied by a substantial catalogue with an introductory text by Bryan Robertson, recalling his first glimpse of Potworowski's work at Gimpel's in 1954, which came as something of a surprise – 'an intensely enjoyable one that I've never forgotten'. His evocation of the

work was typically enthusiastic and enlightening. It's a prime example of Bryan's late style: the product of seemingly perfect recall and affectionate memoir-like reassessment.

The paintings, some quite large, were brilliant in touch, in the projection of an almost abstract imagery, and in their total authority of execution, command of form and play of light. I remember cloud-like areas of intensely strong and light-filled orange, pink and yellow colour loosely tied to figures in landscapes or deserted gardens, terraces, and, although almost vaporous at first sight, not so much impressionist in form as very nearly abstract or on the verge of abstraction. These paintings were also oddly buoyant in spirit, high-pitched in colour, light, and above all, in feeling. The spirit of Bonnard lurked here, but without Bonnard's intermittent sense of lassitude; and quite free of any suggestion of pastiche. These were rather wild and certainly original paintings. It was no surprise to learn later that Potworowski loved the sea with special feeling.

Robertson brilliantly conjured up the context in which Potworowski found himself, in the London of the 1940s and 1950s:

The post-war scene in which Potworowski played his part was enlivened by a number of original artists of considerable distinction: Kenneth Armitage expressed in sculpture something more playful and vulnerable about the human condition than we were used to seeing, although Germaine Richier and Giacometti had in different ways already broken the ice for the London public. Reg Butler was creating strange, fetish-like creatures in welded iron which managed to distance themselves from the earlier precedents of González. In painting, Peter Lanyon was restructuring the whole idea of landscape painting through developing insights from his friendships with Gabo, Nicholson and Hepworth. Adrian Heath extended our idea of the human figure into a new kind of abstract landscape in which the figure and the landscape were one. Alan Davie managed to transform his early love for Chagall and Pollock into a spectacularly rich and wild vision that had no precedent in British art. There were of course other excellent artists working in the fifties, but here I have indicated a few central figures.

In his peroration, Robertson summed Potworowski up:

His work has an utterly poetic and lyrical dimension, dangerous words to use about painting, but I believe them to be just in Potworowski's case. His intense love of life and strong feeling for place, a river, a garden, a beach, a park, the corner of a familiar room – comes through everything he painted, and this love is so distilled, and expressed with such a sexily frugal and charged touch that each painting became a poetic experience, an epiphany.

Later, Anthony Brown, managing director of Connaught Brown, commented: 'I was very grateful to Bryan for bringing this artist to my attention. He understood what I was doing and cleverly identified a forgotten artist who would fit into my programme.' Once again Robertson had proved his worth as the champion of the overlooked and unfairly neglected. On the evidence of the reproductions in the catalogue, Potworowski was an inventive painter of great sensitivity, an *intimiste* in the tradition of Bonnard and Vuillard, and a lyrical colourist. Bryan's essay provoked at least one warm response from an old friend: a letter from Kenneth Armitage (dated 9 April 1999):

It was delightful to have sent to me from the Connaught Brown gallery the catalogue for the Peter Potworowski exhibition. Plus an excellent Forward [*sic*] by your good self. It is something to treasure.

It made me happy to see the Potworowski images again.

While William Scott was also a friend from even before WW2, it was Potworowski and Lanyon who were my closest active friends.

Potworowski was enthusiastic for my sudden acclaim at the 1952 Venice Biennale which, he said, came about without any help from others and which, also, was a surprise for me being before that totally unknown. The result was that we spent much time together and I was happy to know an older and highly talented man whose work well matched his friendship …

Peter Potworowski gave me a lovely drawing (girl with hands covering her face) which is always on the wall here. That, together with a Picasso etching and a tiny Roger Hilton painting and also drawing are my treasures by other artists.

Bryan as collector

Christopher Le Brun described the living room in Bryan's house, with the majestic Lee Krasner painting and

a lot of paintings that had appeared mysteriously on the wall. He had a very charming way of getting you to give him a painting. He'd come into the studio and say, 'I'm very interested in this painting'. They were quite often little, transportable. And he'd say, 'Could I take it away with me and have a look at it?' And as one would be asking him to write something, there would be a faintly transactional aspect to it which was never spoken. And then the painting would never come back. And you'd feel mean for even thinking about it, because he prompted terrific affection.

Stephen Chambers was not so easily won over: 'His house was full of things. I think I was aware that if I gave him something it would end up in the broom cupboard anyway. I was aware that people gave him things.'

Bryan's art collection was a source of cash in times of need. Hoyland remarked on the major Lee Krasner that Bryan for a time owned, saying

that first of all it looked unfinished, but the more you looked at it, the more resolved it became. Hoyland said that Bryan sold it in New York for very little money when he was hard up. Bryan also owned a small Pollock painting around 1960, but that soon went. A beautiful Hepworth wood-carving was also sold. Bryan owned two Warhols in 1969 according to a letter he drafted to John Coplans, a pencil drawing entitled *One Dollar Bill* (*c.*1958–62) and *Self-Portrait* (1964–5), silkscreen on canvas. Neither of these were left in Bryan's estate after his death. He had two big Hoyland paintings in the house, both of which were given to him by the artist, a major Phillip King sculpture, important early pieces by Nigel Hall and Ken Draper, and paintings by Clough and Wragg and Huxley. Much of the best work was bequeathed to museums and the rest divided up by his executors and sold.

Snapshots

Here follows a trio of 'character-squeezes' of artists by Bryan, or short appreciations of their work, rather along the lines of the soundbites, but somewhat lengthier.

Alexander Calder

The following brief excerpt is taken from a draft review of a Calder exhibition that began at the National Gallery of Art in Washington and then travelled to the San Francisco Museum of Modern Art in September 1998. It was written for the *Fine Art Journal*.

I met Calder several times in the fifties and sixties in Paris, New York and in London, where I interviewed him on the then Third Programme at the time of his brilliant and hugely popular show at the Tate Gallery. Calder had an innate dignity with an amiable but not particularly talkative presence. He had a deep pitched, rumbling and rasping sort of voice, and always sounded drunk, which he wasn't – it had something to do with the way he alternately barked and slurred his words. He wore vividly coloured shirts and was something of a dandy, in a rough, haphazard sort of way. He had an exceptionally elegant and beautiful wife, Louisa James. The philosopher William James and his novelist brother Henry James were her great-uncles. Louisa maintained a wonderfully relaxed, amused and laconic presence at all times: she exemplified the attribute 'laid back' long before the phrase was coined.

Ben Nicholson

Bryan first knew Ben Nicholson in the late 1940s and early fifties, well enough for Nicholson to invite him to St Ives for Christmas in 1955. (Bryan declined, saying he had to be with his parents at his sister's.) The following quotation comes from a letter of Bryan's to Nicholson (dated 12 September 1967):

London I must say has never been better in my lifetime. Don't be put off by all the nonsense in *Time* and elsewhere about the swinging city: the plain truth is that it's bright, cheerful, energetic, full of good food, excellent drink, astoundingly pretty girls in mini skirts which have to be seen to be believed (and are, frequently) – a friend of mine calls it 'the free milk generation' come true at last, and everywhere you see these simply stunning clothes, flower children and all. I feel a distinctly middle-aged flower pot myself, though groovy on occasion, still, I'm told.

Bryan goes on to say how much he would love to live on Crete. 'The great journey in my life of recent years was to *Crete*. It is the greatest place I know, & I should like really to just go and live there & cut out all this nonsense. The London art world is full of mediocrity and nonsense, mainly. Crete is a continent when you're there, and quite stunning.'

Another Bryan letter to Nicholson (dated 15 February 1968) apologises for not thanking Ben for a print that arrived while Bryan was abroad, was taken in by his temporary cleaner and found behind a trunk-seat months later. (It had been sent c/o the *Spectator* who forwarded it to Barnsbury Street.) 'Ben, the print is stunning and I love it: so surprising as a form and familiar and yet inexplicable, wholly new, and tough as hell, like stone ... Your line is unique and very inspiriting and cheerful. The scale of this shape, through its placing on the sheet, is also disconcerting.'

Writing to Nicholson in February 1979 about his latest Waddington show, Bryan's explanation for not writing sooner is due to his 'innate diffidence' which can be 'taken instead for indifference'. So he finally plucks up courage and writes a fan letter: 'To say, dear Ben, that those paintings brought back to me, all over again, my deepest beliefs in art and absolute *love* for the radiant, sharp, witty, profound, disturbing, quite *marvellous* things that you make line, colour, shape and space achieve. It is a stunning act of creation and transformation.'

R.B. Kitaj

In his posthumously published *Confessions of an Old Jewish Painter* (2017), R.B. Kitaj acknowledged Bryan as one of the writers and critics to come to his defence when he was so widely attacked over his 1994 Tate retrospective. In a second reference he cites Richard Morphet's and Robertson's reply to Andrew Graham-Dixon in the *Independent*. In fact, these were separate pieces: Morphet's article the response to unfair criticism of the exhibition's curator, Robertson's a letter. Under the title 'An outstanding artist who has been unfairly rubbished', the *Independent* (of 28 June 1994) published the following:

Sir: R.B. Kitaj has made in a large number of paintings – some of the strongest, most original and haunting images by any artist working in

England in my lifetime. *The Ohio Gang*, *Cecil Court* and *John Ford on his Deathbed*, to name only three, have stayed vividly in my memory for years. There are many others. But Andrew Graham-Dixon's dismissal of Kitaj's Tate Gallery retrospective ('The Kitaj Myth', 28 June), rules out any positive achievement of any kind. In effect, he has rubbished a lifetime's work by an artist now in his sixties and an outstanding figure in contemporary art.

As I like and admire Mr Graham-Dixon's criticism very much, I am puzzled by this negative view of so much work and activity. Is there nothing of any consequence whatever in the entire Kitaj output? I should be concerned if it were not for the fact that although all Mr Graham-Dixon's points are reasoned with his customary grace, his review gives no idea whatever of what Kitaj has actually created.

Kitaj offers us a series of images that bring together in odd convergences a good many of the things in art, life, literature, movies, politics and history that touch him as a man. As an artist, he is true to his experience of life. He plays paradoxical games with all this experience in the way that his imagery is presented, even in the way it is handled in design, colour, brushwork, drawing, surface and scale.

What Kitaj achieves at his best is absolutely original, personal and peculiar to him. There is nothing anywhere quite like the finest of the Kitaj paintings. May I add that for years now Kitaj has had a most bracing effect, imaginatively, on students and young artists all over England and in the US; that he is greatly loved and admired here, with all the usual grumbles and reservations, by every artist I've ever known; and that Kitaj first stood up for serious drawing and the retention of the life class not long after the 1968 students' revolt brought artistic discipline into bitter disfavour.

Mr Graham-Dixon's displeasure in the work seems to have been aggravated by the sight of so much text by Kitaj adorning the galleries and in the catalogues and perhaps looking, to him, a bit pretentious. But Kitaj has always been something of a Village Explainer and I think this shows a friendly and trustful nature: visitors to the Tate exhibition are visibly very interested in Kitaj's notes.

Yours sincerely,
Bryan Robertson

Bryan Robertson on Michael Sandle

Like Bryan Kneale, Michael Sandle (born 1936) is a Manx sculptor who came to prominence in post-war England, subsequently making a name for himself also in Europe and America. Sandle and Robertson didn't really get to know each other until the 1970s, but then formed an affectionate and mutually respectful friendship. Bryan's appreciation of Sandle's work is taken from a draft of the introduction he wrote for John

McEwen's 2002 monograph on the sculptor. Sandle's appreciation of Robertson comes from an email of July 2013.

Michael Sandle is one of the most original and powerful sculptors to emerge in Europe in the latter half of the twentieth century. There is no other sculpture to touch the hieratic mystery and ceremonial grandeur of his early strike into history, *Monumentum pro Gesualdo* (1966–9), an intensely imaginative abstract tableau. No other sculpture can match the gleaming, razor-sharp expressionism of Sandle's invocation of the maniacal destructiveness of war and violence which so disfigured the twentieth century and continues to plague our so-called civilization today – all trapped balefully forever in *Mickey Mouse Machine Gunner* (1972–8).

Malta Siege-Bell Memorial (1988–92) is also unparalleled, as an exceptionally calm and elegiac, unrhetorical memorial to the Merchant Marine convoy which saved the blockaded citizens of the George Cross Island of Malta in 1943. A schoolboy at the time, I have vivid memories of the courage shared by sailors and by citizens loyal to England to the last. The loveliest and perhaps the most directly moving of Sandle's public commissions, the memorial – a vast bell in a tower by a long, reclining figure-as-catafalque – is sited at the entrance to the Grand Harbour, Valletta ...

In my view, Michael Sandle is a great man and a great artist with a conscience-stricken sense of outrage at the futility of violence which gives an extra edge to his imaginative genius. The word 'genius' does not exactly spring to mind when viewing some of the recent trivialisations of sculpture in England, but in Sandle's case I am deploying it with precision and from solid comparative evidence.

Bryan went on to recount his meetings with Brancusi, Henry Moore, Hepworth and Caro, and mentioned staying with David Smith at Bolton Landing. He then stated: 'All these sculptors have shown authentic genius and I place Michael Sandle among them, because of the sheer strength of his intensely imaginative, sardonic individuality.'

Bryan continued: 'Sandle has never resorted to easy solutions or to the besetting twentieth-century sin of manufacture or "production" – all of his themes or subjects find their unpredictable form through intensity of feeling, uninhibited by recipe, undimmed by mannerism. Sandle's work throughout shows a large degree of imaginative courage: he is not afraid of any aesthetic or formal eventuality.' Bryan finished this splendid tribute, which in its unedited version appeared as the introduction to John McEwen's 2002 monograph on Sandle, with a word or two of praise for Sandle's drawings, which he regarded as being 'among the most beautiful and haunting of the twentieth century and have to be considered on equal terms with the sculpture'.

Michael Sandle on Bryan Robertson

I first met Bryan Robertson about fifty years ago in the old Dover Street ICA. If my memory is correct he joined in a podium discussion that Terry Setch, Victor Newsome, Michael Chilton, myself and presumably Tom Hudson were having about an exhibition of students' drawings held there from Tom Hudson's pioneering Foundation Studies Department at Leicester College of Art.

I viewed Bryan with some suspicion then, I have to say, as I was not very articulate in those days and also rather defensive. It took a while for me to get to know him – and that was some time after he had left the Whitechapel Gallery because during his tenure there the callowness of youth made me still view him with suspicion, thinking he was a far too powerful taste-maker. And I thought too of that gallery, in my own mind then, as the 'Whited-Sepulchre Gallery'. It is an irony that I had a retrospective there myself in 1988.

It pains me that it took such a long time to realise what a remarkable mind he had and what a wonderfully anarchic sense of humour he had too. However, bit by bit, I got to know him and the more I did the more I liked and respected him. Towards the end of his life he seemed to have a touch of greatness and he seemed to me to have the aura and wisdom of a Roman Senator facing death.

I first got to know him well after taking part in an exhibition curated in 1969 by Michael Compton called *Six at the Hayward*, i.e. Buckley, Flanagan, Milow, Newsome, Sandle and Stephenson. He was extremely enthusiastic about my sculpture *Monumentum pro Gesualdo* which was in this exhibition and which he eventually obtained for the Neuberger Museum in New York State when he became the Director there. After he'd bought it for the museum's permanent collection I went out to oversee its assembly and was impressed that this was done with great care by convicts from Sing-Sing prison – some of whom were apparently murderers.

We eventually developed a firm friendship which I greatly valued – I could see that he was his own man and possessed great integrity. I also learned to quickly value the scope of his erudition as I firmly believe that you learn from other people. I am very grateful to Bryan Robertson for being instrumental in my meeting the critic John McEwen, who has been a life-long supporter of my work. I met the wonderful Irene Worth through Bryan too. In fact he seemed to know everybody – when he was very ill but still at home in Islington he made an impromptu lunch for me with some ham that he informed me Claire Bloom had brought in for him the day before. He told me that her former husband Philip Roth was a close friend too and that he sent him all his books to read. I remember too that Bryan told me once that when he was much younger and lived in Germany – Baden-Baden I think – he was going out with Juliette Greco's sister.

He was very brave when he was dying in hospital – I am deeply touched and grateful that he managed to write the preface to John McEwen's book on my work on what was to become his deathbed – it was the last thing he ever wrote. When John and I visited him in Hospital the day before he died he was drifting in and out of consciousness – however he was able to joke when he opened his eyes and saw us. 'Look what's just come in – two undertakers!' he said. I miss him – there are no Bryan Robertsons anymore.

A brief note from Patrick Caulfield, 25 November 1985

When the painter Patrick Caulfield was going through marital difficulties, and didn't yet wish to commit to living with Janet Nathan, the woman who was to become his second wife, Robertson was supportive and sympathetic, and offered to put him up in his house in Islington. Caulfield's good friend John Hoyland commented:

When Patrick was leaving his wife, or undecided about what to do, he couldn't afford a flat – which is what I thought he should do, give himself a couple of months off. He didn't want to move into Janet's place. Bryan had a very nice spare room where Lee Krasner used to stay. I thought that would be a marvellous solution. Bryan thought about it and then he said, 'Well, she can visit, but she can't stay overnight'. This was Janet. So Patrick went to live there with him and it was brilliant because he didn't have to pay rent and Bryan was rather a good cook in the Elizabeth David style. They'd come home pretty late then sit drinking and talking all bloody night. Those are some conversations I would love to have been part of – or heard at least. Then Patrick decided to move in with Janet, and that was that.

Here is Caulfield's note:

Dear Bryan,

Thank you for your understanding letter and offer of accommodation.

It would be very helpful for me to make this move to neutral territory and I understand that it is inconvenient at this moment, so please expect me on the 3rd December. I may seem to have a lot of stuff, but don't let this dismay you, as it won't signify a prolonged stay.

Fond regards,

Patrick

Bryan on Tate

On the back of a typed-out poem is this scribbled undated note (probably *c.*2001) in Bryan's handwriting (now in the Tate Archive):

I endorse in the strongest terms Frank Stella's denunciation of the curatorial misrepresentations at the NY Museum of Modern Art and aped so tiresomely here at Tate Modern and, in different ways, at Tate Britain. What we are witnessing is nothing less than the betrayal of art itself and all the known intentions of artists through curatorial arrogance in ludicrously schematic games-playing which deceives no-one but the participants.

Ballet and modern dance

Bryan was devoted to ballet and modern dance, saw a great deal of it, and gave much time and energy to promoting links between dance and visual art. His ambition was to oversee a series of collaborations between painters he admired and choreographers. To this end he accepted the position of adviser on design to the Royal Opera House at Covent Garden in 1979, with a brief to suggest artists who had not previously worked for the stage. Interestingly, Bryan's mentor Colin MacInnes was not keen on ballet, and called it 'this sad, prancing art' in his novel *City of Spades* (1957). However, he was converted by the all-black Katherine Dunham Dance Company when it came over from America in the summer of 1952. Robertson, on the other hand, had been keen on dance from an early age and must have greeted his friend's change of heart with some relief.

One of the people most involved with the art-dance link-up was Richard Alston. Another was Ashley Page. I quote extensively here from interviews with both of them, because their reminiscences offer a wonderfully full account of the process of collaboration between artists and choreographers. To round out this section focusing on dance, I interviewed the artists Deanna Petherbridge and Christopher Le Brun about their particular collaborations, and quote from Bryan's writings about two other artists who designed for the stage, David Hockney and Yolanda Sonnabend. A letter from Victor Pasmore about a dance project he worked on gets in here too; and there are more dance words from John Hoyland, John Hubbard and Stephen Chambers.

Richard Alston

The choreographer Richard Alston (born 1948) studied art and theatre design before he began to work in the dance world. The following remarks come from an interview in June 2015 at The Place, a dance and performance centre in London's King's Cross area, where he is Artistic Director.

I think that I am quite visually aware and can notice things because I was taught to look. I began to get interested in dance in the mid-sixties – [in] 1966 Merce Cunningham came to London, and his work was still mostly designed by Rauschenberg then, and then in 1967 Martha Graham came. Heaven knows how they took all the Noguchi stage sets across the Atlantic, but they did. These companies I went to see because of the artists – Rauschenberg and Noguchi. Years later that was a real link between me and Bryan, because Bryan had known Noguchi. The sculptures that he made for Graham were very stylised but incredibly effective.

I was always fascinated when Bryan used to say to me – I won't name names – about an artist, 'Well, actually, I think he or she is not a brilliant artist but they're a brilliant designer'. And these were sometimes the people he'd recommend to work in the theatre. In the same way, I think Noguchi saw his work come alive when people were clambering all over it – it needed that element.

I went to America to study [as a dancer] with Merce Cunningham in the mid-seventies, and when I came back in 1977 I made a piece for a company called London Contemporary Dance Theatre, and Bryan always said to me, 'That's when I met you, Richard, when I came to see *Rainbow Bandit*. I was so excited by it'. We had a mutual colleague and that's how he said he met me afterwards to tell me how much he admired it. And he would have done – he was always generous and had a wonderful enthusiasm. When he loved something he would be almost over-the-top about it in a wonderful way.

But I don't remember that. What I do remember is that a couple of years later I got a commission to make a piece for [Ballet] Rambert. I was very interested in working with the painters I was interested in. If I shoot back quickly: when I was at school, at Eton, we used to come up to London for cultural visits. It was something called the Alexander Cozens Society. A lot of boys used to sign up for this because then they could nip off to Soho and what have you. I used to find my way across London to exhibitions. One of the big ones was *54–64* at the Tate. Somehow I organised myself on the tube to get to Aldgate East, and I went to the Whitechapel. That's where I saw Bryan's *New Generation* exhibitions. The first one I saw had Bridget Riley, David Hockney, Patrick Procktor, Derek Boshier [1964]. It was the most extraordinary thing – it was like the most amazing escape to this wonderful space with this extraordinary and completely invigorating art. It didn't seem like a museum, it was almost like an industrial space – big, white and clean.

I have a sense in a non-cognoscenti sort of way that Bryan arranged wonderful exhibitions. He was fantastic. He cared hugely about lighting, and he would spend ages thinking about where the paintings or sculptures should be. I went to several of those *New Generation* shows and the next one, the next year, was sculpture. The way that sculpture was in the space was just wonderful. So I knew about Bryan. Not long before this commission from Rambert, I went to the Serpentine Gallery, because there was an exhibition of John Hoyland [1979]. So I went there and the paintings were amazingly vigorous, and colourful and very theatrical. I got the catalogue, and it had a long lavish introduction by Bryan. So when this commission came up, I wrote to Bryan, that's how I met him. I wrote and said, 'I keep seeing your name when I see art that I like. I'm a choreographer and I'm really interested in the idea of painters working in the theatre. I have this idea that maybe this exhibition at the Serpentine has huge possibilities for doing something exciting on the stage, and I wondered whether you would help me. If you think this is an interesting idea.' Then Bryan got back in touch and said 'Of course I know you, we met at Sadler's Wells in 1977. What a marvellous idea – this is something which is very close to my heart.' So he introduced me to John Hoyland.

Hoyland was interested but mentioned that he was going to Australia for six months – 'but that probably won't be a problem, will it?' I said yes, so it didn't happen then. That's why I worked with a theatre designer and lighting designer on that piece. Then I actually became attached to Rambert and I think it was the following year that I went back to see Bryan and he said 'You must come and talk about artists who I think would be wonderful in the theatre'. Eventually it all worked out, and he put me in touch with the slightly difficult Howard Hodgkin. So the first artist I worked with in the end was Howard. In fact the first piece, called *Night Music*, was actually the best piece he designed – he did the most amazing set with a collage at the back, a big painted cloth that had blotches of lining paper from inside books. Then he put what looked like giant silver foil along the sides so that all the colour of this amazing backdrop was reflected. I would describe it as purple and yellow houndstooth with lots of green. Once I found myself at a dinner Bryan had organised, I think at the Warwick Arts Trust, and I found myself sitting next to Bridget Riley. I said that I was working with Howard. 'I hope you like red,' she said.

But it did work and Bryan was very helpful, because Howard was tricky. Bryan was hugely supportive. I used to go to exhibitions a lot then. I like painting and I like sculpture that you can touch. At that time, modern dance was always about *things*, so it was the equivalent of figurative painting. I found I always wanted to get away from my feelings being – I thought – invaded, so I found that after the Whitechapel when I was studying I used to go to the Kasmin Gallery a lot. It was a sort of cool neutral space and you would see one Jules Olitski painting on the wall and an amazing Caro sculpture called *Prairie*, which I absolutely adored. It was a terribly important space for me. The Graham work, which was what the training was in those days, was quite emotionally intrusive and dictating what you should be feeling and how deep you should dig. I liked the way that artists at that time were very often just presenting things which I found incredibly beautiful and dispassionate. So I got hugely involved in it.

I think I had seen a sculpture show at the Hayward and there was a beautiful piece by Nigel Hall that moved and quivered slightly. That's when Bryan said, 'Oh, well I'm doing an exhibition of Nigel's work at the Warwick Arts Trust', so the next thing I did was to work with a piece by Nigel called *Soda Lake*. That was because it had this extraordinary hoop and this sort of column of space, and I had just at that moment been approached to make a dance for television and I thought this would be wonderful.

I did several things at Rambert and then I became director, and that's when Ashley Page started choreographing and working with artists. I always felt that Bryan was perhaps unrealistically excited about the establishment, whereas the art that he seemed to promote and nurture ... well, the Whitechapel wasn't the establishment. It was an independent place. I think it was Claus Moser who invited him to be an adviser, to be on the board of the Opera House and to advise on design. Bryan had some very exciting ideas but he didn't really know how to implement them. The thing about Rambert, if somebody came up with a very difficult idea, I would know when it was impossible or how it could be done, and I would liaise with the stage crew, who were not always the most adventurous people in the world and who would rather have had a rock that looked like a rock and a tree that looked like a tree. But I can tell you that really good work was done at Rambert.

At the Opera House, sometimes the designs were wonderful, but the practical people did nothing to actually ensure that they were as the artist wanted. And Bryan then didn't have the knowledge, so you sometimes had conflicts, like Helen Frankenthaler, who quarrelled with the choreographer and they took curtain calls on alternate nights – they refused to be on stage together. And Bryan was right in the middle of all that, and Helen Frankenthaler was quite a diva. She came to dinner and Bryan asked me to come which was fine. She had a sort of rather hen-pecked amanuensis or assistant who was there with her. At a certain point Bryan brought a plate of food over to her then turned away and sneezed. Helen went 'Oh my God' and sent the unfortunate girl out for Vitamin C in the middle of dinner. Bryan used to open himself to impossible people, men and women. But I think he had a hard time. Time and again things went wrong with the Opera House, and that was very difficult. He didn't have the experience, and the rhetorical side of Bryan didn't go down very well with the people in the modelling room ...

There were problems. For instance, Patrick Caulfield did a wonderful set which was taken from the red stripes in the auditorium. It was a box. Bryan used to take me very early on to see these things, and say, 'Look, isn't this exciting?'. And I'd say, 'But that's going to be really difficult – how's that going to happen? It's going to take a lot of time to put up. And what is the music? Oh, Stravinsky's Symphony in D. You do realise that's only ten minutes, Bryan? So you're going to ask the audience to come in, and there's this amazing set and they'll all be thrilled. Then there's a ten-minute dance.' And because the set was so unwieldy, it took forty minutes to take down. It's that kind of thing that used to cause tensions. Or they got all the proportions of Christopher Le Brun's setting wrong. They just would not help.

When I worked with John Hubbard, we went to the scene-painting room together and he saw what they were doing, and he said 'No, no, no – hang on. Can you give me a couple of hours and I'll quieten this down.' They'd taken a cupboard and they'd turned it into Frank Auerbach – completely expressionist and over the top as a piece of scenery. John just got up a ladder in a pair of white overalls and he won them over because he's such a charming man. And he got what he wanted. But that didn't work when he did *Les Sylphides*. It was an amazing idea – a completely new way of looking at a very traditional ballet, but they didn't change the costumes [traditional tutus] so his painted backcloth seemed suddenly very overbearing, at which point the authorities threw their hands up in horror. They actually withdrew John's design. I think it got as far as the First Night. It might even have been the Dress Rehearsal.

I always felt that Rambert was an ideal place for Bryan to see his dreams come true, because I was the director by then and could say 'fine – let's make this work'. So the second time I worked with Howard was for *Pulcinella* [1987–8]. Before, he had invited me down to this beautiful place in the country when he was still with Julia, and we had this idyllic weekend. At dinner on the Sunday evening, Julia lent forward and said, 'Howard, don't you think Richard should see what you've done?' After dinner he showed me. This was *Night Music* and it was wonderful.

But for *Pulcinella* he'd done a wonderful set except it had a white floor and white things at the side. I said, 'Howard, we're a touring company. It's not the Opera House, so we have things at the side that are black. We can't actually have white wings. We go from theatre to theatre and we usually dance on a black floor, but we could have a white floor.' Howard looked at me and said, 'Well, I'll have to start again. I'll just have to start again.'

And he walked out of the room and in the distance I heard a door slam, and eventually, about a quarter of an hour later I rang Bryan and said, 'I'm in Howard's house and he's walked out. I'm not quite sure what to do'. (This was in Hodgkin's house and studio in Coptic Street.) So Bryan said, 'Just stay there, Richard, he'll be back. Don't worry.' He was very kind. Eventually Howard changed the colour and it was wonderful. It was always worth it with Howard – the designs are amazing.

Sometimes in those situations Bryan couldn't cope and sometimes he really would help. He got very angry on behalf of Christopher Le Brun, he got very upset. He'd done wonderful things but they'd got the proportions wrong … It shouldn't have gone wrong: Le Brun's designs were extraordinary. Also he'd done the most amazing front cloth – it was really extraordinary, really wonderful, but because *Ballet Imperial* had gone wrong, the people who were the traditionalists said, 'We can't possibly have a modern painting, we have red velvet with gold'. So that never happened. It was very grand and it would have looked amazing.

Bryan had this wonderful vision, but he didn't know how to actually deliver it. If there were people who weren't interested, they could work against it, and then suddenly at board level they [would] all throw their hands up and say 'Oh, well ...' This put a stop to artists working with the Opera House for a while, with Roy Strong dismissing the designs as very 1940s. What's wrong with that? If you look at the early days of Sadler's Wells there were these amazing big cloths by Graham Sutherland – they were extraordinary – they certainly used artists at Sadler's Wells when they first started. It's a very exciting idea. The other choreographer I've worked with a lot – as a student and then when I was at Rambert – is Merce Cunningham. And he worked with Jasper Johns, Rauschenberg, Warhol. It can be so exciting. So I absolutely believed in what Bryan loved, and we did everything we could to make it absolutely work, and it did.

When I left Rambert, I lost that resource in a way. When I started this company [at The Place] I decided I was going to really concentrate on *music* and dance. We had to be really flexible, going to all sorts of theatres, big ones and small ones, so I haven't worked with artists with this company at all.

Anyway, I did work with Hoyland before I left Rambert. I gave him the music by this composer called Nigel Osborne. I went to his studio one morning and he was in a very good mood and very chirpy, and probably a bit hung over. I asked him whether he'd liked the music. He said, 'Well actually, Richard, I was listening to Aretha Franklin. That's really the kind of music I like.' But he'd done this amazing painting – it was wonderful. I told him I'd like to come back with the lighting designer and discuss what we could do with the painting, rather than have one big painting as a backdrop. So we worked out how you could actually put it on a series of gauzes so that the elements of the painting could be isolated and then layered and revealed bit by bit. I loved that.

I think it's agony for someone like Howard to work in the theatre because the theatre is about co-operation and Howard works in isolation. Probably one of the most exciting projects I did was one with Dick Smith, called *Wildlife*, which he got very excited about. He came on tour with the company – we were in Portugal or Spain I think. There he was cutting out pieces of paper in this hotel and making maquettes of kites, because I'd asked him for something like the kites he made, like the amazing piece I think might have been called *Yellow Pages* which I saw in the Museum of Modern Art in Oxford. So that's what he did. He made these kites that could move and which became an active part of the piece. I think Dick was one of the most generous people that I've dealt with. He was very excited by working with the music, very excited by working with the dancers. Think of the work he did for Conran or for shopping malls in America – he was, in that sense, a designer. He would make these very attractive elaborate things that would be up in the roofs or the rafters, or hanging over people, which lent themselves to being in the theatre.

The lighting designer is hugely important. I used to work with Peter Mumford, who now works in the West End but at that time did a lot of work for me at Rambert. He had a very sure sense of colour, not wanting to distort or mess around with an artist's work. The hardest thing for Peter was when an artist called Kate Whiteford made a red and green design of runic marks. I said to her that red and green were almost impossible to light in the theatre, but anyway Peter dealt with it.

I know that Bryan had a lot of tricky scrapes to get out of. He would put the most unlikely people together. Sometimes it didn't work, which I used to think privately was a blessing. There was a very charismatic performer called Wayne Eagling, a very good dancer, a wild boy in the eighties. Bryan met Wayne, and Wayne said he wanted to do something about the circus. Bryan said he had the perfect artist for it and got in touch with Calder. It would have been such a mismatch: grand old man and clubbing young lightweight. I was quite glad that that didn't happen. That's why things like the Helen Frankenthaler rumpus could happen. She'd done a beautiful job, a really beautiful and enormous version of one of her very delicate paintings. Even though they're delicate, there's lots of detail and lots of texture, and so the choreographer freaked out because he thought his steps couldn't be seen. Bryan couldn't help – he tried, he really tried – so they got to this point when they literally would not appear on stage together. He objected to the costumes which he thought were too fussy. It was quite dysfunctional.

Bryan made most of the artist/choreographer collaborations work. His enthusiasm was so great, that people would get carried away with it. The other thing about Bryan – I used to love reading what he wrote – but towards the end of his life he used to go out to Lindos for the winters, and I went out there, and there were always, always missed deadlines. So you'd be in this idyllic place. He had this little white Greek room with a fax machine in it, which was the most modern thing that existed in those days. And reams of paper appeared to be coming through from people: 'Unless it's here by lunchtime, I can't …' So I'd say let's go for a walk and he'd say 'No, I have to finish this. I should have finished it last week'. But that's why I think he would go in [to the production] a little bit too late. When I worked with John Hubbard, it worked very well. The in-house lighting designer was John D. Reed, very knowledgeable. It was very hard to make what John had done work as there were so many colours and quite subtle. But he really did absolutely the best he could.

In an opera house like that you're in a situation where it's *Aida* tomorrow and in the afternoon they're rehearsing it, so you don't have a lot of time for technical things. So Bryan came to the dress rehearsal and we'd spent a couple of days lighting it. Rather late in the day we watched a dress rehearsal, and I had to give notes and Bryan said, 'I'd like to have a word with you'. He had a pad with him and had made some notes. Bryan started saying, 'Now when that happens, I think there should be a bit more blue, I felt it was a little bit too hot. And now this moment there …' And I said,

'Bryan, this is really wonderful knowledge, but the lighting's done. This is not Rambert. I cannot say we'll look at it tomorrow. We're doing two other ballets and an opera, this that and the other. I didn't know you actually wanted to contribute to the lighting. I'd have been delighted if I'd known (I lied), but I should have got you in earlier.'

I enjoyed Bryan's imperiousness. I never quarrelled with him. Dick Smith never quarrelled with him. I think both of us were unique in that really. He would get quite annoyed with me, and he would send me these hilarious postcards of Gloria Swanson or somebody, with really ridiculous fantasy messages on. Sometimes they would be funny things and sometimes he would be describing a dance he'd seen or why he found it extraordinary. He could use English in the most wonderful way, and make very acute observations. But I would always know when he was annoyed.

Bryan's dinners were always extraordinarily late but what made up for it, sort of, was the extraordinary jugs of Negroni and Bellini and dry Martinis so dry you thought you'd never stand again. So, within twenty minutes you were (I was) completely drunk. So hunger wasn't an issue. There used to be the most amazing people there. He was really good friends with Irene Worth and she had been involved in the setting up of this building [The Place], she was on the board. Claire Bloom was there several times and then came with her then-husband Philip Roth which was tricky, so that was a frosty evening. But Bryan meanwhile held the whole thing together with a cooking spatula in his hand, making marvellous baroque gestures and giving us these lectures. If anyone said a word he'd say, 'I'm saying something important – listen!' Somehow he cooked at the same time, and he'd be describing to you what he was doing. 'I just sweat the onion for a few minutes, then very simply you do this and do that ...'

And he was always recommending things, which I loved. He would recommend books. Stephen Chambers said to me the other evening, 'You know he never read those books!' I don't think that's true. He could be very eloquent about certain books like *The Good Soldier* or *Miss Smilla's Feeling for Snow*. They were always amazing books. Unless he just osmosed and knew they were brilliant. I loved the fact that when you went to dinner you had to pick your way through the books around the dining table. I found him hugely stimulating and really lovable. I think he used to get annoyed that sometimes I didn't do this or that, but I just refused to take offence. I was very fond of him. I still think of him a lot and remember him. I don't think I've ever known anyone be so generously enthusiastic about people. If he thought something was wrong he'd tell you. But very often he would say, 'This is one of the most sublime paintings I've seen in my lifetime.' ('In my lifetime' was a favourite phrase.) 'This is one of the most important artists I've met in my lifetime.' And I used to think, 'Oh, I'd better have a look.' So I'd rush off and see. I found that extraordinary and I miss that. I don't know anyone like him.

He would talk about a young artist starting out, or about an old friend like Nigel Hall or Patrick Caulfield, but then I would see his BBC programme about Stubbs. He was amazing! Talking about the drawing of horses in the same extraordinary flow of enthusiasm that he would have for a young artist now. I always found that so exciting, so stimulating. I suppose for me, being outside the art world, and being younger than most of the people who were at these dinners, I think there was something very special about meeting Bryan and sharing his amazing knowledge, especially because he had been rejected by the establishment. These were not big public statements. His dinner parties were extraordinary because he would perform. I was completely convinced by what he was saying and think it was absolutely genuine and what he was talking about was something he was passionate about. He would sometimes get into great arguments with people if they would disagree with him, but that seemed to be just part of it all, and water off a duck's back to him.

Christopher Le Brun

As mentioned earlier, Robertson was an important figure in Le Brun's early career, and their close friendship made it somewhat inevitable that Bryan would suggest that Le Brun venture into theatre design.

Bryan asked me to design a ballet. I'd been going and looking at things and very good artists had designed – Patrick Caulfield, John Hubbard – so he introduced me to the people. It was called *Ballet Imperial* by Balanchine [the production was performed in 1985]. Covent Garden decided they must ask New York City Ballet because they were sort of the spiritual guardians of Balanchine. They asked this man to come over and look at my designs. Right from the start I had admitted I knew nothing about design and asked for an experienced designer to work with. They said I wouldn't need it and that they were just interested in my vision. All, in retrospect, nonsense. I did my designs and brought them in and this man from New York said (to a friend), 'I told you – it's all Marxist'. We were all exchanging baffled glances. I think he was determined not to like it. Later I discovered that the entire ballet establishment was sharpening the knives. You could hear the sound of the sharpening.

The next thing that happened was that the chief painter went to hospital with some major illness. He disappeared, leaving a very unionised painting crew, including a very stroppy leading painter. So the painting of it was very difficult. It culminated at the point where, with about a week to go, there was something that needed altering on the actual set, and I had to do it myself while the stage hands looked on. We didn't have a director, and it got to the point where I didn't go up on stage on the opening night. The papers probably quite rightly lambasted it. I found it so painful. Bryan couldn't do anything. But it was a fantastic experience.

My design for the safety curtain was a happier story, up to a point. I had a studio in Bethnal Green and I did a big cartoon (which I still have), and all the trustees of the ROH came one by one to look at the design and liked it. Claus Moser, John Sainsbury, Kelly [Colette] Clark, etc. Everybody loved it. At that time there was a technical director and he said it was fine but it needed to say Safety Curtain in big letters right across the middle. I thought this was a negotiation, but it wasn't. He got the GLC to come in and say it needed Safety Curtain on it. It just killed it. Bryan and I put a lot of effort into that.

When we were talking to John Tooley [then Director General of the ROH] about the safety curtain Bryan said to John, 'Oh, you must come and see Christopher in his studio'. 'Fine, I've a terrifically busy diary, but if you can collect me and bring me back I'm sure we can do it.' So Bryan organised for me to go in my car to collect John Tooley. My car at the time was a little yellow-painted Morris Post Office van. They were cheap (£400) and you could put things in the back – perfect artist's van. And there was a network of artists' car repairers that would fix the car. So we turn up at the front of the ROH Covent Garden, with this little yellow van. The back of the van I laid out with foam to cushion it, and some terrible old carpet. Bryan had a bad leg and we arrived and he said to John Tooley, 'I'm terribly sorry, but I hope you don't mind, I have to sit in the front seat. Would you mind getting in the back?' So John got into the small enclosed dark space in the back of the van, which had no windows. You could see into the front, but there was a grille. And Bryan said, 'You know we're kidnapping you, don't you?' And John laughed in a slightly nervous way. Then we drove to Wapping, because my studio was on Wapping Wall. That was typical of Bryan's sense of humour.

Ashley Page

The dancer and choreographer Ashley Page (born 1956) met Bryan as a young man and was soon the beneficiary of Robertson's unique gift for introducing like-minded artists, as he recalled in a telephone interview in April 2016.

As a young choreographer in the early eighties with the Royal Ballet (I was a dancer first), I was commissioned to do something for the Opera House to be performed in 1984. There were quite a few young choreographers they were trying to nurture, and they also brought in Bryan to advise us on fine artists as designers. At that point in the Royal Ballet, Kenneth MacMillan was principal choreographer and he had been using mostly Nikos Georgiadis or Yolanda Sonnabend, and the work started to look a little bit the same – it was either one thing or the other – and they wanted the new group not to fall into a similar trap. So Bryan started to talk to us individually about what we wanted to do to see if he could advise on suitable collaborative partners.

I must have met him first of all in 1983 because I was preparing this work all the way through 1983 into 1984, and I know that when he introduced me to Deanna Petherbridge we had a long time together on the collaborative process. I think it might have been at Le Caprice – the restaurant he loved so much – that he arranged a dinner for us to meet. Afterwards Deanna and I left to go to my car – in those days I had a cassette player in it and wanted to play her a tape of some Purcell music I was thinking of using – leaving Bryan and my girlfriend in the restaurant drinking their coffee. I remember that quite vividly. Deanna plays the harpsichord and loves baroque music. I had a conversation with Bryan before he introduced me to Deanna about what I wanted to do, which was basically to strip down the classical technique in dance, lay it bare, and then start building it up with my own version of that language. I'd been to Greece in the summer of 1983 for a holiday and was struck all over again by ancient Greek architecture, so I wanted to do something that was visually harking back to the classical period. With Purcell we were going back to the ground bass of baroque music and the fact that it provides an interesting rhythmic structure for dance.

Over the course of this collaborative period it became clear to me, and I was advised also by people at the Opera House, that Purcell harpsichord music was not going to come across very well in that cavernous space. I was starting to feel a bit depressed about that and not quite sure what to do. At that point I was going up regularly to Deanna's apartment to talk to her about ideas. She started doing drawings and I knew I wanted to use six dancers. *The Draughtsman's Contract* [the film directed by Peter Greenaway with music composed by Michael Nyman] came out in 1982 but somehow I'd missed it – I'd heard about it but not managed to see it. Then I had dinner with a couple of friends and they played the Michael Nyman music and I realised that it was exactly what I wanted to use. In the end it was the key to the issue, and it all came together like that.

The piece, which was called *A Broken Set of Rules*, was performed in August 1984, at the very end of the Royal Ballet season, and had only four performances. It caused quite a stir actually because there was an absolute racket coming out of the pit – not the sort of thing usually heard at the Opera House – with Deanna's epic designs and some of the youngest and best dancers in the company. Some people were really shocked by it and thought the Royal Ballet ought not to be doing things like this, and others thought it was the beginning of a new dawn. Bryan loved it and was thrilled for Deanna and me that we had such a success with it. He didn't interfere at all. That was the beginning.

Bryan wasn't in the building much. He'd been going regularly to see London Contemporary Dance which was on a high at the time, and he was very familiar with the work of Merce Cunningham and Martha Graham, and the whole Rauschenberg-Warhol world. There had been a history and of course it stretches right back to Diaghilev with the fine artists that worked for the Ballets Russes in the early part of the twentieth century. That's the sort of blueprint really. Even before my experience with Bryan, I'd been in a new ballet at the Opera House by Richard Alston, who was Rambert's resident choreographer. I'd been going to see Richard's and other choreographers' work in places like Riverside Studios and The Place, and he seemed to be the leader of the pack at that time. I'd been very influenced by him in my choreography, rather more than I had by people in the ballet world, because they seemed to be investigating something that had more to do with classicism than the more expressionist dramatic work that was going on at the Opera House.

John Hubbard designed the piece that Richard Alston did at the Opera House that I danced in. That was in December 1983. Richard had already worked with Howard Hodgkin at Rambert. Richard also worked with John Hoyland, Nigel Hall, Dick Smith, maybe others. Just before my piece premiered, another new piece, by Michael Corder with designs by Patrick Caulfield, had premiered: *Party Game* [1984]. Michael also worked with Helen Frankenthaler in 1985 at the Opera House, which had a little bit of drama about it actually because they fell out, Michael and Helen, when it got to the stage calls, and Michael didn't like the costumes. John Tooley, who was General Director at the time, had to step in and they had to agree to have half the performances in the costumes Frankenthaler had designed, and half in plain white leotards. That was rather upsetting for Bryan, I think.

Later on Patrick Caulfield redesigned an Ashton ballet called *Rhapsody* [1995], which I was in the initial cast of in 1980 which was made for the Queen Mother's eightieth birthday. Patrick's design for *Party Game* was like a huge interior. He mimicked the wallpaper in part of the Opera House – what we call the Stalls Circle – which had this black and red striped paper and these wall lights with lampshades, and that was basically the set, with a vast cushioned circular banquette which they tipped over and wheeled around. It was rather wonderful really – very Patrick. *Rhapsody* was a bit more prescribed – they had to have steps at the back and arches, so it was a little less free, I think. Helen Frankenthaler's design was three unbelievably beautiful backdrops, one for each movement of a Prokofiev piano concerto (No.3). David Bintley also worked with Victor Pasmore in 1984 on *Young Apollo*, with Britten's music. There was also the revival of an amazingly famous and wonderful Balanchine piece called *Ballet Imperial*, I think also in 1985, and Bryan was instrumental in that happening. And Jennifer Jackson in 1985 – it was called *Half the House* – and I think it was a fine artist doing that. [The artist was William Henderson.] Bryan would have been involved with that. It was a very interesting time.

By 1986, Richard Alston was Artistic Director of Rambert, and he commissioned me to do a piece for their sixtieth anniversary, me and several other choreographers, Michael Clarke included. I wanted to use a piece of music by Harrison Birtwistle, which I think Richard suggested. He said why don't you talk to Bryan about what he thinks about design. I was very happy to do that, and he came up with Jack Smith. He took me down to Brighton to meet Jack in Hove and we had Sunday lunch I remember. Bryan was very funny. Jack and his wife Sue were a funny couple. They had no children and Bryan said they were like each other's children. He was rather wicked with them actually, but affectionately. They didn't really drink and we took some wine, and I remember them producing tiny little wine glasses. When they were out of the room Bryan said, 'Like an eye bath!'

That collaboration, called *Carmen Arcadiae*, went very well. Bryan was responding with the suggestion of Jack to the spiky, angular nature of the music – it was very jagged – and by then Jack was doing those abstract collages of geometric shapes, like musical paintings – and he designed a backdrop cut in two and overlapping in the middle so that I had an entrance in the back. It was quite simple – just a backdrop and fantastically vibrant costumes. It was exactly what was needed: Rambert are a touring company so they needed to be light on their feet. That was another success.

I then worked with Jack again because the following year I was due to make my second work for the Royal Ballet and I'd found another piece of music by a contemporary British composer, called Colin Matthews. Bryan listened to this music – I remember sitting in that front room at Barnsbury Street – and said 'I think it's Jack again. He would do this wonderfully – he's right for it, and also you'll get more out of a second collaboration – you already know him.' And he was right. This time it was two backdrops and fantastic costumes. I wanted tutus for this, but very modern ones, and Jack loved that idea. Jack went bananas this time and painted twelve possibilities for these backdrops. We went down to Hove again and had another lunch and he just produced all these pictures and I felt spoilt for choice.

That went really well at the Opera House and it came back several times – Anthony Dowell who was the director really liked it. For the next year, Richard had asked me to do a second piece for the Rambert, and I wanted to do a version of *The Soldier's Tale* with Stravinsky, but just the concert suite, not the text. I knew I wanted this time a big piece of sculpture or a big object in the middle of the stage that would dominate the space and that I had to work around. Bryan took me to meet Stephen Chambers who was working away in some very rough studio space somewhere. He was working on these rural landscape pictures, and Bryan thought that would be interesting. I loved the pictures, but it wasn't what I was looking for – I was looking for something much more abstracted and sculptural.

So I asked him about Bruce McLean who I knew had been artist in residence at Riverside Studios while I was doing stuff there. Bryan did know him and actually encouraged him when he was very young, and he told me how to get hold of him, but he said, 'I think that's a mistake'. I went to see Bruce and talked to him and we got on really well, and in fact Bruce did design that piece and I think Bryan was a bit upset about that. I never knew that at the time – somebody told me years later. Bryan never showed it. That piece was a huge success and Richard was very happy with it. Bruce did a brilliant job on it and it was filmed by the BBC as well – badly, I have to say. Bruce McLean and I also did the Stravinsky *Renard*, also for the Royal Ballet, in 1994.

Then I had another piece coming up at the Royal Ballet in 1989, to Beethoven's Piano Concerto No.1. I really wanted to work with Howard Hodgkin. He'd done two pieces with Richard and I loved what he did, and I knew that for what I had in my head for this ballet he would do brilliantly. Bryan said how he was a great supporter of Howard's but that Richard had already used him and that we should be using somebody else. So Nicholas Serota's wife at the time, Angela Serota, who was on the board at Rambert, I think she effected an introduction with Howard, or maybe Richard did. That all happened and Howard was really enthusiastic about it all and designed this amazing set. He wanted to do the model showing at his house, so he set it up in his studio. It was enormous. The technical people from the Opera House came along and sat there in stony silence. Then Howard walked out and slammed the door and we all sat there. He did come back and the design had to be pared down, but Howard was hurt and disappointed, and had to be cajoled back into it.

What did echo on from my association with Bryan and Stephen Chambers was that later, in the nineties, in the mid-nineties and right through to 2001, I did a series of ballets at the Royal Ballet which were inspired by Stephen's work. Eventually in 2001, my last piece at the Opera House before I came up to be director of the Scottish Ballet, was with Stephen and a theatre designer working together because Stephen was worried about costumes and how you achieved the technical side of it, all of that. I put him together with a theatre designer I'd been working with for a while called Jon Morrell and they did an epic job together at the Opera House. It was the most amazing piece of design I've seen, called *This House Will Burn*. It was based on three paintings by Stephen, quite different ones but from the same kind of period.

There was one which was a sort of portrait of the writer Alina Reyes, that was like a front gauze with a doorway cut in the bottom left-hand corner of it. That was near the front of the stage. There was a mid-stage backcloth with a woman semi-reclining backwards, and Jon cut into her stomach a big glass box in 3D that people could access from behind, so they could just appear in it, like in this figure's stomach. And it also had a bigger doorway, like an archway but squared off, cut in it at bottom left. Finally there was another right at the back, of another amazing bright orange vibrant painting.

But also Jon designed some furniture: the Opera House made the bed in Stephen's painting *Around My Spanish Bed*, slightly larger than life. That was right in the middle of the stage. Then there was a very Stephen Chambers wardrobe, and piles of junk furniture around as well. It had a domestic feeling to it which a lot of Stephen's work does. It was the culmination of a series of pieces I'd based on his work. Jon and I did a thing called *Room of Cooks* in 1997, which is based on that painting by Stephen. Orlando Gough wrote an amazing smoky, filmic, jazzy score for it. It was nominated for an Olivier and it was only twelve minutes long. And in 1996 I made a piece based on a painting called *Sleeping with Audrey*, from a slightly earlier period of Stephen's work with a slightly rural setting. That was a series of work which wouldn't have happened if Bryan hadn't introduced me to Stephen back in 1987.

Ashley himself designed *Sleeping with Audrey* because there was not much money.

I did the costumes and I did the backdrop which was just very abstracted blocks of colour in browns and greens. I learned the difference between working with artists and working with theatre designers the hard way, because I started with artists who weren't used to the theatre, and most of them were abstract artists. I was making at that point mostly abstract pieces – they weren't narrative works – to do with unbelievably strident colours and amazing bold shapes. In a way it was like the paintings blown up to a large scale, but because of the collaborative dialogue, it was affected by the choreography and the music. A real collaboration. I'm known for my collaborations as much as my own choreography. All my pieces have had fantastic design.

At one point Bryan was talking about me possibly doing something with Paul Huxley, but that didn't happen. What I found when I started working with theatre designers was how much easier it was because I knew I could leave all of the technical side of it to them. Costume – choice of fabric and cuts. How a theatre designer works with a costume maker is a fluid relationship – a bit like me working with the dancers. And although I still have a big say in it all, and I'm there at the fittings and all that, I can just put my worries aside because I know they know what they're doing. With the artists I had to be there. But given that lack of experience, the artists created some of the best costumes in my whole body of work, because they were unusual. Sometimes a lack of knowledge is quite a good thing. You're not constrained by the rules – like Orson Welles and *Citizen Kane*. My work always stood out mainly because of its unusual visual appearance, and the fact that I used excruciatingly difficult music most of the time.

By the time we got to *This House Will Burn*, it was very sophisticated work. By then I'd been choreographing for eighteen years and working with these two men, Jon Morrell and Stephen. People either loved it or hated it. I remember people like Nicholas Hytner, who was just about to take over the National Theatre at the time, coming along to see it. I bumped into him in a restaurant later and he said, 'My God, that's fantastic that work'. It was very gratifying that people from other forms of theatre and the arts would come to see what I was going to do next. And that all started with Bryan.

Stephen Chambers recalled in an interview at his East London studio in March 2014:

Bryan brought the choreographer Ashley Page to my studio when I was quite young. I would go and see contemporary dance with Bryan – he loved contemporary dance. Conversations went on for years with the production about to happen. Eventually it did, but it was the best part of ten years before it was actually realised. By which time Bryan was not very well, and in Greece, and I don't think he ever saw it. And I didn't consult him too much on it because I knew that he would want involvement. I didn't want to go through that. But I think he was pretty upset.

Ashley Page continued:

Bryan was very happy that I worked with Stephen eventually. I remember I hadn't seen him for a while and he said 'We need to go out to lunch'. He took me to L'Escargot, to that room upstairs and we had a long boozy lunch. Bryan – and this was very important for me – was always suggesting books and giving me books to read, telling me which films I should go and see, and also introducing me to new music as well. It must have been an anniversary of Webern, or something like that, and Bryan took me to a concert of his music at QEH, and both of us were in raptures. He knew his music. He also knew his films, his directors – sometimes not the obvious ones, the quieter films. My summer reading invariably came from Bryan. He'd often not read the book he recommended and would ask you to tell him what happened in it. He was a great magpie in that way, he'd sample things and then spread the word. And a great raconteur. I got to know the art world through him – openings at d'Offay and places I'd never heard of. At one time a lot of my friends were from the art world. I miss that.

John Hoyland

John Hoyland recalled in an interview in his London studio in May 2011:

Bryan was constantly trying to engineer design work for artists, but he was up against professionals at Covent Garden. They didn't want artists, they wanted stage designers and he'd always be pointing out that the best designs ever done were by artists not stage designers. He managed to squeeze us in: I think Patrick did two, I did one, Howard did one. Patrick was so funny. He said, 'I'm doing this ballet – I'm going to insist the men wear trousers'.

And they did! And the girls all wore kind of summer dresses. Mine was much more abstract. I wanted to paint the costumes on the girls, but they wouldn't let me. It came out very well – I was surprised. Bryan gave me a very good tip. Helen had done one at Sadler's Wells or somewhere and given him absolute hell. By this time she was becoming more and more the Jewish Princess, rich and powerful. Bryan said that she just thought it was an opportunity to paint the biggest Frankenthaler there's ever been, and that everybody should be there at her beck and call to do this. He said, 'No – when you get into anything like this it's to do with working together: with the lighting man, the choreographer and so on. You're not the most important person. And what you've got to remember is that they're not trying to make your show crap, they're trying to make it better.' I took that on board. What really got me going was seeing when they got the lighting man on it, backlit it and stuff, he did all kinds of things that I hadn't even thought of. I thought it was a good experience.

John Hubbard

Another close friend of Bryan's who was drawn into the world of theatre design was John Hubbard, as he recalled in an interview in November 2012:

One area in which Bryan's success was chequered was in his relationship with the Royal Opera House company. He was passionate about it – he wanted it to be positive and it should have been positive – but he had this determination to improve the standard of the visual aspects of production. He was right, but he wasn't good at politics. He didn't understand the politics of an opera house – byzantine at the very least and full of backbiting and underhand dealings, full of mistruths and people being very deceptive. Bryan was fooled by all this, and went about it in his usual way, which was a mixture of charm and insistence. If he didn't get the response he wanted he would just keep on. This didn't succeed. If he got depressed he'd go to talk to somebody who said I'll sort it out, but didn't intend to, nor try to. Without naming names, he was let down by those he thought would help him.

But he had some great success with Patrick Caulfield, Deanna Petherbridge. None of the things he did were liked by the official ballet people. They saw him as an outsider, an intruder who was pushing these things on them. Chris Le Brun had a lot of trouble with his, and the Helen Frankenthaler one didn't go down at all well. The Pasmore was good – that was a success – and it was seen as a success. But none of those ballets have been seen more than once – it's a terrible shame. Probably now all those sets have gone. Patrick Caulfield's was complicated – I never saw it but I think that was one of the very best. They only did four performances and then it was scrapped.

The ballet I did with Richard Alston got good reviews and that was seen as a success but again it was resented. As an example of this I remember one day when I was working with Richard, I went to the canteen to have lunch. I'd met de Valois several times and she was terrific, a wonderful character. She was sitting by herself so I said, 'Can I join you?' 'Yes, yes.' She said, 'What are you doing?' I said I was doing a ballet with Richard Alston, that I was designing it. 'Oh,' she said, 'lovely, lovely. It's so nice we're not having one of these awful artists who come here all the time.' Of course it wasn't anything to do with her. It was the time of Norman Morrice, who was weak but nice. John Tooley was in charge. The first ballet I was supposed to do was *Les Sylphides*. They'd used the same old Benois sets for years. They asked me to do a new backcloth and so on. I wanted another designer to redo the costumes very simply. But it ran out of time and was sabotaged. Bryan was very despondent about that, very let down. The lighting man was very upset, had a heart attack and died. The ballet was shelved but they used the backcloth several times. So it was seen but only as a backcloth, not a decor. Richard actually wanted to work with an artist.

Deanna Petherbridge

The artist Deanna Petherbridge (born 1939) was to become close to Robertson through theatre design. She recalled their friendship in an interview in her north London studio in December 2015:

I was so fond of Bryan and I miss him so much. What I miss most is him laughing. Bryan did have the most extraordinary and outrageous sense of humour. In a way that was always the thing that was so wonderful about him. There were occasions when Bryan and I were lying on the floor – he could do that: go into a total and complete laugh, laugh so much that you nearly wet yourselves. He devoted a lot of energy to making people laugh. It was quite contrived in a way, thinking back on it. It was a generosity of spirit and it also covered up the fact that he didn't want to talk much about himself. He was very opinionated but he was also quite private. So I think this thing of entertaining you and keeping you laughing was also to control where he wanted to meet up with you. Laughter was a defence mechanism.

I remember another time when Bryan and I lay on the floor in gales of laughter – it was a scurrilous story about a German art historian then teaching in Manchester. Bryan started taking him off – completely politically incorrect and absolutely shameless. The story spiralled as he took him off – in a kind of performance. We lay on the carpet and laughed and laughed and laughed. We cried with laughter. That bonded me to him forever.

He could be impossible too. He would say, 'Now, Deanna, stop interrupting!' when I hadn't been able to get a word in. We had a bit of an interregnum in our relationship. At some point he got very cross with me and wouldn't talk to me and then we made it up at the end. He was terribly cross that I was publishing, that I was researching, in a way that I was in a competitive field. And he kept saying to me with both affection and manipulation – which was always the double thing with Bryan – 'You're an artist, what are you doing all these other things for? You should be in the studio.' He felt it distracted me too much. Of course it did – I've had a double career. It's been like that all my life. But he didn't approve of it. I never had any animus towards him.

I loved and adored him. I used to invite him around and he'd never come, or he would say yes and then phone at the last moment and cancel – after you had prepared the meal. When I think about people I miss in life, I think of Bryan and Peter Townsend [Sinologist and editor of *Studio International* and later *Art Monthly*]. Both were knowledgeable. Peter was cynical, but Bryan wasn't at all. He was always into defusing negative things, like his not getting the Tate, with a funny story. I do feel now – and this is probably grumpy old age – that the people I knew in the art world in the seventies, eighties and nineties were huge figures. They were big mad grand figures. (Mad is a word I picked up from Bryan – it was a word he often used about other people, like Vera Russell. When I use it, I always hear his voice. Swanning was another of his words.) I'm not often as generous as I am about these figures – because somehow they were bigger, they weren't petty people ... I can't think of anyone nowadays who is so unfrightened to be themselves, to be so grand.

He wrote in the catalogue of an exhibition I had up in Manchester in 1982. [This exhibition travelled to the Warwick Arts Trust in January 1983.] I knew him by then. I think I must have met him through Vera and the exhibitions she organised in Covent Garden (the Artists' Market). He did have an astonishing memory: he could tell you what he'd heard in a concert or seen in a play, who had performed, what he'd had in the meal afterwards, what his guests had said ... He could tell you all those sorts of things if they added up to an amusing story. Or a disgraceful story – but he was so funny when he said all those disgraceful things. Scurrilous. He was very mischievous. He did say things like that about everybody. He used to say to me, 'I'm just an old eunuch, darling!' I think the implication was that by the time I knew him his sex life was behind him. I think he fell in love with younger men in a completely platonic manner. He needed to have them around him, but he didn't need to touch them.

The Whitechapel exhibitions for me changed the world – the American work, the quality of how they were displayed – they were extraordinarily important, those exhibitions. But I only got to know him when he came back from America. It was *folie de grandeur* with Bryan [printing too many catalogues, running up the bills at Warwick Arts Trust]. I used to say to him, 'Bryan, you're not a Queen, you're an Empress!' He would chuckle. He was very grand, thought big on everything and didn't want to be troubled with practical things like money. So all his life he was up against it.

He didn't open his mail and on the long table in his dining-room would be piles and piles of books, and piles and piles of correspondence. He wouldn't open it, and at some point he would collect it all up and put it in a black sack. One day a cleaning lady managed to throw out one of these black sacks – with everything in it: letters, uncashed cheques ... He would then tell this story as the funniest thing in the world. He mocked himself with great style. He could be terribly pompous but then he would immediately deflate it. Fantastically self-aware. But he wasn't necessarily interested in understanding about other people's lives ...

When he wrote in a chatty, conversational way it wasn't great art history, but it had a certain quality and it didn't pretend to be anything else. He spoke in fantastically beautifully measured phrases. He constructed his sentences. He was in fact a better talker than writer. When he wrote – when you could finally get him to do the writing – he wrote in a really beautiful and elegant and rather slow handwriting.

I remember him saying to me, about selecting an exhibition, 'It's really important that you don't make choices as artists get it wrong. Artists always like the latest thing they're doing. They find it very difficult to look back and make the right choices.' I would learn from him and it didn't get in my hair. I've always been told I'm a difficult woman, but I realise that I completely accepted that Bryan was the dominant person in that relationship. That's the way he wanted it and that's when he played it best. He didn't want to be challenged at all. He'd make pronouncements and I'd say 'Bryan, that's absolute nonsense!' And he'd say, 'Deanna, don't interrupt me!' and it would have been the only word I'd said in a three-hour monologue. Unless it was dinner. He did encourage others to talk at dinner, as he'd be cooking and serving the food.

Bryan approached a number of people to design for the ballet. I've a feeling that Bryan came on to the board of Covent Garden through Colette Clark. She obviously had a vision too: let's bring in Bryan, he knows everybody in the art world, let's open this whole thing out. He loved the position of being able to do something for you – the grandeur of giving all of this to you – and by God it was a gift. It was a surprising time for me and absolutely wonderful. I did three ballets with Ashley Page. Ashley was doing his very first ballets and Bryan had taken him on board. I was at least twenty-five years older than Ashley, but Ashley accepted that he could work with someone so much older than him. But of course I was a novice, in the sense that I'd never designed for the theatre before. So there was never anything heavy in the way I came to him. Bryan had used incredible skills to put people together. He was extremely good at it.

My work – or so I've been told – is quite cerebral. It uses line, it's quite stern work, it's very complex work. It doesn't give. It's not about gesture, it's not about warmth, it's not about colour. We were put together – this absolutely unlikely couple – and it was extraordinarily good for me. I became terribly fond of Ashley and really admired him. The first ballet we worked on was called *A Broken Set of Rules* [1984]. Before I started designing I went regularly to ballets. I attended everything – all the rehearsals, when Ashley was choreographing with his troupe. I became a kind of resident of Covent Garden. But I was so attracted by working with a live performance. I drew the auditorium a few times – rather schematic drawings – and I remember thinking 'I need to draw myself into the place, into familiarity with something so strange'. The total magic of all those workshops on the other side of the road in Floral Street. It was so exciting. And for the first time I was learning about collaboration. I was teaching myself a skill.

We were working with classical structures and we must have argued this together with Bryan, there must have been meetings when the three of us developed these notions. Ashley took the classical language that he knew and just started breaking it, disrupting it. So the theme behind the ballet was the disruption of the classical. I did a set where the pediment is on the ground instead of up in the sky, and the columns, instead of being supportive at right angles, are all at funny angles. There was a fantastic very free column that worked like a drawing in three dimensions. We worked so well together, it was just wonderful. I designed the costumes as well. The next ballet I had someone help with the costumes. There were no budgets at Covent Garden then – too vulgar. Anything you wanted to do there was some brilliant person in some unbelievably exaggerated mad little corner of Floral Street who could do it for you.

I think Bryan was a facilitator – he put together people and helped us to get on just as people. An incredible skill. He never interfered and said, 'Oh no, you can't do that'. I don't think Bryan ever found a designer for a long ballet. They were all short ballets – which was fair enough as they were all experimental. Young choreographers and very established artists. But the opening nights, the rehearsals, the excitement of working with all these people, made it the most magical time for me. Maybe that's also why I feel so fond of Bryan because this was entirely due to his generosity of soul.

Letter from Deanna Petherbridge (**dated 7 August 1984**)

Dear Bryan,

I think that you are one of the most amazingly generous and large-souled people I have ever known, and I love you and am grateful for knowing you. Thanking you, my dear, for:

Your perfume
Your flowers
Your brandy

Your kaolin-and-morphine-mixture (perhaps that should have been top of the list?)
THE CHANCE TO DO IT
Your support, your back-up, your tact
Your walks around the courts
FOR EVERYTHING
With much love and deep admiration
Deanna

Victor Pasmore

Victor Pasmore (1908–98) was not a great friend of Bryan's, but he was yet another artist who Bryan advised and promoted in the world of theatre design. In the following letter he consults Bryan about David Bintley's production of Stravinsky's ballet *Apollo*, choreographed by George Balanchine, for which Pasmore had been commissioned to produce designs.

Letter from Victor Pasmore, Malta (dated 10 July 1984)

Dear Bryan,

I have now received a letter from David Bintley explaining that the postponement and long delay in producing his Apollo ballet has led to changes and modifications in his ideas about the form of the dancing. As a result he does not want two contrasting backcloths symbolising a transition from dionysian to apollonian forces. Instead he wants the whole ballet danced before the blue linear symphony, but in two or three variations depending on the number of movements the ballet finally takes – he thinks now that it may be three.

As it happens I have a second blue variation because I made two versions as alternatives, but chose the one you know. The second version is equally attractive and would do very well. As to a third; well I have this also if necessary.

I appreciate the developing process and inevitable changing of ideas; I behave in exactly the same way in respect to painting! I feel, therefore, that the visual setting should develop likewise because it is essential that the ballet, as a whole, is a mutual creation. In these circumstances I am quite happy to drop the dionysian image and have informed both David and Anthony accordingly.

Yolanda Sonnabend

An exhibition of Yolanda Sonnabend's stage designs and paintings was mounted at the Serpentine Gallery from November 1985 to January 1986. Bryan wrote one of the essays in the catalogue, entitled 'The Studio and the Stage'. The following paragraphs, full of general wisdom about designing and specific assessment of Sonnabend's gifts, are taken from it:

Good designers, let alone the great designers, can also use colour in this way, like an artist, but at a lower level there can be something raw, un-lived-in and not properly experienced or felt about the colour in what I call an ordinary 'design job'. This can be effective but also peculiarly shallow and unsatisfying in its crucial lack of an imaginative dimension. What I am trying to explain is really one of the signs of the difference between a good artist and an indifferent one in any métier. Artists can deploy colour just as inadequately as designers. When Matisse uses bright blue, that blue has come out of Matisse's whole experience of the physical world of sea and sky and flowers and birds, as well as a good many centuries of specifically French awareness of nature, with its special elements of serenity, sophistication and purity. The blue is inhabited, experienced and felt by Matisse and it glows with a spiritual and imaginative depth. When a weak artist or designer uses blue it is just blue and it doesn't breathe or exist in the same way. It lacks that extra dimension because its juxtaposition with other colours lacks the edge and bite of the heightened juxtaposition achieved by Matisse. The difference between design-job colour and an artist's colour is profound, but the difference vanishes when we are confronted by the work of an inspired designer. Bérard was as much of an artist as he was a designer; the often enjoyable Oliver Messel was not.

Sonnabend's handling of abstract shape and, above all, colour in this first version of *Symphony* (the work has since been re-designed far more sparsely with no backdrop, in a white space, for its 1975 revival – the original set having been destroyed for storage reasons) was plainly the work of a true artist/designer and everything Sonnabend has done since has confirmed that view. *Requiem*, another great MacMillan ballet, is certainly one of Sonnabend's best inventions also, but what we see on stage in England is quite a considerable degree removed from what the artist intended. In its original production for the Stuttgart Ballet in 1976 (it was choreographed by MacMillan in memory of John Cranko) Sonnabend set seven, square, translucent pillars on the otherwise bare stage – a plain white space – and these pillars, at certain responsive moments in MacMillan's choreography to Fauré's gentle music, become iridescent in rainbow-like columns of light. The effect is extraordinary. At Covent Garden, for technical reasons, the lighting is equally inventive, but different in certain aspects so that there are no iridescent, rainbow-like effects. (When the work was first seen in England at the Coliseum, danced by the Stuttgart Ballet in 1979, the set was held up in Customs, so that only two pillars ever appeared on stage.)

Bryan on David Hockney's theatre designs

Bryan included David Hockney in *The New Generation* shows of 1964 and 1968, but only rarely wrote about his work. The following assessment of his stage designs comes from a typescript with Robertson's corrections in the Tate Archive:

The big show of Hockney's theatre design at the Hayward Gallery in 1983 was so enjoyable and gave intense pleasure to such rapt crowds that it is hard to believe now that it nearly didn't come to London at all. I became Chairman of the Art Council's Exhibitions Committee in 1980 in time to discover that the proposal for the show had been turned down just before I accepted the new honorary role. Suspecting that a vague sense of a surfeit of Hockney had compounded with that English puritan mistrust of success to add its own negative note to a genuinely tight schedule at the Hayward, I persuaded the Committee to manipulate everything and reconsider its decision. An official flew off to view the show at the Museum in Minneapolis where it originated: he returned with overwhelming enthusiasm for the project. The rest is history: a hugely popular show at the Hayward Gallery at a time when its crucial role in London's artistic life was under fire.

I refer to this retrieval not only to bask in the light of my own shining action but because it illuminates also the peculiar difficulties which, marginally but persistently, have faced Hockney in recent years – above all, probably, in his own country. In sequence, as I recall the successive little waves of discouragement, it has been said that Hockney is really a draughtsman and not a painter at all; that Hockney has lost his peculiarly nervy powers of invention and become an academic; that Hockney finally found his proper vocation as a stage designer at just the moment when his painting began to decline; that his photography was an excuse for his inability – running out of creative steam – to either paint pictures or design for the stage; that his photography was his only genuine invention which made everything else seem trivial, and so on. There are still those who cannot bear to contemplate the example of an entirely popular modern artist, although the recent crowds milling through the Tate's late Picasso show demonstrated that modern art long ago abandoned its exclusive association with a rarefied minority.

The truth about Hockney, of course, is that he is an astonishing figure as a painter, draughtsman, designer, an artist in the round: an authentic magician in the figurative art of this latter part of our century of whom the worst that can be said is that occasionally – and only very occasionally – the magic gives place to slighter conjuring tricks, but the magic is real and constant. Hockney also fulfils my long held belief that a strong artist should feel able to move freely from one discipline to another without being constrained by type casting or the restrictive labels that critics seem to love. Which is why I am so fond of Dufy: apart from the intrinsic pleasure in Dufy's work, there's his gutsy ability to paint, draw, illustrate books, design for the stage, engrave, design fabrics, create huge murals, work in ceramics – and all this long before the liberating example of Picasso could provide extra courage for such an adventure. Hockney shares my love for Dufy's magisterially delicate touch and command of colour and you can see it, in his own terms, in some of Hockney's best theatre work.

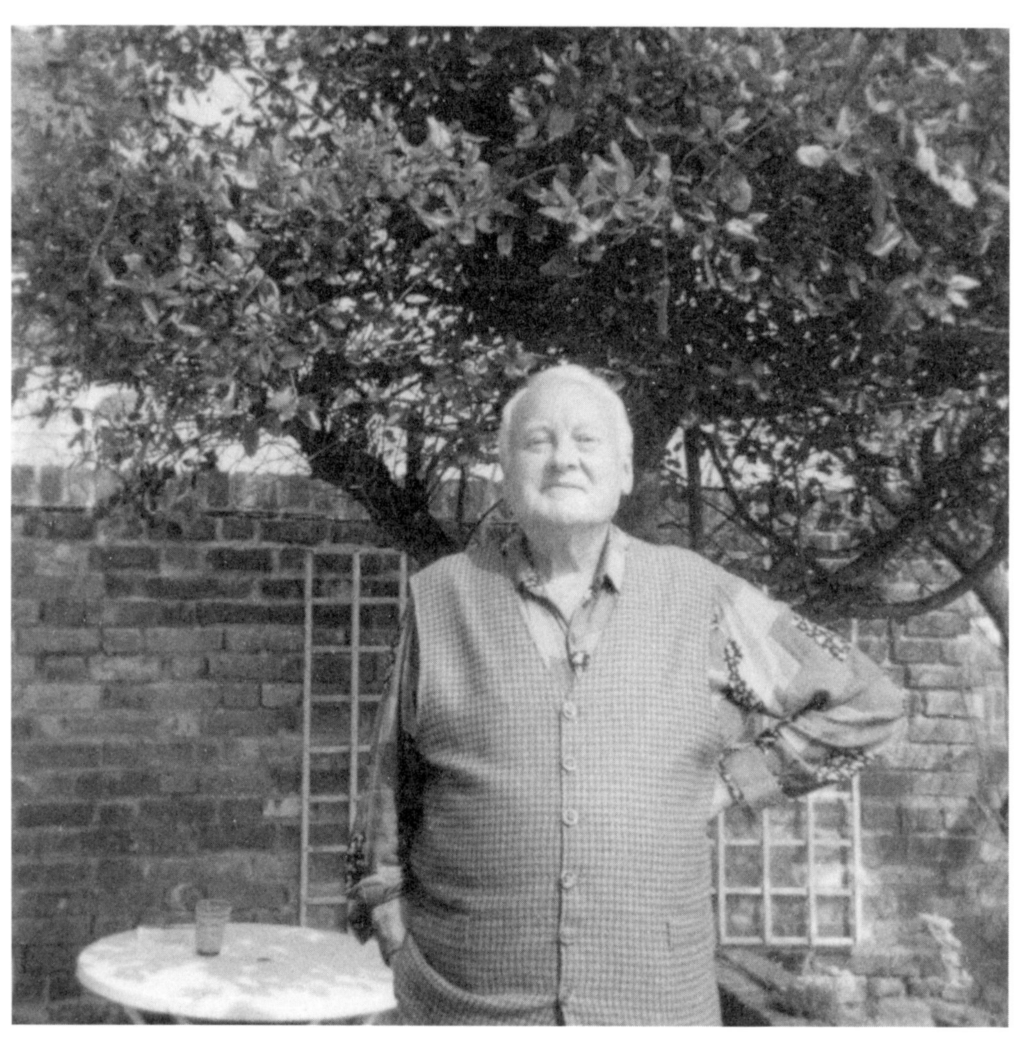

30 BR in the garden of his Islington home, *c.*1990.

Last years

Bryan's active engagement in the art world inevitably diminished as he grew older, and although his friendships with a wide circle of artists never dimmed, and may even have occasionally blazed into a row, his sociability was as flamboyant as ever. Meanwhile he still did his best to promote those he believed in, and one of his later sites of influence was the art magazine *Modern Painters*.

Modern Painters

The following text by the novelist William Boyd, himself an extremely perceptive writer about art, recalled Bryan in a different context: at editorial meetings of the magazine *Modern Painters*, founded by the radical critic Peter Fuller in 1987 and edited by him until his untimely death in a car accident in 1990. Fuller's associate editor, Karen Wright, took over the editorial chair until the magazine was sold to Louise Blouin Media in 2001 and subsequently moved to New York City. Boyd wrote in 2016:

I didn't know Bryan Robertson at all well and I suppose I probably met him a dozen or so times in the 1990s and the very early 2000s. But, interestingly enough, they were always at the same occasion – the editorial board dinners for the magazine *Modern Painters*, then under the editorship of Karen Wright. I remember the first ed-board dinner I attended very vividly. It was in the private room at the Ivy Restaurant in February 1994. I found myself sitting beside David Bowie who, like me, was the new admission to the board. Bryan might well have been there but, not surprisingly, I can only recall the conversations I had with Bowie – a delightful, self-effacing, very clever man, by the way.

However, over the following years of *Modern Painters* business I came to know Bryan better. I was something of an outsider to the art world and only knew a little about Bryan's reputation – the famous years at the Whitechapel Gallery in particular. There was sometimes a rather fierce intellectualism about our discussions round the table – no prisoners were taken – but there was also a lot of banter and gossip, not surprisingly, with other ed-board stalwarts like Howard Jacobson, Patrick Wright and Bill Packer present. Bryan, it was clear, seemed to know everyone but his presiding spirit was almost entirely genial, in my experience, at any rate. I realise he must have been in his seventies during our encounters in the second half of the nineties: grey-haired, anonymously dressed (jacket and tie) with a soft husky voice that was never raised, in my hearing, and a fully functioning sense of humour. Hindsight now tells me that he might have had good reason to feel somewhat bitter or resentful at the way his career in the art world had progressed since his apotheosis at the Whitechapel, but at the time I knew him I saw someone who was open, friendly, interested; who wore his great learning lightly and always seemed quietly self-assured.

The only time I really picked his brains was over the painter John Hoyland (whom Bryan had shown twice at the Whitechapel when it was under his tenure). I had bought, at auction, a large 1960s Hoyland abstract for, it seemed to me, almost nothing – a few hundred pounds. I absolutely loved it but was a little alarmed that I had been the sole bidder. There was another even larger Hoyland coming up for sale. I asked Bryan if I was wasting my money. No, no, he assured me, Hoyland is the real deal – snap up anything you can from the sixties and seventies – a wonderful painter. You wait and see. And of course Bryan was right and, prompted by him, I bought three more big Hoylands in subsequent sales. It was both sincere and shrewd advice.

Modern Painters was sold in 2001 and the new owner promptly rid herself of almost the entire ed-board, including me, David Bowie and Bryan Robertson. And so our irregular encounters ended and I never saw Bryan again. He died shortly afterwards in 2002.

With characteristic self-deprecation, the author and art critic Charles Darwent recalled not knowing Robertson, in an email (dated 9 June 2015):

Bryan wrote me a fan letter when I was a baby critic on the *Independent on Sunday*, and I'm ashamed to say I'd never heard of him. A year or so later, I sat next to him at a *Modern Painters* dinner and he pointed out that I hadn't replied. (Most unlike me, but there you are.) I blushed furiously and said that I'd assumed the letter had come from my mum. He looked at me with cold contempt, said, 'I can assure I am not your mother,' turned away and didn't speak to me again. Ah, well.

Craig Raine, writing in *Modern Painters* (autumn 1999 issue), described Bryan at the 1999 Venice Biennale doing an imitation of a Claes Oldenburg soft sculpture: 'At the mention of Oldenburg, Bryan announced, "Old grey dusty things. Every museum in America has an obligatory soft drum kit gathering dust in a corner." Whereupon he sank like a soufflé into himself. The legendary Boneless Wonder. A puffball short of puff.'

The following is a draft letter from Bryan to Karen Wright (dated 9 November 2000):

Dear Karen,

I'm v. unhappy about the way that Modern P presents itself these days.

1. The covers are appalling and misrepresent the character of the

magazine; if they do represent the mag, then I'm devastated – it's all bad art.

2. There are far too many articles with over-small colour repro's. It looks bitty, and in some cases immense paintings are reproduced smaller, much smaller, than a little one reproduced on a facing page. There should be fewer articles, of decent length and type size, and big repro's.

3. The inclusion of adverts in the same pages as contents is confusing and lowers the tone of the whole publication.

4. Headings of articles are a bit brash and commercial, multi-colour type etc. Bleeding off images – vulgar.

B. Robertson

An independent view

Richard Shone, author, critic and former editor of the *Burlington Magazine*, wrote in an email of June 2015:

On the whole I had a genial, warm acquaintance with BR over quite a long period – from the late 1970s to his death. I did not know him at all well but greatly respected what he had achieved at the Whitechapel. He commissioned one or two pieces from me for the *Spectator* – reviews of contemporary shows and he was always appreciative and would send a note – 'Just the job!' or some such phrase. I think he only wrote once for me at the *Burlington* – a short article on Christopher Le Brun's stage curtain for the ROH, Covent Garden. I remember his being pernickety and rather difficult over this, like a mother hen over a favoured chick. He once asked me for dinner at his house in Barnsbury Street and there were a number of people but the star favourite eclipsed us all in BR's eyes – the young Tim Marlow who was writing about modern British sculpture and had thus got in touch with BR. He always had his protégés and favourites – why not? Paul Huxley was one – earlier, I think Patrick Procktor was another. Twice he contributed to round-table reviews on the radio, of books I had published. Both times he was complimentary and I was pleased.

Once he rebuffed me and I have no idea why. It was in the Royal Festival Hall and he was with Huxley and we met on the stairs. He was dismissively curt. I was rather upset, especially as I knew no reason for it.

The last occasion on which I spent any time with him was in Lisbon in 1997 for a show of British modern art at the Gulbenkian; we were guests in the same hotel and BR and I had a very nice tête-à-tête in the café-bar after breakfast. This was enjoyable. He asked me if I'd been to Lisbon before and I said I had been with Duncan Grant in 1972. BR remembered meeting Grant several times at Christabel, Lady Aberconway's annual summer parties and had always enjoyed talking to him. I don't know how he came to know Lady A – that powdered, amusing and affected woman from an earlier age (perhaps through Kenneth Clark, also often at the parties, I remember).

I think BR said that he even went to the cinema with her, chauffeured from North Audley Street. In my diary I wrote (6 February 1997) that BR was 'pink and white and looking like a cousin of Danny La Rue; he lives in Rhodes in the winter and had thus had a difficult journey via Athens and Rome'.

Looking back

Old friends were dying, and the art world had a new order, even if some of the wire-pullers were Robertson's protégés. It wasn't a question so much of looking back in anger, but of looking back questioningly, of trying to find a pattern and make sense of the past. In this frame of mind, Robertson wrote evocative articles about the artists he'd known, and contemplated writing his memoirs.

Bryan had been friendly with John Rothenstein, going to dinner at his house in Chelsea and meeting occasionally. And perhaps Robertson had been Rothenstein's favourite to succeed him at the Tate, though his sponsorship may have been of little help, given his own later unpopularity. It was thus appropriate that Bryan should give the eulogy at Rothenstein's memorial in 1992, noting that he had been unorthodox in his views on artists, with 'a soft spot for the awkward ones'. There was much fellow-feeling here: this could be Robertson talking about himself. Bryan called Rothenstein 'a serious and gifted writer' and a 'great stylist'. There was also the experience they had in common of running a public gallery with a trustee structure, and Bryan knew from his own Whitechapel years that Rothenstein had stayed too long at the Tate. (He was Director from 1938 to 1964.) Bryan wittily outlined the phases of the love affair between directors and their trustees: a honeymoon period when they can do no wrong; a middle period when some trustees are for them, some against; and a final phase when the director is regarded as 'a monster, a villain, totally incompetent' and they can't wait to get rid of him.

The mood of retrospection was deepened by the deaths of two people Bryan had been close to, and about both of whom he wrote perceptive obituaries in the *Independent* newspaper. The following is taken from his obituary of Liz Frink (18 April 1993):

Elisabeth Frink was a woman of great courage, integrity and style who gambled continuously against the odds, both in her work – against stylistic fashion or any kind of comfortable or ingratiating image – and in her life. She achieved the extraordinary distinction of becoming, without any compromise, a genuinely popular sculptor whose work is admired by a broad public in Britain and abroad. Her dogs and horses have their own authenticity, but the images of a single naked male figure, standing, walking or running, say something about endurance, vulnerability and essential human nature that haunts the memory …

After Frink's early, quiet but very real success in the fifties, her most testing time came in the sixties and seventies. An 'academic' work of art, in the pejorative sense of the word, merely leans on tradition or feeds upon convention without energising or expanding that tradition. As figurative imagery, Frink's sculptures always avoided the negatively 'academic' label through their extreme individuality of mood, given life through a highly personal approach to form. Frink consistently carved the wet plaster after rough preliminary modelling, creating a particular surface tension and concentration of form, and this remained her only debt to Moore – for there are no stylistic similarities. Her personal lodestar, if she had one, was always Alberto Giacometti. But in the sixties, the *New Generation* of sculptors in England, following Anthony Caro's precepts, abandoned both modelling and carving in favour of assemblage, the art of creating form by the additive process – as opposed to the reductive process of carving or modelling – of putting together disparate elements, steel sheets or bars or found component parts from factories or steelyard waste. Brilliant colour and transparent materials were also involved and, although the new sculpture had its own variable mood, it was entirely abstract.

To some, Frink's sculpture looked increasingly old-fashioned rather than academic, with its recognisable imagery and insistence on the traditional substance and properties of bronze. But Frink continued to explore her expanding vision, ignored the strong pressures of fashion and proceeded to make her strongest and most characteristic work. Her public grew, together with critical recognition ...

Elisabeth Frink's strong feeling for the wretched suffering that seems so persistent in the modern world was extremely dry and unsloppy. She was wholly unsentimental as an artist, and her manner and way of talking was laconic, impulsive, full of humour, but also very decisive and rigorously practical. Privately, she was endlessly generous to good causes.

Alex Gregory-Hood was a distinguished art dealer working with contemporary British painters and sculptors, but he had previously been a career soldier (1935–60) in the Grenadier Guards, ending up as Colonel. Bryan wrote Gregory-Hood's obituary in the *Independent* (14 July 1999) from which this is taken:

Nothing could have been more surprising and in its own way more exotic for the London art world than the sudden arrival on the British contemporary art scene in 1962 of Alex Gregory-Hood as director of a new gallery in Lowndes Street, Belgravia ...

The artists selected by Gregory-Hood for exhibitions during the Rowan Gallery's first five years remain among the most remarkable English painters and sculptors of the post-war period. Among the earliest were the painters Paul Huxley, Jeremy Moon, Brian Fielding, Antony Donaldson, John Edwards and Anthony Green and the sculptors Phillip King, Isaac Witkin, William Tucker, Garth Evans and Barry Flanagan. Bridget Riley joined the gallery in 1967, followed by Sean Scully, John Golding, Brian Young, Michael Craig-Martin and Mark Lancaster.

Phillip King's first great inventions, *Genghis Khan*, *Tra-la-la*, *Rosebud* and *Twilight*, moody coloured sculptures which hugged or straddled the ground and dispensed with bases, were first seen at the Rowan, and so were Paul Huxley's majestic excursions into an original synthesis between colour-field painting and purely abstract forms animated, like King's sculptures, by a kind of Surrealist ripple of unpredictability.

The sixties were a time without precedent in painting and sculpture in Britain, a time of vitality, confidence and constructive contact with important developments abroad. The Rowan enjoyed a receptive climate created by the first three or four American shows and *The New Generation* exhibitions at the Whitechapel Gallery and major shows at the Tate Gallery and the ICA.

Loxley Hall [Gregory-Hood's family home] is a William and Mary stone house built *c.*1700 with a substantial red-brick Victorian extension, a courtyard with outbuildings and barns and a series of large, enclosed gardens of varied aspect and character, well planted with trees, bounded by a stream which separates the house and its substantial grounds from the gently undulating Warwickshire landscape.

The grounds also contain a small, pretty church with discreet decorations by Anthony Green. Weekend visitors were invited to attend the Sunday morning service, where Gregory-Hood sometimes dutifully read the lesson clad in a black leather bomber jacket, but most did not. Instead, they found themselves bemusedly learning the names of the flowering plants in the herbaceous borders or learning how to play croquet with Gregory-Hood as an amusingly vicious opponent.

Gregory-Hood liked to relax in the country and it was disconcerting after getting used to him as an art gallery director dressed in impeccably conventional dark suits, shirts and ties to find him sweeping into dinner at Loxley in a patterned flowing caftan worn in a highly *dégagé* manner over purple tights.

In the gallery Gregory-Hood radiated enthusiasm, expressing opinions on art amiably but forcefully in an extremely loud upper-class drawl which brooked no opposition, rather as he had no doubt cajoled the ranks and junior officers in the Army. He had a keen sense of the absurd, and although quite democratic and classless in many ways in his dealings with the world as a whole, with a keen distaste for pomposity or self-importance in others, he also retained a real love for the lineage of ancient country families, and he adored genuine aristocrats with an intense dislike for those who, in his view, failed in their duties by selling off parts of their estate or great paintings.

The Robertson memoirs

A number of people had for some time been suggesting that Bryan write an autobiography (there's an expression of interest, for example, in a 1991 letter from Alexandra Pringle, then Editorial Director of Hamish Hamilton), and it was ostensibly to do so that he began spending his winters in Lindos. Although various episodes from his life in art were adapted as articles for *Modern Painters*, Bryan doesn't seem to have progressed much beyond a draft proposal for his memoirs (alternatively entitled *Art Memories*), which projected a volume of some 150,000 words with about 16 black and white plates. He then subdivided this notional book into five sections, though – according to his extant notes – this wouldn't have taken him beyond 1960.

The first section was to deal with his three main mentors, Kenneth Clark, Colin MacInnes and Merlyn Evans. It was to be an account of the young Robertson at the age of nineteen – 'background, intentions, character (deficiencies), education, childhood in bed till sixteen and lack of formal education; concern for identity, with novelist's eye at work, and concern for art in society rather than art in a vacuum'. The idea was to splice the record of his early years with a memoir of his trio of mentors 'in terms of character, achievement, standards, intellect, eccentricities, and what I learned, and continue to learn, from them'. In a letter to K Clark (dated 17 July 1977) he mentioned the mentor section of his proposed memoirs, listing the protagonists in order of knowing them: '1. Merlyn Evans, artist/philosopher/ poet – true artist, true intellectual. 2. Yourself, as guide and lodestar as intelligence, creative, imaginative intelligence (also something to do with disinterested kindliness, *not* self-interest I mean) & 3. C MacInnes who I know was the only true successor to Orwell – & a better novelist.'

The second section was to focus on Paris in 1947, when Bryan lived there and met the likes of Sartre, Picasso, Dora Maar, Alice B. Toklas, Matisse, Braque, Brassaï and Cocteau. Split into two main parts, this would feature first Brancusi, then the 'New Look', the style of clothing introduced by Christian Dior in the city that year. Bryan was always very keen on Brancusi, whom he loved to talk about. (The painter Trevor Felcey remembered Bryan giving his moving and impressive Brancusi lecture at the Byam Shaw School of Art in the early 1990s.) In this proposal Bryan describes the Romanian thus:

> The greatest, most totally innovative sculptor of this century – from him come 'streamlining' and most of the best modern shapes. About 30 visits [to his studio] from 1947 on, until Brancusi's death in 1955. An account of his studio, the man, his talk, many aphorisms, ideas on art, identity, philosophy. Henri-Pierre Roché, author of *Jules et Jim* and *Two English Girls*, introduced me to Brancusi as well as Alice B. Toklas. Accounts of Toklas and Roché – he was the Maharajah's secretary, also commissioned Brancusi.

The section on the New Look he described as:

All about clothes, at that time and since. About Dior and above all Chanel, and a meeting with her, Balmain (an old friend and protégé of Gertrude Stein's), Jacques Fath, Lanvin, Balenciaga – and about Juliette Greco and Charlotte Greco, her sister (an old girlfriend of mine) now Mme Emile Aillaud (he's the French architect who builds new towns), Dietrich [Marie Laure] de Noailles, Suzanne de Tezenes, Alex de Rothschild.

Bryan wrote that this examination of style would also deal with the difference 'most important and never described between designers/innovators, who change and mould women's shapes, and costumiers/revivalists'.

Sections three, four and five were to be devoted to Jackson Pollock, one of Bryan's great subjects. He noted:

Pollock was nearly always under analysis, always conscious of dreams and dream imagery, always aware of dualities in heads, and the push pull stuff between male and female. In my view also – and a very objective one – Pollock was unquestionably a latent homosexual: his deep affection for and closeness to a few homosexual friends, his intensely close friendships with men, and 'strong mother, weak father' background and the resultant need for a strong woman and excursions against that authority.

The proposal peters out at this point as if Bryan had lost interest or simply run out of steam.

Looking forward

In April 1995 Nick Serota hosted a party at the Tate for Bryan's seventieth birthday. Paul Bailey remembered it thus: 'On the great occasion all his old friends were there, particularly Bridget Riley, who adored him as you know, and Bryan gave this speech. Bryan said: "It's so lovely to be here among one's old friends, brilliant acquaintances", pause, "and some very interesting riff-raff". Everybody was looking round for the riff-raff!'

Then in August Bryan entered the Tyringham Naturopathic Clinic at Newport Pagnell in Buckinghamshire for a month in order to lose weight before an operation on his oesophagus. He had attended health farms and spas regularly in recent years to lose weight, but this was more serious, though in a note he wrote at the time he tended to play it down:

It's not a major operation, [but] to improve a relatively common problem in swallowing I've had all my life, but I'll be out of action for a couple of weeks. I then return to Greece as usual in the first week of October to get on with writing, until next April. I am working on a book of memoirs, essays on artists and others that I've worked with, and I can now write each winter in seclusion at a friend's house on Rhodes.

This new pattern of six months in England and six months in Greece started in 1994. Sadly the Greek interludes, though presumably very enjoyable, did not give rise to the much-vaunted memoirs.

Bryan continued his campaign to found a sculpture park in London, writing to Jocelyn Stevens (then Chairman of English Heritage), on 30 March 1998, as follows:

I want more than anything to establish in London the finest national British Sculpture Park. There is nowhere at present in our capital city where visitors and residents can get an idea of the great achievements of British Sculpture in this country. To me and to many others, this is a serious omission.
I presented British Sculpture at Whitechapel very often.

He proceeded to outline his ideas in some detail, suggesting that there should be,

in my view, no more than seven or eight works on view at any one time and, wherever the site may be, the sculpture should not be presented as 'an exhibition' but sited with subtlety and care so that individual works might be encountered almost by chance, unobtrusively and tactfully sited. An independent committee should be set up and funds sought with which to make purchases, although works might occasionally be on loan from the Tate or from the Moore Foundation, if suitable. Every four or five years, a single work might be suitably re-sited outside London, in the regions.

Despite all Bryan's efforts, a permanent sculpture park in London is still only a pipe dream.

Illness had long pursued Bryan, limiting his energy and compromising his life. Now it began its last relentless stalking. If Bryan was daunted by the prospect of death, he gave no sign of it, and began to plan for the disposal of his goods and chattels in a characteristically generous manner. In a draft letter to Chris Smith (then Secretary of State for Culture, Media and Sport) from the Middlesex Hospital, dated 29 March 2001 and marked Private and Confidential, Bryan wrote:

Lying on my back with drips in, etc., everywhere, I'm writing this above me, somewhere in the sky, so hope your great kindness in writing to me is not answered with indecipherable scrawl. Your last equally kind letter about my (successful, so far) plans to make London's first permanent Sculpture Park at Kenwood, alas went unanswered because this health nightmare had begun and since then I've had three operations in two hospitals and for past five weeks daily chemo-therapy and radio-therapy. It's working and my specialist tells me that there's every prospect of a complete recovery – I've had an anal cancerous lump (sarcoma?) going from one inside buttock to the other and across the (but outside) anal sphincter. A nightmare and it entailed a colostomy before they could even begin treatment. Everyone tells me that I look v. well and have infectiously high spirits.

I saw by chance a nicely made and enjoyable film on your walks in John Smith's old terrain – the Munroes? – and I found it rather moving as well as likeable, and as always with you, unpretentious and straightforward. Lovely places of course, but I want you to know that the film, your low-key Christian example, and my invincible belief – without any faiths, alas – have been a tremendous help for me through the past months. I've no faiths but absolute belief, and it's a bit barmy and unintellectually advanced, but I'm sustained by it.

I got old piranha-teeth [*Private Eye*'s nickname for him] Jocelyn Stevens's agreement to the idea of a known base for Brit Sculp before he retired but his second in command, Julius [Bryant], tells me that it's permanently open and on the record – all I have to do is to re-convene my committee and raise some funding. (Jocelyn thought it meant a big temporary show, but Julius and I think this is a good, English, unalarming way of getting the thing started.) I plan to buy an occasional big work, and borrow from Tate and elsewhere if work in question is right for outdoors. Never more than 6–7 sculps at Kenwood very discreetly sited. I'd have to search to find them. Essential look and 'feel' of Kenwood rigorously respected. Wilfred Cass, Arts Council lady – Audrey Wayton – Julia Peyton-Jones, Nick Serota etc. all aboard the Committee. (We plan to make Reg Butler's *Unknown Political Prisoner* and Epstein's *Rock Drill*.)

I go from here to a nursing home for at least three weeks in late April; then, home!!! but with two nurses alternating etc. so I reckon I'll be home for a formal meeting in late June or early July. Might you, could you, come too and advise us. Or is this premature? Perhaps best to wait for carefully drafted memo.

But I'd love to see you both sooner, when I'm up to it in my nursing home in Battersea sometime in early June? It's near Battersea Park and the river. David Sylvester recommended it, nice food and a trained nurse or two and good physiotherapy, badly needed as I can't walk yet, although standing at last.

I want to set my affairs in order and hence this perhaps overlong letter. As a bachelor, I have a ludicrously low income of art earnings but a house worth around £750,000. Also a lot of paintings and sculptures – and nobody to leave it to. Must do something constructive – some famous, others of less value but together worth a lot. And nobody to leave it all to, apart from a few small personal bequests. I want to leave an executor plus small and youngish committee of personal friends, to administer annually the 'charitable trust' funds from the sale of the house and everything in it. Do you know of a youngish solicitor or lawyer to draw up a will and help annually to administer it?

I have behind-the-scenes been sending young artists to the US and to Europe each year for over 30 years now with about £3000 in hand plus return air tickets – in honour of Mark Rothko. And other annual bursaries of my own devising to help other artists. I want to keep this sort of help going, anonymously.

Which is why I'm asking your help in getting my name taken off the official list as an 'OBE'. I accepted it reluctantly at the time to cheer up v. aged parents – and it did. But it went against my grain as an aspiring socialist (British Empire? etc. etc.) and instinct for decent anonymity. Now, of course, it positively rankles because I'd only just begun at Whitechapel and it doesn't take into account decades of getting artists' work on stage (Royal Ballet, Rambert etc.), building an important collection for British art in the US – 12 foot × 14 foot H Moores and other masterworks, buying for half million dollars collection for Canadian govt and so much else.

I'll get the embarrassing OBE out of *Who's Who* and anywhere else if you'll square it at HQ. Anyway, it got a heartwarming group of tributes from artists in Sunday Tel 2 Suns back. Really touched.

Don't want to bore you but please do help me out. All thanks – best – Bryan.

John Hubbard recalled that a couple of Bryan's American friends, Elaine and Ray Malsin, who were anglophiles and came to London a lot, tried to help at this juncture.

Elaine constantly worried about Bryan. They always did whatever they could, in the right way [helping him with money]. So when Bryan was ill at the end of his life and Elaine discovered, to her horror, that he'd never slept in a proper bed (he'd slept in a cheap divan, like a school bed) – they turned the dining room into his bedroom so he wouldn't have to go upstairs, and she whipped off to John Lewis or somewhere and a bed appeared. But unfortunately by that time Bryan had already moved into hospital and I don't think he ever slept in it.

Bryan was known to be a sybarite who believed in luxury – so why didn't he buy himself a decent bed? Hubbard responded: 'He was old-fashioned. One thing one always forgets about Bryan is that in his youth he was ill for years, and I think he must have come to hate being in bed.' The abiding memory of many of the friends who visited Bryan as he lay dying was how he was still making them laugh, though himself in considerable pain.

Bryan Charles Francis Robertson died of cancer at the Chelsea and Westminster Hospital, London, on 18 November 2002.

Paul Huxley gave the following address at Bryan's funeral in St James's Church, Piccadilly, at 1.30pm on Thursday, 28 November 2002, a ceremony to which Bryan himself (in a delayed hearse) arrived characteristically late.

Bryan was a rare, larger-than-life person. He had a prodigious knowledge and memory, a boundless enthusiasm, an unchallengeable capacity to win and convince an audience and an immoderate generosity, both of spirit and of material things. You might say he was a 'Renaissance man', but not in the multi-creative sense of that term, he didn't paint or play a musical instrument.

But he wrote; always winningly and eloquently, with the desire to express admiration and support rather than negative criticism. In a way his greatest art (that is, apart from the great range of exhibitions he created) was, in my opinion, the spoken word, in radio broadcasts and in conversation, when the full range of his advocacy, erudition, vision, humour and storytelling could take flight unchecked. I use the word 'unchecked' advisedly. It was a brave person who would contradict him at such times, even if they could get a word in edge-ways. He was a polymath of the arts and the senses, because of his astounding knowledge of, and sensitivities to, those areas. He had a profound knowledge of architecture, painting, sculpture, music, opera, fashion, dance, film, poetry, theatre and literature, he could also cook superbly, he knew the great restaurants of the day, he adored gardens and flowers, was able to remember their characteristics and names and could even identify a woman's perfume and recommend others she would like to wear.

If this conveys someone who was overbearingly authoritative, then, yes, there was certainly an element of that, but always compensated for by a largesse, a humanity and, above all, humour. He was a sharer and an educator. He wasn't really censorious of people so much as towards the establishment and received opinions. He had a capacity to love and respect people as individuals. For instance, he didn't much like couples, preferring to treat his married friends as two separate individuals. He knew his own weakness in being liable to become over sympathetic to creative people. So, he would do his best to avoid meeting an artist if he had no feeling for their work; on the other hand, if he liked and respected the work, he would seek out the artist and inevitably become a great friend and supporter.

He was hopeless with money and never had any, but he certainly knew its value as a lubricant to life, and he used his considerable influence, where possible, to help artists to achieve what they needed; the time and space to work, the chance to exhibit and the chance to travel. Bryan's own immediate surviving family is relatively small: his dear sister, Peggy, her son, Marcus, and Bryan's niece, Janet; but no single person is likely to know the full extent of Bryan's circle of friends and the worlds in which he was made welcome, even though his mission was often to bring us all together. He made his artists read books and hear opera, actresses look at sculpture, dancers see paintings, writers watch ballet and all of us meet each other to eat well and laugh a lot. One of the many lasting memories we shall all have is of Bryan's wheezing euphoric laughter, usually at his own infectious jokes, slapping his asthmatic chest for a gasp of air. I certainly have never laughed so long and hard, so that my sides stabbed with pain, than I did in Bryan's company and I doubt that I ever shall again.

Bryan was a life-enhancer, a sensualist, a connoisseur, an entrepreneur. In his lifetime he owned a mountain of books, beautiful objects and wonderful works of art, but he could rarely afford them and didn't care much to be acquisitive. The works of art were often sold to keep the wolf from the door, and the books would be given away. He believed books should travel rather than stay, gathering dust, on the shelf. To cheer himself up he liked to fill bowls full of fruit for his kitchen counter; he would arrange his dining table like a miniature garden with little posies of freesias or anemones, Victorian candlesticks with cut-glass pendants, a tiny Vietnamese Buddha, a turquoise bowl for lemons and green Georgian wine glasses. Well before dusk could even make its presence felt in his house he would turn on all the lights, as if the shadowy side of life should be kept at bay.

Those of us who spent time with Bryan as a friend, or who worked with him, are privileged to have known him; he was our mentor. We should do our best to make sure he is credited for his influence. The important way he changed us and our world may all too easily go unrecorded. And we should, however modestly, try to carry his light and his enlightenment on to the next new generation.

Selected afterwords

One of the last catalogue texts that Bryan wrote was 'The Gentle Illumination of the Present' for Nigel Hall's wife, Manijeh Yadegar (1951–2016), published six years after Bryan's death as the introduction to her Gallery Art Link exhibition in Seoul, Korea, in 2008. It was written in hospital when he was ill and dying, but is characteristically upbeat and optimistic.

The paintings of Manijeh Yadegar are as simple as breathing, in the way that warm and cold densities of a narrow range of colours, pale ochres, soft greys, are set against each other in horizontal bands of paint. A mature artist working steadily in comparative seclusion since student days in the 1970s at London's Camberwell School of Art, Manijeh Yadegar suggests in all her work some kind of philosophical equilibrium but in a way that is quite free of the abstract calligraphy which this artist's Iranian ancestry might well have developed as a subliminal influence and predisposition.

She does, however, in my view, share some ground with that great twentieth-century inventive genius, Mark Tobey, who did indeed exploit abstract calligraphy from Sufic as well as from Japanese models but who also floated quite freely in some abstract stratosphere of his own devising. Like Tobey, Manijeh Yadegar is quite free of any stylistic formal devices; her visual world has a characteristic serenity, a composure that is wholly personal to this artist.

These paintings have a contemplative beauty of their own; they also transmit light and, miraculously, a sensation of calm, but strong feeling. And feeling rather than sensation is what good art is about: feeling, and freedom from nostalgia if we consider the best twentieth- twenty-first-century art from Mondrian to Matisse. Manijeh Yadegar's paintings gently illuminate the present, the living, breathing, continual present, in no need of history or cultural alibis.

And here follow two extracts from Mel Gooding's affectionate and perceptive entry for Bryan in the *Oxford Dictionary of National Biography* (published online 2006).

After a sporadic primary education in Streatham, Robertson attended Battersea grammar school, where he first developed the vital awareness of the common culture of classical and Christian mythology indispensable to his later enthusiastic appreciation of European art. Thereafter largely self-educated, he was to hold education to be an absolute value in all its manifestations, and actively promoted it in his every professional capacity. Exhibitions, writing, broadcasting, and free access to museums and collections were equally regarded by him as having that essential educative value. In the convivial conversation that was central to both his professional and his private life he often effortlessly assumed the Johnsonian role of cultural mentor. Many people, artists and others, found their intellectual and aesthetic lives forever enhanced by his expansive table talk, which was deeply informative but never didactic ...

An unabashed homosexual, Robertson was both witty and robustly humorous, an ebullient conversationalist of Wildean brilliance and profundity. He was immensely kind and thoughtful, if sometimes unreliable in such small matters as turning up for dinner, or even, at times, being at home when guests arrived for dinner. He sometimes went for weeks without opening his mail, including envelopes which might contain much-needed cheques. Careless of money and often without a great deal of it, he was unfailingly generous. Prodigal of his own gifts, he was appreciative of those of others; acute in his judgements, and never sentimental, he could be hilariously acerbic about those he felt to be dishonest or inauthentic. He had a radiant intelligence and catholic critical instincts, repeatedly celebrating in writing and exhibitions the artist he admired, regardless of their fame or obscurity. Through his own experience and his many friendships with artists and writers, he came to a deep understanding of the mixed fortunes of the creative life and a keen insight into the vagaries of fashion. His love of art, literature, music and dance went together, as he wrote, 'with a life-long concern for pleasure, beautiful places, good-looking people and frivolous living'.

Bridget Riley on Bryan

Bridget Riley recollected her friendship with Bryan in October 2018:

I first met Bryan Robertson in 1963 at a party given by John Russell just after my second exhibition at Gallery One. This was the first art-world party I'd been to. Bryan came up to me and his opening line was, 'I've been wanting to meet you. I am Bryan Robertson'. I was too shy to say that I did not know who Bryan Robertson was. We began to talk and were soon joined by Francis Bacon, whom I did recognise and was especially thrilled to meet. Francis Bacon gave me some extraordinary but very good advice, presumably about art dealers: 'Let them cheat you, it gives them such pleasure.' After Francis had moved on, Bryan, seeing that I was rather surprised, said, 'You see, he's treating you as an equal'. Before we parted Bryan asked me for my phone number, which I couldn't remember, so I said 'I'm in the Book'. Bryan laughed and a few days later rang me up. It was the beginning of a wonderful friendship.

Bryan was planning the first of his *New Generation* shows at the Whitechapel. It was an exciting time, full of optimism and opportunity – the war and the years of austerity were behind us and there was a feeling that we could now at last begin. Bryan was working very hard with all the painters on the selection of their work. He wanted four paintings from me and he hung them on the right-hand side of the gallery at the far end. I was very happy with that because it meant the visitor would encounter them last of all. David Thompson, who was the art critic of the *Times*, wrote the Introduction and notes on each of us. Bryan also asked each of us to make a statement for the catalogue, so that our own voices were present as well. I sent him mine, which was '1 + 1 = 1'. Bryan rang and asked me, 'Do you really want to say just this?' 'Yes, I do,' I said. Bryan paused and said, 'But it doesn't, Bridget'. I said, 'If you read it again you'll see that one thing added to another one thing becomes one thing'. He laughed and my statement stood.

Whether the artist Bryan was working with for an exhibition was just starting out or was one of the new heroes of American painting, Bryan took the utmost care in presenting their work in the way they wanted it. He said, 'Good artists always know their strengths and weaknesses better than anyone else', and he always made it his practice to listen. Mark Rothko, for instance, felt that his work needed a very low level of light; the mysterious nature of his work is to do with an emerging presence. Bryan understood this and toiled to achieve the conditions Rothko wanted, taking special care with the lighting. It was a beautiful exhibition. Rothko himself asked for the exact heights and intervals of the hanging for a later exhibition elsewhere.

Bryan saw to it that we met people like Mark when they came over to show at the Whitechapel. Sometimes American artists who back home were not on the best of terms with each other or hardly knew each other, found themselves next to each other at one of Bryan's dinner-parties.

It was very much part of Bryan's philosophy that sometimes friendships under strain could be repaired by meeting afresh on new ground and with new people. It was on one such occasion that he invited me to dine with Ad Reinhardt and the Motherwells. Helen [Frankenthaler, Robert Motherwell's wife at that time] wanted to go to the revolving restaurant at the top of our new radio tower [now the BT Tower, in London's Fitzrovia], at that moment the highest in Europe. But although we 'revolved', there was no service. Robert joked that it was probably too far from the kitchen and insisted that we all moved on to another restaurant where we could have something to eat.

The fact that I had already met a number of American artists made a huge difference to my first visit to America. I remember a party that Bryan gave for Jasper Johns just after the opening of his show at the Whitechapel [in 1964]. His flat in Draycott Place was basically one large room with a sofa that doubled as a bed. Into that room was packed the whole American art world with attendant Brits. It was a terrific party; however I left before the end. The next day I rang Bryan and asked him how it all went. He said, 'Oh, very well! One sculptor made love to another sculptor's wife in my clothes cupboard.'

Bryan resorted to many different ways of helping artists to meet each other and extended this to emerging critics, curators and art-lovers. At lunch-time private views he would gather a group of people he hoped would like each other and take them round the corner to the Great Eastern Hotel [next to Liverpool Street station], notable for its brightly coloured tartan carpet and the silver trolley bearing a huge joint of roast beef under an enormous cover. These events were much loved by all of us, especially the Americans. Enjoyment and intellectual exchange were very much part of the package Bryan offered; he was well aware that as the first post-war generation of artists freed from the constraints of austerity, we had much to discover about the values and aspirations of the pre-war art world. He would cross-question me about the poets I'd read and later introduced me to Proust, giving me the first volume, saying, 'If you like it, there's more to come. But if you don't, try it again later, it might be too soon.' In fact, *Remembrance of Things Past* has become part of my life. Dinners with Bryan – at least when he was younger – were conducted along these lines; the more guests he had and the more of a cultural cornucopia they provided, the happier Bryan was. He went to great lengths to lay on a feast at every level. But all this took a great toll. He suffered from severe asthma all his life and his childhood memories were of days confined to bed. Nevertheless, Bryan would always make the effort – spiritual, physical, financial and even medical – to rise to the occasion of giving everyone a treat. These were the heydays, when under his direction the Whitechapel was taking the lead in exhibition-making on this side of the Atlantic, kick-starting in effect the whole engine of British art in the sixties.

Our friendship continued after Bryan left both the Whitechapel and England. There were several visits to America, one memorable trip to my studio in France and we met up in Australia, a country of which he was very fond and whose interests he had much at heart. Wherever Bryan went he showed a great appreciation of those he met. He had an almost uncanny sense of place and occasion, quick to see latent talent and to recognise individual achievement. He is much missed by all of those who knew and loved him and, as Paul Huxley said to me recently, 'No one has taken his place'.

Let me conclude this celebration of Bryan Robertson with a final quote from '45–'99, his Kettle's Yard exhibition:

for me visual art, with science and music, is one of the supreme expressions of the human spirit and has to be experienced on its own terms. But if art were to be taken seriously enough for it to be used as the basis for education, then students could learn all about astronomy, mathematics, history, geography, religions, costume, agriculture – everything – from the greatest visual sources. And if they did this and learned subjects backwards, beginning with the present day for a clear sense and understanding of the present, and tracing things back through history to their source, the world might be a better place. And on this sententious note of high-minded near-bathos, I am reminded of Dorothy Parker's immortal poem:

Oh life is a glorious cycle of song,
A medley of extemporanea;
And love is a thing that can never go wrong;
And I am Marie of Roumania.

Appendix I
Bryan's Whitechapel catalogues

Bryan was rightly proud of the catalogues he produced for the Whitechapel in its heyday, between 1955 and 1968, which mark the roll-call of remarkable exhibitions he mounted. These handsome publications are still valid today – although the illustrations are mostly in black and white, there is usually some useful text from the artist or from Bryan himself, sometimes from another expert. There might be an interview or a biographical note, but the overall tone was a blend of scholarship and accessibility. Practically for the first time, exhibitions were properly documented. The format was generous, a near-square measuring 9 by 8 inches, and at 30 pages or so, offering seriousness and weight to each subject. The look was much imitated and raised the game for British museums, which could no longer make do with a skimpy brochure. Maurice de Sausmarez, in *Studio International* (February 1969), wrote of 'Whitechapel-style' catalogues having 'a tonic effect on the prevailing standards of catalogue production in many of the smaller public galleries'. Robertson used these catalogues not only to promote his exhibitions and his artists but to expand his audience and increase the possibilities of funding for the visual arts. This kind of ambitious but serious publicity was unusual and unexpected; it was also effective.

In fact there were two basic formats: the larger 9 × 8 inches, and the smaller 8½ × 7¼ inches. The latter tended to be the choice for the late 1960s publications (Hoyland, Craxton, Parsons), but a smaller squarer variant was also used. This near-square (7½ × 7¼ inches) seems to have originated with the *New Generation* exhibitions, and then been used for other shows, such as Mary Potter, Harold Cohen and Bryan Kneale. Of course there were exceptions to this general pattern. The 1954 Hepworth catalogue, before the series got established, was a more upright format, 10 × 7½ inches. Caro's 1963 catalogue is, by contrast, landscape: 8½ × 9½, a shape reflecting the work illustrated. So is Jack Smith's 1959 catalogue, again chosen to best accommodate the work. Phillip King's 1968 publication is less obviously a horizontal rectangle: 8 × nearly 9 inches. It's almost as if Bryan slightly changed the format when he wanted to emphasise the originality of a particular artist.

Paul Huxley commented when I interviewed him in 2016:

Bryan used to design the Whitechapel catalogues himself. He knew quite a bit about typography and was very particular about the fonts that he'd use. He was adamantly opposed to the concept of grids. He said, 'The trouble with modern-day typographers is that they're obsessed with grids, and everything has to fit into a grid'. He was wrong to have such a deep prejudice, he was right to recognise that typography had become very conformist and lacked daring and inventiveness. Bryan was always keen to depart from any grid format – sometimes it worked, sometimes it didn't. He did invent the near-square format for exhibition catalogues, which I still think to this day are the best proportion. But then I would, wouldn't I, because I make square paintings. They were a nicer proportion and very original for their time. Gordon House was the best-known typographer then doing catalogues and he made very elegant pieces, but Bryan was an original, because he understood typography through sensibility.

Richard Wentworth, writing about his own arrival in London as a student in 1965 in his essay 'The Slick of the Eye, A Slip of the Tongue', in the catalogue for Waddington Custot's 2017 show *David Annesley: Kurumidza*, had this to say:

Bryan Robertson's Whitechapel was the easternmost site of pilgrimage, a traipse. I had seen the 1964 Rauschenberg show there as a schoolboy. This young Robertson evidently loved publishing, evangelising. A posse maker, perhaps? As a student I had his *New Generation* catalogues. Devouring them, I admired their simple design. Layouts. Display. Making things stand up. Making them visible. Welding the precarious. Correcting the colour balance. I can no longer say whether I saw these shows or not, something about fusing images on the page and the spaces and works they represent. Casualties of the mental archive, slipperiness and slippages.

'Catalogue introductions are the No Man's Land of criticism'.

Bryan was justifiably proud of the fact that he personally designed and edited all the Whitechapel catalogues, posters and invitation cards, and oversaw all the press releases. He developed the press release as a very effective tool with which to shape public response. Meanwhile he used his catalogue prefaces as declarations of intent, almost manifestos, discussing his ideas and aims, his philosophy of showing art. This was all part of the new professionalism so particularly evident in the *New Generation* shows. The catalogues were evidence that the exhibitions had existed, that the myth was real.

Bryan was equally celebrated and teased for his great and free-wheeling gift for digression. When supposedly writing about a particular artist, he would often provide a potted history of one or other (possibly) related developments in contemporary culture, or happily expatiate upon

a tenuous linked theme, before settling down to make a few well-chosen comments about the artist intended to be under discussion. At first sight, this generously imparted knowledge might seem to be largely irrelevant or beside the point. But, in actual fact, much of interest and importance can be relayed in this process of deliberate diversion and deviation. And Bryan was a master of it.

Here are selected passages – all written by Bryan – from a cross-section of Whitechapel publications.

British Painting and Sculpture, 1954

For some reason not easy to define or understand, many contemporary artists are producing, or are anxious to produce, much larger pictures and sculptures than the public has been conditioned, in recent years, to expect. This conditioning has largely been the result of economic pressure and the simple fact that today most people live in small flats or houses with limited wall and floor space. It could be that the instability of the times we live in and the current process of revaluation of existing artistic aims, in all their many forms, has made it imperative for artists to make these more amplified statements; and it may partly be a reaction against the narrow constrictions of the established art market as it has been for some years in this country – a market that has demanded small pictures and small sculptures that somehow merge very often into *objets d'art* or tasteful items of interior decoration.

What is clearly needed is far more patronage for artists from every possible source so that they may work on large projects and the more general and frequent embodiment of works of art in existing public buildings of all kinds, and in new buildings.

Nicolas de Staël, 1956

De Staël's paintings are of particular interest at the moment. Imaginative images – sometimes fetishes – are still devised which stem from the great period of emancipation achieved by Surrealism and are obsessionally inspired: witness Evans and Sutherland; but there is a feeling in some quarters, possibly generated by the pressure and tension of life today, that painting should now concern itself more directly with reality and with an immediacy of impression. I do not mean social realism, which is pictorial journalism. The resulting image, whether representational or non-figurative, must appear to be indivisible from its technical projection. Image, paint quality, colour, texture, and two or three-dimensional structure are thus synthesized. There is nothing new here but as a point of view it is fashionable. De Staël's work throughout embodies this conception of art: a conception much sentimentalized by onlookers who fail to see that intellectual manipulation always takes precedence in painting: for example Turner, Daumier, Ensor, Soutine or Kokoschka. More extreme practitioners, like Jackson Pollock, are no exception to the rule. Pollock's best canvases like those of Mathieu or Riopelle are most carefully contrived, as self-conscious as any other kind of painting and as objective. The tyranny of reason is not easily discarded.

Expressionism has produced great art. It is an attempt to purge the soul of the artist of some intense emotion; in so doing to disgorge a powerful generalized image. Success or failure in this operation depends upon the degree of generalization achieved by the imagery. Van Gogh achieved it, many have stood upon the awful threshold of success. This activity is tragic in implication, its practitioners can pander overmuch to experience and be ravaged by it. I shall never forget listening to the French poet Artaud's farewell speech to the world after many years in an asylum: the snarling, roaring voice and its message punctuated by drum beats, cymbal clashes and blasts from a whistle handled by the poet were terrible to hear. The limits of human expression were shattered. Passion and great feeling, however, are not the special prerogatives of expressionism: Brancusi and Mondrian share an equally fervent emotional content and manner of delivery.

Two kinds of artists have always existed: those who are caught up in the world around them, remember the past and anticipate the future and find themselves committed to a philosophy and course of action, and those who are conscious of the same things but remain detached and uncommitted. The work of the former can easily descend into ephemeral propaganda, incoherence or psychopathic imagery; the work of the latter, in attempting to rise above actuality and find in an abstract way new forms with which to mask a personal identity, can equally easily descend into a kind of passive private ritual. Both kinds of artist today face the problem of antique-mongering; but they do not have to face problems of communication, as some suppose, for art is not in itself a means of communication any more than scientific research (much painting at the moment can be related to contemporary moral philosophers who think it is their function only to analyse the logic and language of existing moral generalizations and not to formulate new ones); neither is it a substitute for religion or any kind of absolute. Art is quite simply an act of revelation. The spirit of our time is myriad-faced and neither kind of art relates specifically to this spirit.

Charles Howard, 1956

Very slowly, working with intense care and concentration, Charles Howard has created a series of paintings in the past fifteen years which will find, I believe, a place among the other major works of our century that have come from Brancusi, Mondrian, González, Miró, Picasso, Hepworth and Moore. These are some of the innovators of our time: Dutch, Spanish, English and Rumanian. Howard is American. For the past ten years he has lived in England ...

I saw Charles Howard's pictures for the first time eight years ago, at his studio in the country. They impressed me then; studying them ever since and watching their evolution, they seem to me to be even more extraordinary now. Howard's aristocratic and technically brilliant handling of pigment; the concentration and power of his imagery; his profound use of colour and, above all, the clarity and conviction of his pictorial sense combine to make a world. This world is not easily or quickly entered: the pictures have a greater spatial depth, exist on more levels of the imagination and contain a larger number of visual metaphors than are at first apparent. It is possible to live with pictures by this artist for several years and yet not know all there is to know about them. Such a display of polite obliquity and so lengthy and protracted an introduction to a man's vision might well seem excessive. In fact, the process is engrossing and rewarding.

The curious anonymity in the presentation of the images in Howard's work, the impersonality that becomes so highly personal, is in sharp contrast to the style of painting at present 'en vogue', a style that has set handwriting, as it were, at a high premium and frequently at the expense of content. This contrast is not the result of a reaction by Howard against the present tendencies but is, rather, the outcome of a consistently held point of view: the deeply rooted, intuitively formulated and directed. Unable to improvise or design in a mechanical sense, Howard produces about twelve pictures each year and rarely works on a large scale.

The content of Howard's pictures is less private than the manner of their execution; and in a sense their content could be described as Emersonian, with Whitmanesque embellishments. Painting of this kind is concerned with ideas or dreams or shape-obsessions that cannot be expressed in either words or music. Images spring into being to surprise or stimulate the spectator; and the creator hopes that the images will delight his eye, as well as sound a chord somewhere inside him, or remind him of some shared experience. E.M. Forster recently made a short, informal speech in Cambridge and with immense good humour and insight referred to this process which dismays some people still because they want art to be an act of confirmation – confirming their prejudices or what they already know – and not an act of discovery or revelation.

Bryan continued to promote Howard's work wherever possible. In a draft letter to Freddy Gore (dated 1 November 1977), he wrote:

A belated note to thank you most warmly for allowing the inclusion of Charles Howard in the Academy show [*British Painting 1952–77*, curated by Gore at the Royal Academy], and to apologise for having pushed him so assiduously at the eleventh hour. I do know very well how difficult this whole business of selection must have been and I am grateful to you for having made things possible with your usual good humour.

S.W. Hayter, 1957

To put it simply and accurately, Hayter is the greatest living engraver. His technical methods and innovations have radically affected the many faceted art of print making all over the world. His recent book on modern methods of engraving is a unique document and an essential source of reference for all students. The Atelier 17, which Hayter founded in Paris in 1927 as a centre for research in print making, has become equally unique as an institution with a formidable international reputation. Quite apart from these achievements, a certain range of formal expression invented, elaborated upon and refined in paintings, drawings and prints over the years by Hayter has become common visual currency from Tokyo to London: absorbed into their vision and used almost unconsciously by innumerable artists working in different countries. Hayter has, in fact, left his mark on the art of the century as an original, inventive artist with the highest and most unswerving professional standards as a craftsman and technician …

He has accomplished a great deal for the prestige of English culture abroad and with Henry Moore and Ben Nicholson has helped other English artists to receive attention in foreign countries. As an artist, his sympathies are broad and varied: he has an engaging loyalty to other members of his profession, even when their work and interests differ from his own. As a highly articulate teacher he is held in great esteem and affection. His personality, intelligence and way of life are integrated with his work to an exceptional degree. Above all, he has thought constructively about the problems of an artist in this century and always with a sense of historical perspective.

A letter from Bryan to a potential collector (dated 7 November 1957) states that the Hayters are 'beautiful, and very important'. He continues: 'As you probably know, Hayter is representing England at the Venice Biennale next year. He is one of the very few English people to have influenced modern European painting. I don't often enthuse about modern English painting, but these – especially the recent – pictures are very fine indeed.'

Kenneth Armitage, 1959

In general, it is true to say that the activities of the Fine Arts Department of the British Council in sending British art abroad are not well known to the general public in this country except among the artists concerned and a handful of officials or specialists. British artists are fortunate in having an official body of this kind empowered to propagate their work abroad, freed from the complications of commerce and as part of a generally enlightened attempt to show foreigners what we are doing in the fields of the arts, the sciences, or education in general. Any policy adopted by such a department could be criticised; and indeed artists and their friends talk from time to time of the work that the Council sends overseas in the widest sense and criticise the Council's choice – and deprecate the choice of X and wonder why Z was not selected, and so on; all this minor and entirely amiable controversy is natural. But it is essentially irrelevant when set beside three remarkable accomplishments which will always stand to the credit of the Council. First, the Council has secured a sympathetic and interested audience abroad for our artists' work, so it would follow that the Council's choice must be fairly perceptive. Before the war, there was little interest abroad in British art, and if the Council since the war had sent indifferent work overseas or made too many wrong decisions this foreign apathy would have continued. Second, the Council has indirectly consolidated, in Europe and America, a number of expanding reputations, and this has been immensely beneficial to the artists concerned. Thirdly, a number of major art prizes with international implications have been secured by British artists whose work has travelled under British Council auspices. Hovering over all this is the immaculate professional standard maintained by the offers of the British Council's Fine Arts Department, and the real enthusiasm, integrity and energy brought to bear upon a prolonged campaign that sometimes embraces as many as forty-five travelling exhibitions in one year and conducted with an exemplary degree of economy and restraint.

This professional standard is a direct reflection of the enlightened and unflagging work of the Department's chief, Mrs Lilian Somerville, OBE. In putting the Council's policy into practice, Lilian Somerville has done a very great deal for British cultural prestige abroad; and whilst keeping on unusually direct and intimate terms with artists of all kinds in this country and abroad has retained an unswervingly detached and level gaze on the international scene in the arts.

Kazimir Malevich, 1959

The Trustees welcome this exhibition and hope that the East London public will see again, as with the Hepworth, Mondrian, de Staël and Pollock exhibitions, that modern art is less remote from life than its detractors suppose: for our buildings, interiors, typography, industrial design, most articles of daily use, posters, magazine covers and shop window displays have all been affected by the work of artists who originally created their pictures and sculpture for its own sake. Artists give shape and expression to our lives and continually expand our vision of the world. Looking at the streets of East London, and the objects masquerading as furniture and fabrics that are still foisted on to a public limited in the knowledge that produces taste, it is clear that we are still roughly fifty years behind the artists and our manufacturers and promoters are still trying to ignore their existence.

Ida Kar, 1960

The books, paintings and sculpture, or music of a very large number of artists in Europe, or for that matter in America, have become an easily obtained experience for a large public compared with fifty years ago when horizons were narrower. We owe this marvellous influx of experience to lending libraries, broadcasting and television, gramophone records, and public art exhibitions. During the past twenty years, the artists themselves

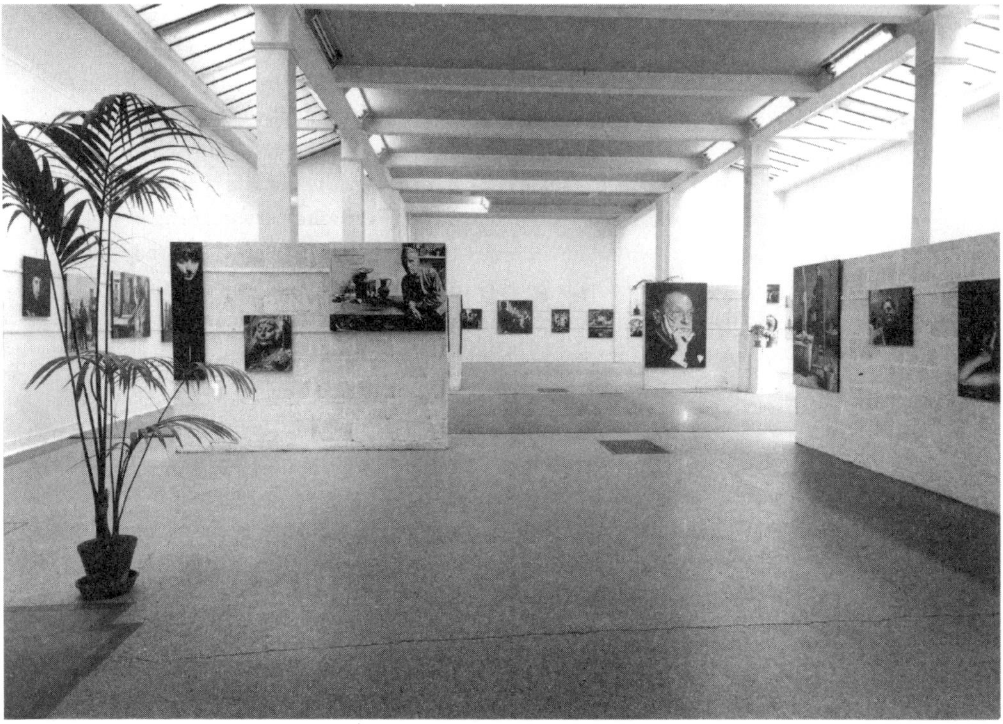

31 Installation view of the Ida Kar exhibition at the Whitechapel Gallery, photographed by the artist in March 1960, 11 × 15.8 cm, vintage bromide print
© National Portrait Gallery, London

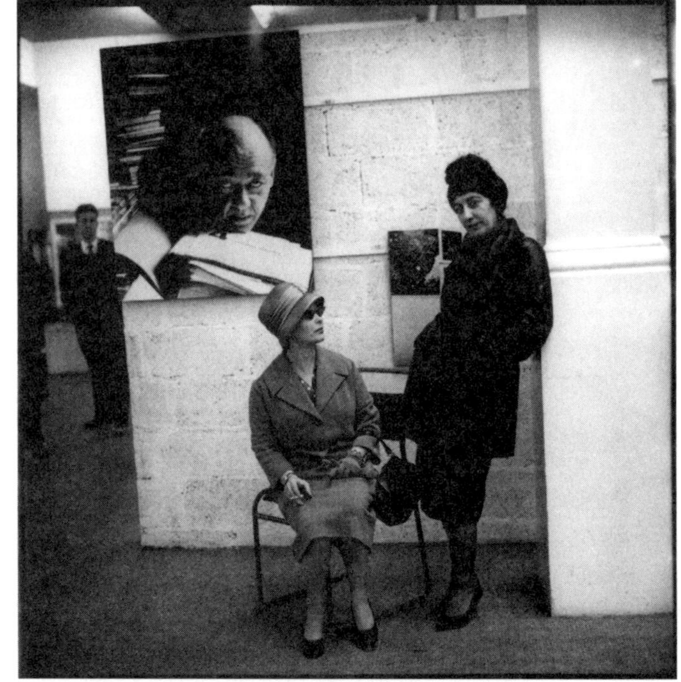

32 Ida Kar and an unknown woman at her Whitechapel Gallery exhibition in 1960, photographed by Ida Kar, 5.7 cm^2 square film negative
© National Portrait Gallery, London

have come a little nearer to most people because the methods and purposes of publicity have brought the physical images of these artists into millions of homes. We take this easy access of familiarity for granted, but it is really quite extraordinary that some young sculptor – or anybody just interested in sculpture – living and working in Wisconsin should be able to have in their head, without ever leaving their home town, a clear picture of Henry Moore's face; or that an enthusiast for American fiction living in Poland should have an equally clear picture of William Faulkner in mind whilst reading one of his novels. But our contact with illustrations of celebrities in magazines and newspapers is only glancing and temporary, and it is very agreeable to find a rich collection of photographic portrait studies assembled together is one exhibition, registered and caught for us to contemplate at leisure. For we are all inquisitive about our fellow human beings, or we should be, and inquisitiveness has an extra depth when we sympathize with their work.

The value of Ida Kar's own work as a photographer is self evident as a record for us and for the future, but her intelligence and integrity are behind every picture and so her photographs go further than records: we look at these faces and are engrossed by them because each face seems to be formed by that effort to project a particular life and experience into a particular kind of work which we find reflected in artists' faces. We feel, in fact, some slight sensation of what it is to be an artist.

Mark Tobey, 1962

Tobey's paintings need slow and thoughtful attention, at close quarters: they are not display pieces and their quiet spirit is not helped by the artificial framework of a temporary exhibition. They need a humanized interior to come fully to life. Although there is no comparison between the two artists, the work of Morandi has a similar intimacy and more than most contemporary painting relies upon an appropriate human context.

Robert Rauschenberg, 1964

Robert Rauschenberg's work has been of key significance for young artists in Europe and America during the past decade. For young artists especially, because they are on his wave-length, they speak his language, and although they do not always share his American experience they understand his references. And the point of view which animates and gives fresh meaning to this experience is universal. Rauschenberg has, in fact, evolved a new vocabulary, a new sentence construction even, that has permanently enriched our language. But it is probably only now, in the early sixties, that the general public is beginning to appreciate his contribution to recent art. And to see that when one has looked beyond the stuffed goat and the tyre, the winking light bulbs and the built-in sets, Rauschenberg is, in fact, a classical artist with a fastidious sense of structure and a hypersensitive understanding of space.

Thirty years later (in *Modern Painters*, summer 1996) Robertson reminisced:

Working with Robert Rauschenberg on the installation of his retrospective show at the Whitechapel Gallery in 1964, we broke for lunch and I took the artist on a devious route to a pub to show him the street life of Brick Lane. We had left at the Gallery the stuffed goat with a rubber tyre, the chimney cowl on a trolley, the paint-soaked bed and other strange works of the period, including the then new 'combines' which included disparate elements, chairs, or implements, dangling in front of canvases with silk-screened images on them. Turning a corner, we saw a large chair suspended by a long rope from a high window and dangling against a tall building plastered over with luridly coloured posters and graffiti. It was quite a shock and seemed very funny at the time, as if a huge combine had followed us out from the Gallery.

Franz Kline, 1964

Franz Kline was one of the main handful of artists to give an absolutely new momentum, and significance, to American painting in the late nineteen forties and fifties. He found himself, and his image, a little later than one or two other American painters of approximately his generation, but his impact on art throughout the world has been no less great. It is wretched to have to write of Kline in the past tense. Words can conjure up nothing of the man's warmth, gaiety, wit, tremendous feeling for life and for people, complete honesty and courage. It was a privilege to be with him – only too rarely, in my case – and his rich sense of occasion and freewheeling, uninhibited enjoyment of people made every meeting with him memorable.

Marzotto Prize, 1964–5

A main characteristic of recent work by the young generation of painters in England is an unexpected dissolution of the old barriers which used to divide figurative and abstract art. Even three years ago, painting in England could be separated approximately into those two groups; but today that distinction seems to have disappeared and a new kind of painting is produced which, although abstract both in formal construction and in spatial implications, still contrives to project or imply figurative or representational references.

John Craxton, 1967

One of the more positive results of the isolated position of England during the 1939–1945 war was the belated recognition, among those elements of the art public left in London, of the fact that artists did not have to wait until they were forty or fifty to produce remarkable work. Before 1939 a young English artist had to possess an extraordinary personality, or to project some kind of glamorous personal legend like Christopher Wood, before his work could secure any measure of serious assessment. Talent was almost coincidental to those extraneous factors. It was as if the English levelled at artists the same standards of maturity strictly equated with age

'Craxton's generation made it possible for younger artists to get serious consideration: he and his contemporaries raised the whole temperature of art in England.'

that were demanded from political figures. But the war brought a new sense of urgency to the English attitude to art in general: the creation of the Arts Council, in the initial form of the Council for the Encouragement of Music and the Arts, and the National Gallery lunch-hour concerts, were two active results ...

The great allure of Craxton's work in general, for me, was the sophistication of its references to Miró and Picasso and the crisp, clean vitality of its design. Above all, perhaps, the colour seemed more tonic, cleaner and fresher, than the prevailing mood of English painting then. Picasso affected everyone, of course, but Miró was exotic ground for speculation in this period ...

In consistently following the work and careers of young artists I have learned more than I can express here. My love for the English school, and belief in its strength, is very deep, from Moore, Hepworth and Nicholson through to King, Riley and Hoyland. One of the minor ironies of my life is to have aroused vexation in some quarters for what is believed to be consistent or excessive championing of American art. The fact that among over a hundred Whitechapel shows since 1953, all large and elaborate, exactly ten have been devoted to American art, should speak for itself. But in talking about 'young artists' and 'generations' a plea must be entered here for dropping altogether this excessive use of the word generation, at least in critical talk. It has become an irrelevant bore: an octogenarian can paint just as well as a twenty-two-year-old arrival from Huddersfield. This pious truism should not have to be stated, but in fact successive generations are turning their backs on each other with increasing alacrity with the result that English art will soon be doomed to bright eruptions, in a series of vacuums, wholly lacking in organic continuity or any real depth. It is a consistent shock to discover how ignorant English artists are of work by other English artists in their own lifetime. Cliques produce only a false sense of security for those involved: ultimately they are self-consuming.

British Sculpture and Painting from the Collection of Leicestershire Education Authority, 1967

Bryan was official buyer for the Leicestershire Education Authority from 1965 to 1968, and thus responsible for all purchases of paintings and sculpture for the collection. Although he strongly believed in the educational value of what he was doing, it was also another way of distributing patronage to the artists he admired and valued. As buyer for the Contemporary Art Society in 1959, Bryan was similarly able to support a number of friends, including Prunella Clough, Elisabeth Collins, Robert MacBryde, Ceri Richards, Jack Smith and Richard Smith, but there are also some less expected purchases. He bought Craigie Aitchison's *Triptych*, Peter Blake's seminal early painting *On the Balcony* (now in the Tate collection) and Bryan Wynter's *Under Mars*. These artists do not quite fit within the accepted parameters of Robertson's taste, despite

some support for Aitchison (see pages 279–80) and the inclusion of a painting by Wynter in the exhibition *British Painting and Sculpture* at the Whitechapel in the autumn of 1954. But Peter Blake is the real surprise, particularly as Bryan later turned down a proposal from Jann Haworth for an exhibition of pop art at the Whitechapel featuring, among others, Blake, Hockney, Allen Jones, Colin Self and Joe Tilson. (He didn't want an exclusively pop show and put on *The New Generation* instead.) Robertson was never known to be a supporter of either the St Ives school or pop art, yet he chose Wynter and Blake. Clearly he was interested in individual paintings rather than categories, and was quite happy to confound his own preconceptions and habits of thought.

The aim of this exhibition is to show the London public what has been accomplished by one County Education Committee in making contemporary art an integral part of the daily experience of schoolchildren, in England, at different stages of their education …

Organizers of art exhibitions, reassured by enlarged attendance figures, were possibly disconcerted by Kenneth Clark's sober reminder, some years back, of the essential decline in public taste since the middle of the nineteenth century, when manufacturers and industrialists in the Midlands chartered trains to send their employees to London to see the most advanced works of their time in art and design at the Great Exhibition of 1851. There is no single authority at work in the present age with the penetration and insight of Prince Albert who, in his urgent sense of the dangers confronting the English in their isolation from the creative spirit in the art of their own time, made the Royal College of Art and the Victoria and Albert Museum an integral part of English life.

Appendix II
Bryan's *Spectator* articles

The following excerpts from Bryan's *Spectator* articles convey something of the range and spirit of his writings and provide an appendix to Hilary Spurling's essay (pages 139–44).

Mike Bolus

17 SEPTEMBER 1965

Michael Bolus, currently showing at the Waddington Gallery, is among the recently established small number – it isn't a group – of young sculptors hell-bent on redefining not only the entire character of sculpture but also its particular function, the specific part it can play in life at this moment. Not life last year, or last week, but now. Exasperatingly enough these young sculptors are so far condemned to project their discoveries only within the restricted and totally artificial orbit of dealers' galleries or, with occasional luck, as part of a wider corporate or shared demonstration like the recent *New Generation* show which the Peter Stuyvesant Foundation made possible earlier this year (trustfully, I must say, considering the new-planet nature of most of the work in question). To use the word 'condemned' for almost any averagely gifted young artist nowadays is to strike, perhaps, an unnecessarily sentimental note: young artists have never had so many chances of financial backing or amiable opportunities for going through their paces in an occasionally almost mindlessly permissive situation. And that 'artificial orbit' of the dealers' galleries has never been more alert, encouraging, crisply intelligent or useful – in financial backing and general encouragement for the artists themselves, and in providing all the opportunities we need for assessing the situation as a whole at any given moment. No complaints in either of these quarters, but the fact remains that until our livelier artists are used, up to the hilt, and released from the incessant show biz circus, their creative strength can only be enjoyed and understood by a very limited public. For anyone like myself, trying to act as a flexible transmission station (and occasional commentator), this basic lack of reality is a sad compromise with what should be a new age of enlightenment. That is, a time like the present when England is bristling with talent (and some flashes of sheer genius) and an unprecedented breakthrough has been achieved which could transform all our lives, believe it or not; totally disrupt whatever vestiges of a dull English image may remain in some quarters abroad – and back up our scientific and technological advances with an equivalent glow of recharged imaginative insight and verve.

Jim Dine

23 SEPTEMBER 1966

There are some fascinating insights in Jim Dine's new show at Robert Fraser's gallery. An American bouquet to London, where Dine stayed earlier this year, this latest work is less concerned with an amiable fetishry of shoes and clothes, Quant-like gear, and spreads out into a celebration of signs, symbols, emblems and appurtenances of English everyday life indoors, in stores, on the streets, in the gardens – and in bed, as there's a vivaciously erotic core to the show. In particular, a series in pencil, wash and collage (all bewitchingly employed with edgy restraint) of penises – genitalia sounds like a creeping rock plant in relation to these funny and charming divertissements. The ladies are to the fore, too, with a galaxy of lips on coloured papers.

But, as twenty-one exhibits, including the entire *London* series, have been removed by the police, it is now impossible for London to assess the show. This is a major exhibition by a distinguished foreign artist; and officialdom might recall that practically every artist of any consequence has made strenuously erotic drawings and paintings at some time; if disapproval is carried to any logical conclusion, Picasso, most notably, should have been in and out of jug for the past thirty years. All this is, or should be, marginal: the show, until it was tampered with and wrecked, was a beaming, relaxed tour de force. If art is meant to enhance our sense of life, let along expand perception and apprehension, then the show succeeded on all fronts.

Henri Cartier-Bresson

24 MARCH 1969

The big Cartier-Bresson show at the Victoria and Albert Museum is so overwhelmingly exact in its attitudes and responses to life that any other exhibition in town is bound to seem muffled by comparison. This will be one of the memorable events of the year. The old argument as to whether photography is an art or not seems especially irrelevant when confronted by the noble realities of Cartier-Bresson's insights into life, place and time. As a photographer he is quite simply supreme. What he finds for us adds, time and again, to our awareness of life in the most concrete terms, even when heightened by such a fastidious concern for texture, light and dark, and the relationships at work in any given scene. And what he finds is so consistently positive, and affirmative of life itself, that I cannot imagine why he hasn't been given the Nobel Prize: Cartier-Bresson is plainly one of the great men of our age. What he has made as a documentation of life, all over the world, is a priceless gift to us all. He renews belief in the meaningfulness as well as the casual, infinitely graceful rewards of existence.

The reality presented by his work is too strong for argument. It reminds us, rather necessarily, that a photograph can convey something which nothing else can. A written description is a literary act, quite separate from what it describes; eye-witness accounts are their own opera or plainchant; a painting is a painting. A photograph is some kind of selective record, and in Cartier-Bresson's case the dominant theme is the quality rather than the stuff of life: the quality of life, that debased phrase bandied around so easily by politicians, busily erecting barriers across it, or educationalists in short cuts and economies which will diminish it. Cartier-Bresson never swerves for an instant from his awareness of it.

Pop Art

19 JULY 1969

The pop art show at the Hayward Gallery, ably selected by John Russell and Suzi Gablik for the Arts Council, is for me a lead balloon – or at least kapok-filled, to keep the apt metaphor inside the right media. It may be the heat that creates for even the youngest visitors a mood of lethargy, readily perceptible in their tour of this truly dreadful gallery: itself becoming for the occasion a monstrous pop art fortress of concrete architectural non sequiturs, and dull lighting that is lethal for most of the exhibitors, especially downstairs. The greater part of the exhibition covers transatlantic pop; the English contingent includes Richard Smith, Peter Phillips and Allen Jones who survive the ordeal with distinction.

Charles Biederman

11 OCTOBER 1969

The galleries were deserted during my two-hour visit, though the show is being hugely enjoyed by the attendants. This is no comment on Biederman; more esoteric shows have found a public here, but it is an indictment, I believe, of our impoverished mass media: where are the accounts and pictures of the show in our national press, where is the TV programme in colour which might relate Biederman to everyday city realities and possibilities in a way that few artists can be; and where are the organised parties of art students, invincibly ignorant as they are nowadays, with instructors? Aren't schoolchildren taken to art galleries any more? There should be bus loads of architectural students piling up along the South Bank, but this historic show at the Hayward Gallery seems to be taking place in a pool of silence, surrounded by the faceless, eggbox architecture that is gradually devouring London. Just one architectural façade in London that had profited by Biederman's example would swerve the course of what appears otherwise to be a future with the shape of a Kafka prison compound.

A few more soundbites

'Many have stood upon the awful threshold of success.'

A colourist, 'a term which always sounds cheerfully mindless applied to any artist'.

'Artists give shape and expression to our lives and continually expand our vision of the world.'

'Drawing is not copying. Drawing is a supreme act of visual probity demanding direct co-ordination between eye, nervous system, imaginative response, and hand and wrist.'

'No artist can make eloquent and concise marks on paper or canvas with pencil or brush, to delineate and trap the promptings of either his imagination or subconscious dream life without the ability to draw with absolute ease and precision any object, mass, volume, space, form or substance in front of him, in the physical, verifiable world.'

'The familiar and dreadful trap that so many gifted young artists fall into, because of a false macho concern for virility as a numbers game of output played as a sign of health, a need to belt out the work like playing crack table tennis, the trap of manufacture.'

'An academic artist always coarsens or diminishes whatever is selected from tradition.'

'Surrealism ripples through so much twentieth-century art: despite Breton's efforts, it was never a doctrine or a method so much as an unstoppable fresh consciousness of disparate relationships.'

Writing of Louise Nevelson: 'The sculpture made me think of Emily Dickinson's tough poetry: bristling with feeling and yet lightly, drily, unsentimentally articulated in formal terms, speaking of love, nature, stoicism and its fearful retreats, faith and scepticism.'

'Vision is unique, comes only from an individual, and emerges gradually through the patient physical slog of solitary day-to-day work heightened by imaginative thinking and a will to explore. Vision is not a group activity.'

'The Books of Hours, enamels and ivories mostly from the early fourteenth century are shown here with the later French paintings because ancient art, classical or medieval art is for me not remote or dead but totally alive forever, making a continuous whole with the best art made yesterday or today. All great art lives in a continuous present: the links between these jewel-like paintings and enamels and ivories in cases and the paintings on the walls are to me quite touchingly clear in their radiant sense of life and harmonious equilibrium between man and nature or man and a trustful Christian faith.'

'French art has a particular sophistication, an astringent tenderness, an integral sense of luxury as a part of life and a perennial invocation of light which brings to life the French unsentimental love of nature and its cultivation. A love above all of order, balance: an alert response.'

Bryan's chronology

This was largely compiled by Bryan, so is slightly inexact at times, and of course ends long before he did.

1 April 1925 Born in Paddington. On his birth certificate his father's occupation is listed as caterer's manager.

1936–42 Attended Battersea Grammar School. Lists art and literature as his main interests.

1942–4 Oxford University Press, at the Neasden office in north-west London, working as a publishing assistant in various departments. He also studied typography and book production. Attended classes at London College of Printing.

1944–6 Editorial assistant at *The Studio* magazine (also Studio Publications Inc.) involved in general production. Wrote occasional essay and book reviews. General literary ambition concentrated on art criticism. His first feature article in *The Studio* covered the new generation of British artists.

1946 First met K Clark 'whose advice, role as mentor and friendship, have remained constant to the present time'. (Other information dates their meeting to the summer of 1948.) 'Studied, in weekly sessions, medieval illuminated books and mss with Sir Sydney Cockerell (retired Director of Fitzwilliam Museum and executor of Kelmscott Press: Authority on Morris) from Cockerell's private collection of medieval art. Began interest in American art, through *Documents of Modern Art* series (edited by Motherwell) arriving for review in England.'

1947 Lived and studied in Paris. Attended art lectures at Sorbonne; visited Brancusi frequently and met many French artists and writers. Became fluent in French language. For three months, lectured at university level in French-occupied zone of Germany: courses on English literature and British art. K sent him a cheque for £30 out of the blue. 'I was on the verge of leaving for Paris having discovered to my mortification – but very necessarily – that I knew practically nothing about painting.'

1948 Worked for one year at Lefevre Gallery in London, then the principal centre for nineteenth- and twentieth-century French art. In addition to showing the work of Nicholson and Hepworth, the gallery exhibited the most advanced British artists at that time, particularly a younger generation.

1949–52 Director of the Heffer Gallery, Cambridge. 'Among other shows organised the first exhibition for a university public of modern French art from Gauguin to Picasso and his contemporaries.' Also exhibited Henry Moore for the first time, and was in frequent contact with the sculptor thereafter. Showed other contemporary artists. Instigated the formation of the Cambridge Society of Artists. Worked with Cambridge Contemporary Art Society (giving lectures, etc). 'Much contact with Joseph Needham, and other scientists and scholars.' In his introduction to the 1999 Peter Potworowski catalogue, Bryan observed that running a gallery in Cambridge meant missing shows in London, so that he was not as *au fait* as he wanted to be.

1952 Appointed Director of the Whitechapel Gallery, aged twenty-six. Wrote a letter to K outlining his plans: twentieth-century form; Mexican and Columbian art (a show then in Paris); a Picasso retrospective; a big show of Turner. K put him off the Picasso, thinking that it 'would be rather mystifying to your regular visitors', but encouraged him to do Turner.

1953–70 Contributed essays to *The Listener.*

1954 Appointed art buyer for collections at Jesus College and Clare College, Cambridge.

1954 'Stimulated interest in American art in England for the first time by presenting shows of work by George Catlin, from the Smithsonian Institution, and American primitive art from the Garbisch Collection.' The exhibition, *American Primitive Art 1670–1954*, opened at the Whitechapel Gallery in 1955.

1956 First trip to America, after being awarded the US State Department grant for an extensive tour of the country for a period of four months.

1957 Invited by the Polish government to visit the country to organise a Bernardo Bellotto exhibition at Whitechapel. At the urgent request of the Polish government, he also secured a Henry Moore exhibition for Poland.

1958–60 Lectured on modern art and design at the Royal Ballet School.

1958–62 Member of the Art Panel of the Arts Council (Bryan's CV has 1955–60, then 1965–70).

1958–70 Appointed to the Executive Committee of the Contemporary Art Society (CAS).

January 1959 Appeared on the BBC Radio arts programme *The Critics* four Sundays in a row (as he tells Barbara Hepworth in a letter).

1959–62 Appointed a Trustee of Digswell Arts Trust, a charity established by Henry Morris for artists in the early phase of their careers.

1960 Lecture tour for the British Council throughout Australia at state galleries and museums, and in South-East Asia. Visited Thailand, Cambodia, Angkor Wat, Ceylon.

1961 Organised first exhibition in London of contemporary Australian art at the Whitechapel Gallery.

1961 Awarded Ford Foundation grant for research on American art.

1961 Awarded an OBE in the New Year's Honours List (his CV has 1962). (A letter of congratulation from his mother in Hythe on the OBE reads: 'You must know your father and I have watched your progress in life with wonder and awe, often saying where will he be next?')

1963 Made film for New York TV on Jackson Pollock.

1963 Contributed an essay and notes on Mantegna's *Triumphs of Caesar* to *Enjoying Paintings* (1964), edited by David Piper.

1964 Made film for NY TV on Robert Motherwell.

1964 Contributed essay, 'An Artist in our Times', to *Topics & Opinions*, an anthology of critical writing edited by A.F. Scott.

1965 Honorary Fellow, Manchester College of Art & Design.

1965–8 Member of Governing Council of Royal College of Art (CV has 1963–6).

1965 Selected and installed (with Robert Melville) *The English Eye*, an exhibition of painting and sculpture at Marlborough-Gerson Gallery, New York, the first there to show the younger generation in terms of their seniors such as Henry Moore, Ben Nicholson, etc. Opened by Lord Snowdon and Princess Margaret.

1965 Invited by Israeli government to attend the opening of the Israel Museum in Jerusalem and subsequently took a tour of Israel as a kind of cultural ambassador.

1965–70 Art critic of the *Spectator*. Contributing, by his own estimate, approximately thirty essays on art for the magazine a year, as well as other reviews.

1965–8 Appointed official purchaser of painting and sculpture for Leicestershire Education Authority.

1966 Installed Hepworth exhibition in New York when she was ill.

29 September 1966 Moved into new house at 73 Barnsbury Street, Islington, London N1 (from 51 Draycott Place, SW3).

1966 Ambassador Award (of a Kenneth Armitage sculpture) for services to art.

1967–8 Invited by the Art Institute of Ontario to be the sole juror in selecting and purchasing contemporary Canadian art for a centennial exhibition, with a budget of $150,000. Also organised, with Herbert Read, a large exhibition, *New British Painting and Sculpture*, at UCLA Art Galleries, Los Angeles, with subsequent American and Canadian tour. Further study and lecturing in America and Canada, the latter leading to Canadian artists showing at Whitechapel.

January 1969 Retired from the Whitechapel Gallery, with an invitation to install two or three future shows there, including one on Helen Frankenthaler.

A note on his CV in 1969 reads: 'The action that has pleased me most, and is perhaps the most useful thing to have achieved in the English environment, was to obtain a firm commitment to the visual arts from industry in the form of the *New Generation* exhibitions, conceived and implemented by me at Whitechapel each year since 1964. These shows are financed by Peter Stuyvesant: a Foundation was formed on my advice, and this awards substantial bursaries for travel in the US to artists participating in the exhibitions. The Foundation also purchases works by these artists for its collection. This will not seem remarkable to an American reader, but England has been regrettably dilatory in this field.'

1969 'Invited by Keele University to propose and consider implementing general scheme for the visual arts at Keele. Appointed by Arts Council of Great Britain to purchase, for one year, sculpture for its collection (£10,000). Currently working on volume of selected essays on art; and an introduction for volume on Ian Hamilton Finlay and concrete poetry movement; to be followed by long-planned and gestated monograph on Robert Motherwell.'

1969 'Gave opening lectures at first conference of art teachers in Africa, at Stellenbosch University, S Africa. Travelled in Africa. Travelled and studied at length in Italy.'

1970–5 Director, Neuberger Museum, Purchase College, State University of New York, Purchase, New York. The museum opened in May 1974, with a gift from Henry Moore of the sculpture *Large Two Forms* (1969), as well as the Neuberger Collection of American Art, a collection of New Guinea art (nearly 200 items), a major collection of African art, also donated; a gift from Hans Richter of his own works and those by contemporaries (Ernst, Arp, etc.), and a collection of constructivist art donated by George Rickey.

1970 Associate Editor, *Art in America*; contributor, *New York Review of Books*.

1971 Participated in panel discussion on modern art with Clement Greenberg and others at Detroit Institute of Arts.

1972 'Invited by Royal Academy to plan and install exhibit British Painting 1890–1970 – temporarily postponed through opening of Neuberger Museum and exhibition schedule in London.'

1975–7 Back to the *Spectator*. Also writing for the *Times*, the *Times Literary Supplement*, the *New Statesman* (where he was a guest critic for six months), *London Magazine*, the *Listener*, *Encounter*, *Studio International*, etc.

1975 'Invited by British publishers to write book of "autobiographical" account of development of art in England since 1945; also invited to write history of activities at Whitechapel Gallery.' Talk also at this point of writing an extended account of the Philip Johnson Compound at New Canaan.

'While at Whitechapel, also invited to other countries such as India and Bulgaria to study national contemporary art, but declined. Admiring leader by Maurice de Sausmarez in *Studio International* (Feb 1969) about BR's achievement at Whitechapel, recalling his first meeting with BR in a Queensway coffeehouse in January 1946, when BR was researching an article on the younger English painters (pub. *The Studio*, March 1946). M de S concluded his article: "It will be a dismal confession of our society's inability to profit from proven talent if an opportunity does not present itself for his gifts to be engaged in some way in the promotion of the visual and plastic arts – faith of the kind he has exemplified is too rare."'

Select bibliography

This book would not have been possible without recourse to the Whitechapel catalogues that Bryan published when Director, and to the catalogue essays he wrote subsequently. These, along with his books, are not listed here as they appear in the text.

Adrian Clark, *Fighting on all Fronts: John Rothenstein in the Art World* (London 2018)

Richard Cork, *Everything Seemed Possible: Art in the 1970s* (London and New Haven 2003)

Penelope Curtis (ed.), *Sculpture in 20th-Century Britain: A Guide to Sculptors in the Leeds Collections* (2 vols., Leeds 2003)

Ian Dunlop and Hester R. Westley, *New Generation Revisited: British Sculpture from the Sixties and Seventies: A Tribute to Bryan Robertson at the Whitechapel*, exh. cat., New Art Centre, East Winterslow, Wiltshire (2008)

Mel Gooding, *John Hoyland* (London 1990)

Mel Gooding, *Merlyn Evans* (Moffat, Dumfries and Galloway, 2010)

Tony Gould, *Inside Outsider: The Life and Times of Colin MacInnes* (Harmondsworth 1983)

Gerard Hastings (ed.), *Drawing to a Close: The Final Journals of Keith Vaughan* (London 2012)

Anthony Hepworth and Ian Massey, *Keith Vaughan: The Mature Oils, 1946–77* (Bristol 2012)

Andrew Lambirth, *Stephen Chambers* (London 2008)

Marco Livingstone, *Peter Blake: One Man Show* (Farnham 2009)

Colin MacInnes, *England, Half English: A Polyphoto of the Fifties* (Harmondsworth 1961)

Ian Massey, *Patrick Procktor: Art and Life* (Norwich 2010)

Robert Medley, *Drawn from Life: A Memoir* (London 1983)

Victoria Newhouse, *Art and the Power of Placement* (New York 2005)

Simon Pierse, 'Bryan Robertson, Abstract Expressionism and Late Modernism in Recent Australian Painting' (1961), from *Impact of the Modern: Vernacular Modernities in Australia, 1870s–1960s*, ed. Robert Dixon and Veronica Kelly (Sydney 2008)

Simon Pierse, *Australian Art and Artists in London, 1950–1965: An Antipodean Summer* (Farnham 2012)

Patrick Procktor, *Self-Portrait* (London 1991)

Frances Spalding, *Gwen Raverat: Friends, Family, and Affections* (London 2001)

Frances Spalding, *Prunella Clough: Regions Unmapped* (Farnham 2012)

Roger Stonehouse, *Trevor Dannatt: Works and Words* (London 2008)

James Stourton, *Kenneth Clark: Life, Art and 'Civilisation'* (London 2016)

Keith Vaughan, *Journals 1939–1977* (London 1989)

Mary Yule, 'A Place for Living Art: the Whitechapel Art Gallery 1952–1968', from *Artists and Patrons in Post-War Britain*, ed. Margaret Garlake (Aldershot 2001)

Acknowledgements

My chief vote of thanks must be to Stephen Chambers, John Spurling and the Bryan Robertson Trust for commissioning this book, and for granting copyright permission to quote so extensively from his writings. When it became clear that a biography of the great man was neither really appropriate, nor what he would have wished, the suggestion of a more general celebration of his diverse talents was received with enthusiasm, and this book resulted. I began my career interviewing artists, so am reasonably familiar with the business of transcribing taped conversation, but the many hours of Robertsoniana I have listened to and edited in the pursuance of this project nearly floored me. Yet I do not begrudge the midnight oil spent deciphering recordings with my finger on the pause button: so much of the material was joyous and uplifting. So a sustained thank you to all those friends of Bryan who have given so unstintingly of their time and memories in recalling him. Without them, this would have been a less personal and entertaining book, though Bryan's anarchic spirit would still have shone though it. Inevitably, there were people I wish I'd managed to speak to about him, including Robert Hughes and Anthony Caro, but the wealth of hilarious and appreciative anecdote I did obtain from others has helped to compensate for any gaps. I was fortunate to talk to John Hoyland and John Hubbard before their deaths, and everywhere was met with heart-warming enthusiasm for the task of celebrating one of the best-loved of curators and critics.

On the technical side let me thank the publishing team of Hugh Tempest-Radford and Unicorn Press, nobly assisted by the editorial skills of Mary Scott, the picture research of Susannah Stone, the meticulous indexing of Judith LeGrove and the inventive design of Robert Dalrymple. This is not a picture book: it would have been impossible adequately to feature the work of all the artists discussed herein, so we decided to plump for several wonderful portraits, a handful of personal snaps, and a representative selection of installation shots from the Whitechapel. I take the opportunity here to thank Bridget Riley and the executors of the Estates of Ida Kar, Lord Snowdon, and Elisabeth Vellacott for their kind permission to reproduce portraits of Bryan.

I would also like to thank the staff of the Whitechapel Gallery Archive for all their help in sourcing photographs, and the Tate Archive (which now holds Bryan's personal archive) for their assistance in making his papers available. For permission to quote extensively from the Journals of Keith Vaughan let me thank Professor Jonathan Gosling of the Keith Vaughan Estate. Thank you also to Denis Conti for allowing us to reproduce his evocative photograph of Bryan and friends in an Oxfordshire garden.

A separate and heartfelt vote of thanks to the Bridget Riley Art Foundation for generously assisting with the publishing costs of this venture.

Once again I wish to pay a special tribute to my wife Sarah, who has been my tireless researcher, fact-checker and editor, without whom I would not have been able to write this book. But however much I owe to her, any mistakes or misunderstandings in the text must be firmly placed at my door. AL

Index

Numbers in *italics* indicate illustrations

The Bryan Robertson Trust

He may not have written his memoirs, but Bryan did manage to set up the Trust to make use of his bequeathed wealth in helping artists, especially those with an interest in dance. The Trust defined its purpose thus, under 'Aims & activities': 'Nominators are invited by trustees and advisers each year to nominate artists, or an artist working with a choreographer, usually mid generation, who might significantly benefit in their artistic practice from a grant. Meetings take place once a year to discuss and decide on the recipients (usually two artists) each year.' Former trustee John Spurling noted:

In the codicil to his will in which he left his money to the Bryan Robertson Trust to give awards to artists, he particularly asked that we should give awards to artists doing work for dance companies. But that's extremely difficult to bring about, trying to find a ballet company that wants to work with an artist rather than their usual designer. We have managed it once. One of his specifications for the Bryan Robertson Award was that it should only be given to artists over forty.

The Trust is funded out of the sale of Bryan's house in Barnsbury. Trustees include or have included: Richard Alston, Stephen Chambers, John McEwen, Nigel Hall, Tim Marlow, Ashley Page and John Spurling. Richard Alston commented:

I can tell you that compared to choreography, or performing arts, in the world of visual arts there's a lot of clashing going on. Bryan set it [the Trust] up in the most extraordinary way – it's so Bryan really, bless him. When I went to the first meeting, there were eleven men, not a woman in the room. I was astonished. Bryan liked women! That's partly why they appointed Ruth Rattenbury so there would be a woman. Now there are women. He probably wanted trouble, he probably wanted us to have terrible quarrels.

After the annual trustees meeting, there is dinner in a good restaurant, another Robertson stipulation. This meal is, according to John McEwen, 'the point of the whole thing really'.